The Qashqa'i of Iran

Young man dressed in Qashqa'i hat, cloak, and cummerbund

The Qashqa'i of Iran

LOIS BECK

Yale University Press
New Haven and London

Library of Congress Cataloging-in-Publication Data

Beck, Lois, 1944–
The Qashqa'i of Iran.

Bibliography: p.
Includes index.
1. Kashkai tribe. 2. Iran—History—Qajar
dynasty, 1779–1925. 3. Iran—History
—20th century. I. Title.
DS269.K3B43 1986   955'.004943   85–23404
ISBN 0–300–03212–9

Designed by Susan P. Fillion
and set in Garamond #3 type
by Graphic Composition, Inc.
Printed in the United States of America

*The paper in this book meets the guidelines for
permanence and durability of the Committee on
Production Guidelines for Book Longevity of the
Council on Library Resources.*

10 9 8 7 6 5 4 3 2 1

IN MEMORIAM

Naser Qashqa'i
Khosrow Qashqa'i
Abdollah Qashqa'i
Ayaz Darrehshuri
Sassan Kazemi

Contents

Illustrations

xi

FIGURES

MAPS

TABLES

Acknowledgments

I cannot adequately express my debt of appreciation to many members of the Qashqa'i tribal confederacy for their support during the research connected with this book. Members of the Shahilu family—particularly Houman Qashqa'i, Malek Mansur Qashqa'i, Mohammad Hosain Qashqa'i, Naser Qashqa'i, Homa Qashqa'i, and Golnar Bayat—were generous with the time they spent with me discussing Qashqa'i history and politics, despite the duress they and all other members of their family were experiencing. I also appreciate the assistance offered by my hosts in the Darrehshuri tribe of the confederacy, especially Jehangir Darrehshuri, Sara Darrehshuri, Manuchehr Darrehshuri, and Nahid Sitork Darrehshuri, and, in the Qermezi section of the Darrehshuri tribe, Borzu Qermezi and his extended family.

The impact of Fredrik Barth, who wrote a pioneering study of a tribe in southwest Iran, and Pierre Oberling, who wrote a valuable history of the Qashqa'i, is obvious in this book. A conference on tribes and the state in Iran and Afghanistan, organized by Richard Tapper and David Brooks at the University of London's School of Oriental and African Studies, came at a point when my own ideas for this book were forming.

To Gene Garthwaite, Dale Eickelman, Leonard Helfgott, Jon Anderson, Carter Bentley, Daniel Bradburd, and Mary Hegland, each of whom offered an insightful, detailed critique and analysis of earlier versions of this work, I am most grateful. I also appreciate the efforts of Patty Jo Watson, Richard Watson, Nikki Keddie, Richard Tapper, Reinhold Loeffler, Robert Canfield, Rebecca Torstrick, Dorothy Grant, and Maxine Schwanke, who read all or parts of earlier versions and offered many useful comments and suggestions. The final version has benefited from all these individuals. Erika Friedl, Eric Hooglund, Floreeda Safiri, and Jerrold Green made general comments on relevant issues; and Richard Cottam, Ann K. S. Lambton, Oliver Garrod, Yassi Amir-Moez, Sassan Kazemi, Rahmatollah Moqaddam-Maraghe'i, Carl Lamberg-Karlovsky, Bahman Abdollahi, and Bahram Azadeh provided specific information otherwise unavailable. Richard Tapper, Mary Hegland, Henry Munson, and Gerhard Kortum furnished personal manuscripts or documents. Gerhard Kortum generously allowed me to use his maps of the province of Fars at a time when I needed to prepare a map of Qashqa'i territory. Yit Lee supplied his cartographic skills, and Adria LaViolette provided some research assistance. Rebecca Torstrick was helpful at the early stages of the writing of the manuscript and continued with her support through the final stages.

I acknowledge the financial assistance of a postdoctoral Fulbright-Hays fellowship, initially awarded for research in Iran in 1979; when it was determined that conditions then did not permit research there, officials responsible for administering these fellowships graciously allowed me to transfer the allotted funds to essential archival research in London. The Department of Anthropology at Washington University, under its chair, Patty Jo Watson, along with Washington University faculty research grants, helped financially to support various phases of the preparation of the manuscript.

I appreciate assistance given me in London by the staffs of the India Office Library, the Public Record Office (where Foreign Office documents are stored), and the library of the University of London's School of Oriental and African Studies. Finally, editors at Yale University Press—Charles Grench and Barbara Folsom—have been most helpful.

PART I

Introduction

Tent encampment in winter pastures near Kazerun in the foothills of the Zagros
Mountains; sloped-roof winter tent dusted with snow

MAP I. Iran

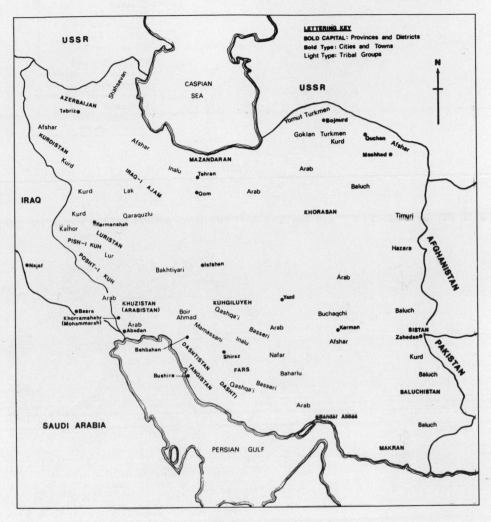

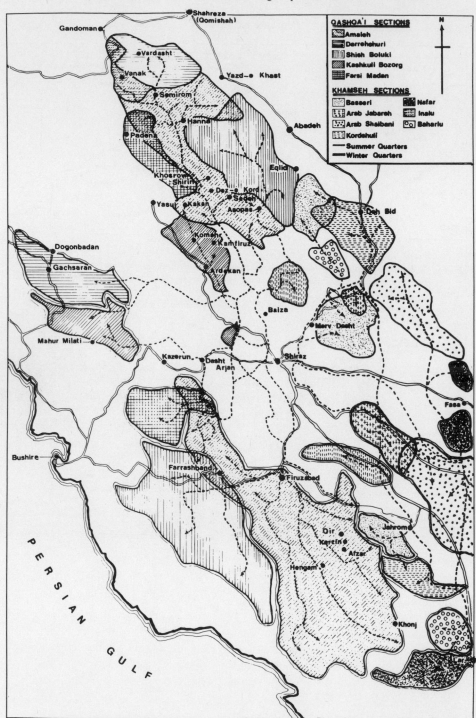

Note: Data from Kortum (1980), Tribal Development Office (1967), Demorgny (1913a, maps 1–3), Bani Hashimi et al. (1977, map 2), Field (1954), Monteil (1966:12).

1

❖

Introduction

*I*n 1982 a small group of Qashqa'i in the mountains of southwest Iran were defending themselves from military attacks by Khomeini's Revolutionary Guards, who had commandeered American-made helicopter gunships (left over from Pahlavi rule) to use against them. The Qashqa'i group included paramount leaders who had spent years in exile under the last shah and had returned to Iran to resume tribal leadership in the aftermath of his departure, together with their most loyal supporters. They held little hope of success; yet they were determined to resist. These leaders traced descent from men who had founded the Qashqa'i tribal confederacy many generations ago. This book is their history, as well as being a historical and anthropological account of the Qashqa'i people.

After a statement outlining the issues and a brief overview, the study is divided into three parts. The first part presents a history of the Qashqa'i confederacy based on new sources and on a reinterpretation of primary and secondary sources according to my anthropological field research on the Qashqa'i and to my reexamination and rejection of many conventional notions about tribes and confederacies. A major part of this history concerns the nineteenth century and stresses Qajar administrative practice, which is essential to an understanding of the formation and transformation of the Qashqa'i confederacy and its leadership. The second part presents a social anthropological analysis of the

Qashqa'i confederacy based on my anthropological field research and on my appreciation of historical materials and analysis. The third part represents an integration of anthropological and historical materials and analysis to highlight the most recent events involving the Qashqa'i.[1]

The Qashqa'i tribal confederacy is not a survival of ancient times or an unchanging, anachronistic, primitive form of organization in a modernizing world, but is, instead, a dynamic development in the context of dynamic forces, a response to prevailing and changing conditions. The confederacy arose in response to historical, political, and strategic circumstances relating to Iran as a whole rather than from autochthonous factors, and it has changed as these circumstances changed. This study, based on anthropological, archival, and other historical research on the Qashqa'i, including oral histories collected from contemporary Qashqa'i leaders, is an account of the connections between their tribal confederacy and the Iranian state during the eighteenth, nineteenth, and twentieth centuries. It focuses on the interrelated processes of Qashqa'i political development and the state's indirect rule of the Qashqa'i people, and it links a discussion of long-term transformations in tribal leadership and identity to state and dynastic politics.

Nomadic pastoralists in Iran and other parts of the Middle East have been organized in different ways, ranging from small groups of families with no formal political leaders and no wide sociopolitical ties to huge tribal confederacies of hundreds of thousands of people having elaborate, hierarchical sociopolitical ties.[2] For the Qashqa'i, the process of political centralization involved the attachment of small sociopolitical units to larger ones and the affiliation of individuals and groups to a hierarchy of political leaders. The result of centralization was a tribal confederacy, a political system composed of a leadership and a means of organizing people beyond the local household and resource-utilizing level that arose primarily for the purpose of standing between these people and competing forces, including those connected with the Iranian state. The confederacy contained a ruling elite that participated in national politics and played a role in international politics during part of the nineteenth and twentieth centuries. A major task of this

1. For recent discussions about the integration of anthropology and history, see Wolf (1982) and Cohn (1980, 1981).
2. For examples of groups in Iran at each end of this spectrum, see Bradburd (1980, 1981) on the Komachi of Kerman and van Bruinessen (1978) on the Kurds.

study is to explain how and why a highly developed sociopolitical institution emerged among these nomadic pastoralists in southwest Iran,
and, by implication, not among most others in Iran and elsewhere.
While the Qashqa'i are unique in many ways, the processes of tribal
and confederacy formation for them are typical of patterns found elsewhere in Iran and the wider region.

From well before Islamic times, probably even extending back millennia (Frye 1963), nomadic pastoralists, semisedentary pastoralists
and cultivators, and sedentary cultivators inhabited the southern Zagros Mountains in a region bordered on the north by Isfahan, on the
east by the deserts of the central plateau, and on the south and west by
the Persian Gulf. After the eleventh century A.D., these rural inhabitants—Persian, Luri, Laki, Kurdish, and Arabic speakers—were
joined by Turkic speakers from the north, northeast, and northwest.
Until late Safavid times in the late seventeenth and early eighteenth
centuries, in fact until possibly the late eighteenth century, we know
of no form of comprehensive political organization for these various
peoples. We know that during this period the Shahilu family (which
became the Qashqa'i ruling elite) grew in prominence and power, apparently through its connections with Safavid and Zand rulers and possibly through local support which may or may not have been rooted in
tribal nomadic pastoralists. Gradually an entity or polity containing
many of these people developed, characterized by centralized authority
and hierarchical leadership. Over time a sociocultural system evolved,
drawing from both the Shahilu family (and its Turkic and probably
tribal heritage) and the local, primarily Turkic yet still heterogeneous,
population. By the late nineteenth and early twentieth centuries a distinct Qashqa'i identity was forming. Thus, concrete Qashqa'i identity
is a rather late development rooted in the complex history of late Safavid and post-Safavid Iran but emerging in the modern period, a situation true both for the Qashqa'i as a political unit in Iran and as a
sociocultural system that we now identify as the Qashqa'i.

The Qashqa'i polity emerged during a period of political instability
and decentralization of power occurring from the end of the Safavids to
the rise of Reza Shah in the 1920s, a period characterized in the southern province of Fars by a decline in agriculture and a settled rural population and the abandonment of many rural settlements. Qashqa'i history, involving connections among the Shahilu family, Iranian state
rulers, and peoples residing in the rural southern Zagros, can be divided into two coherent periods that correspond with the major period-

ization of Iranian history. The first period, between the late Safavids and early Qajars, corresponds with dynastic decline, tribalized civil war, the rise and fall of short-lived dynasties, and the early impact of capitalism (especially in south Iran). During this period connections between the Shahilu and rural inhabitants were established and took an early and loose but coherent form. The second period extends from the mid-nineteenth century to the present—that is, the period coextensive with modern nation-state formation in Iran as the result of the impact of capitalism. During this period the Qashqa'i polity took very specific, concrete form.

The history of Qashqa'i political centralization is a history of attempts by the Iranian state, foreign powers, and competing elites and polities to exercise power in and extract wealth from the Zagros Mountains of southwest Iran. The Zagros are located at the western edge of the vast Iranian plateau and consist of parallel mountain chains running northwest to southeast, separated by valleys and plateaus, which are sometimes fertile and well watered but are more often suitable only as pasture because of their considerable altitude (Barthold 1984:166). The specific area inhabited by the Qashqa'i within these mountains, valleys, and plateaus was of great, possibly indispensible, importance to political centralization. Its features include rich natural resources, proximity to trade routes and a major city, distance from the national capital and national borders, isolated and widely separated seasonal pastures, long and vulnerable migration routes through non-Qashqa'i territory, and the dominant, surrounding Persian society. This combination of features is unmatched elsewhere in Iran. More specifically, the Qashqa'i straddled an area of communication between the Persian Gulf and the major population centers of Iran, a strategic location that proved to be vital to expanding British interests via India and the gulf in the eighteenth, nineteenth, and early twentieth centuries. Elites, often relying on military strength, have competed for control over the region's resources, products, and labor throughout Iranian history; this competition is a central theme of that history. One capital of the Persian Empire of the first millennium B.C. was located in the southern Zagros, as were several local dynasties in the twelfth through fourteenth centuries A.D. and the Zand capital of the eighteenth century.[3] This important agricultural and commercial region contrasts with the territories of some of Iran's other nomadic pastoralists, who inhabited

3. The Salghurids (1148–1284) and the Muzaffarids (1313–93).

economic backwaters and peripheral desert environments. Although part of the southern Zagros has been effectively exploited only by nomadic pastoralists, as is true for other areas of Iran, the region also contains rich agricultural lands, heavily settled areas, the city of Shiraz, and important trade routes.[4]

The rich pastures and cultivable land on which the Qashqa'i relied permitted surplus production and contributed to the emergence of socioeconomic stratification and a wealthy and powerful elite, who assumed control over land use, helped to coordinate migrations, and dealt with outside forces. People who regularly used pastures in widely separated locations in the area became part of a coordinated system of migrations and land use that enabled them to compete successfully with others in the region, and they were provided with a system of mediation for interactions with state officials, competing elites, settled society, and foreign powers. For any power to attain and maintain control in the region, a well-developed, locally based, centrally linked political system was essential. For at least two hundred years, the Qashqa'i tribal confederacy proved to be a viable means of organization for its members, who rarely needed directly to confront intruding, competing polities and organizations, including those connected with the Iranian state. The confederacy prevented the state from subordinating or assimilating the Qashqa'i people, while at the same time it enhanced their exploitation of resources and permitted a high degree of local political, economic, and cultural autonomy.

The history of Qashqa'i political centralization is a history of the parallel processes of centralization in the Iranian state. The Qashqa'i emerged as a polity at a time when rulers of Iran were attempting to establish and extend authority over the territory they claimed and were developing mechanisms for ruling—however indirectly, in some cases—the people within their borders. The polity emerged simultaneously with the attempted extension of state structures into areas heretofore relatively free of them, two dynamically connected processes, and not a historical coincidence.

From at least early Islamic times until the centralizing rule of the Pahlavi shahs beginning in the mid-1920s, and to some extent thereafter, rulers of Iranian states attempted to govern large groups of nomadic pastoralists through indigenous and appointed leaders. In ex-

4. For a cultural geographical study of historical patterns of settlement in Fars, see Kortum (1975).

change for functions performed on behalf of the state—collecting taxes, organizing armies, and maintaining law and order—these leaders became de facto state officials and received land grants and other privileges. State rulers, who often lost their positions to rivals with more powerful tribal backing, depended on tribal leaders for the maintenance of their rule over the realm. Tribal leaders were essential agents of the state, as were other elites who also performed state-related functions, such as the Muslim clergy. But in the fragmented and inefficient Iranian state, often characterized by few if any autonomous structures of authority, these functions were often carried out sporadically and according to local self-interest. Therefore, until the late 1920s, rulers of Iran encouraged and depended upon competition between and among local elites and organizations, which enabled them to retain overarching control without having either an effective centralized bureaucracy or a strong standing army. The Qashqa'i polity is thus one of a number of often competing entities that have played important roles during various phases of the history of state formation and state centralization in Iran. After the 1920s, centralizing state rulers attempted, through modernizing bureaucracies and military forces, to rule tribally organized nomadic pastoralists more directly and to end competition among local groups. Although the higher Qashqa'i leaders were banished or executed, others continued to perform state functions. The revolution of 1978–79 introduced a regime that initially lacked the ability to rule tribally organized nomadic pastoralists even indirectly but one that gradually consolidated its power through coercive means. Once again, higher leaders were banished or executed and lower ones left to deal with the state.

The Qashqa'i confederacy also developed as a polity during a historical period when foreign powers were interfering in Iran's internal affairs. In the nineteenth and twentieth centuries, other states attempted to develop ties with Iran; it was a period marked by the economic and political penetration of south Iran. The commercial and strategic importance of the region offered interests for the British, Germans, and most recently the Americans to attempt to secure and defend. The inability of Iranian rulers to govern south Iran effectively influenced the degree of foreign involvement in the area. Foreign powers distrusted Iran's ability to protect their interests and hence acted aggressively on their own behalf, contributing further to the state's inability to rule. Foreign powers not only manipulated Iranian rulers, they also attempted to remove Qashqa'i leaders from office, encouraged the formation of a tribal confederacy to rival that of the Qashqa'i, organized and imported military forces to fight Qashqa'i forces, and encouraged and supported changes in pastoral land tenure and other "modernization" programs. During some periods, foreign powers rather than Iranian rulers constituted the effective local power and authority. It is therefore essential to understand the foreign connection in Qashqa'i history.

Qashqa'i identity and ethnicity also emerged within this politically dynamic context. Although the Qashqa'i today have belief in and concrete expressions of cultural unity, they have roots in ethnolinguistically diverse peoples and are still culturally diverse. They developed and enhanced notions of cultural identity not only in the context of defense against attempted state penetration but also when the state weakened or collapsed, as it did in 1979. Qashqa'i leaders explicitly carried forward and elaborated institutions, ideologies, and symbols that served to set the Qashqa'i apart from others in the region and nation. Such cultural processes, which help to explain the affiliations that were essential to the confederacy's longevity, did not occur in a vacuum but in the context of an expanding Iranian, Persian-dominated nation-state. Notions of Qashqa'i cultural identity and desires for greater political autonomy were vitally connected. The changing nature of the integration of the Qashqa'i into the Persian/Iranian state and within the Persian-dominated national political economy through the nineteenth and twentieth centuries is a major focus of this work.

The terms *tribe* and *state* indicate complex sociopolitical phenomena having variant forms and components. Both terms stand for a variety of leaders or rulers, institutions, practices, and ideologies that are historically variable, situationally specific, and contextually defined. A state is broadly defined on the basis of institutionalized power in the form of socioeconomic stratification (differential access to strategic resources) and the centralized arrogation and control of force, and it is institutionally expansionistic, a trait linked directly to the centralized control of force (Price 1978:170, 179; Fried 1967). Throughout Iranian history the centralization of state authority and tribal authority involved parallel and interrelated processes; both entailed the expansion in scale of sociopolitical systems, the coalescence of smaller systems into larger, more complex ones. As predominant patterns in Iranian history between the eleventh and twentieth centuries, tribes coevolved and coexisted with states, states broke up into competing tribal factions, and tribal systems formed complex polities, including states.

The expansion of state structures into areas occupied by non-state-organized people has a number of possible results. State rulers can pacify and encapsulate, exterminate, or force the people to flee from the area. Or these people can, in response, form tribes or secondary states (Price 1978:180–81). In the case considered here, Iranian rulers were unable for at least two centuries to pacify and encapsulate, exterminate, or expel the Qashqa'i nomadic pastoralists found in the southern Zagros—all actions which in other locations and historical periods rulers did take with respect to nomadic pastoralists.

The formation of a tribe solves several political problems.[5] It enables people to escape certain aspects of state encroachment, and it enables state rulers to govern—however indirectly—people within their territories and to extract from them wealth and labor. Tribes usually emerge on the periphery of effective state control, either on the actual physical borders of the state or in ecologically marginal areas or difficult terrain such as mountains, where state rulers lack the physical and material forces to exert power and authority directly or deem such an expenditure of energy of dubious worth. State rulers cannot afford to neglect these areas completely or for long periods, however, without risking their own, often tenuous, monopoly on physical coercion. They need to prevent internal competitors and imperialist—often neighboring—states from taking control, especially because the areas are often important buffer zones, and they usually require resources and labor from the areas. As a compromise, state rulers seek ways to rule indirectly, although ultimately they aim to rule directly. They have two possible strategies, both of which help to centralize power and authority in these areas.

First, state rulers can select one or more individuals from local populations to be responsible to the state for maintaining law and order in the area. This action can result in people being subsumed under a single authority when they had not been previously. Political organizations present among the indigenous people are transformed in this process, and a new polity may emerge. Initially a tribe is often administratively defined as the people for which the state-appointed leader is responsible. These indigenous individuals are usually existing leaders

5. Ernest Gellner notes that "the creation of a tribe solves a political problem"; personal communication, 4 July 1979, London; also Gellner (1983:442).

of some people in the area, who now have their population base expanded and their position legitimized and enhanced through state conferral. If state rulers do not approve of the actions of established indigenous leaders, they can bestow power and authority on rival leaders. Second, state rulers can assign their own officials to be responsible for law and order in the area and possibly to serve as leaders of the people there. This strategy also results in people being subsumed under a single authority when this had not previously been so, and this too may involve the formation of a new polity, for previously existing political organizations among the indigenous people are transformed. While this strategy theoretically offers more direct rule than ruling through indigenous leaders, the fact that the officials serve other than local interests and are nonindigenous individuals, usually of a different linguistic and cultural background, inhibits rapport and usually prevents effective rule. Garthwaite, in his work on the Bakhtiyari tribal confederacy in west-central Iran (1983:15), labels these two strategies jointly as "designation" (in contrast with "amalgamation," when an indigenous leader welds successively larger and more effective units under his own authority), but the differences between the two strategies seem significant enough to warrant separate treatment.

State structures, in other words, can encapsulate indigenous, politically centralized societies more easily than they can indigenous decentralized societies. State rulers unable or unwilling to rule directly their peripheral territories enhance or create political leaders and institutions for the indigenous people there, actions that place a uniform political umbrella over diverse peoples and initiate tendencies toward political centralization. State rulers then rule them indirectly through these authorities and associated institutions, have easier access to resources and labor, and can more easily prevent competitors from seizing control of the area. State rulers, requiring agents at the local level and relatively stable groups to administer, often owe their survival to the success of these activities. Rulers of weak or decentralized states are especially dependent on alternative polities in the areas they cannot rule directly or effectively (Blok 1974, Godelier 1977:89); such states might collapse without these polities.

State rulers, while enhancing or creating authority structures for the purposes of ruling territory and extracting wealth and labor, simultaneously enhance or create the potential on the part of these same people for anti-state actions. This development poses a serious dilemma for state rulers: in order to extend their authority to an area, they must first politically unify the people there, a process that can make the resulting polity a political threat. The history of the Middle East and central Asia, and Iran in particular, contains many examples of tribes rising against the states in which they were formed and state rulers being forced to develop strategies to control the tribes they originally strengthened or created. The Qashqa'i are but one of many cases. This situation explains the seemingly contradictory behavior of state rulers who both bestow leadership titles and carry out reprisals (Ahmed 1980:63). Such a double-edged strategy creates tension and insecurity for both interacting parties. In a somewhat different although still relevant context, Yapp astutely remarks that "to destroy a tribe a state must first create it" (1983:186).

The development of tribes can also lead to the rise of states. Tribal leaders can successfully challenge state rule in their own territories and form their own states, and they can expand to challenge and take over state rule in other territories. In the fourteenth century, the Arab historian Ibn Khaldun wrote eloquently about the cyclical process involved (Rosenthal 1967, Mahdi 1957). The agrarian societies of much of the Middle East were formed under the circumstances of repeated conquests by militarily organized tribal polities, which for centuries, possibly for millennia, competed with one another for the right to dominate agrarian societies that were reduced to the status of subject peoples (Meeker 1980:687). In the case of the Turks and Mongols of central Asia in the eleventh through fifteenth centuries, tribes were a prelude to the rise of large-scale states; their success is largely explained by military prowess and technological superiority. In Iran, all major ruling dynasties from A.D. 1000 to 1926 were tribal in origin, except the Safavids, and all, including the Safavids, based their military strength on tribal forces. Ruling dynasties developed when tribal leaders on the peripheries of states grew in military and political power, conquered existing states, and became state rulers.

I define the term *tribe* as a polity emerging out of the contact between local resource-sharing, non-state-organized people and larger, more complex polities, states in particular. A tribe develops in the context of a particular sociopolitical environment; it is an adaptive strategy adopted by people to mitigate encapsulation or avoid extermination, and it is a form of manipulation by states and imperial powers in order to rule indirectly. A tribe is an authority structure that emerges in response to another or other authority structures. It contains a political system composed of a leadership and a means of organizing people beyond the local household and resource-utilizing level. The primary function of this political system is to mediate between affiliated members and competing forces and to ensure some degree of autonomy and security in the utilization of resources. It provides protection to the group in the face of competition and incursion, and it creates the means for organized defense and offense. Membership in a tribe is defined dynamically, largely in terms of allegiance to political leaders and affiliation to sociopolitical groups. The degree of political development in a tribe is correlated with the degree of competition and external pressure. A tribe as a sociopolitical entity is a means by which its members relate to similar or more complexly organized societies. It sometimes stands in opposition to other polities, particularly states. A tribe can be viewed as the dialectical expression of the conjuncture of affiliated people undertaking one or more modes of production, externally imposed pressures, and mediating agents. Its history is therefore internally generated as well as shaped by external forces.

Other features are often associated with a tribe, but none is the principal defining feature, nor do all taken together serve to create or define a tribe. In addition, all occur in nontribal society. A tribe usually has a territorial basis and orientation because land is the primary resource and needs protection. A tribe usually has some common ethnolinguistic features and notions of cultural distinctiveness, even though the people may be culturally diverse; members of a tribe, although they often speak a common language, may share this language with their neighbors. A tribe often has a name or names, but so do its component parts. Members of a tribe often use kinship idioms to unite them; they invoke one or more common ancestors, recite genealogies, delineate lineages, and stress their common kinship ties. A symbolic complex—usually composed of a name, language, customs, notions of common ancestry and "blood," genealogy, and possibly a ritual or religious system—is often associated with a tribe. Other kinds of sociopolitical entities, such as ethnic and religious groups, castes, and some occupational categories, also have symbolic complexes. In all cases they reflect political processes and facilitate political unity (Krader 1968:60, Cohen 1974). There is no necessary association between a tribe and a particular ecological adaptation, mode of production, economic system, pattern of mobility, or life-style (Asad 1979). A common error of many scholars, especially of the Middle East and Iran, and others is the facile equation of tribes with nomadic pastoralists, probably because of the frequent association of the two. Nothing inherent in either nomadism or pastoralism, or their combination, generates a tribe. In Iran and elsewhere, some nomadic pastoralists have no historical or current tribal associations, and many settled agriculturalists are tribally organized and affiliated.

Eickelman outlines four forms in which people make tribal identities. Two concern the identifications of the people themselves ("the elaboration and use of explicit 'native' ethnopolitical ideologies by the peoples themselves to explain their sociopolitical organization" and "implicit *practical* notions held by people which are not elaborated into formal ideologies"); one concerns the concepts used by state authorities for administrative purposes; and one concerns anthropological concepts (1981:88).[6] Anthropologists, however, do not agree about such concepts. The entities they often define as tribes have not proven to have enough common characteristics to warrant a single label (tribe) for all of them, while the definitions themselves have been overly broad.[7] In

6. Anthropologists have also defined tribes in ways that served political ends and provided practical guides to action. By choosing certain people to study and by affixing a tribal label to certain people, they have given national governments, imperial powers, indigenous people, and social scientists the basis for acting in terms of these units.

7. Sahlins's overview of tribal societies (1968) unintentionally demonstrates that the extent of political, economic, social, cultural, and religious diversity in the world's so-called tribes is so great that the term is rendered practically useless. In the literature, the term *tribe* commonly covers the range from totally acephalous societies to kingdoms. For some scholars (Leacock 1972, Fried 1975, Godelier 1977), a term that is supposed to apply so broadly has no true meaning. "Tribe . . . has been too loosely used. . . . It has been applied alike to societies which are no more than a loose aggregate of autonomous villages to societies where there is a relatively centralized administrative and judicial apparatus" (Leacock 1972:266–67). If the term *tribe* encompasses "all primitive societies" (including acephalous societies as well as chiefdoms), then classless and class societies are lumped, and the category is "hardly distinct from two other categories of society opposing each other: the 'bands' of hunter-gatherers on the one side, 'state' societies on the other" (Godelier 1977:88–89). The structural differences between classless and class societies are more important than their similarities, one of which is the use of kinship in the relations of production. Despite the publication of excellent critical statements about the anthropological use of the concept of tribe, as generally applied (Fried 1975, Helm 1968, Godelier 1977, Southall 1970) and as applied to the Middle East (Gellner 1981:1–85, Asad 1972, Eickelman 1981:63–104), many anthropologists continue to use the term in an uncritical fashion. Most anthropologists view a tribe as a "primitive" society, a resource-sharing, culture-sharing, kinship-based, and socially bounded population. And, for this reason, some believe that tribes no longer exist in the modern world. Many anthropologists assume that a tribe is not part of more complex polities such as states,

addition, the definitions typically describe phenomena that may never have existed; they conjure up an improbable past (which is often euphemistically termed the "ethnographic present")—as, for example, "a tribal society . . . is a whole society, with a high degree of self-sufficiency at a near subsistence level, based on a relatively simple technology without writing or literature, politically autonomous and with its own distinctive language, culture, and sense of identity" (Southall 1970:28). Such highly discrete polities probably did not exist before the emergence of states. Pre-state societies must have been loosely knit, without clear-cut boundaries or centralizing economic or political institutions (Fried 1975:76). Members of pre-state and non-state societies interacted regularly with other societies in their regions, a fact that cuts against the closed, self-contained nature often ascribed by anthropologists to tribes (Paynter and Cole 1980).

> Although we are accustomed to think about the most ancient forms of human society in terms of tribes, firmly defined and bounded units of this sort actually grew out of the manipulations of relatively unstructured populations by more complexly organized societies. The invention of the state, a tight, class-structured political and economic organization, began a process whereby vaguely defined and grossly overlapping populations were provided with the minimal organization required for their manipulation, even though they had little or no internal organization of their own other than that based on conceptions of kinship. The resultant form was the tribe. [Fried 1975:i]

Some scholars identify tribes as socially egalitarian units, while others see greater complexity. Tribes are not static units, however, but are historically and situationally dynamic and have decentralizing and

---

although the issue is not usually addressed explicitly. Some scholars reject the use of the term *tribe* for political reasons (Diamond 1970, Southall 1970). They, as well as some others (Asad 1972), believe that tribes are Western reifications serving the interests of imperialist powers, that they are myths created by colonists who are assisted by obliging anthropologists. They demonstrate how imperialist powers have manipulated names and categories in order to rule people under their domain. This type of influence by foreign powers is compatible with my discussion of tribes, and the work of these scholars, who note that politically complex polities such as Western imperialist states generate tribes, supports my own notions of how some tribes are formed. British policy in parts of Africa and the Middle East, for example, was to create tribal administrative units by recognizing or selecting and then sanctioning particular leaders.

egalitarian as well as centralizing, inegalitarian, and hierarchical tendencies. The task of the analyst is therefore not to define tribes rigidly but, instead, to discover the conditions under which a decentralizing or a centralizing tendency is dominant within the society at any given time and then to trace the transformations through time. Several scholars suggest a continuum of possibilities in this regard (Gellner 1981:38, Garthwaite 1983:12–16, van Bruinessen 1983:369), while others see cycles of political centralization and decentralization (Sahlins 1963:298) and oscillations between tribal formation and state formation (Krader 1968:100). A continuum can cover the range from decentralized society (egalitarian or "kinship" society) to centralized society (inegalitarian, hierarchical, and possibly class-based society). The stages of political evolution (egalitarian, ranked, stratified, and state societies) suggested by Fried (1967) are possible points along this continuum, as are Service's (1975) stages of social evolution (band, tribe, chiefdom, and state). A continuum for Middle Eastern nomadic pastoralists can include kin group or lineage, tribe, confederacy, and state, in which a confederacy is a centralized, hierarchical, non-kinship-based polity analytically positioned between less centralized entities and a state.[8] Each of these terms can also be construed analytically as a continuum. States in Iran, for example, demonstrated many variant forms in the eighteenth through twentieth centuries. They ranged from fragmented polities to centralized states maintained by a bureaucracy and a standing army and claiming a monopoly of the legitimate use of power (the modern state in the Weberian sense) (Garthwaite 1983:15). For much of the period of Iranian history under discussion here, it is difficult to consider the state as if it were an analytically distinct entity, for autonomous structures of authority, separate from other existing polities and political forces, did not exist. The Iranian state was often little more than the expression of the interests and activities of such groups as the royal or ruling family, wealthy commercial and landowning elites, military leaders, Muslim clergy, leaders of tribes and confederacies, and foreign powers.

Recent hypotheses concerning political development among nomadic pastoralists focus on interactions with states, complex and hier-

8. Kinship does, of course, remain important among people organized into confederacies; the development of complex political organizations does not eliminate kinship but rather leads to its reinterpretation (Fried 1967).

archical societies, and other external stimuli (Burnham 1979, Lindner 1982, Khazanov 1984). Irons suggests that

> among pastoral nomadic societies, hierarchical political institutions are generated only by external political relations with state societies, and never develop purely as a result of the internal dynamics of such societies. . . . In the absence of relatively intensive political interaction with sedentary society, pastoral nomads will be organized into small autonomous groups, or segmentary lineage systems. Chiefly office with real authority will be generated only by interaction with sedentary state-organized society. [Irons 1979:362, 372]

Because all pastoral nomadic societies interact politically with sedentary state-organized societies, however, and take part of their form from this interaction, their "internal" dynamics cannot easily be isolated. Also, a determination of the time when interaction between the two societies becomes "intense" is problematic. Tapper explains two ideal types of tribal leaders—"brigands" and "chiefs"—in terms of the relative weakness or strength of the central government (1983:55–57), while Garthwaite suggests that "the potential for tribal confederation is directly proportional to the strength of an external stimulus" (1983:4), a general and broadly applicable hypothesis.

Stress on the influence of the nontribal or external domain corrects earlier explanations of tribal polities, which presented them as generated by endogenous factors. Because descriptive and analytical difficulties emerge in attempting to separate external and internal domains while simultaneously focusing on the process of change, an analyst can, instead, stress the processes involved in the interactions of state and non-state polities, which will enhance the utility of hypotheses concerning tribal formation and tribe-state relationships. Helfgott's characterization of the "constant dynamic in Iranian history involving the structured relations between two distinct socioeconomic formations— one characterized by the natural division of labor and kinship relations and the other characterized by a more complex division of labor and class rule" (1977:54–55) is relevant in this regard. Finally, an adequate explanation of the interaction of state and non-state societies is not possible without an understanding of the historical, political, economic, and ecological context, which introduces factors that affect both state and non-state polities, structures their interaction, and increases

or decreases the possibility and extent of centralization occurring in
each one. For example, the opening of a trade route, incursion of a
foreign power, or development of a commercial enterprise may restructure the interaction of a state and a non-state polity to the extent that
the state decentralizes and the non-state polity develops hierarchical
political institutions. Without such contextual factors, neither change
might have occurred.

In this analysis of the Qashqa'i tribal confederacy, I rely heavily on
information gathered during four periods of research and residence in
south Iran. From 1963 to 1964 I was in Iran as a student at Pahlavi
University (now Shiraz University) in Shiraz. Qashqa'i individuals were
my classmates and friends, and I traveled extensively in their region. I
returned to south Iran from 1969 through 1971, in 1977, and in 1979
to conduct anthropological research on current and historical Qashqa'i
politics. During part of this research, I lived with the khan family of
one of the component Qashqa'i tribes, with whom I have enjoyed a
long-term personal relationship. Most of my doctoral research and part
of my postdoctoral research were conducted among members of a
Qashqa'i subtribe whose headman was closely linked with khans of his
tribe and with the confederacy's paramount leaders. This association
gave me an appreciation of the impact of different levels of leadership
on the local level. Data gathered during these four periods have contributed significantly to my understanding of archival and other historical materials.

I have interviewed members of the Qashqa'i confederacy's ruling
family, members of the ruling families of the component Qashqa'i
tribes, nonelite Qashqa'i of various political affiliations, and Iranians
who knew Qashqa'i leaders and/or were knowledgeable about the confederacy. I observed the political activities of the paramount leaders
shortly after their return to Iran from exile in 1979, spoke and corresponded with them periodically from 1979 to 1985, and interviewed
many Qashqa'i and other Iranians about the resumption of this leadership. I have observed each level of the political hierarchy in operation,
from the bottom up and the top down, under different conditions (the
Pahlavi state in 1963–64, 1969–71, 1977; revolutionary Iran and the
Islamic Republic in 1979; political exile in Europe in 1979–82) and
in different contexts (nomadic camps, seasonal migrations, villages,
encampments and urban residences of khans, government offices, gen-

darme posts, residences of khans in exile). Just as I have utilized anthropological experience in interpreting the historical record, so have I used history to interpret my firsthand observations as an anthropologist.

2

An Overview

*T*he dominant members of the Qashqa'i confederacy were Turkic, probably derived from western Oghuz people who began entering Iran from central Asia in the eleventh century A.D. Although the confederacy may have begun to develop in the seventeenth century, or even earlier, little historical information exists until the eighteenth. Karim Khan Zand, who ruled in south Iran in the second half of the eighteenth century, appointed a Qashqa'i khan as *ilbegi* (tribal leader) of the province of Fars, and Qajar shahs after him regularly appointed Qashqa'i khans as *ilkhani*s (paramount tribal leaders) and ilbegis of Fars. Whether rulers earlier than Karim Khan also designated Qashqa'i khans as ilkhanis and ilbegis is not known, although ancestors of these khans are reputed to have performed state functions for Shah Isma'il Safavi in the early sixteenth century and for Nader Shah Afshar in the mid-eighteenth century. The proximity of the Zand capital, Shiraz, and the nature of Karim Khan Zand's rule undoubtedly contributed greatly to what locally amounted to centralization among nomadic pastoralists in the region. Many tribal people brought by Karim Khan to Fars to serve as his standing army remained behind after the Zand collapse and came under the authority of the Qashqa'i khans.[1]

1. This chapter constitutes a general statement; greater detail and references are included in later chapters.

The Qashqa'i are distinguished from other tribal, nomadic pastoral, and settled agricultural peoples in southwest Iran by their political allegiances and affiliations. Many of the Turks, Lurs, Laks, Kurds, Arabs, Persians, and gypsies who utilized and who sought resources in the region aligned themselves with Qashqa'i leaders and over time assumed Qashqa'i identity. The primary basis of this identity was political allegiance to leaders and affiliation to political groups (subtribes, tribes, and the confederacy). In the twentieth century, the major Qashqa'i tribes were Amaleh, Darrehshuri, Kashkuli Bozorg, Shish Boluki, and Farsi Madan; smaller tribes and other sociopolitical units were also part of the confederacy. Identity also came with residence in Qashqa'i territory and the assumption of associated rights and duties of control and defense. Cultural features such as Turkic speech, dress, and custom were also important, especially in the twentieth century, and, although not uniform among the people, were sufficiently recognizable to distinguish most Qashqa'i from most non-Qashqa'i in the region. The identifying labels "Qashqa'i" and "Turk," which in Fars are virtually synonymous, are associated with these political affiliations.

The contemporary leaders of the Qashqa'i confederacy trace descent from Amir Ghazi Shahilu (reputed relative of Shah Isma'il who established Shi'i Islam as the state religion in the early sixteenth century) and from his descendant in the eighteenth century, Jani Aqa, who is considered the founder of the confederacy. The Shahilu patrilineage provided every paramount leader of the confederacy. The time period this represented was longer than that experienced by any other tribal or confederacy leadership in Iran and exhibited a longevity comparable to some of Iran's nontribal, urban-based elite families. Through this history, paramount Qashqa'i leaders enjoyed the support of their followers and exercised considerable charismatic influence over them. In the twentieth century and possibly earlier, they consistently identified with Qashqa'i culture and life-style, certain aspects of which they helped to form. In tribal territory and often in cities, leaders wore distinctive clothes. They did not often dress like members of Iran's upper class, of which they were a part, nor did they identify with them, despite superficial similarities. They established tent-camps in the seasonal pastures of nomads, perfected hunting and riding skills, worked personally on their properties, and were available—whether in tent-camps or urban residences—to any tribesperson who came to them. They delighted in wedding celebrations, in which central elements of the Qashqa'i cultural system were expressed, and they set themselves

apart, when possible, from Persians, whom they privately ridiculed.
They associated Persian culture with corruption, deceit, and disingen-
uous politeness, to which they had been subject in their interactions
with members of the dominant society. The paramount leaders' identification with the Qashqa'i cultural system was one reason they enjoyed the loyalty and allegiance of the Qashqa'i people. In contrast to
the Bakhtiyari (Brooks 1983:357), cultural connections between these
leaders and the Qashqa'i people were strong and overt, their relationships respectful and emotional. Both groups were proud to be
Qashqa'i, and each acknowledged the importance of the other.

THE SETTING

The setting in which the Qashqa'i confederacy developed contains
many features that help to explain its particular character and was especially favorable for the political forms that emerged. It is noteworthy
that the tribal groups immediately to the northwest and southeast of
the Qashqa'i, residing in different settings, developed different political systems. Nomadic pastoralism in the relatively lush Zagros Mountains of western and southwestern Iran is somewhat surprising because
the physical environment seems to favor a settled agricultural way of
life. The Qashqa'i in the southern Zagros occupy territory ecologically
varied and rich in natural resources. While parts of the region are suitable only for seasonal occupancy, given constraints of climate, water,
and natural vegetation and fuels, others are permanently occupied, and
population density is relatively high. Through history the ecological
setting has contributed to socioeconomic stratification among the region's inhabitants, and wealthy elites have competed for control of resources, products, and labor. Pastoralists (tribal and nontribal), agriculturalists, and collectors of natural resources, often forced to compete
for access to and control over land, have exploited the southern Zagros
throughout history. The Qashqa'i polity, emerging in the eighteenth
and nineteenth centuries under the authority of a wealthy ruling elite,
was a centralized political system enabling the affiliated nomadic pastoralists and cultivators to maintain sustained use and control of a large
portion of the region and to produce at maximum levels with relative
freedom from predatory incursions. The system also facilitated the ability of elite and nonelite Qashqa'i to extract wealth from others, a practice augmenting their economies, especially in times of regional political instability and drought. Both maximum production and the

ability to extract surpluses contributed to the overall, long-term power of the Qashqa'i polity.

The Qashqa'i have also been strategically located. Shiraz, the major city in southwest Iran and a center of Qashqa'i political and economic affairs, lies between their winter and summer pastures, south and north of the city, and most Qashqa'i migrate past it twice annually. The Qashqa'i elite established residences and extensive networks in the city which, combined with tribal backing and wealth, made its members major figures in local politics. Tribal and urban politics often overlapped. Some members of the elite used their positions in the region as the basis for national prominence. Much economic activity in Shiraz was geared toward and supported by the economic production of its hinterland, an important part of which was Qashqa'i territory. Qashqa'i economies were tied to this market center and through it were integrated into regional, national, and international economic systems. Important trade routes linked Shiraz and its hinterland with national and international markets. At least since the late eighteenth century, the link between Shiraz and the Persian Gulf port of Bushire drew the attention of the state and foreign powers and figured prominently in the struggles among these powers and regional ones. The growth of Western influence, interest, and power in the Persian Gulf appears to be precisely the "event" that created the economic and political conditions facilitating the Qashqa'i polity's formation in the eighteenth, nineteenth, and early twentieth centuries. Had Qashqa'i territory not intersected the principal routes of south Iran, a much different tribal history would have resulted.

Qashqa'i territory did not touch or overlap with Iran's borders, unlike the territories of many of the nation's other tribal and non-Persian groups. Distance from state borders was conducive to Qashqa'i autonomy and prosperity in the long run, and the absence of competition over the Qashqa'i by bordering states helped the Shahilu lineage to retain leadership for a long period. The state did not use the Qashqa'i to defend its borders, and they were free from pressures that might be applied by neighboring states and by fellow tribespeople across frontiers. The Qashqa'i were, however, encircled by Iranian territory and constituted a minority enclave within a strategic part of Iran, and hence their integrative, protective political system provided borders of another sort.

Proximity to the Zand capital at Shiraz was important in the early development of the Qashqa'i confederacy. With the fall of the Zand dynasty in the 1790s and the rise of the Qajars, the central government moved to Tehran, where it has remained. This move allowed the confederacy, after the formative years under the Zands, a high degree of autonomy from state control and interference. Proximity to the capital can bring influence in national affairs, but it can also sever tribal leaders from their tribal base; both happened to the Bakhtiyari (Garthwaite 1983). Except for a brief period during the constitutional era (1906–11), state rulers did not view the Qashqa'i as a military threat to the capital. Before Reza Shah, Qashqa'i leaders did not seriously pursue national leadership; most used their Tehran connections to serve their class and tribal interests in Fars. Beginning with Reza Shah's reign, they attempted to strengthen their position in the state, and a few did seek national leadership. The Qashqa'i people were too distant from the capital to be much involved in their leaders' quests for national leadership, except when the state brought sanctions against them in order to punish these leaders.

Qashqa'i winter and summer pastures are isolated and virtually inaccessible to outsiders, and their mountain territories are particularly defensible. Before the advent of Reza Shah's improved roads and mechanized army, state forces could attack the Qashqa'i in their pastures or directly threaten their lands only with difficulty. State and foreign forces made no efforts to dislodge the Qashqa'i from their pastures until the 1960s, and no other tribes or confederacies seriously threatened their control of land. In the modern age of aircraft, paved roads, and tanks, however, military forces have had enhanced abilities to assault the dispersed, mobile Qashqa'i people, usually with the intention of defeating their leaders.

The strategic isolation of Qashqa'i pastures contrasts with their vulnerable migration routes, which have been their Achilles' heel because pastoralism depended on the seasonal movement of herds between low altitude (one to five thousand feet) winter pastures (*qishlaq* in Turkic, *garmsir* in Persian) and high altitude (up to twelve thousand feet) summer pastures (*yailaq* in Turkic, *sarhad* and *sardsir* in Persian) separated by 200 to 350 miles. Migration routes took the Qashqa'i past Shiraz and through heavily settled, nontribal agricultural areas. Regional, national, and foreign armies attempted, sometimes successfully, to block migration routes, thus threatening Qashqa'i economic survival. Migrating Qashqa'i were also vulnerable to raids and attacks by non-Qashqa'i populations. Qashqa'i leaders coordinated these movements, and hence the nature of migrations relates to the development of centralized leadership.

The geographical distribution of the Qashqa'i in vast, widely separated seasonal pastures has always caused problems for state administration, but it also facilitated coordination through both centralized and locally based Qashqa'i leaders. While some of Iran's tribal groups reside and migrate within single provinces and can be administratively contained within a single jurisdiction, Qashqa'i are found in five areas (Fars, Isfahan, Kuhgiluyeh-Boir Ahmad, Khuzistan, the gulf coast), and many fall under different provincial governments at different times of the year. The government's administration of the Qashqa'i was almost always indirect, even during periods of strong, centralized state rule, and government policy was by necessity relayed from state officials to tribal mediators and hence was vague and usually unimplemented.

The Qashqa'i occupy a minority status in the dominant Persian society of the region and nation. Tribal leadership and confederacy organization coordinated and protected Qashqa'i activities and served as political, military, and cultural counterforces to intrusions and to expanding Persian control of nearby centers of power and wealth—the state apparatus, the bazaars, and the religious institutions. Although of diverse linguistic, cultural, and tribal origins, the Qashqa'i express their common identity as "Turks," affirming group solidarity and creating boundaries between themselves and members of the surrounding society, who are predominantly Persians and Lurs. Qashqa'i leaders shared this Turkic cultural identity and used its associated symbols and institutions to support their leadership.

PRESSURES FROM OUTSIDE

The more complex and multifaceted a pastoral nomadic society's interactions are with external powers, the greater the potential for the development of hierarchical political institutions and the formation of a tribal confederacy. Why external powers were interested in the Qashqa'i and their territory, and how the tribal people and their leaders responded, must be considered. Qashqa'i leaders, often in a position to initiate interaction, cannot be seen as passive victims of external forces. External powers include the central government, provincial government, foreign powers, other tribes and confederacies, and institutionalized religion. Although two or more powers occasionally cooperated in order to ally with or confront the Qashqa'i, their respective interests did not necessarily coincide. In fact, much of the drama in the history of southwest Iran derives from the opposing interests and resulting confrontations and conflicts between and among these powers; and the relationships of tribal, provincial, national, and international politics through time are complex.

The central government's interest in the Qashqa'i, centering on taxes and revenues, military service, and law and order (especially near settled areas and trade routes), would have applied to any people occupying the rich southern Zagros. But its interest was also drawn by the fact that the numerous, tribally organized, armed, mobile, and sometimes politically independent Qashqa'i were able to resist imposition of government control and could interfere with administration. Some governments were not able to govern the Qashqa'i, while others worked through, rather than against, Qashqa'i leaders in order to facilitate their own administration. Still others intrigued and battled against them, sometimes quite effectively. The government exercised indirect but proximate rule over the Qashqa'i under Karim Khan Zand in the second half of the eighteenth century, indirect decentralized rule under the Qajars in the nineteenth century, virtually no rule during the first two decades of the twentieth century, more direct and centralized rule under the Pahlavi shahs between 1926 and 1979, and weak but sporadically hostile rule under the Islamic Republic of Iran. Some early Shahilu figures may have fought for Safavid rulers, and two later figures accompanied Nader Shah Afshar on his conquest of India in 1738. Karim Khan Zand assigned one of them authority over the tribes of Fars. The first Qajar ruler was hostile to Qashqa'i leaders, but later Qajars governed the Qashqa'i indirectly by instituting the office of paramount tribal leader, and Qashqa'i troops and commanders were part of the Qajar armies. The Pahlavis worked to eliminate Qashqa'i leaders and destroy tribal power. The Khomeini regime, initially supported by Qashqa'i leaders, crushed a Qashqa'i insurgent movement after two years of military attacks but as of 1985 had failed to establish its authority in many Qashqa'i areas. During each period, paramount Qashqa'i leaders dealt directly and personally with state rulers, a major characteristic of Qashqa'i relations with central authorities through history. Relationships between tribal leaders and state rulers ran the gamut from intermarriage and parliamentary service to imprisonment and execution, sometimes for the same individuals. In attempts to exercise control, rulers occasionally exiled Qashqa'i families to distant locations, held tribal leaders or relatives as court hostages, and arranged marriage alliances between court and Qashqa'i families.

From at least Qajar times, the central government's appointment or confirmation of the paramount Qashqa'i khan as ilkhani made him a government official responsible for handling nontribal as well as tribal affairs in Fars, including tax collection, conscription, and the maintenance of order. While the formal appointment almost always coincided with internal tribal recognition, the powers and privileges accompanying the title of paramount leader were considerable, and ilkhanis were able to enhance their already strong positions. On occasion, the government—under pressure from other powers—deposed a tribally favored ilkhani and tried to seat a rival, intending to create internal tribal crises, but most tribal members refused to pay allegiance to such appointees.

The central government held the Qashqa'i ilkhani and ilbegi responsible for the collection of taxes from the Qashqa'i and from other tribes and villages under their authority. They did not always collect taxes nor did they always transfer collected taxes to the government, hence officials were interested in amicable relations with them. Qashqa'i leaders were also obliged to provide levies for the shahs' armies, a service offering them arms, legitimated military action against competitors, captured property, and enhanced tribal power. The government at different periods entrusted to Qashqa'i leaders the task of securing the countryside, and as a result much of Fars was under their control or influence. Their territory was often considered an autonomous administrative region—Vilayat-e Qashqa'i—and the ilkhani was held responsible for it. The ilkhani and other members of the ruling family were assigned district governorships and the duty of bringing order to neighboring tribes and territories, which added to their wealth and power. The loci of government concern were the rich agricultural areas of Fars, from which it could then safely secure taxes and conscripts and its officials could become wealthy, and the trade routes to Bushire and Isfahan, from which the government and its officials could profit by their foreign and mercantile interests. The central government rarely reached the Qashqa'i people directly; but when it did make the attempt, officials holding assigned duties assumed additional, more profitable ones on their own initiative. Qashqa'i leaders handled these officials and protected tribespeople from their predatory incursions. Many people, including non-Qashqa'i agriculturalists in and near

Qashqa'i territory, affiliated with Qashqa'i leaders in order to escape the harassments and extortions of officials. Those who fell under Qashqa'i protection held advantages that others did not, and leaders in turn gained agricultural surpluses, clients, and territories.

Provincial government, the second external power and the expression of local and national politics, was not always organized to serve national interests, as in tax collection and military activity. The two governments often used the Qashqa'i in their power struggles, and Qashqa'i leaders actively promoted their connections with each to further their own interests. As a check on provincial autonomy, the central government installed its own representatives, often relatives of the monarch, in the south. The governor of Fars was a state appointee, although local mercantile families, foreign powers, and Qashqa'i leaders could influence the appointment. When the central government was weak, provincial governors were able to act in their own interests, a situation exploited by regional and foreign powers. The governor of Fars and the Qashqa'i ilkhani were often considered the two top political figures in the south. A third powerful figure in Fars was the Qavam ol-Molk, head of a wealthy merchant-landowner family and frequently chief magistrate of the province. Through the nineteenth and early twentieth centuries, this family's interests and those of the Qashqa'i ruling family often conflicted.

Foreign powers, forming the third category of external power and including the British, Germans, and Americans, have long interfered in the affairs of south Iran. Except for forays by the British-organized South Persia Rifles during World War I, foreign powers have never invaded Qashqa'i territory, but their maneuvers and intrigues against one another and with and against national and local governments, other tribes, and some dissident Qashqa'i groups were major elements in Qashqa'i political history. The Russians, who were the major power in north Iran in the nineteenth and first half of the twentieth century, had little direct impact on the southern Zagros tribes, while the British, motivated by concern for the strategic importance of the area from the Persian Gulf to India, played major roles in south Iran. From the late eighteenth century to the mid-twentieth, especially during the constitutional revolution and the two world wars, British commercial and strategic affairs intruded into the political and economic life of the region. While pursuing their own interests, the British claimed to act on behalf of the Iranian government, whose apparent inability to bring order to south Iran disrupted their strategies.

The first clash between the British and the Qashqa'i was when Qashqa'i troops assisted in the defense of south Iran during the Anglo-Persian war of 1856. Thereafter, British irritation with the Qashqa'i focused on what they believed to be Qashqa'i disruption of British trade and other vital communications in south Iran, including their newly installed telegraph line. In 1861, partly because of British pressure, Naser ed-Din Shah created the Khamseh tribal confederacy and placed it under the leadership of the Qavam family to provide a balance of power in the south. The Qavam family's commercial interests corresponded with those of the British, who financed and employed this confederacy's leaders and forces for their own ends. When the British threatened to create their own local army, the central government, apparently lacking other options, entrusted the maintenance of safety on the roads and stability in the province to the Qashqa'i ilkhani. When the British still could not find safe passage for their commerce, they pressured the government to create a Swedish-officered gendarmerie and financed the Qavam's efforts to attack the Qashqa'i.

During World War I, politics in Fars reflected the British-German struggle. The British were mainly concerned with the safety of the Khuzistan oil fields to the northwest of Qashqa'i territory, but they also had strategic interests in Fars to defend. The German General Staff, acting in terms of its own national interests, sent Wilhelm Wassmuss to provoke tribal uprisings against the British and their allied Khamseh tribes. The British, agitated by these developments, formed a new military force for south Iran, the South Persia Rifles, which was British officered and contained imported Indian troops, and used it to attack Qashqa'i forces. One reason why Reza Shah victimized Iran's pastoral nomadic tribes in the late 1920s and 1930s was his fear of tribal and foreign collusion against his new nation, a fear justified by events prior to and during his reign. The foreign presence thus directly contributed to his oppression of the tribes. During World War II, the Qashqa'i ilkhani and the Germans reestablished ties, largely to counter renewed British interference in the area, and the Germans sent Berthold Schulze-Holthus to the ilkhani's camp to organize anti-British activities.

The United States became deeply involved in Iran beginning in 1942. The paramount Qashqa'i leaders, having supported Prime Minister Mohammad Mosaddeq who was ousted through CIA intrigue in 1953, were forcibly exiled from Iran. American officials, motivated by concern over oil and the Soviet presence and acting on notions that tribes are threats to the state (and hence threats to American interests) both because of their relative autonomy and because of their vulnerability to manipulation by foreign powers, suggested and helped to implement programs for pacification, sedentarization, conscription, and education. Under the American-encouraged land reform of the 1960s, the government nationalized Qashqa'i pastures, distributed many of their cultivable lands to non-Qashqa'i, and removed the second level of khans from office. With the top levels of their political system now largely dismantled, most Qashqa'i fell vulnerable to external pressures.

The southern Zagros contains many tribally organized people who compete for land, resources, supporters, and links with external powers; their tribes and confederacies constitute the fourth category of external power. The Qashqa'i confederacy was particularly successful in this competition; its size and heterogeneity, indicating the mobility of people, resulted from popular perceptions of political effectiveness. Intertribal alliances and conflicts in south Iran, largely provoked by other powers, form an important part of the region's history. The Khamseh confederacy, to the east of the Qashqa'i and of mixed tribal and linguistic origins, was created by the state to counterbalance Qashqa'i power and foment conflict in the area; British and local mercantile interests used it against the Qashqa'i. Previously its tribes had been loosely affiliated with the Qashqa'i for administrative and military purposes. The end of British support and the state's removal of indigenous and externally imposed leaders after World War I signaled the effective end of Khamseh power. The Boir Ahmad and Mamassani, both Kuhgiluyeh Lur tribes and the major tribes to the northwest, occasionally allied with the Qashqa'i against government troops, the British, and the Qavam's Khamseh troops. But the government also used Qashqa'i forces in military campaigns against these Lurs, and several governors appointed from the Qashqa'i ruling family were responsible for security in the Kuhgiluyeh region. Intermarriages among the Qashqa'i and Lur khan families attest to their complex political relations. The Lur tribes never possessed the centralized, coordinating political system of the Qashqa'i or the Bakhtiyari, largely because they were not as strategically located in terms of cities, trade routes, rich agricultural areas, and oil fields, and as a result foreign powers and state authorities were not much interested in manipulating or controlling them. Many Qashqa'i are Lur in origin, indicating the extent to which the Qashqa'i confederacy attracted and retained people in the region.

The Bakhtiyari, also Lurs, are found to the north of Qashqa'i summer pastures. The paramount khans of the Bakhtiyari and Qashqa'i confederacies were frequently at odds, partly because of Bakhtiyari links with the government and the British. On occasion they supported dissident movements in each other's confederacies, and Bakhtiyari and Qashqa'i tribespeople have periodically sought refuge in one another's territories. In 1910 a Bakhtiyari khan in a position of national leadership pressured the government to depose the Qashqa'i ilkhani, and hostility between leaders of the Bakhtiyari and the Arab tribes of Khuzistan, fostered by British manipulations, led to a formal alliance among Qashqa'i, Arab, and Lur tribal leaders. The Dashtistani, Tangistani, and Dashti tribes of the Persian Gulf coast, to the west of the Qashqa'i, were each a heterogeneous group named after the district it occupied and consisted of Arabs, Persians, and Lurs as well as Sunni and Shi'i Muslims. They frequently allied with the Qashqa'i in efforts to fight the British and exploit trade routes. Many other, smaller tribes in Fars also occasionally joined forces with Qashqa'i leaders.

Institutionalized religion is the fifth category of external power. The Qashqa'i are Shi'i Muslims, unlike many of Iran's tribal, ethnic, and national-minority groups. Qashqa'i leaders occasionally allied with Muslim clergy in Shiraz, Tehran, and Najaf (Iraq) during national political struggles. In 1906–11 Qashqa'i khans and Muslim clergy supported the constitutional movement; in 1918 Qashqa'i troops allied with clergy-inspired Shirazis to fight the British; and in 1946 tribal and religious leaders jointly protested against government policy and foreign interference. In 1978 Naser Khan Qashqa'i, the exiled ilkhani, visited the Ayatollah Khomeini in France but, although they remained in amiable contact during the early months of the new Islamic revolutionary government, they later had a falling out. Qashqa'i khans, having little use for organized religion in the conduct of internal and most external affairs, allied with Muslim clergy only when it was politically expedient. They did not rely on persons of religious eminence as advisors or mediators, and few were devout, practicing Muslims.

Economic forces represent an additional set of pressures on the Qashqa'i. Pastoralism and cultivation were very productive in Qashqa'i territory, and competition for control of land and profit flourished. The khans, as owners of land and herds and allocators of usufructuary rights over land, prospered from the proceeds of production, and they and other wealthy Qashqa'i were among the regional elite. Urban merchants and commercial brokers competed for their business and negotiated contracts for the production of animals, grain, fruit, wool, carpets, opium, and gum tragacanth, some of which were exported abroad. These activities facilitated capitalist expansion in Qashqa'i territory, and the influence of national and international markets was felt throughout the region. Qashqa'i pastoralists, who gained exclusive and secure use of pastures through the support of the tribal system, were facilitated in production. Qashqa'i who raided trade routes, collected road tolls, and sold protection to commercial transport derived economic advantage even from facilities they did not use and had no part in creating. Membership in the tribal system facilitated the many economic activities of both wealthy and less wealthy Qashqa'i and connected them with broad economic and political forces.

INTERNAL TRIBAL DYNAMICS

Discussion of the Qashqa'i as a political force is essentially a discussion of the paramount Qashqa'i khans, for they were the power brokers who interacted with other powers. Much Qashqa'i history is therefore a history of these khans. It is clear, however, that they could not have been the political figures they were without the supporting political hierarchy or the support of the numerous Qashqa'i tribespeople. An account of internal tribal dynamics is therefore essential to the discussion of the formation and function of the confederacy.

The Qashqa'i people were organized in a hierarchy of sociopolitical groups, each represented by one or more leaders. At the base was the household, whose head represented it in most domains beyond the encampment or village. For the vast majority of Qashqa'i who were nomadic, the encampment was a flexible, temporary association of households; the oldest, most respected men made some decisions concerning this coresident group but households exercised considerable independence. The pasture group, a collection of encampments in a geographically defined area, was also a flexible arrangement of tents and camps. A subtribe, consisting of a number of pasture groups in winter and summer quarters and sometimes some villages and village sections as well, was a political group defined largely by kinship ties and affiliation to a headman. A tribe was a collection of subtribes headed by a family of khans, one of whom often held the title of *kalantar* and the role of providing liaison with the ilkhani. The khan families were a small, distinct socioeconomic group with dynastic, aristocratic features. Finally, the confederacy, a collection of tribes and other sociopolitical units, was headed by a male member of the ruling Shahilu lineage, who was usually titled ilkhani. The chain of political authority extended from household head to elder, headman, khan, kalantar, and ilkhani, and it paralleled a functional hierarchy of groups formally recognized by having spokesmen. Each tribe had its own winter and summer pastures, and khans allocated usufructuary rights to their associated subtribes, via headmen, who in turn allocated pasture rights to member households. All leaders coordinated the long seasonal migrations, especially under conditions of political instability in the region. Khans, often through headmen, handled general tribal affairs; they designated local leaders, administered tribal law and justice, resolved intratribal and intertribal disputes, negotiated with sedentary authorities, collected taxes, coordinated economic redistribution, and organized defensive and offensive activities. Given the strategic setting and the many external pressures, as outlined above, a centralized, coordinated, and effective leadership was essential if the Qashqa'i were to maintain control of their territory and compete successfully against their neighbors and intruding forces.

The ability of the Qashqa'i to act as a quasi-independent polity rested on the coordinating and mediating efforts of the confederacy leader, the ilkhani. His main functions related to external powers and the confederacy's administration, and he also served as khan to the Amaleh, the tribal body supporting his office. An ilbegi, usually his brother, often served as his lieutenant, and other close relatives also performed leadership functions which were informally assigned according to personal skills and interests. Under Isma'il Khan Soulat ed-Douleh, ilkhani from 1904 to 1933, the Qashqa'i enjoyed some of the main attributes of sovereignty—an army, an economy, and a foreign policy (Oberling 1974:195)—and he functioned as the head of a political group that was often beyond the state's control. He depended on the support and loyalty of the tribal khans, and these khans often depended on and profited from his wider leadership functions. That he could and occasionally did act without their consent or knowledge was his prerogative, based upon his wide-ranging provincial, national, and international connections. One of his bases was Shiraz, where his activities were similar to those of many nontribal elite, but he differed from them in that he could utilize the tribal support behind him. The ilkhani's presence in Shiraz and other settled areas stimulated interaction with powers external to the confederacy; his position as a power broker was a major factor in the degree of interaction that occurred.

Limits were placed on the power of the ilkhani and the activity of the confederacy. All tribal leaders, especially the ilkhani, were restricted by the fact that their political activities held consequences for, and generated reactions from, other powers. As part of the state, the Qashqa'i were always vulnerable to its instabilities, internal power struggles, and foreign intrigue. When the ilkhani engaged in regional and national politics, and when other powers attempted to engage the Qashqa'i as a political or military unit, he functioned as confederacy leader, consulting other Qashqa'i leaders and planning joint action in large tribal gatherings. But he never controlled the other tribes of the confederacy or their khans, and the confederacy itself was never a totally united political or military force. Some tribal activities were always independent of the ilkhani's leadership, and many continued uninterrupted when he was removed from the scene, as was the case during much of Pahlavi history. Also, khans could act independently, and some, including members of his own family, overtly opposed him. Finally, the most concerted military effort by the Qashqa'i involved, at most, five thousand horsemen (at a time when the total population approached four hundred thousand), and these were drawn primarily from only one of the confederacy's many tribes.

Membership in tribes and the confederacy benefited the Qashqa'i people sufficiently that leaders rarely needed to rule by coercion. Through allegiance and loyalty to tribal leaders, the Qashqa'i gained secure and protected access to pastures, which facilitated pastoral and agricultural production. They profited economically from raids and other actions coordinated or supported by their leaders, and, if in economic need, were assisted by leaders who expropriated and redistributed surpluses. They escaped having to interact with external powers, including extortive government officials, and they often benefited in their individual interactions with non-Qashqa'i because of the superior political position and reputation created by the Qashqa'i khans as exemplary Qashqa'i.

As members of tribes and the confederacy, Qashqa'i households and subtribes owed certain obligations. Khans occasionally collected an animal tax to support their office, and the ilkhani levied an additional tax when the state demanded taxes or he needed revenue for warfare. The ilkhani and the khans had ready access to military force in their personal retinues and occasionally relied on additional support from their associated sections as well as from allied non-Qashqa'i forces in the region. Tribesmen who fought for ilkhanis and khans in battle were summoned by headmen whose responsibility was to supply a certain number of warriors, mounted and armed. Some tribespeople also owed labor and tribute to khans and headmen on special occasions.

The extraction of surplus from the Qashqa'i people by tribal leaders was not exploitative, especially compared with practices found elsewhere in the region where landlords extracted 20 to 80 percent of their peasants' yearly agricultural yields. The tax occasionally collected from the Qashqa'i was not burdensome and at any rate was a small proportion of household capital that reproduced regularly. Household economies, based on pastoralism, agriculture, and weaving, were not controlled by tribal leaders except that access to pastures derived from tribal ties and obligations. Matters of animal ownership, allocation of labor, production, and exchange were solely in the hands of individual households. Qashqa'i in economic difficulty were exempt from the tax and could expect some help from leaders. The ability of dissatisfied followers unilaterally to sever ties checked the actions and demands of leaders who depended on political and military supporters, while leaders dissatisfied with followers were also able to apply sanctions and punishments. Denial of access to pasture was the strongest sanction, although those forbidden by one leader could obtain land from another who was anxious to increase his following. Allocation of poor pastures and the temporary imposition of high taxes were still other sanctions. The khans' secretaries, overseers, and gunmen enforced tribal law and the policy of leaders.

The wealth of the ilkhani and khans did not derive primarily from their tribal supporters. These leaders depended on other, more profitable and dependable sources of wealth and avoided heavy extractions from the tribal people, which would have undermined and weakened their support. The state assigned tribal and territorial governorships to the ilkhani, enabling him to acquire private property and collect government taxes, some of which he held back. Most khans were wealthy landowners, having acquired land through government service, investment of income from other economic activities, and confiscation. They extracted part of the yearly production of their sharecroppers and tenants, who were usually Persians and Lurs. The ilkhani received land and cash payments from the state for his administrative functions and for arming and supporting a tribal army. Foreign powers also paid him and other khans to protect trade routes and conduct military operations, and merchants paid these leaders to guarantee safe passage for commercial traffic.

The ilkhani and khans used their various political positions for their own class and personal interests in ways that prevented them from being economically dependent on tribal followers. They derived political and economic power from domains beyond the confederacy, where they were able to use the threat of tribal action to buttress their regional and national positions. The ilkhani and khans established themselves in an interstitial position between the state and the Qashqa'i people, whom the state lacked the means to govern directly. They exploited this position for their own benefit by extracting profits from services offered to both sides, but they avoided exploiting the Qashqa'i people, upon whom they depended for political and military backing. The ability of the Shahilu and the supporting khan lineages to occupy and maintain such an interstitial position facilitated the formation and enduring political power of the Qashqa'i confederacy.

PART II

The Historical Development
of the Qashqa'i Confederacy

Woman and child preparing to mount a horse

3

Qashqa'i Origins

*T*he Qashqa'i originate from peoples having diverse linguistic, cultural, and tribal backgrounds who were part of large- and small-scale movements in southwest and central Asia from Islamic times forward. For most of their history they have not constituted an ethnic group in the common use of the term, and their paramount leaders have always been distinct from those they have led. Practically all references to the Qashqa'i in the literature, however, involve the assumption that a single entity (a "tribe") exists. It is assumed that, as a tribe, the Qashqa'i had an identifiable time and place of origin, that the group's movement through time and space can be traced, and that it did and does consist of ethnolinguistically homogeneous people. It is also assumed that the Qashqa'i people and the Qashqa'i paramount leaders shared a common history and stem from the same group. Scholars and journalists, in writing of the activities of leaders, often phrase their accounts in terms of "the Qashqa'i." These assumptions mask important issues that are central to this study.

HISTORICAL SPECULATIONS

Most sources are correct in noting that the Qashqa'i are not indigenous to southwest Iran, but they focus on establishing their previous locations and the timing and circumstances of their movement into that region. The Qashqa'i were not a single group elsewhere, however, nor did they migrate as a unit.

Some sources place the origin of the Qashqa'i among the Khalaj, a Turkic people originating in central Asia, one of twenty-two branches of the western Oghuz, and one of the Middle East's largest Turkic groups.[1] At the end of the fourteenth century, the Mongol ruler Timur moved some Khalaj from Asia Minor, where they had settled in the eleventh and twelfth centuries, to central and eastern Iran, at which time a group of them was said to have fled and settled in Fars. This group was called "Qashqa'i" ("Fugitives," or "Those Who Fled," from the Turkic verb *kačmak*—to flee). Another theory connects the Qashqa'i with Iraqi Turkmen who escaped from Ghaznavid rulers (994–1040) and settled in western Iran.[2] A nineteenth-century Iranian historian states that the Qashqa'i are a branch of a Yomut Turkmen tribe named Qashqah that accompanied the Salghurid Atabegs to Fars in the twelfth century (Khurmuji 1859). A related notion is that the Qashqa'i descend from the Qara Khitai, who were sent to Fars by Mohammad Khwarazm Shah (1199–1220) to spy on his rival, the Salghurid Atabeg Sa'd (Oberling 1974:27). The dynasty of the Salghurid Atabegs (1148–1284), who ruled in Fars as the tributaries of the Seljuqs, Khwarazm shahs, and Mongols, was of Turkic origin and based its power on nomadic tribes near Gandoman in northern Fars (Haig 1934, Bosworth 1968:172, Lambton 1960:1099), which is regarded as the ancestral pastureland of the Shahilu lineage. Southern Fars provided an "inexpugnable haunt" for Turkic tribes under the Muzaffarids (1313–93), and a certain Ibn Sihab Yazdi noted the presence of Qashqa'i (?) nomads in summer pastures at Gandoman in 1415 (Aubin 1955:497, 504). Nineteenth-century Qashqa'i leaders stated that the Mongol Hulagu Khan brought the Qashqa'i to Iran from Kashgar in Turkistan (Abbott 1857:170, Curzon 1892:112), while more recent ones recount the popular legend that the Qashqa'i originally were cavalrymen whose families tended flocks for Chengiz Khan in eastern Turkistan and who participated in his westward campaigns. Another theory is that the Shahilu lineage descends from the Aqquyunlu ruler Uzun Hasan (d. 1478), but it does not address explicitly the issue of

1. Fasa'i (1895–96b:312), Picot (1897:82), Demorgny (1913a:92), Minorsky (1939–42), Sümer (1978:705), Bosworth and Doerfer (1978), Garrod (1946b:294, 296).

2. Malek Mansur Khan, personal interview, 28 August 1979, Tehran.

the origin of the Qashqa'i people, unless it is assumed that they also descend from Aqquyunlu groups (which were diverse). Finally, a Soviet scholar states that the Qashqa'i were part of the Turkic-speaking Shah-sevan tribes of Mughan in northwest Iran at the end of the sixteenth century and that Shah Abbas (1587–1628) moved these Qashqa'i to Fars to assist in military operations in the Persian Gulf area (Balayan 1960:351, 359ff.).

Elements of truth may exist in each of these theories. Remnants of each group mentioned could be part of the Qashqa'i today, and each group along with the relevant historical circumstances could have played a role in the formation of an early Qashqa'i entity. Many names of groups within the Qashqa'i confederacy today are identical with or similar to names found in other locations and at other times in Iranian history, which, if current groups can be connected with historical ones, does suggest the presence within the Qashqa'i of a diverse set of peoples. Some examples are Qaraquyunlu, Aqquyunlu, Bayat, Afshar, Shul, and Shabankara. This approach does, however, tend to an etymological literalism that is inadequate to the complexities of the process by which tribes and confederacies are formed. A popular method of establishing Qashqa'i history and connecting Qashqa'i people to other groups in Iran has been through weaving styles and certain design elements in woven goods. These attempts are unsatisfactory and inconclusive, especially given market pressures to produce certain styles and designs and the ease and speed with which weavers invent and adopt new ones.

Historians have tried to address the issues of previous locations and movement into Fars through etymological analysis. The word *Qashqa'i* has been connected with geographical and tribal names and Turkic verbs and nouns (Oberling 1974:32–34). Etymologies also serve political purposes, for Persian sources (Fasa'i 1895–96b:312) tend to prefer an unflattering etymology, while Qashqa'i sources prefer more noble ones. Qashqa'i people, especially leaders, find the derivation of *Qashqa'i* from "Those of the Horses with the White Spots on Their Foreheads" (*Qashqa Atlilar*), which they regard as an auspicious sign, more pleasing and acceptable than "Those Who Fled." They argue not only that the Qashqa'i have always held their ground against aggressors and would never have fled, but also that the use of animal-connected names for groups is common. They say *Qashqa Atlilar* was shortened to *Qashqalu,* which when Persianized becomes *Qashqa'i*. Malek Mansur Khan, a member of the Shahilu lineage, believes that *Qashqa'i* means

"Invincible Place," derived from *qash* ("animal pen in an encampment") and *qa'i* ("invincible").[3] In short, such etymologies are more a part of the processes of identity formation than they are its residue.

THE SHAHILU LINEAGE

It is essential to separate the establishment of the ruling dynasty (the Shahilu lineage) of the Qashqa'i confederacy in southwest Iran from that of the political association of groups forming the confederacy, however much the two processes are interdependent. While it is probable that ancestors of today's Shahilu family did enter southwest Iran at a specific historical point, given their claimed Oghuz Turkic ancestry and identity, it is unlikely that a Qashqa'i entity made such an entrance. The Shahilu family was apparently not originally part of a Qashqa'i tribe, nor in all probability did such a "tribe" exist at this time. Some segments of what later became the Qashqa'i confederacy had already been in southwest Iran for centuries, and others were dispersed throughout Iran and adjacent territories. Western Oghuz (Ghuzz) Turkic people, who were part of a loosely joined confederacy of tribes, had been moving from central Asia into Iran from the eleventh century (Cahen 1965, Minorsky 1943:186), and from the middle of the twelfth century, particularly in conjunction with the Salghurid Atabegs, some took up residence in Fars, while Persians, Lurs, Laks, Kurds, Arabs, and others had long been present in the region.[4] For centuries, state rulers had relied on the region's tribal forces for military support and had moved tribal groups into and out of the area. The southern Zagros, ideal for nomadic pastoralism, had often been utilized as pastures for the royal flocks, and many other groups as well had exploited its resources long before the appearance of the Shahilu family or a Qashqa'i polity in the area.

Members of the Shahilu lineage today claim that their ancestors had a tribal background but are unsure of any specific affiliation beyond the broad Oghuz Turkic one. They believe they descend from Oghuz Turks who once lived in the Ural Mountains and who were slowly pushed south into the Caucasus and the gap between the Caspian and Black

3. Ibid.
4. The primary tribes of Fars just prior to the emergence of the Seljuqs (1040–1157) and their Atabeg governors were the Shabankara and affiliated Kurdish groups (Le Strange 1905:266, 288; 1912:6–13).

seas by the expansion of Slavs.[5] They eventually settled in what is now Iranian and Turkish Azerbaijan, where they formed part of the Aqquyunlu confederacy and empire (1378–1502). The Qaraquyunlu (1378–1469) and Aqquyunlu dynasties had drawn back to the east and consolidated many Turkic groups that had moved west into Armenia, upper Mesopotamia, and Anatolia under the Seljuqs (1040–1157). Members of the Shahilu lineage believe they are related by blood to Uzun Hasan (d. 1478), the famous Aqquyunlu ruler, and by marriage to Shah Isma'il Safavi (1501–24). Uzun Hasan's son (Soltan Ya'qub) had a son (Soltan Morad) whose two sons (Ya'qub and Hasan) ruled the remnants of the Aqquyunlu empire between 1498 and 1508 (Woods 1976:227). Qashqa'i sources claim a third son was Amir Ghazi Shahilu (the first Shahilu name known), although his name is not found in Aqquyunlu genealogies. Soltan Ya'qub's daughter Tajlu married Shah Isma'il Safavi, who, if Shahilu family tradition is correct, is Amir Ghazi's father's sister's husband. Amir Ghazi Shahilu, said to have been a religious figure, possibly a sufi, is believed to have helped Shah Isma'il Safavi establish Shi'i Islam as the state religion of Iran. Most of Shah Isma'il's supporters belonged to Turkic and Kurdish tribes from Asia Minor, Syria, and Armenia mixed with tribes detached from the Qaraquyunlu and Aqquyunlu confederacies (Minorsky 1943:188). One of Amir Ghazi's descendants is referred to in documents by the expression *sufizadeh* ("born of a sufi"), which may refer to him.[6] Amir Ghazi's grave is in northern Fars near Gandoman and is still a place of pilgrimage. The only other information about him is that a Safavid shah may have given him the title of ilkhani.[7]

The significance of these and other connections with known historical figures is not in their historical accuracy but rather in the legitimacy they give to the contemporary status of the Shahilu. The name Shahilu means "Those of the Shah," indicating service to rulers. This title precedes any historical evidence connecting the lineage with nomadic pastoralists, and the Shahilu family apparently had no Qashqa'i name at this time. Excepting the Azeris, whose origins and background are unknown, virtually all Turkic people in Iran emerged from and retained

5. In the tenth century, the western Oghuz occupied territory bounded to the south by the Aral Sea and the lower course of the Syr Darya, to the west by the Ural River or the lower Volga and the Caspian Sea, and to the northeast by the upper course of the Irtysh (Cahen 1965:1107).

6. Malek Mansur Khan, personal interview, 28 August 1979, Tehran.

7. Ibid.

connections with tribal units that were in whole or in part pastoral nomadic, which may suggest a tribal background for the Shahilu family as well. Lists of prominent tribes under the early Safavids do not include the Qashqa'i or any comparably named group (Le Strange 1926:45–46, Minorsky 1943:193–95).

Members of the Shahilu family believe that Shah Isma'il or another Safavid shah sent one or more of their ancestors to be governor of the tribes of Fars and to help protect the area from Portuguese incursions, specifically to prevent the establishment of Portuguese trading posts and to stop their penetration inland.[8] The Portuguese first entered the Persian Gulf in 1506, when they occupied Hormuz and established dominion on both sides of the gulf—including the coastal portions of the province of Fars in Iran. Portuguese dominance in the area ended in the early 1600s as the Safavids established rule in Iran and as the British and Dutch established a commercial and strategic presence in the region (Marlowe 1962:4–5). The interpretation by the Shahilu family of its history as a mandate from Iranian state rulers to govern the tribes of Fars seems to provide justification for Shahilu domination in the area and probably served as a tactic to acquire additional state favors.[9] On its way south to assume the governorship, the Shahilu family passed through what later became the territory of the Bakhtiyari confederacy, which it regarded as having unsuitable pastures, and came to settle in the Zagros Mountains southwest of Isfahan near the settlements of Gandoman, Semirom, and Nokhuddon, in what are now the most northern summer pastures of the Qashqa'i. In this region at about the same time were found two large tribes, Dadekai and Rahimi, both western Oghuz Turkic groups and each headed by leaders called kalantars;[10] later, both groups became part of the Qashqa'i confederacy. Safavid rulers had given the governorship of the neighboring Kuhgiluyeh region to Afshar and Shahsevan leaders from northern Iran, which brought additional Turkic tribal groups to Fars (Minorsky 1934a:42, 45), some of which also became part of the Qashqa'i confederacy.

The first known use of the Qashqa'i name in connection with the Shahilu family is during the late 1600s, in a government document

8. Naser Khan, personal interview, 29 August 1979, Tehran. He also recounted this history to Ullens de Schooten (1954:77).

9. As suggested by Bestor in her analysis of the Kurdish elite in Iranian Baluchistan (1979:28).

10. Malek Mansur Khan, personal interview, 28 August 1979, Tehran.

deeding property in northern Fars to the family and referring to it as Qashqa'i.[11] The name of Hamid Beg Qashqa'i occurs in a list of prominent persons during the reign of Shah Hosain Safavi (1694–1722), but his connections with the Shahilu are not known (Asaf 1969:105). Only the names of five generations of Amir Ghazi's direct descendants are known (see fig. 1).

Jani Mohammad Aqa (Jani Aqa), said to be six descending generations from Amir Ghazi Shahilu, is considered by Qashqa'i to be the founder of the Qashqa'i confederacy. Historians have never explained what this process or event actually entailed. Jani Aqa may have fought for Safavid rulers in the late 1600s and early 1700s, but it is only with his sons, Isma'il Khan and Hasan Khan, that specific evidence appears. Isma'il Khan followed his father as the Shahilu's leading figure, while Hasan Khan, who held the government-bestowed title of Mo'tamad os-Soltan (Trusted of the Sultan), was a distinguished warrior who fought against the Afghan invasion of Fars in 1724.[12] From this time in history, prominent members of the Shahilu family held the title of khan, representing a status higher than *aqa* and often awarded for bravery in battle. Aqa (gentleman) was the usual male honorific title of address in Iran in the eighteenth century. The government conferred the title of khan on tribal leaders who performed military and other state services (Malcolm 1829:412); the title also often implied a relationship with an underlying population.

Nader Shah Afshar (1736–47), who followed the Safavids, had originally been a tribal leader. He relied on tribal, primarily Turkic forces for his army and military campaigns (Lambton 1977:110). In 1730 he relocated fifty to sixty thousand tribal families from Fars and other provinces to Khorasan in northeast Iran (Lambton 1953:131); some of those associated with the Shahilu family were said to be included. He took Isma'il Khan, Hasan Khan, and possibly some of their affiliated warriors on his military campaign against India in 1738–39. Nader Shah and the two Shahilu brothers had a falling out, and in punishment Isma'il Khan was blinded and exiled to Khorasan, while Hasan Khan was mutilated and died of his wounds.[13]

11. Ibid.
12. Ibid.
13. Ibid.

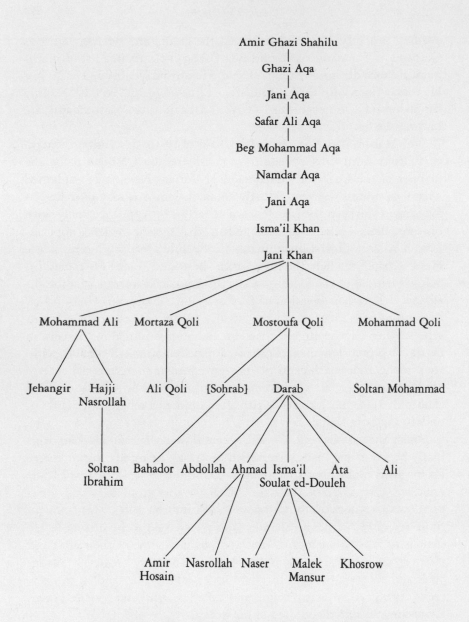

FIGURE I.   Genealogy of Qashqa'i Ilkhanis and Ilbegis

48

The founder of the next dynasty, Karim Khan Zand (1756–79), had also been a tribal leader who based his power on tribal forces.[14] The death of Nader Shah in 1747 had led to a struggle for power, and Isma'il Khan (still in exile in Khorasan) requested permission from the up-and-coming Karim Khan, then based in Isfahan (early 1750s), to return to his "ancestral" lands in the Semirom-Vardasht region. Karim Khan gave permission in writing for the return and noted that the specific pasturelands mentioned rightfully belonged to Isma'il Khan's family: "These lands have been the inheritance of the family of Isma'il Khan for hundreds of years."[15] The phrasing represents a stylized formula used for recognizing and bestowing rights and should not necessarily be taken literally.

Shortly thereafter, Karim Khan bestowed upon Isma'il Khan the title of Tribal Leader of Kuhgiluyeh, Fars, and Isfahan (Ilbegi-ye Kuhgiluyeh va Mamlakat-e Fars va Dar al-Saltaneh Isfahan).[16] The phrase, "Dar al-Saltaneh Isfahan," refers to the state capital and indicates that Karim Khan was still based in Isfahan at that time. Isma'il Khan may have helped Karim Khan in a battle against Azad Khan Afghan.[17] Karim Khan Zand established state rule in Shiraz in 1756, and this became his capital. The ruling dynasty was supported by Zands, Laks, and Lurs, many of whom he brought to Fars. Karim Khan's initial supporters were Kurd and Lur tribespeople from western Iran, and as his strength grew, Turks and Bakhtiyaris joined him. His standing army consisted primarily of tribal and provincial levies (Lambton 1977:110–11). As state ruler, he was reported to have been "surrounded by friendly tribesmen" (Oberling 1974:39). Lambton in-

14. Karim Khan Zand began his career as an "obscure local brigand" in northwest Iran (Perry 1979:31). Leonard Helfgott (personal communication) notes that it is somewhat misleading to label Nader Shah Afshar and Karim Khan Zand as "tribal" leaders, on the grounds that, although they led minor clans, their success was the result of freebooting during troubled times and drawing diverse collections of tribal and probably nontribal scavengers, adventurers, paupers, and plunderers to them on their way to seizing state power. My use of the term *tribal,* however, does not exclude such activities and coalitions, and, in fact, I suspect that most tribes during the historical period under consideration consisted of such disparate components. "Tribes as we know them today are fortuitous conglomerations" (Cunnison 1966:6), a situation applying, as well, to the past.

15. Malek Mansur Khan, personal interview, 28 August 1979, Tehran. Farrokh Bibi possesses the document.

16. Malek Mansur Khan, personal interview, 28 August 1979, Tehran.

17. Ibid.

cludes Karim Khan Zand "in the tradition of the great tribal leaders, Tughril Beg and Uzun Hasan" (1977:109), and writers report favorably about his rule (Perry 1979).

Isma'il Khan was influential in Karim Khan's court, possibly even as minister of court, and appears to have had wide-ranging duties and activities. Karim Khan changed his title to Tribal Leader of Fars (Ilbegi-ye Mamlakat-e Fars) and named another person ilkhani of the Lur tribes in the Kuhgiluyeh, although Isma'il Khan continued to have responsibilities there.[18] Karim Khan also entrusted Isma'il Khan with the care of the young Qajar hostage, Aqa Mohammad Khan, who later became the first Qajar shah and founder of that dynasty (Asaf 1969:338). As shah, Aqa Mohammad took revenge on the Shahilu for this period of captivity.

Circumstances during and immediately following the rule of Karim Khan Zand contributed to the process of centralizing rule in Fars on both the state and tribal levels. Karim Khan needed a governor of the tribes of Fars, and Isma'il Khan was a suitable candidate: he was of Turkic ancestry (as were many tribespeople in Fars), already had vested interests in the northern tribal areas, and was loyal to Karim Khan, just as his ascendants had been loyal to previous rulers. The proximity of the state capital at Shiraz allowed Isma'il Khan to play simultaneous roles as court minister and tribal administrator, each role enhancing the other. Karim Khan was sympathetic with tribal people and always considered himself one of them, in contrast to other Iranian rulers who, despite their own tribal backgrounds in many cases, needed to free themselves from tribal control and hence oppressed tribal people. Karim Khan had moved tribal people into Fars to serve as his standing army; many remained in the region after his death and were susceptible to control by another popular leader. The Zand dynasty did not survive long, and Isma'il Khan and his descendants were already established leaders of the tribal people of Fars. The Qajar dynasty, based far from Fars, was not able to rule these people effectively, and Qajar rulers continued the Zand policy of delegating authority to the Shahilu khans.

In his book on Karim Khan Zand, Perry mentions many tribes in Fars but includes the Qashqa'i as a people only once,[19] which is initially puzzling because of the reputedly close connections between Karim

18. Ibid.
19. Karim Khan Zand "had left Nadr Khan Zand with a thousand men to garrison Shiraz and punish Qashqa'i and Mamassani raiders" (Perry 1979:62).

Khan and Isma'il Khan. Isma'il Khan, however, probably functioned as governor rather than "tribal leader," and his ability to centralize tribal groups in Fars probably arose from his state administrative functions, at first under Karim Khan's auspices and then on his own behalf in the confusion created by the struggles over a successor state in the area. During Karim Khan's rule, Isma'il Khan appears to have been more important in court than in the countryside; his presence in historical records appears to be a function of his role as governor. Little record of the Qashqa'i as an entity of consequence appears at this time. It was possibly only after Karim Khan's death and during the resulting power struggles that Isma'il Khan, and then his son, were able to translate the role of administrator of tribes for the state into a more direct political role at the tribal level itself. The process of confederacy formation under the centralizing rule of the Shahilu family appears to have received its major impetus at this time.[20]

The broader context is important to summarize here. Fars was increasing in importance during the reign of Karim Khan Zand, due primarily to its proximity to the Persian Gulf and Western commercial interests. The process of state formation in Shiraz under Karim Khan encouraged the formation of ties between government officials with tribal backgrounds, such as the Shahilu, and the diverse tribes in the region. Cultural heterogeneity had been intensified by Zand policies of relocating diverse tribal groups in Fars, and when the interregnum and civil war occurred, the Shahilu took the opportunity to form a confederacy of local tribes and those recently imported by the Zands.

That there is no evidence of Qashqa'i in Karim Khan's army is also initially puzzling. If Karim Khan and Isma'il Khan were closely allied, why did Isma'il Khan not contribute Qashqa'i forces to Karim Khan's army? Part of the answer is Karim Khan's reliance on the tribal people he brought with him from other locations, but it is also possible that Qashqa'i forces were not yet adequately coalesced for such a purpose.

THE POSITIONS OF ILKHANI AND ILBEGI

The central figures in the relationship between the Qashqa'i people and the state have been the ilkhani (paramount tribal leader) and ilbegi

---

20. Sümer suggests an earlier formation: "Whilst we have no knowledge of the causes leading to the formation of the Qashqa'i, it is probable that many Turkmen communities living in Fars gathered around the strong Shahilu tribe of the Khalaj during the Afghan invasion [1724], thus forming this people" (1978:705).

(deputy tribal leader). Discussion of these positions is especially important because of the lack of historical information on practically all other aspects of tribal organization and structure until the twentieth century. The subject also has theoretical implications for the role of the state in tribal formation. The many centuries of formalized political relationships between Iranian states and large tribal groups before the Qashqa'i appearance helped to structure the relationships emerging for the Qashqa'i. The particular circumstances of the Qashqa'i, however, allowed the position of the paramount tribal leader to become more highly developed than in any previous or future tribal groups, with the possible exception of the Bakhtiyari.

The identity, date, and circumstances of the first Qashqa'i ilkhani is a matter of some controversy, particularly because of Fasa'i's (a nineteenth-century Iranian historian) authoritative but possibly incorrect comment concerning the bestowal of the ilkhani title on Jani Khan: "Up to that year [1818–19] nobody in Fars had been called by the title 'Ilkhani'" (Busse 1972:160).[21] (see table 1) Members of the Shahilu lineage today believe that a Safavid shah sent their ancestors to govern the tribes of Fars and to help police the area against the Portuguese. Their names and titles are unknown. The first known named member of the Shahilu lineage, Amir Ghazi, is said to have been closely associated with Shah Isma'il in the early 1500s, and this or another Safavid shah may have given him the title of ilkhani.[22] Five generations separate him from Jani Aqa, reputed founder of the Qashqa'i confederacy. Jani Aqa's son, Isma'il Khan, was closely associated with Nader Shah, Karim Khan Zand, and Aqa Mohammad Qajar (before he became shah). Such high-level contact, within the context of the strategic and political importance of the region and the state's dependence on governors to administer tribes, seems to have been central in establishing Isma'il Khan as a powerful figure on the state and provincial levels and in establishing his connections with tribal people in Fars.

The best available source on the positions of ilkhani and ilbegi is Malek Mansur Khan, who possesses family documents. He says that although his seventeenth- and eighteenth-century ancestors possibly held ilkhani and ilbegi titles, the first solid evidence is for the reign of Karim Khan Zand, who bestowed the title of ilbegi of Kuhgiluyeh,

21. Oberling uses the ilkhani title for Jani Aqa (late 1600s) and all succeeding paramount rulers (1974:35, passim).
22. Malek Mansur Khan, personal interview, 28 August 1979, Tehran.

TABLE 1. Historical Sequence of Qashqa'i Ilkhanis and Ilbegis

Ilkhani	Ilbegi	State Ruler
	Isma'il Khan 1754–79 (executed)*	Nader Shah Karim Kand Zand
	Jani Khan ? – ? (became ilkhani)	
Jani Khan 1779?–1823 (death)	Mohammad Ali Khan 1818–23 (became il- khani)	Aqa Mohammad Shah Fath Ali Shah
Mohammad Ali Khan 1823–52 (death)	Mortaza Qoli Khan 1823–33 (died in prison)	Fath Ali Shah Mohammad Shah Naser ed-Din Shah
	Mohammad Qoli Khan 1833–52 (became il- khani)	
Mohammad Qoli Khan 1852–67 (death)	Jehangir Khan 1852–67 (reappointed)	Naser ed-Din Shah
Soltan Mohammad Khan 1867–91 (death)	Jehangir Khan 1867–71 (death)	Naser ed-Din Shah
	Ali Qoli Khan 1871–76	
	Darab Khan 1876–91 (death) de facto ilkhani	
Hajji Nasrollah Khan 1891–96 (death)	Soltan Ibrahim Khan 1891–96 (became il- khani)	Naser ed-Din Shah
Soltan Ibrahim Khan 1896–98 (overthrown) Abdollah Khan was de facto ilkhani	none	Mozaffar ed-Din Shah
Abdollah Khan 1898–1902 (replaced) Isma'il Khan was de facto ilkhani	Isma'il Khan and Bahadur Khan (joint ap- pointment) 1898–1900 Isma'il Khan 1900–02 (became il- khani) de facto ilkhani	Mozaffar ed-Din Shah
Isma'il Khan 1902 (became ilbegi)	none	Mozaffar ed-Din Shah
Abdollah Khan 1902–04 (imprisoned, executed)	Isma'il Khan 1902–04 (became il- khani)	Mozaffar ed-Din Shah
Isma'il Khan 1904–06 (dismissed)	none	Mozaffar ed-Din Shah
Ahmad Khan 1906 (militarily de- feated)	none	Mozaffar ed-Din Shah

Ilkhani	Ilbegi	State Ruler
Soltan Ibrahim 1906 (not accepted)	none	Mozaffar ed-Din Shah
Isma'il Khan 1906–10 (attempted replacement)	none	Mozaffar ed-Din Shah Mohammad Ali Shah Ahmad Shah
Ahmad Khan 1910 (not accepted)	none	Ahmad Shah
Isma'il Khan 1910–11 (dismissed)	none	Ahmad Shah
Ahmad Khan 1911–12 (not accepted and resigned)	Ata Khan 1911	Ahmad Shah
Isma'il Khan 1912–18 (dismissed)	none	Ahmad Shah
Ahmad Khan 1918 (resigned)	Ali Khan 1918–20 (lost Qashqa'i support)	Ahmad Shah
Isma'il Khan 1918–33 (executed)	none	Ahmad Shah Reza Shah
Naser Khan 1920–28 (post abolished) nominal ilkhani Isma'il Khan was de facto ilkhani	Amir Hosain Khan 1920 (forced to resign by Isma'il Khan) Nasrollah Khan 1920 (unable to gain support)	Ahmad Shah Reza Shah
Malek Mansur Khan 1929–31 (resigned)	none	Reza Shah
Ali Khan 1931–33 de facto ilkhani	none	Reza Shah
Ilkhani title abolished by Reza Shah in 1928	**Ilbegi title abolished by Reza Shah in 1928**	Reza Shah
Naser Khan 1941–54 (exiled)	Malek Mansur Khan 1946–56 (exiled)	Mohammad Reza Shah
Ilkhani title abolished by Mohammad Reza Shah in 1955–57	**Ilbegi title abolished by Mohammad Reza Shah in 1955–57**	Mohammad Reza Shah
Naser Khan 1979–82 (banished) Khosrow Khan 1980–82 (executed) de facto ilkhani	Khosrow Khan 1979–82 (executed)	Ayatollah Ruhollah Khomeini

*Phrase in parentheses indicates reason for end of officeholding

Fars, and Isfahan on Isma'il Khan.[23] At this time Karim Khan had not yet completed his quest for state leadership, and this appointment probably cannot be considered a formal state appointment so much as a promise made as part of a bargain struck between the two men. Later, when Karim Khan established state rule in Shiraz, he modified Isma'il Khan's responsibilities and title to ilbegi of Fars, which included some responsibility over the Kuhgiluyeh.[24] Lambton notes "two apparently new appointments relating to the tribes" during Karim Khan's reign: an ilkhani of all the Lur tribes (who may have replaced the governor of the Bakhtiyari, an important frontier government under the Safavids) and an ilbegi of all the Turkic tribes of Fars (1977:110–11).

The label "tribal leader" (ilkhani, ilbegi) is itself ambiguous. It could represent one or more of the following: (1) a state-appointed administrator of tribal people; (2) a state-appointed tribal person as leader; or (3) an indigenous leader of tribal people recognized with the title by those people. The issue is whether a tribal leader was appointed from within the tribe(s) to be governed or whether he was an outsider simply assigned this jurisdiction. Moreover, how tribes were defined at this time is also unknown. Most nineteenth- and twentieth-century sources equate tribes with nomadic pastoralists, particularly non–Persian-speaking ones, and do not address the issue explicitly. It is also unclear whether the first ilkhanis and ilbegis were administratively responsible only for tribal people within the provinces mentioned (Fars, Kuhgiluyeh, Isfahan) or whether they were also responsible for the territories in which tribal people were located, which would have included agricultural land, villages, and towns.

Historical evidence indicates that the state appointed prominent members of the Shahilu lineage to govern tribal people in Fars (for a short time in Kuhgiluyeh and Isfahan also), and that this appointment was the key factor in the lineage's becoming politically based in and identified with these people. The prominence of the Shahilu family at the time when the state first gave its members gubernatorial responsibilities seems to rest primarily on prior service to and close ties with state rulers, rather than on their ties with nomadic pastoralists and other rural people. Members of the family were wealthy landowners in the rich pastures of northern Fars, however, and undoubtedly had ties with nomadic pastoralists who also utilized pastures there. Their own

23. Ibid.
24. Ibid.

Oghuz Turkic ancestry provided ethnolinguistic links with Turkic no-madic pastoralists, and the Shahilu family seemed to have favored these groups over others in the granting of pastoral and agricultural rights in the region.

Historians have stressed the fact that the state's nomination of il-khanis and ilbegis was confined to leading tribal families. A shah, ac-cording to Malcolm (1829:412), could alter the succession by placing an uncle in the place of a nephew, or a younger brother in the place of an elder, but usually he had no choice but to appoint as leader of a tribe a man belonging to the family of the chief. Given the lack of historical evidence, however, one cannot state unequivocally that Qashqa'i il-khanis and ilbegis of the eighteenth century were leaders indigenous to the governed tribal people. The processes of state appointment and in-ternal tribal selection were interrelated in the nineteenth century, but until, and perhaps through, the reign of Karim Khan Zand, the title-holders may simply have been those individuals to whom the state as-signed administrative responsibilities for tribal people in the province.

Some or many tribal people in Fars may have accepted certain Shah-ilu figures as ilkhanis and ilbegis before state conferral occurred. These titles had also been used by some politically centralized Turkic and Mongol tribal groups elsewhere in Iran and adjoining areas. The first state appointments of an ilkhani and ilbegi of Fars possibly recognized positions already in existence rather than established them; such ap-pointments could have been cooptations of roles with roots in earlier times and could have provided de jure recognition of prior indigenous systems. Although these positions had always served in a mediatory capacity with regard to the state, formal state recognition and support did greatly enhance them in terms of power and authority, and legiti-mized them for the people involved and other powers. The state, by assigning administrative responsibilities for a region's people to Shah-ilu individuals, helped to foster bonds between them, and in turn en-abled them to see themselves and become seen by outsiders as a single entity. In time, by means of this process, the Shahilu became truly representative of the Qashqa'i people. It is interesting to note that not until the 1860s did the state appointment of ilkhani refer specifically to a Qashqa'i people.

Historians and others stress the supposedly tribal nature of Qashqa'i ilkhanis and ilbegis, whom they perceive as mountain-dwelling, no-madic, rustic warriors, but their similarities to state-appointed gover-nors in general were significant and deserve emphasis. Close ties with state officials and membership in wealthy landowning and urban elites were especially important for both tribal and nontribal governors, who depended on outside support and adequate resources for the acquisition and retention of their posts. Governors lacking local ties, however, changed frequently in response to the instabilities of state and local politics, while the Shahilu who served as governors did so under continuous and enduring conditions. Governors supported only by the state appointment could be and were expendable, while tribal governors such as the Shahilu, especially after Karim Khan Zand, more easily established local support than nontribal governors. Given the state's perpetual fear of tribal unrest, tribal governors exercised more leverage in dealing with both the state and tribal people than did nontribal governors, even as they posed a more serious potential threat to the state.

The status of the Shahilu family during the eighteenth century raises some basic questions. Who, exactly, were these figures and how did they live? The political distinction between the family and the tribal people they governed must have had socioeconomic correlates and undoubtedly corresponded with distinctive life-styles. Mid-twentieth-century Shahilu stressed the cultural features they shared with Qashqa'i tribespeople, and yet they also enjoyed the luxuries of their often urban and always elite life-style, a privilege that may also have been characteristic of the family during earlier periods. Because the first Shahilu known to history were closely connected with state leaders, they probably established permanent urban residences. Where other family members resided is not known. The ancestral land of the Shahilu lineage was said to be near Semirom, which had excellent pastures. The first known document noting the Qashqa'i name concerns land, and a document written by Karim Khan Zand lists pastures belonging to the family,[25] so at least by the mid-eighteenth century prominent members of the Shahilu lineage were wealthy land- and herd-owners. But did they directly participate in agricultural and pastoral production, or did they simply rent their lands to others to work, in a fashion similar to other landed, often absentee elites? Had they risen from the tribal ranks through good fortune and smart husbandry, or were they outsiders who were assigned to the area as governors and awarded land assignments for their efforts? The twentieth-century connections of the Shahilu with land, animals, laborers, and political supporters suggest

25. Ibid.

interpretations for earlier periods, but no concrete conclusions on this early period can be stated.

Contemporary Shahilu recognize the sparse and conflicting nature of the evidence concerning their origin and identity. Some suggest that members of the family did not actually reside with tribal people in rural areas until the beginning of the twentieth century and that earlier they were based in Shiraz and visited their assigned territories and lands periodically, as did other governors and many large landowners. From the 1860s to the rise of Reza Shah in the 1920s, members of the family were entangled in the power struggles of the Iranian state centered in Tehran, the provincial government centered in Shiraz, growing British and then German interference, other provincial elites, the powerful Bakhtiyari confederacy to the north, and the rival Khamseh confederacy to the east. Malek Mansur Khan states that the ilkhani was often *forced* to live in Qashqa'i territory during this period for the protection that it provided. Should he remain in Shiraz, as had been the custom of his ancestors, he would be vulnerable to political competition; by seeking a safer, securer residence in the mountain pastures of tribespeople, he could possess certain distinctive strengths. Malek Mansur Khan says that only *then* was a close bond established between the ilkhani (and his family) and tribespeople.[26] The intimacy of this relationship, as depicted by mid-twentieth-century travelers such as Duncan (1946, 1982), Douglas (1951), and Ullens de Schooten (1956), may be a fairly recent phenomenon rather than a centuries-old tradition, despite what the literature implies.

Mirza Mohammad Kalantar-e Fars, a contemporary of Isma'il Khan, served as kalantar (overseer) of Fars under Karim Khan Zand. Isma'il Khan, returning to his ancestral pastures in Fars from exile in Khorasan, confiscated the kalantar's land. The kalantar indignantly comments, "Isma'il Khan thought *I* had burned the black tents of his father [Jani Aqa] and has seized my lands in revenge, when instead Nader Shah had burned the black tents of Jani Aqa."[27] The reference to "black tents" offers some evidence, according to Malek Mansur Khan, that these early Shahilu figures were indeed tent-dwelling nomadic pastoralists much like their tribal supporters.

26. Ibid.
27. A paraphrase of the kalantar's written remarks, according to Malek Mansur Khan; personal interview, 28 August 1979, Tehran. See also Oberling (1974:36n.).

In summary, I suggest this interpretive analysis: During the eighteenth century, Iranian state rulers, being unable directly to administer and control rural, largely nomadic, tribally organized people, sought the services of prominent members of the Shahilu family, who, because of their tribal background and Turkic ancestry, were well qualified for posts as governors of rural, tribal, largely Turkic people. The Shahilu profited from this service because regular formalized contacts with the state and with a revenue-producing population were established. From this base, they were gradually able to extend their influence and control, and by the mid-nineteenth century they were consolidating their position as leaders of the culturally diverse but largely Turkic peoples in the rural southern Zagros. No available evidence suggests that the Qashqa'i as either a political or sociocultural unit predates the establishment of members of the Shahilu lineage as agents of the state. During the unsettled period of the first two decades of the twentieth century, this identification became more complete, with shifts in the primary residence of the Shahilu from Shiraz to the countryside. The processes underlying these events remain to be considered.

4

✦

The Qashqa'i in Qajar Iran

*T*he history of the Qashqa'i during the major part of Qajar rule (1796–1906) is inextricably interwoven with the general history of Iran. Although the Qashqa'i tribal confederacy took form in this period, little specific information is available about the Qashqa'i people or their coalescence under the leadership of the khans of the Shahilu lineage beyond their military role. Accounts are limited to sources describing military engagements and the interactions, almost exclusively in urban settings, of the paramount Qashqa'i khans with state authorities, agents of foreign powers, and leaders of other tribes.

THE TRANSITION FROM ZAND TO QAJAR RULE

The interregnum period from Karim Khan Zand's death in 1779 to Aqa Mohammad Shah's coronation in 1796 was unsettling for the Shahilu family. Ali Morad Khan, the successful contender for Zand leadership, executed Isma'il Khan because he had supported another contender. Jani Khan, Isma'il Khan's son, succeeded his father as the leading figure of the Shahilu family and allied himself with Ja'far Khan, who took over Zand leadership in 1785 upon Ali Morad's death. Jani Khan supported Ja'far Khan's efforts to defeat the Qajar chief Aqa Mohammad Khan. Although Ja'far Khan was repeatedly defeated, his Shahilu allies were more fortunate. Aqa Mohammad conducted three campaigns against Fars in order to establish his rule. In 1788 he sought specifically to defeat the Qashqa'i tribes but was unsuccessful; twice he attempted surprise attacks against the Shahilu and their affiliates in summer pastures (Gandoman and Khosrow Shirin), but they evaded him by moving elsewhere (Busse 1972:29, 36n.; Oberling 1974:40).

The Qashqa'i tribes rarely appear in accounts of Zand history, yet within a few years of Karim Khan Zand's death they and their leaders apparently warrant a special campaign by a major contender for state rule. Geography helps to explain this apparently sudden rise to prominence of a Qashqa'i polity. Aqa Mohammad Khan Qajar, based in north Iran and having ambitions to rule, needed to defeat the Zand dynasty contenders based in Shiraz. Tribal forces assembled by Karim Khan as military units had lost cohesion on his death, but tribal people brought under the authority of Isma'il Khan and Jani Khan, including some Zand forces, had risen in importance. Jani Khan, who was closely allied with the Zands, resided in summer pastures on the northern frontier of Fars province and would encounter a force coming from the north to conquer Shiraz. Also, Aqa Mohammad sought revenge on the Shahilu for his many years of captivity under Karim Khan Zand.

Ja'far Khan was assassinated in 1789, and his son, Lotf Ali Khan, was recognized in Shiraz and by tribes in the region as the legitimate Zand ruler. His enemy, Hajji Ibrahim Shirazi, seized Shiraz in 1791 in the name of Aqa Mohammad Qajar, and twelve thousand men from the "military tribes" posted in the city were tricked into leaving town and were unable to oppose the seizure (Malcolm 1829:116–17). What role, if any, Qashqa'i tribesmen played in these events is not recorded, although an involvement is possible (Oberling 1974:42). With the beginning of Qajar rule in 1796, the state capital was moved from Shiraz to Tehran, where it has remained.

TRIBES AND THE STATE UNDER QAJAR RULE

A major problem for the Qajar state concerned the tribal people within and on its borders, but as the nineteenth century progressed state rulers developed rudimentary mechanisms for ruling and thus gained some increased power and authority over them. Nomadic and settled tribal people during this century may have equaled in numbers the state's settled, nontribal people (Sheil 1856:393). Tribal contingents, along with the shahs' personal force and the forces of provincial governors which also contained tribal levies, made up the military during the early Qajar period. Each major tribe had its own division in the army, and armed horsemen and foot soldiers served six months of any year in which the shah required their service. Levies appeared at the royal camp every New Year's Day (the spring equinox) and would either be kept on or dismissed for the year if their services were not needed. Wages passed through tribal leaders, who took a portion. Military service offered protection to soldiers' families from other government incursions (Malcolm 1829:355–58; Morier 1816:118, 239–41, 1837: 236–38; Waring 1805:81–84). After 1830 tribal levies, although still important, were no longer the exclusive elements in the Qajar military that they had been earlier, for the shahs' sons and other relatives who served as provincial governors began to develop military forces that were not tribal in organization and only partially tribal in origin. After 1850, Naser ed-Din Shah attempted to undermine further the military's tribal base.

The Qajar central government maintained a weak hold on the provinces, and the shahs' sons, uncles, and nephews who served as provincial governors often exercised relatively autonomous rule. Large areas of the Qajar state were defined as tribal regions, which Qajar rulers at the national and provincial levels attempted to administer through local tribal leaders. Over the larger tribes, shahs and governors appointed ilkhanis and ilbegis who were responsible for collecting government taxes and administering tribal affairs and who in return received land grants and other privileges. Tribal leaders, especially in vulnerable frontier areas, often received free land in exchange for levies and owed no state taxes. Qajar rulers bestowed the title of ilkhani on the paramount leaders of at least four tribal confederacies: Qashqa'i, Bakhtiyari, Kurd (in Khorasan), and Gunduzlu (in Khuzistan). The post of the ilkhani of the Lur tribes was apparently not filled after Karim Khan Zand's reign. The first ilkhani of the Bakhtiyari was appointed in 1867, and the office was effective until the 1920s (Garthwaite 1983). In the early seventeenth century, Shah Abbas had relocated some Kurds from northwest Iran to Khorasan in the northeast to defend that frontier against Uzbeq and Turkmen incursions. In the process these groups were reorganized into new tribes and confederacies, and their leaders owed their positions primarily to appointments by the shah. When the Kurds proved to be an additional disruptive force in the region, Shah Abbas appointed one of their leaders as ilkhani, held him responsible for the Kurds' conduct, and made him governor of the district. Later in the century, two ruling families emerged (the Zafaranlu of Quchan and Shirvan and the Sadlu of Bojnurd), and in the nineteenth and early twentieth centuries the heads of both families held the title of ilkhani and served as governors of their districts (van Bruinessen 1978:215–20; Fraser 1825: Appendix, pp. 42–53). Leaders of the Gunduzlu, a Turkic tribe in Khuzistan derived from the Afshars, held the title of ilkhani from at least the early 1840s until 1934 (Layard 1846, Oberling 1964:170). Iranian authorities created the office of ilbegi for the Shahsevan in 1839 in response to Russian complaints about Shahsevan incursions (Tapper 1971:512).

The policy of Qajar rulers in tribal regions was divide and rule—"in setting one tribe against another, fomenting family feuds and jealousies, and bribing chiefs with gifts or promises of support in their struggles, one with another for the headship of the clan or tribe" (Lambton 1960:1104). Tribal leaders were "both from birth and influence, the first men in the empire; they are always mutually jealous and hostile; and the king, by fomenting their quarrels, and thus nicely balancing the power of the one against the other, insures his own safety and the peace of his dominions" (Kinneir 1813:45). In the attempt to undermine tribal power, shahs dispersed groups, killed or held leaders or their relatives in court as hostages, and arranged marriages that brought about substantive alliances as well as networks of relationships with tribal leaders.

The Qajars assessed taxes on land and flocks and occasionally collected poll or family taxes. Nomadic pastoralists were sometimes taxed on their animals and crops, and those who did not cultivate were obliged to offer military service to the state. Tribespeople paid taxes through leaders who levied the amounts and were responsible to the government, and who could hold money back for their own benefit. Labor service to the state, required of peasants, was not required of nomadic pastoralists. Tribal leaders and followers who owned or held land were sometimes subject to land taxes. The government and tribal leaders frequently came into conflict over taxes. If the government possessed sufficient force, it collected taxes during military expeditions, and it farmed out tax collection to others, which increased the amounts extorted. Officials oversaw large tribal migrations and, to control revenue collection, attempted to prohibit tribes from moving to new provinces without permission. Interregna and other periods of political uncertainty allowed groups to change locations. The government considered pastures as tribal property, although its ruling elite enjoyed free access to them on demand (Morier 1837:236–38, Lambton 1960: 1104–05).

GOVERNMENT OFFICIALS OF THE QAJAR PERIOD

Much of the information on the paramount Qashqa'i khans during the nineteenth century is contained in the history of competitions and alliances among government officials at the provincial level. Provinces of the Qajar state were administered by Governors (var. Governor-General) of different ranks. (Governor is capitalized from this point, to distinguish it from governor, an administrator of a subprovincial district.) Major provinces, including Fars and Azerbaijan, were administered by a *farman farma,* those of lesser importance by a *vali* or a *beglarbegi.* The shah appointed the Governor of Fars, who was usually his son, uncle, or nephew because of the province's importance. The second major state-appointed position was that of the vizier of Fars, receiver-general of the state's (the shah's) revenues and manager of crown lands. Governors and viziers came and went rapidly during the Qajar period; few served more than several years, and many served less than a year.

The third important position was that of the kalantar (overseer or chief magistrate) of Fars, who served as the main representative of the people of Shiraz and the province vis-à-vis the central government (Morier 1816:234–35, Lambton 1977:121n.). He was also a state-appointee, although local interests figured in his choice more than they did with the Governor and vizier. The kalantar of Fars during most of the Qajar period was the senior male of the family of Hajji Ibrahim Shirazi, who as kalantar had seized Shiraz in 1791 in the name of Aqa Mohammad Qajar. His service as grand vizier (chief minister) of Iran under Aqa Mohammad Shah and Fath Ali Shah ended in 1801 when Fath Ali Shah had him boiled in oil. The shah also killed all male members of his family except Hajji Ali Akbar Khan, who became kalantar of Fars in 1811. In 1829, Fath Ali Shah bestowed upon him the title of Qavam ol-Molk (Pillar of the Kingdom), and both office and title later became hereditary. Members of the Qavam family wielded considerable political and economic power in the city and province and were able to survive interregna and periods of state decentralization (Royce 1981:292–96).

The final major provincial position was that of the ilkhani (paramount tribal leader) of Fars, who sometimes exercised power comparable to that of the kalantar or even the Governor of Fars. Members of the Shahilu lineage monopolized this post and that of ilbegi (deputy tribal leader), second in importance to the ilkhani. At least from 1818, state appointments of ilkhani and ilbegi often occurred simultaneously. The ilbegi was often the new ilkhani's son and often became ilkhani on his death. Many Qashqa'i ilkhanis and ilbegis enjoyed long political reigns despite unrestful interregna and changes in state rulers, and many were officially recognized by successive state rulers. This situation contrasts with the high rate of attrition in many other political positions in Iran. In contrast to twenty-seven appointments of Governor of Fars and thirty-three of vizier between 1791 and 1881 (Busse 1972:422–25), the government appointed only four ilkhanis. Longevity in the rule of single Qashqa'i leaders, combined with the autonomous power base, is correlated with continuity in Qashqa'i power and authority. Governors dealt directly with and relied heavily upon the ilkhani, who as a long-term officeholder and prominent local figure was often more knowledgeable about local politics than Governors and viziers who were brought from outside to rule the province. Governors played off the ilkhani and the kalantar, also a local figure and powerful in local politics, against one another, a practice that increased their rivalry.

On New Year's Day, the shah summoned to Tehran state-appointed figures such as Governors, viziers, and kalantars, accepted their tributes, and confirmed or changed their positions. He often ordered those who were not reconfirmed to stay in the capital. Whether or not the Qashqa'i ilkhani was usually included in the New Year's rite is not known; only one occurrence, in 1863, has been found (Busse 1972:347).

Fars was divided into some sixty-three to sixty-five administrative districts (*boluk*) during the Qajar period, a rather arbitrarily defined number varying according to administrative manipulations and instabilities and power struggles among provincial elites.[1] The Governor of Fars appointed a governor to each district, and individuals occasionally

1. The borders of Fars proper were also vague and variable. Fasa'i notes 64 administrative districts in Fars (Busse 1972:87), Demorgny more than 63 (1913b:18), and Field 65 (1939:209–10). Lane's 76 may be incorrect (1923:209). Seven of the 63 districts were more closely tied to neighboring provinces and areas than to Fars (Demorgny 1913b:18). Demorgny provides demographic and descriptive information on each district (1913a, 1913b), and Field notes their locales, sizes of their sedentary populations, and chief towns (1939:209–10).

also sought these positions directly from Tehran. District governors were ordinarily chosen from the ranks of the area's economic and political elite. Many competed for these posts because of the accruing benefits. Large landowners sought to be governors of the districts where they owned or controlled land in order to expropriate additional surpluses and assert more power and authority. Other members of the elite, including clergy and state appointees recently assigned to Fars, sought these posts in order to acquire land. The Governor, vizier, and other state officials, who were large landowners throughout Fars, arranged for their relatives to acquire governorships. The Governor bestowed these posts on those who were loyal to him and who performed admirably in military campaigns and other state-related functions, which meant that entrance into the ranks of this elite was possible. Some district governors enjoyed long terms and their posts were passed to their male descendants, while others were changed yearly or even more frequently, according to political whim in Shiraz or Tehran and the intrigues of the Governor, vizier, kalantar, and ilkhani. Many district governors lost their posts when state or local government changed; their positions were vulnerable to political struggles. District governors who were unable to "subdue" their inhabitants or pay assessed taxes were liable to be dismissed. The Governor consistently conferred governorships on Qashqa'i ilkhanis, ilbegis, and other members of the Shahilu family. When a new ilkhani was appointed, he was confirmed or reconfirmed in his governorship of certain districts. This practice constituted a means of support and of financing the necessary military contingent; it offered an opportunity for the personal accumulation of wealth. The administrative duties of ilkhanis, ilbegis, and district governors were similar. The ilkhani, ilbegi, the Qavam ol-Molk, and others were often appointed governor of more than one district at a time, and some prominent families administered many districts simultaneously.

The duties of district governors centered on taxation and law and order. The Governor of Fars regularly summoned them to Shiraz to fix the amount of their taxes and tributes, and they often had to pay in tribute an amount equivalent to a third or a half of the assessed tax in order to retain their posts (a practice applying to most official posts; Malcolm 1829:341). Qajar administrative policy assessed taxes on places rather than on individuals. Each district was assessed a fee, which its governor was responsible for paying yearly. The most common abuse involved governors collecting more taxes than they were required to pay, then retaining the difference. Governors could pay district taxes out of their own pockets and become creditors of the inhabitants, which often led to additional expropriations and eventually to land confiscations. Farming out taxes to others also increased the sums extracted, often many times the amount of the assessed tax. The state's policy of assessing taxes on places rather than on individuals increased competition among governors and other tax collectors to expand the local population base and hence collect more revenues. Such competition affected the location and organization of people in the area, especially nomadic pastoralists who could be easily moved.

When the Governor of Fars was displeased with the ability of district governors to establish law and order in their areas, he replaced them or sent his own militias on punitive expeditions. Fasa'i rather idealistically reported that Mo'tamad ed-Douleh, Governor of Fars in 1841–43 and 1876–81, "appointed honest men financial agents and governors of the districts and tribes and took from them a written statement in which they promised to pay the taxes and to administrate the affairs of the subjects in an orderly manner. . . . He appointed governors of the districts and tribes on the condition that they seize the thieves and evildoers. Every governor who arrested a thief or an evildoer was granted special favors and a robe of honor. . . . By these means thefts, lies, crime, and oppression were eradicated in the province of Fars within a short time. The revenues collected from the oppressed people were taken away from the oppressors" (Busse 1972:405). The newly appointed governor of Kuhgiluyeh and Behbahan, two regions frequently causing difficulties for the government, traveled through his districts with tribal and Azerbaijani soldiers. There he "calmed down the people by doing good and talking gently; he united the Lors . . . and allowed no encroachments. If in a tribe two men were enemies, he would inquire into their behaviour, remove one of them, and assign him a living, because most depravities and most cases of disobedience were the outcome of financial troubles. By these means he calmed all the rebels of the Lors within a short space of time; the tribes of the region . . . who had been dispersed by the unseemly behaviour of the [former] governor, were united by persuasion and promises of tax remittance and subsidies and became engaged in agriculture" (Busse 1972:349).

District governors, as agents of the state as well as private entrepreneurs, defended both state and private interests in their regions in order to maintain their privileged positions. They were not able to count on state or provincial military forces to defend their territories and enforce their rule and hence were compelled to establish their own militias, which also affected the location and organization of tribal and nomadic people. District governors utilized existing tribal forces, relocated tribal and nomadic people to their areas to serve as military forces, and created military forces out of existing settled inhabitants. In the local competition among the regional elite, governors with tribal forces already in their districts exercised a considerable competitive edge over governors of settled nontribal districts because of the readily available, mounted, armed, mobile population. Governors of both tribal and nontribal districts assembled horsemen and gunmen from their districts, which strengthened or created these forces as political groups. Although the contingents were often small (fifty to one thousand), compared with the populations from which they were drawn, they were unified in relation to governors and acquired specific identities in performing military functions. The process created bounded groups, in some cases tribes, where they had not earlier existed and strengthened preexisting ones. The Governor of Fars called upon district governors who were particularly effective in assembling their own militias to assemble forces for his use also, a practice fortifying ties between these officials. The success of the Shahilu khans in recruiting their own and the Governors' militias, as well as detachments for the shahs' armies, helps to explain the formation of the confederacy and the rise in the khans' power in the nineteenth century.

The Shahilu khans differed from many other district governors because of the added responsibilities of administering tribal groups, and the way they combined these two positions resulted in a powerful political and economic base. Their governorship of certain districts, especially those where tribal groups predominated, was often fairly permanent, while many other governors lost their appointments when higher-level state officials lost their posts or were weakened in political struggles. Also, their ties with the governed population extended beyond the administrative one, which was generally not the case for nontribal governors. As governors, the Shahilu khans strengthened existing ties and forged new ones with local inhabitants, thereby strengthening local identities. The special character of tribes and why they were historically important partly rest in these patterns.

Qajar rulers assessed taxes on the Qashqa'i tribes, to be paid in kind (sheep) or more usually in cash, and held the Qashqa'i ilkhani and ilbegi responsible for their collection and payment. In the 1830s Mohammad Shah assessed the Qashqa'i tax, based on their animals (sheep, cattle, donkeys, horses), as 13,000 tumans a year (Demorgny 1913a:95–96, *Gazetteer of Persia* 1918:812), and in 1850 Naser ed-Din Shah assessed the Qashqa'i 10,000 tumans and the other tribes under the ilbegi's authority another 13,000 tumans (Abbott 1857:170).[2] The annual tax assessment on Fars is unknown for 1850, but it was 360,000 tumans in 1841 (de Bode 1845:180), which, if the two years were comparable, would mean that these tribal taxes constituted approximately 6 percent of the province's revenue. In the 1870s the Governor of Fars added 30,300 tumans to the Qashqa'i tax, which brought the amount due to 43,300 tumans, a sum said to be high compared with that assessed other nomadic tribes in Iran and apparently remaining constant until 1912 (*Gazetteer of Persia* 1918:812). As district governors, the Shahilu were also responsible for district taxes, which totaled more than 71,000 tumans annually, a sum larger than tribal taxes.[3] These districts contained Qashqa'i seasonal pastures and villages as well as non-Qashqa'i villages and agricultural land. Once state officials began to consider the Qashqa'i as a single entity for tax assessment purposes, the tax assessments of the districts in which Qashqa'i utilized pastures were probably based on the sedentary non-Qashqa'i inhabitants. Given the khans' vested interests in the tribal Qashqa'i, they could also utilize taxes collected from non-Qashqa'i tribes or from non-tribal areas to pay the Qashqa'i tax.

Administrative divisions in Fars during the Qajar period often varied and were ambiguous, a situation probably used to good advantage by the Shahilu and others. The government gradually formalized administrative distinctions between districts and tribes, and between territories and groups of people, during the nineteenth century. It increasingly treated the Qashqa'i and other large tribal groups as distinct social entities, rather than continuing to include these people within

2. These amounts are similar to the tax assessed on the Bakhtiyari, who were probably of comparable size. The Bakhtiyari were assessed 14,000 tumans, an amount remaining constant through the nineteenth century (Garthwaite 1983:65), although the tax in 1884 was 20,000 tumans plus a unit of horsemen (Napier 1900:70). The Bakhtiyari paid their tax in mules, and the Shahsevan in camels (Garthwaite 1983:49). The tax on the Khamseh tribes was 21,000 tumans in the latter part of the nineteenth century (Demorgny 1913a:107).

3. The tax on 13 of the 16 districts administered by the Qashqa'i ilkhani and ilbegi in the latter part of the 1800s totaled 70,740 tumans (Demorgny 1913b:23–34; he includes no tax figures for the other three districts).

districts, as had been the case earlier in the century. Those holding vested interests in the matter, such as the ilkhani, aided this process by creating ties with governed people and by informing state authorities that these people represented distinct social entities. In both circumstances—tribal people included in districts and regarded as separate entities—ambiguity clearly existed because district and tribal populations overlapped. Tribal leaders and governors could exploit this situation by defining what the administrative unit was at any given time and who was included in it.[4] In addition, tribal and nontribal land was not clearly demarcated (Lambton 1960:1105), and those with power could add land to or subtract land from tribal and district jurisdictions. Demarcation of land between tribes was also a matter of the relative strength of the bordering groups.

The ilbegi also collected taxes from other tribes under Shahilu authority. In 1861 the government entitled the Qavam family to collect the taxes of four of these tribes (Nafar, Baharlu, Inalu, Basseri) (Abbott 1857:170), and a fifth (Chahardah Cherik, "Forty Guerrillas") became part of the Qashqa'i confederacy. As holders of the titles of "tribal leaders of Fars," the ilkhani and ilbegi appear to have been responsible for tax collection from other tribes of Fars as well. It is not known if district governors, other than the Shahilu and the Qavams, collected the taxes of tribal people within their territories.

AQA MOHAMMAD SHAH, 1796–1797

Aqa Mohammad Shah, the first Qajar ruler, attempted to establish order and security in the state. Lambton notes, and probably over-states, that "the leaders of the tribes were ambitious, had become accustomed to revolt and plunder, and were reluctant to submit to any kind of authority. The countryside had been ruined by repeated pillage. The people had been reduced to ruin and driven to exile. Security on the roads was virtually non-existent and commerce had greatly declined" (1953:134). Aqa Mohammad Shah, basing his power on tribes

4. Nomads in Fars in the tenth century were divided into five districts called *zumm* in Kurdish (Kurds being the largest group in the area at the time), with each district headed by a tribal leader responsible for collecting taxes and ensuring road safety. Barthold (1984:166), in noting that the Kurdish name of these districts was replaced by the Turkic "counterpart" *il* (territory, tribe), is apparently equating an administrative district of nomads with a tribe and appears to be applying the same kind of analysis to tribal units in Fars that I have employed in this book.

from northern Iran (Goklan and Yomut Turkmen, Afshar, and others), moved quickly to reduce the power of tribal leaders. He relocated tribal people, as had his predecessors (Perry 1975:211–12), moved tribes into and out of Fars, and dispersed many groups brought by the Zands to Fars. Some of these had affiliated with the Shahilu and joined the Qashqa'i tribes (Oberling 1974:43), and most of their names are found today among the many Qashqa'i subtribes. He forcibly moved seven thousand Qashqa'i families to central and northern Iran (Oberling 1974:42), but no major Shahilu figure was sent with them. Many people dispersed by Aqa Mohammad returned to their previous locations after his death (de Bode 1845:118). The other known connection between Aqa Mohammad Shah and the Qashqa'i concerns Jani Khan, who had escaped the Qajar's campaigns and gone into hiding with his family in the Zagros, where he remained until Aqa Mohammad's death in 1797. Through the offices of Fath Ali Khan, Governor of Fars (and shah on Aqa Mohammad's death), the shah attempted to induce Jani Khan to establish relations with the new regime but failed (Oberling 1974:42–43).

THE ERA OF FATH ALI SHAH, 1798–1834

Under Fath Ali Shah, provinces were ruled by his sons and other close relatives, who were often able to establish relatively autonomous rule when their local interests became entrenched and he was too weak to dislodge them. As with his predecessor, Fath Ali Shah aimed to weaken the tribes within his realm, in part by attempting to coopt tribal leaders. In 1818–19, "by mediation of Hajji Mirza Reza Qoli Nava'i, vizier of Fars, the title 'Ilkhani' was bestowed upon Jani Khan-e Qashqa'i, ilbegi of Fars. His son Mohammad 'Ali he appointed ilbegi. Up to that year nobody in Fars had been called by the title 'Ilkhani'" (Busse 1972:160). Jani Khan was the leading figure of the Shahilu family in the period spanning the rule of the Zand contenders, Aqa Mohammad Shah's rule, and most of Fath Ali Shah's rule, another example of longevity in Qashqa'i leadership.

For years, state rulers had used leading figures of the Shahilu lineage for purposes of tax collection and administration of law and order, but no specific accounts are found until 1821, when disputes between Qashqa'i and Bakhtiyari tribesmen erupted over pastures near Semirom in northern Fars. Both groups had just migrated into summer pastures, which apparently were then, as they are today, adjoining. The Governor of Fars (and son of the shah) heard about the trouble and sent Jani Khan Qashqa'i, "ilkhani of the tribes of Fars," to arbitrate. The Bakhtiyaris rejected the ilkhani's solution and appealed to Fath Ali Shah, who sent an emissary to negotiate another (Busse 1972:163). Given his administrative position, Jani Khan was an appropriate official to settle a dispute between two of the province's tribes. If his connections with the Qashqa'i people at this early point in Qajar history were known more precisely, it might also be known how much of a conflict of interest his mediation created.

On Jani Khan's death in 1823, his four powerful sons assumed leadership of the Qashqa'i tribes. A fifth son, the eldest and the one expected to be leader, demonstrated no interest in tribal politics. Three of the four sons held ilkhani and ilbegi appointments in the next decades, and the fourth died young in battle. The second son, Mohammad Ali, became ilkhani on his father's death and held the position for nearly thirty years, a period spanning the rule of Fath Ali Shah, Mohammad Shah, and Naser ed-Din Shah. He was considered the most powerful individual in south Iran and was active in conflicts involving local and state elites, including the Governor of Fars and the crown prince, both sons of Fath Ali Shah (Busse 1972:196, 206–07).

One of the first accounts of Qashqa'i tribespeople occurs in 1829, when a blood vendetta developed in Shiraz. The vizier, a member of the Nuri family that had come from Mazandaran in 1799 in order to serve the Governor of Fars, exercised harsh rule over Shiraz, tribes, and districts. When a Qashqa'i tribesman was killed in Shiraz as part of the vendetta, the Governor held the vizier responsible. After many Qashqa'i occupied the Nuri quarters in Shiraz, the Governor expelled the Nuris from the city (Busse 1972:92, 192–94). This occasion may be the first time that Qashqa'i tribespeople occupied Shiraz; they were also to use Shiraz as a political arena in the future, often in alliance with its inhabitants, as in this case. The incident demonstrates the growing military potential of the Qashqa'i tribes and their actual involvement in urban and provincial politics. Although the report contains no mention of the ilkhani or ilbegi, Governors did often oppose one political figure with the help of another; the ilkhani and the Governor, amiably connected at this time, had just arranged a marriage alliance between their families.

In 1832, thousands of Qashqa'i moved en masse to the province of Kerman to the east (Busse 1972:208–16, Oberling 1974:49–54), an event illustrating the activities of the ilkhani and ilbegi and providing the first specific evidence of the nature of the ties between these khans and the Qashqa'i people. It also demonstrates interactions among state and provincial officials, tribal leaders, and religious authorities that typify Qashqa'i politics from this date on (and possibly earlier). The event illustrates the benefits and detriments to the government of a large tribal, pastoral, and nomadic constituency. The protagonists were: Hosain Ali Mirza Farman Farma, Governor of Fars and son of the shah; his arch-rival and brother, Abbas Mirza, crown prince; Hajji Ali Akbar Khan Qavam ol-Molk, hereditary kalantar of Fars; Mirza Mohammad Ali Moshir ol-Molk, vizier of Fars; Mohammad Ali, ilkhani of Fars; and his brother Mortaza Qoli Khan, ilbegi of Fars.

The Governor of Fars, who distrusted the ilkhani's support of his rival Abbas Mirza, married his daughter to the ilkhani. While the Governor was absent, the ilkhani and the Qavam ol-Molk also arranged a marriage alliance to improve their relations. The vizier, who was disliked for causing administrative disorders, warned the Governor that such an alliance would be to his disadvantage. Responding to the warning, the Governor arrested the ilkhani and confiscated his family estate in Shiraz. In retaliation, the ilbegi ordered the Qashqa'i tribes to move out of Fars, beyond the Governor's authority, and into the province of Kerman. The Governor then released the ilkhani and ordered him to stop the Qashqa'i move, but it was already well underway. Joining the Qashqa'i tribes on their trip east were leaders of the Nafar, Baharlu, and Inalu tribes of eastern Fars and their groups. The Governor of Kerman (son-in-law of Abbas Mirza), welcoming the arrival, allotted winter and summer pastures for one hundred thousand families. The ilkhani and the Governor of Kerman sent emissaries to Abbas Mirza in Khorasan, who wrote to his father, the shah, to defend the Qashqa'i move and encourage them to remain in Kerman permanently. The shah asked the Governor of Fars (his son) to resolve his problems with the ilkhani. With fifteen thousand soldiers, an artillery force (eight cannons), and a retinue including the Qavam, the vizier, and the Muslim leader of Fars (shaikh ol-Islam), the Governor of Fars prepared to force the Qashqa'i to return. The Qavam and the shaikh, sent as mediators, reported that the tribes would remain in Kerman unless the vizier was deposed.

When the Governor dismissed the vizier from office, the ilkhani instructed the ilbegi and the other tribal leaders to move the tribes back to Fars. The Governor of Kerman, regretting the loss of tax revenues that the departure of these tribes would mean, sent a military force to block the roads, which angered the Governor of Fars (his uncle), who ordered an additional five thousand troops and sent a threatening message to the Governor of Kerman. The people of Kerman welcomed the messenger and prevented their unpopular Governor from entering the city, and the Governor of Fars expelled him from Kerman province. The ilbegi and the tribes of Fars then marched back to Fars. Before the ilbegi left, he placed his younger brother, Mostoufa Qoli Khan, and two thousand horsemen in the service of the Governor of Fars, who had been asked by the Kerman elite for help in ridding the city of the joint control of the wife of the deposed Governor (daughter of Abbas Mirza) and a Qaraquzlu general (from Hamadan in western Iran) who had run afoul of the central government and had sought refuge in the Kerman citadel with one thousand of his Qaraquzlu tribal soldiers. The Governor and Mostoufa Qoli, supported by fifteen thousand soldiers, prepared to oust them from Kerman. Mostoufa Qoli, who considered it shameful that the citadel should be conquered by craftsmen and merchants (the Governor's soldiers recruited from Shiraz), attacked before the other force was in position and was killed. Avenging their commander, Qashqa'i forces seized the citadel from the Qaraquzlu forces.

After this episode the animosities among the central figures continued, and when Crown Prince Abbas Mirza died in 1833, the Shahilu lost a powerful ally. The Governor of Fars, fearing the khans' support of the new crown prince, sent a force to arrest them. The ilbegi was tricked into a meeting, and in the ensuing battle he was wounded, then bound in chains and taken to Shiraz as a prisoner, where he died. The ilkhani was arrested and imprisoned, his son-in-law blinded, and the ilkhani estate in Shiraz plundered of "several centuries" of possessions; family graves were unearthed and money was found concealed inside (Busse 1972:223–25).

Shortly thereafter, the Governor released the ilkhani from prison, reconfirmed him as ilkhani, and entrusted him as before with the "governorship of the Qashqa'i tribes" and six districts (including Firuzabad and Farrashband) (Busse 1972:223–26). Mohammad Ali's brother, Mohammad Qoli, was confirmed as ilbegi. Designating the ilkhani as governor of the Qashqa'i tribes was apparently a new usage, although his title as paramount tribal leader of Fars still held. The new designation marks a distinction between the Qashqa'i tribes and the administrative districts in which they used pastures, which also contained towns, villages, agricultural land, and non-Qashqa'i people. The dual role as governor of tribes and districts gave the ilkhanis power and authority and made them virtually unmatched political figures in Fars.

In 1832 the Governor appointed Jehangir Khan, the ilkhani's son, commander of a new detachment in the army consisting of forces drawn from the Qashqa'i, Arab, Nafar, and Baharlu tribes (Busse 1972:221). The appointment followed immediately upon the Governor's use of Qashqa'i forces under the ilbegi in his attack on Kerman, which apparently demonstrated to him the utility of the group and its leaders. Two of the other tribes in the new detachment had also participated in the Kerman venture. No mention of Qashqa'i commanders or levies in state armies has been found before 1832. Possible exceptions include Nader Shah's use of forces associated with the Shahilu in the 1730s and the use of "Turks" from Fars in a military campaign against the governor of a gulf coast port in 1817 (Busse 1972:153).

THE ERA OF MOHAMMAD SHAH, 1834–1848

The death of Fath Ali Shah created a struggle over the succession to Qajar rule. The major contenders were Mohammad Mirza (the rightful heir), the Zell os-Soltan, and the Farman Farma (Governor of Fars) who declared independent rule in Shiraz. Mohammad Mirza, assisted by British and Russian forces, marched to Tehran, forcing the submission of the Zell os-Soltan, and then south to Qomishah (later Shahreza) with British forces to defeat the Farman Farma (Sykes 1930:327). The Farman Farma, who had recruited an army from the tribes and the city, was defeated at Qomishah and returned to Shiraz, where the leader of the Nafar tribe prevented his escape (Busse 1972:233, 237). Mohammad Ali, the ilkhani, supported the rightful heir and arrested the Farman Farma's family in Shiraz (Oberling 1974:55–56). The Farman Farma summoned the ilkhani, who sought refuge with the Imam of Prayers of Shiraz (the first documented alliance between the Shahilu and Muslim clergy). The ilkhani was almost killed and the "rabble" of Shiraz plundered his house (Busse 1972:237–38). A force sent by Mohammad Mirza captured the Farman Farma, who died on his way to prison.

In 1835 the vizier of Fars arrested Mohammad Ali, the ilkhani, "on mere suspicion" (Busse 1972:243). After practically a year in prison, he was sent to Tehran under heavy guard, but before he arrived Mohammad Shah ordered his release. He made the mistake of continuing his journey to Tehran, where the shah held him hostage (keeping him for the next thirteen years despite the ilkhani's support during the crisis over succession and despite a marriage alliance between them). In 1836 the vizier also harassed Mohammad Qoli, the ilbegi, but the shah sided with the ilbegi and dismissed the vizier (Busse 1972:250–52).

A European traveler commenting on the political rivalries in Shiraz in 1841 noted that the city was "divided into two rival camps," one headed by the ilbegi and the other by the Qavam ol-Molk, and that other powers had a vested interest in preserving the conflict (de Bode 1845:180–82). The Governor (the shah's son) and his vizier "hope to uphold their own authority by keeping alive the animosity between the two rival parties, and in this respect they only follow the policy pursued all over the empire, and that which appears from time immemorial to have been the system of government in Persia. . . . the Prince, who is named governor of a province, embraces the cause of one party, while his minister [vizier] sides with the adherents of the other. One can easily imagine what sort of order and harmony can exist, when such elements compose the administration" (de Bode 1845:181–82). In 1843 the newly appointed Governor of Fars toured the province with a military escort to assert his authority. In his absence, members of the Fars elite, including the ilbegi, traveled to Tehran to complain about him to the shah, who then named a new Governor. The Qavam ol-Molk and the ilbegi were ordered to remain in Tehran (Busse 1972: 273–74).

Conflict within the Shahilu lineage among sons of the ilkhani and ilbegi, exacerbated by the retention of both men in Tehran, is reported for the first time in 1846. When the fathers failed to settle the dispute, in which one of their sons was killed, the ilbegi escaped from Tehran in order to handle the problem personally. The Governor of Fars attempted to apprehend the fugitive ilbegi in Qashqa'i summer pastures and, although unable to locate him, settled their difficulties (Busse 1972:276–78).

The Qashqa'i selected their own pastures during the reign of Mohammad Shah (Sheil 1856:398–99), which implies considerable military power. A major task of Fars officials during this period was "subduing" the province's "rebels." The Qashqa'i were not included in this category, but the Mamassani Lurs in particular frequently challenged the government, which attempted to punish them (Busse 1972:268).

THE ERA OF NASER ED-DIN SHAH, 1848–1896

By the middle of the nineteenth century tribal influence, although still powerful, was more localized than previously, and few tribal leaders except the ilkhanis of the Qashqa'i and the Zafaranlu in Khorasan were said to exercise a "preponderating influence in the affairs of the country" (Sheil 1856:395). Under the long reign of Naser ed-Din Shah, the government continued to attempt to assert power over the tribes. Amir-e Kabir, the shah's famous prime minister, enjoyed the support of Mohammad Qoli, the ilbegi, in his efforts to rid Fars of its Governor. To achieve this end, the ilbegi and the Qavam formed a short-lived military alliance. The ilbegi assembled troops from the tribes and districts of Fars, which indicates he did not rely solely on Qashqa'i forces. The Governor agreed to leave his post if his opponents would meet several demands, to which the ilbegi complied. When the Governor did not depart as promised, fighting broke out in Shiraz between his Azerbaijani troops and the Shirazi insurgents and their tribal cobelligerents. With mediation of the shah's representative, fighting ceased and the Governor was dismissed from his post (Busse 1972:283–87, Oberling 1974:55–59). Mohammad Ali, the ilkhani who had been held hostage in Tehran for thirteen years, escorted the new Governor of Fars to his post. In 1851 Naser ed-Din Shah granted "royal favors beyond the usual" to the ilbegi (Busse 1972:300) to indicate his support. When Mohammad Ali died, Mohammad Qoli became ilkhani, and Jehangir, son of Mohammad Ali and commander of the tribal detachment, became ilbegi.

Qashqa'i troops were a major part of many military expeditions taken by state and provincial authorities in south Iran in the mid-nineteenth century. Between 1832, when they were part of a detachment, and 1868, when their own detachment was permanently disbanded, the Qashqa'i supplied the central government with a body of armed men under its own commander (*sartip*), a post held by sons and nephews of the ilkhani. In 1832 the Qashqa'i, Arab, Nafar, and Baharlu detachment contained eight hundred men and was trained in Shiraz by a British citizen (Busse 1972:221–22). By 1852 (the exact year is unknown), a specifically Qashqa'i detachment had been formed (Busse 1972:301–02), consisting of one to two thousand cavalry and one thousand infantry (Pelly 1865a:182, Demorgny 1913a:94). An 1856 treaty appointing the Imam of Musqat as governor of Bandar Abbas required him to prevent people from settling in his district, which intended to prevent nomads in Fars, who supplied a major part of the Governor's military forces, from leaving the province. The Governor of Fars in 1852 took two detachments, one of Qashqa'i soldiers under the command of the ilkhani's son and another of Arab soliders from Fars under the command of an Arab tribal khan, to "settle the affairs" (which included quartering a rebel and sending each part to different officials) of the southern districts. In 1855 the Qashqa'i detachment participated in the occupation of Bandar Abbas, and the government rewarded its officers (Busse 1972:301–02, 307–09, 316).

In 1856–57 British forces captured and occupied the Persian Gulf port of Bushire in specific response to Iran's occupation of Herat in Afghanistan (but also reflecting their commercial and strategic interests in Iran). Qashqa'i troops formed a major part of the army used against the British, in this first of many military conflicts between the British and the Qashqa'i. Other detachments came from Azerbaijan, Shiraz, Isfahan, and the Arab and Shahsevan tribes. British forces in the occupation included thirty warships and forty thousand British and Indian soldiers. The Governor of Fars dispatched the ilkhani of Fars (Mohammad Qoli), the Qashqa'i detachment with its commander, one thousand additional Qashqa'i horsemen, and artillery to the Dashti districts near Bushire to await the call to battle. In the meantime, the inhabitants of nearby Tangistan were singlehandedly facing the British attack, which demonstrated to state officials and the British the vulnerability of south Iran and the inefficiency of assembling diverse detachments after a foreign army had already invaded. When the British marched on Borazjan, the ilkhani organized the assembled detachments as a counterforce and urged courage by sending them two severed British heads mounted on lances. They engaged the British and helped to force their retreat. The bravery of the Qashqa'i cavalry was reported to have been an inspiration to the other fighters. Although British forces outnumbered the Iranians five to one, they fled to Bushire and ceased fighting; they had lost fifteen hundred men on this small excursion. According to the peace treaty signed in Paris in 1857, the Iranian army agreed to retreat from Herat and the British army from Bushire. Honors were bestowed on the Qashqa'i ilkhani for services rendered (Busse 1972:260, 319–38).

In 1864 the new governor of Kuhgiluyeh and Behbahan took Qashqa'i and Azerbaijani soldiers to his districts and to the Posht-e Kuh in order to assert authority, settle tribal affairs, and collect taxes (Busse 1972:348–50). The Qashqa'i detachment was permanently dis-

banded in 1868–69. Naser ed-Din Shah wanted to create a nontribal
army, or at least one in which tribes were not separate units, but his
attempts to modernize the army and increase the reliance on artillery
were only partly successful. In 1879 the Cossack Brigade, instructed
and commanded by Russian officers, was formed, but it contained only
a small force (Abrahamian 1982:39–40, 52–53). The transition to a
nontribal army was not completed until the 1930s.

In 1861–62 Naser ed-Din Shah formed the Khamseh tribal confederacy in order to oppose the growing strength of the Qashqa'i confederacy and create a balance of power in Fars. The British, whose recent
defeat (1856) had been partly caused by Qashqa'i military strength,
apparently urged this measure in order to weaken Qashqa'i power, and
their interests in this regard coincided with those of the shah. The new
confederacy consisted of the five major tribes found to the east of the
Qashqa'i tribes—the Arab, Nafar, Baharlu, Inalu, and Basseri—and
it took its name from the Arabic word for "five." As with each of the
Qashqa'i tribes, each Khamseh tribe was a composite group consisting
of people of diverse tribal, linguistic, and cultural backgrounds. Members of the Arab tribe, composed of two main sections (Arab Jabbareh
and Arab Shaibani), traced their origins from bedouin Arabs of the
Arabian peninsula and Iraq who came to Fars during Umayyad and
Abbasid times. Their language became a mixture of Arabic, Persian,
Turkic, and Luri. Members of the Nafar, Baharlu, and Inalu tribes were
said to descend from Turkic groups from Turkistan who settled in Fars
in the twelfth and thirteenth centuries and who furnished soldiers for,
and assisted in, Safavid, Afshar, and Zand rule. Members of the Basseri
tribe, who spoke Persian, Turkic, and Arabic, claimed origins from
indigenous as well as intrusive populations: Persian ("Farsi") nomads
who had utilized pastures in the area for hundreds of years and Turks
from Khorasan. All members of the Khamseh tribes and confederacy,
regardless of their language or reputed origin, came to be called "Arabs," a political label distinguishing them from "Turks" (Qashqa'i) in
particular but also from "Tajiks" (Persians).[5]

Naser ed-Din Shah placed the Khamseh confederacy under the leadership of the Qavam ol-Molk family, whose members were wealthy and
powerful merchants and landowners in Shiraz and Fars. He appointed
Ali Mohammad Khan, son of Hajji Ali Akbar Khan Qavam ol-Molk,

5. Fasa'i (1895–96b:309–15), Demorgny (1913a:100–07), Lane (1923:210–15), Field (1939:213–17), Oberling (1960:123–70), Barth (1961:passim).

as administrator (*hakim;* he was never appointed as or considered an ilkhani) of the confederacy and as governor of the large district of Darab, in line with state policy to provide tribal governors with means of support and enrichment. The Qavams, whose international commercial interests and plans for capitalist expansion promised greater profit than administering tribes, sought the governorship of the new confederacy for its military use in policing trade routes and countering Qashqa'i military strength, both of which facilitated their commercial and political interests and those of their British allies.

Other factors also explain the creation of the new confederacy. By 1861 the five eastern tribes had become increasingly anomalous in a setting in which power was being centralized. They had grown "difficult" for state and local governments to handle, which would seem to stem from their military activities on behalf of other powers and their ambiguous political attachments in the region. In 1859, after the Baharlu and Inalu tribes rebelled against Nafar leaders, the Governor of Fars appointed the shah's son as governor of the three tribes, and he brutally suppressed the rebellion (Busse 1972:340–41). The Qavams had taken military support from these tribes on many occasions, but the tribes had also been connected with the Qashqa'i confederacy for many years for purposes of taxation, administration, and military levies. Some of their pastures were far from Qashqa'i pastures, however, and effective control over them by the Shahilu was impeded. In addition, the Qavams and the shah's relatives administered many of the districts utilized by the five eastern tribes, which meant potential conflicts of interest. As governors of important districts in Fars and a major power in Shiraz, the Qavams had in the past been able to draw military forces from these areas, but escalating conflict in Fars and a new alliance between the Shahilu and the five Ni'mati wards in Shiraz (Abrahamian 1982:45) increasingly threatened their expanding economic and political interests.[6] The Qavams needed a larger, more accessible and dependable military force that could compete with that of the Shahilu. Although khans led the five eastern tribes (Fasa'i 1895–96b:309–15, Picot 1897), these figures were not nearly as powerful as the Shahilu khans. The Qavams, in order to utilize these tribes (and control their

6. The Qavams were said to own a third of Fars at the turn of the twentieth century, and the districts in eastern Fars they administered were assessed from 170,000 to 200,000 tumans in annual taxes (Demorgny 1913a:107, 134; *Additions and Corrections to Who's Who in Persia* 1924:88).

territory) more effectively, needed to exercise centralized, state-allocated authority over them, which coincided with the efforts of state and provincial rulers to gain greater control in the region.

With the five eastern tribes now under their administration, a degree of parity was created between the Qavams and the Shahilu. The only two consistently powerful local figures during most of the nineteenth century were the Qashqa'i ilkhani (or ilbegi) and the Qavam ol-Molk, and state officials fostered conflict between them in order to preserve their own tenuous hold over the province. The formation of a second confederacy enabled state officials to divide and rule, a regular state policy in this and other periods. Thereafter, the ruling elites of the two confederacies opposed one another and competed in escalating regional, national, and international conflicts. The Qashqa'i and Khamseh confederacies did, however, also constitute a "permanent repository of power in Fars," as compared with the transitory authority of the Governor and other state officials. One Governor after another appeared in Shiraz, allied with one or the other of the tribal groups, and then "vanished in a welter of confusion" (O'Connor 1931:217, 184).

In 1866, only four years after the formation of the Khamseh confederacy, a European who visited the Qashqa'i ilkhani commented that the Qavam ol-Molk was "the chief of a powerful and rival tribe of this region" (Mounsey 1872:254), an example of how quickly, at least in Western eyes, "tribes" could be created. By 1868 the Baharlu and Inalu tribes were formally complaining to the Governor of Fars about the Qavam's oppression and tyranny. In response, the Qavam promised the Governor that he would persuade the Baharlu to be obedient or he would "fight and exterminate them" (an attitude typical of many non-indigenous governors), and he attempted to subdue them by military force. The vizier, the Qavam's major competitor, had secretly ordered the Baharlu to disobey the Qavam, however, and the Governor transferred the governorship of Darab from the Qavam to the governor of Fasa and added the governorship of the Baharlu and Inalu tribes to that district. The Qavam responded by using his influence in Tehran to increase the taxes of Fasa, add its governorship to that of Darab and the two tribes, and have these governorships conferred upon him (Busse 1972:361–64), all of which overrode official decisions made at the provincial level.

The rapid changing of governorships of districts and tribes illustrated in this case simultaneously created and reflected instability at the local level and increased the opportunity for misrule. Given instability in tenure, governors taxed and extorted heavily in expectation that any particular year would be their last in office (Stack 1882b:298). In 1868, for example, the inhabitants of Darab experienced at least four changes of governor. For many rural inhabitants of Fars, protection under strong, established leadership was preferable. In the nineteenth century the Qashqa'i confederacy offered security in a context in which instability in the province was the norm; this trait was a key factor in the confederacy's growth and importance.

The claim of the Qavam family to the leadership of the five tribes was weak and differed from that of the Shahilu khans, as indicated by the apparent ease with which state officials could appoint new governors of the tribes. By this period, the Qashqa'i tribes were clearly regarded as an entity separate from districts, while the Baharlu and Inalu were still being added to and switched between districts. The Shahilu were molding a sociopolitical unit with a distinctive identity, while the Qavams, who remained urban politicians, utilized the five tribes for military and revenue-generating purposes only. The Shahilu were developing close political and cultural ties with the tribal people they administered, while the Qavams, partly for reasons connected with their entrenched urban Persian identity and life-style, made no such effort.

The creation of the Khamseh confederacy and its administration by the Qavams significantly changed the balance of power in Fars. Because this change occurred simultaneously with deepening British involvement in south Iran and because the Qavam family was a British ally, the Shahilu were suspicious that British influence was involved. They had previously collected taxes from four of the eastern tribes, and the severance of these groups economically affected both Qashqa'i tribespeople and khans because these revenues had helped to offset the Qashqa'i tax and other financial responsibilities of the khans. The Shahilu could no longer draw on the eastern tribes for military purposes, and, more crucially, these tribes now became a military threat to them. For decades to come, competing powers in Fars pitted the two confederacies against one another. In the early 1870s, five thousand Qashqa'i families under economic duress joined the Khamseh confederacy (Curzon 1892:113), indicating that this new confederacy threatened the Shahilu in yet another area. The Qavams encouraged such additions because they increased potential tax revenues and military support.

The creation of the Khamseh confederacy and subsequent British pressure for its use were major factors restricting the ilkhani's official responsibilities after the 1860s. The shah changed his formal title and role from Tribal Leader of Fars (Ilkhani-ye Mamlakat-e Fars) to Tribal Leader of the Qashqa'i (Ilkhani-ye Qashqa'i), which may have been British-inspired.[7] Until 1861 Qashqa'i ilkhanis and ilbegis had administered, apparently successfully, the tribal people of Fars on behalf of the state. Thereafter, competition over wealth and power increased substantially, and many powers demanded that the province's inhabitants be administered and controlled. Creation of the new confederacy both caused and reflected the dramatic escalation in such competition in Fars after the 1860s. The British, frustrated by the inability of the Iranian state to protect their growing commercial and strategic interests in south Iran, increasingly relied on their long-term ally, the Qavam ol-Molk, and his new tribal confederacy to defeat what they viewed as their major obstacle, the Qashqa'i confederacy, and the Khamseh and Qashqa'i confederacies were set in opposition to one another. Because of these changes, Qashqa'i politics and political development after the 1860s (and until the 1920s) were less related to issues of the Iranian state than to the British presence. The Shahilu-Qavam struggle has been viewed as a major axis of political unrest in Fars, but this ignores the broader context of increasing foreign interference.

A major source of conflict between the British and the Qashqa'i from 1865 well into the twentieth century was the rugged mountainous road between Shiraz and the Persian Gulf port of Bushire. The British were agitated about the Iranian state's inability to secure the safety of the route and their newly installed telegraph line running adjacent to it, both essential to their communications and their expanding interests in south Iran, and they blamed the "lawlessness" on the tribes in the vicinity, especially the Qashqa'i. The first reported conflict occurred in 1865 near Kazerun, where miles of telegraph wire was cut, insulators were broken as a result of target practice, and poles were used as firewood. The British, who had just completed this section of the line, demanded immediate government action against the perpetrators. One suspected offender was a Qashqa'i "clan chief," whose prominent position made his punishment politically important to the British. The shah's agent seized him and levied a fine on the ilkhani, possibly the

7. Malek Mansur Khan, personal interview, 28 August 1979, Tehran.

first historical record of an ilkhani's being responsible for the actions of an individual tribesman. The alleged offender held the title of *beg,* one of the first accounts of a Qashqa'i leader below the level of khan. British officials asked the government not to execute him, which had "the happy effect of securing the friendship of the Kashkai chiefs to the English Telegraph officers." The telegraph in Fars in the next few years suffered less damage than in the rest of Iran (Goldsmid 1874b:253–55), which implies that the ilkhani exercised some control in the region.

In 1871–72 a famine caused great hardship and misery in south Iran, and many people died of starvation (Goldsmid 1874a). Some of those devastated by the famine-related economic crisis resorted to raiding and robbery, which leaders in the region were hard-pressed to curtail. As a result of the famine, "the wandering tribes have lost from want of feed their herds of cattle; but of course have had to pay the revenue. These people depend solely on their cattle and sheep for a livelihood, and have now reached a pitch of desperation which leads them to commit any atrocity."[8] In 1872 the Governor of Fars executed three Qashqa'i for the robbery and murder of a British telegraph inspector (Wills 1883:293–95).

Leadership is tested in crisis, and this period was not to be one of the Shahilu's finest hours. Soltan Mohammad Khan had become ilkhani in 1867 on the death of his father, Mohammad Qoli, regarded as second in importance only to the Governor of Fars; the government had required Mohammad Qoli to live in Shiraz as a hostage for the good behavior of his "clan," but he was otherwise free to conduct his life according to his needs (Mounsey 1872:274). Soltan Mohammad, the new ilkhani, was also held hostage in Shiraz (Bell 1885:109). He was a weak leader and retired from active leadership, although he retained his title and the governorship of two districts, and a succession of three ilbegis exercised power in his place. "Tribal affairs fell into the hands of smaller khans, which resulted in internal dissension" (Curzon 1892:113—one of the first accounts of khans other than those of the Shahilu family). In the late 1860s and early 1870s Sohrab Khan, a member of the Shahilu family and son of Mostoufa Qoli, who had died in the attack on Kerman, organized a rebellion against the Governor and government exactions. He was then deceived by a promise of a

---

8. An employee of the Indo-European Telegraph Department, *The Times* (London), 1872:7, as quoted in Oberling (1974:69).

governorship from the succeeding Governor, was captured through treachery, and was executed on the shah's orders in 1874–75 (Oberling 1974:71). (This sequence of events also happened to another young Shahilu khan in the 1960s.) This rebellion is the first historical account of organized resistance to the state by a Shahilu khan. The Qashqa'i confederacy, which until this point had steadily increased in numbers of people and affiliated groups, now lost members. In the mid-1870s four thousand Qashqa'i families settled, five thousand joined the Bakhtiyari confederacy, and five thousand the Khamseh (Curzon 1892:113). The Governor of Fars placed the administration of the Lashani tribe under the care of his nephew, which severed it from the Qashqa'i confederacy (Christian 1919:62).[9]

The long, effective rule of Naser ed-Din Shah was responsible for establishing an unprecedented degree of government control in Fars. The British-installed telegraph assisted the government's efforts by linking the capital with Shiraz and Bushire, thus speeding communications that had previously taken days or weeks. In 1876 the shah limited the powers of Governors, abolished the road-guard corps, released the army from gubernatorial functions, and offered Governors the choice of either taking full responsibility for road safety, which was expensive and caused greater exactions of revenue and labor from the districts, or allowing the central government to handle it, which introduced into the area forces competitive with those of provincial and district governors (Oberling 1974:63–64). The Governor of Fars responded by assigning salaried musketeers to the roads for protection against robbers and held them financially responsible for goods stolen from travelers (Busse 1972:405). By these centralizing actions of the state, district governors were relieved of some responsibilities for security in their areas. The Governor, still lacking an adequate military force of his own, successfully acquired the support of the Qavam ol-Molk and his Khamseh troops in ending the rebellion of a Baharlu tribesman who, along with five hundred followers, had evaded government forces for eighteen years (Busse 1972:387n., 390–91).

9. The Lashani was one of the Lak tribes Karim Khan Zand brought to Fars from northwest Iran to serve as his armed guard. With the end of Zand rule, it was absorbed into the Qashqa'i confederacy and was gradually Turkicized (Oberling 1960:109–12). After being severed from the confederacy in the 1870s, the Lashani remained independent and during World War I harassed the British, who considered them "the most notorious robbers" in south Iran (Sykes 1930:482).

In 1882 the Governor of Fars ordered the Qavam ol-Molk to assemble a body of five hundred horsemen from the tribes of Fars to present to Naser ed-Din Shah in Tehran. They included Qashqa'i, Arab, Baharlu, Inalu, and tribesmen settled in Shiraz. The shah offered royal favors to the Governor and confirmed the Qavam's grandson as commander of the force, which remained in Tehran in the shah's special service and as hostage for the good behavior of the "unruly tribes" of south Iran (Busse 1972:418). In the same year the shah executed the Bakhtiyari ilkhani and feared a rebellion in the south as a consequence. The Qavams had often been Bakhtiyari allies, and hence one of them may have been appointed commander, rather than a Shahilu khan, to ensure Qavam support for the Qajars and not the Bakhtiyari in the expected uprising.[10] In 1896 the shah proposed a Superior Council of Tribes of Iran, to be based in Tehran with its principal branch in Shiraz (Demorgny 1913a:90). No concrete steps toward its formation appear to have been made.

In 1896 Naser ed-Din Shah was assassinated, and Iran was not to have a strong state ruler until Reza Shah in the 1920s. Mozaffar ed-Din Shah, who became head of state, was a weak ruler, and the Shahilu had few contacts with him. Abdollah Khan, eldest son of Darab Khan who had served as de facto ilkhani for sixteen years, became de facto ilkhani and then assumed the position himself, but his younger brother, Isma'il Khan, who served as ilbegi, increasingly took over power. From 1898 until 1933 Isma'il Khan Soulat ed-Douleh drew national and international attention to the Qashqa'i, and Qashqa'i affairs were largely his orchestrations.

Stack's comments about the Qashqa'i ilbegi and ilkhani in 1881 are typical of European accounts in demonstrating little understanding of Qashqa'i leadership: the ilbegi "seems to be a kind of brigand on a magnificent scale" (1882a:86), while the ilkhani is "perhaps too refined for a leader of nomads" (1882a:100). Qashqa'i ilkhanis and ilbegis were prominent national figures, upper-class urbanites, wealthy landowners, district governors, and strong tribal leaders, a combination of features that stymied Europeans, who were expecting rough-hewn steppe warriors in their stereotypic images of Chengiz Khan and Timurlane. Oberling contrasts the luxurious, corrupt life of the urban, effete, and sophisticated Qashqa'i elite with the "tribal world," where leaders were ascetics and tribe-oriented and where "the continual presence of a

10. Gene Garthwaite, personal communication.

leader who enjoys the austere modus vivendi of the nomad is deemed essential for effective leadership" (1974:73). Such a "tribal world" never existed for the paramount Qashqa'i khans. These urban-oriented, sophisticated leaders had helped to create a massive tribal confederacy in the context of national struggles over power and wealth and had forged contacts with state rulers and foreign powers that ensured their place in written history. It is ironic that the only time the paramount Qashqa'i khans lived as ascetic mountain warriors was when they had virtually no tribal support, and this occurred in the most modern of times— 1980–82.

THE IMPACT OF TRADE ROUTES

The British East India Company signed a treaty with Karim Khan Zand in 1763 giving the company "a monopoly of the import of woollens into Persia, freedom from all taxes, either on imports or exports, and a promise that no other European nation would be allowed to establish a trading station at Bushire as long as the British remained there" (Marlowe 1962:10; also Perry 1979:258–67). In 1778 the company made Bushire, which had gained prominence under Nader Shah (1736–47) as Iran's main port on the Persian Gulf, its gulf headquarters.[11] Bushire was a commercial center, to some extent an extension of the British commercial presence in Basra (Iraq), and a naval base that protected British interests from pirates who "infested" the gulf and that allowed surveillance over the Ottoman navy. The routes inland from Bushire were of great importance. British trade with Iran flourished in the nineteenth century, especially under conditions fostered by Naser ed-Din Shah, but trade declined rapidly thereafter because of foreign interference, loss of state control, and competition among local groups.[12]

11. Previously, the main ports on the gulf for Iran had been, in successive order, Siraf (near the current Bandar Tahiri), Kays Island, and Hormuz Island. The route of travel from Siraf to Shiraz passed through Jur (later named Firuzabad).

12. Goods exported from Bushire in the second half of the nineteenth century included: cotton, cotton goods, wool, silk, carpets, gum arabic, hides and skins, mother of pearl, opium, spices, grain, rosewater, tobacco, lemon juice, nuts, dried fruit, and horses. Goods imported at Bushire in this same period included: cotton goods, woolen goods, silks, drugs, medicine, hardware, metals, indigo, porcelain, china, glassware, grain, sugar, tea, and spices (Pelly 1865b:158–65, Curzon 1892: 559–61, Napier 1900:47).

MAP 3. Nineteenth-Century Trade Routes in Southwest Iran

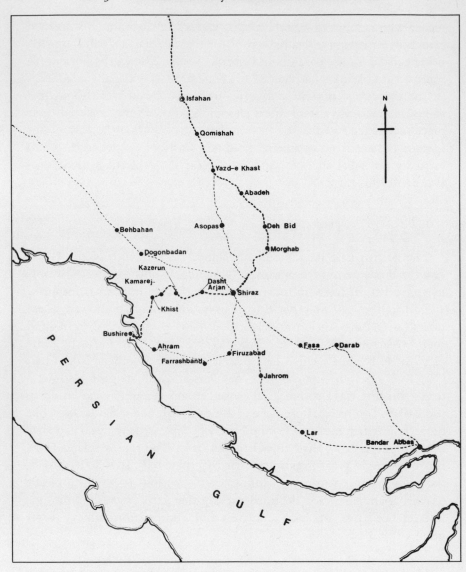

The main route of trade and travel from the Persian Gulf into the interior of Iran was called the Royal Road and ran from Bushire, through Kazerun, to Shiraz, and then north to Isfahan and Tehran. It offered caravansary services at regular intervals. The main alternate route between Bushire and Shiraz ran through Farrashband and Firuzabad, the hereditary domain of the Qashqa'i ilkhanis.[13] This southern route, 210–22 miles long, was sometimes used to avoid the disruptions frequently occurring on the more regularly used, more direct, shorter (165–80 miles long) northern route through Kazerun, but it offered no services. Both routes passed by and through pastures used by Qashqa'i pastoralists, but the southern route was more under the control of the ilkhanis because of their winter headquarters at Firuzabad and Farrashband. Qashqa'i leaders and tribespeople were drawn directly into the affairs of those using and depending on these routes. Had Qashqa'i pastures not abutted and intersected these routes, a much different history of the Qashqa'i would have resulted.

Two main routes connected Shiraz and Isfahan. The main route through Abadeh and Deh Bid, the continuation of the Royal Road, was the post road; it provided caravansaries and post houses. The alternate route, called the sarhad or hill route, provided no services and could not be used in winter; it lay to the west of the main route and passed through Asopas and Qashqa'i summer pastures. The two routes met at Yazd-e Khast, and a single road continued to Isfahan. After the creation of the Khamseh confederacy, the Royal Road separated the two confederacies, and south-north travel, no longer cutting through pastures under Qashqa'i control, now occurred in the relatively neutral territory between them. It could be speculated that concern over security was partially responsible for the creation of separate confederacies, one on either side of the route.

A road-toll system, called *rahdari,* was an integral part of travel along the Bushire-Shiraz route in the nineteenth century. Travelers paid tolls in exchange for safe passage, and caravans were assigned night watchmen and armed escorts to the next toll station. Caravansary services, including food, lodging, animals for transport, and shelter for trade goods, were also available. Provincial and district governors were responsible for assigning specific toll stations to individuals and groups, and some sections of the road were auctioned off to the highest

13. Other, less used routes from Bushire to Shiraz also existed. The route from Bandar Abbas was much longer and not as popular.

bidders. Many competed for the often lucrative privilege of collecting tolls. When government in the region was strong, the route was regulated and payments fixed. As the government became increasingly unable to handle local affairs at the end of the nineteenth century and into the twentieth, the rahdari system became less regulated and more subject to local powers, who competed among themselves for the opportunity to control stations (which increased fees and numbers of stations), to ally with those responsible for "guarding" the road, and to raid caravans. Iranian merchants and officials exploited a situation they were increasingly unable to control and arranged possibly half of the robberies themselves (Safiri 1976:182). Many of those accused of theft had been paid to rob.

Lack of road safety irked British commercial interests, and British officials regularly issued complaints to Iran's central authorities. Arms and ammunition were items of trade coming into Iran from Britain, and some of the first commercial interests to complain to the British government about disruption of trade were the Manchester arms manufacturers. The British inadvertently supplied the means by which they were often separated from their trade goods, and the number of arms available to people along the route as well as the number of robberies rapidly increased. Civilians (tribal and nontribal) were better armed than the government (Wilson 1916:40, 1942:177). In 1903 the Iranian government ordered local powers along the road to arm and equip more guards but failed to supply funds, which enabled those who collected tolls to increase rates to support extra guards. As a result of the raised tolls, more robberies, and higher insurance rates charged by British companies, travel and trade along the road became increasingly, then prohibitively, expensive. British and other foreign commercial powers, as well as commercial interests in Shiraz and elsewhere in Iran, found that their margin of profit, which had been substantial, steadily decreased and eventually disappeared.

The "most troublesome" of the "bandit tribes" for foreign and Iranian traders and travelers were said to be those of the Qashqa'i confederacy, which, under the "able leadership" of Isma'il Khan, the Qashqa'i ilkhani, were "giving vent to their marauding propensities by raiding the caravans from Abadeh all the way down to Dashtestan" (Oberling 1974:86–87). Actually, all local powers along the route, the Qashqa'i included, were involved in its traffic, and many were serving larger interests. Some individuals exerting power along the route were called *khan,* which deceived many Europeans into thinking that they were tribal leaders. Khan, however, was a commonly found honorific title that could be self-assumed, inherited, or group-bestowed as well as being government-appointed, and it was not restricted to tribal leaders. Many khans living in towns and villages along the road had no tribal affiliations or attachments. Most were medium and large landholders, whose families had profited from commercial traffic along the route for generations. As traffic on the route increased in the nineteenth century, local powers profiting from it sought armed road guards, toll collectors, muleteers, providers of food and lodging in the caravansaries, and commercial agents. The population in the vicinity of the road increased in proportion to the level of traffic, and travelers often mistook these inhabitants for the "tribes" of the khans who were in charge of toll stations. As a result, identities were attributed to blocks of people along the road, who were believed to be represented by khans in the area. By the beginning of the twentieth century, the range of powers along the route included single highway robbers, small groups of "bandits," professional brigands, road guards who were "more or less legalized and established robbers" (O'Connor 1931:189), rural and urban elite backed by rural supporters, settled and nomadic tribesmen, and tribal confederacies. British officials tended to lump them together in a single category, equating the activities of a highway robber with that of the Qashqa'i confederacy. Ironically, the traffic of goods and the commercial competition among foreign and Iranian interests were responsible for the creation of many of these groups and for the increased political unification of others, including the Qashqa'i confederacy.

The perceived role of the Qashqa'i ilkhani changed along with the development of trade routes. The government held him officially responsible for safety on roads passing through or by what was regarded as his domain, an area much broader than Qashqa'i winter and summer pastures and increasing in size as trade routes increased in importance. The ilkhani was given power and authority that he previously lacked over people and territories in the area, and the land under Shahilu and Qashqa'i control and the number of people affiliated with the confederacy increased. The state, in other words, delegated authority to him in a way that no amount of politicking among the involved people could have established. Given the context of local competition, these people were probably not averse to such state action. The ilkhani was a leading political figure in the south, and through him they received sole rights to collect tolls and police the road to their economic advantage.

THE PARAMOUNT QASHQA'I KHANS AND PROPERTY
AT THE BEGINNING OF THE TWENTIETH CENTURY

During the nineteenth century Qashqa'i ilkhanis and ilbegis were appointed governors of at least 23 districts in Fars covering both winter and summer pastures.[14] Given that Qashqa'i pastoralists occupied at least 39 districts in Fars (27 in winter pastures and 12 in summer pastures), out of a total of some 63 to 65 in the province as a whole, it is probable that Qashqa'i ilkhanis and ilbegis were governors of other districts as well; historical evidence is, however, lacking.[15] Several of the 23 districts were also placed under other governors during the century, and the important district of Darab, which the ilkhani's family administered, was transferred more or less permanently to the family of the Qavam ol-Molk upon the creation of the Khamseh confederacy. Darab is in eastern Fars near the Khamseh tribes and outside the political domain of Qashqa'i ilkhanis from that period. All 23 districts (except Darab) contained winter and summer pastures utilized by Qashqa'i pastoralists in the twentieth century and, apparently, the nineteenth. Two districts in winter pastures, Firuzabad and Farrashband, were regarded as the hereditary domain of the Qashqa'i ilkhani. Both contained towns, and both were located on the southern route between Shiraz and Bushire. Semirom, an important agricultural district in northern Fars containing a town of the same name, was considered the tribal capital of summer pastures and was owned in part by the Shahilu family. The Shahilu controlled pastures near Semirom during the reign of Karim Khan Zand, and during the nineteenth century they also controlled pastures south of Semirom near Khosrow Shirin.

The paramount Qashqa'i khans regarded some land in most of the districts they governed as private property, and much of the rest was

14. The districts in winter pastures include (north to south): Mahur-e Milati, Kazerun (Kuhmarreh, Mashgan), Kamarej, Khisht, Famur, Jereh, Firuzabad, Farrashband, Darab (until 1861), Maimend, Qir-o Karzin, Mahalleh Arba' (Dehram, Rudbal, Hengam, Dehrud), Afzar, Khonj, and Ala Marv Dasht. In summer pastures they include (north to south): Shish Naheya (Falarod, Vardasht, Vanak, Semirom, Padena, Hanna), Khosrow Shirin, Dez-e Kord, Chahar Danga (Asopas), Kakan and Komer, Kamfiruz, Ardekan, and Mashhad-e Morghab.

15. The districts in winter pastures utilized by Qashqa'i pastoralists, in addition to those in the previous note, include (north to south): Khairabad, Mishun and Bidkarz, Shapur, Tangaram, Sar Mashhad and Hosainabad, Simakan, Laghar, Siakh, Duzdgah, Gallehdar, Jabal Anaruyeh, and Bidshahr. In summer pastures they include (north to south): Garmabad, Nokhuddon, Baiza, and Ramjerd.

MAP 4.   Nineteenth-Century Administrative Districts of Fars Province

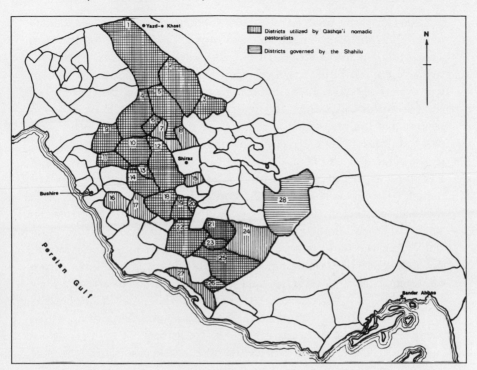

Note: Data from Demorgny (1913a, maps 1–2).

Key:
1. Shish Naheye
2. Chahar Danga
3. Morghab
4. Kakan
5. Kamfiruz
6. Ardekan
7. Baiza

8. Ramjerd
9. Mahur-e Milati
10. Kazerun
11. Khisht
12. Kuhmarreh
13. Famur
14. Jereh

15. Siakh
16. Ahram
17. Boluk
18. Farrashband
19. Firuzabad
20. Maimend
21. Qir-o Karzin

22. Mahalleh Arba'
23. Afzar
24. Bidshahr
25. Khonj
26. Ala Marv Dasht
27. Gallehdar
28. Darab

regarded as communal tribal land which they allocated to Qashqa'i tribes and subtribes. The khans also moved nomadic pastoralists and agriculturalists into districts over which they had been assigned administrative responsibilities, which resulted in their firmer political control over these areas. Many people became "Qashqa'i" upon being assigned usufructuary rights in the districts governed by these khans, a process that is a major part of this confederacy's formation. When new pastoral groups affiliated, additional communal land was often added to the confederacy's political domain, and in this way territory under its control expanded. Each of the districts the khans governed also contained agricultural land, villages, and at least one town, over which they had jurisdiction and some opportunity for acquiring property and wealth. They profited from their tax-collecting responsibilities, especially from the non-Qashqa'i inhabitants under their administration, and they acquired private property by investing income held back from tax revenues and confiscating land when holders fell in arrears. They also purchased, acquired, and rented land in other areas in and bordering Fars, including Kuhgiluyeh, Dashtistan, and Tangistan, which often fell under the authority of other tribal leaders.

Toward the end of the nineteenth century, specific territories were associated with each of the four branches of the Shahilu lineage descending from the four sons of Jani Khan. Competition among the branches partly centered on land and other wealth, especially because the person appointed ilkhani was also appointed governor of the major Qashqa'i districts. Ilkhanis emerged from three of the four branches during the nineteenth century, and ilbegis from all four; each time positions changed, property also changed hands. Soltan Ibrahim Khan inherited the property of two of the four branches, which constituted eleven of the twenty-three known districts under Shahilu administration. Marriage with other prominent families in Iran could also increase land and property, although in at least one case it meant loss of property.[16]

The ilkhani's estates in Shiraz were also important properties: Bagh-e Eram (the summer house), Bagh-e Ilkhani (the winter house), and possibly other residences. There is no evidence that the lineage held any commercial properties in Shiraz or that its members trafficked

16. Mohammad Qoli, ilkhani from 1852 to 1867, married the Qavam ol-Molk's sister, and, when the ilkhani died, the Qavam expropriated his property at the expense of the son and heir, Soltan Mohammad (Stack 1882a:86).

in real estate there, two features distinguishing them from the Qavam family and other elites. The Shahilu estates in Shiraz were vulnerable to political struggles; city officials occasionally plundered and confiscated them, and the "rabble" of Shiraz ransacked them. Some ilkhanis and ilbegis in the Qajar period were forced to live in Tehran or Shiraz. Members of the Shahilu family always owned residences in Shiraz, but whether or not they moved seasonally or regularly between urban residences and mountain encampments, as their descendants did in the twentieth century, is not known.

Land holdings in winter and summer pastures, Shiraz, other parts of Fars, and adjoining territories placed ilkhanis, ilbegis, and their families in the ranks of the wealthy landholding elite of nineteenth-century Iran. This economic base contributed to their ability to wield power on the provincial level. But their power was also based on their tribal and rural affiliates, and in this they differed from many other wealthy elite of the time. The Shahilu also possessed wealth in flocks and especially agricultural production. Rural Fars was rich in the production of grains, fruit, nuts, cotton, and tobacco, which were traded locally and nationally. Major items of overseas export in the nineteenth century were wool and gum tragacanth and, after 1870, carpets and opium. The Shahilu participated in all these ventures, usually through their (almost exclusively non-Qashqa'i) brokers and commercial agents in cities.[17]

CONCLUSIONS

The evidence suggests that by the beginning of the twentieth century the Qashqa'i confederacy had been established by the interplay of four forces: the Iranian state, prominent members of the Shahilu lineage, affiliated tribespeople, and (after the 1850s) foreign incursion. It was especially the interaction of the Shahilu with state and local officials that helped to form the confederacy; the Shahilu were not passive in the face of state and foreign encroachments but, instead, played a direct role in the structuring and outcome of the interaction. By the beginning of the twentieth century, the Qashqa'i confederacy was defined from the outside as a taxable and administrative unit, military force, rival political/military unit to the Khamseh confederacy, and

17. Many of the Shahilu's commercial agents are listed in *Who's Who in Persia* (1923) and *Additions and Corrections to Who's Who in Persia* (1924).

enemy of British commercial and strategic interests. Economic changes in south Iran, especially increased foreign commercial penetration and the creation of new regional and national market structures, figured in the realignments of power in the region and help to explain the formation of the Khamseh confederacy and the further solidification of the Qashqa'i confederacy.

No actual political unity of the Qashqa'i apparently existed during the nineteenth century, and the Qashqa'i polity, especially in the early Qajar period, may have been little more than an aggregation of groups whose unity consisted primarily of coallegiance to the Shahilu khans and acceptance of their authority. The ilkhani's ability to mobilize support in the confederacy was limited, and the Qashqa'i people never acted as a corporate body. The tribes and subtribes of the confederacy conducted many of their own affairs independently, and, short of general directives concerning migrations and pasture utilization, their leaders may have interacted with the ilkhani infrequently. That the Iranian state and local and foreign powers perceived the Qashqa'i as a single entity, however, contributed to confederacy formation. Outside powers dealt with the Qashqa'i as a unit through the ilkhani, and in so doing helped to form it as one.

Problems in administering nomadic people were different from those met in administering settled ones, and over the centuries Iranian rulers had developed indirect means. Their concerns focused on taxation and law and order, and they assigned these responsibilities to prominent individuals and families. In the case of Fars province, they selected members of a lineage that had historically served state rulers. The Shahilu—"Those of the Shah"—lineage was ideally suited for the task, for it held a combination of crucial and unique characteristics. It possessed a Turkic and tribal heritage, it was a local unit (as compared with one brought from outside), its members were sophisticated urbanites as well as rural-based landholders, and it had a long history of service to state rulers. As state administrators, the Shahilu did not view their service only as a means for extortion and profit, partly because they relied on tribal support, and as a result they offered a contrast to those state officials who were corrupt and avaricious and who lacked interest in the well-being of governed people (see Lambton 1953). As a result, people adhered readily to the Shahilu as administrators, and in time the Shahilu were able to consolidate them under their authority. The context of this consolidation involved competition over pastoral and agricultural land in sometimes quite heavily settled areas, and competition over labor to put this land into production from which revenue could then be secured. Because the Shahilu were regularly confirmed as district governors and exercised that form of control over these and other territories, those who supported them gained secure, predictable use of land.

Iranian state rulers defined their administrative divisions through territorial districts and then through districts and tribes. Faced with a large rural population, part of which ignored or resisted attempts at administration, these rulers utilized tribal blocs as a partial solution. The Qashqa'i became a single taxable entity, and one person was held personally responsible for it, whereby in the past state rulers were fortunate to tap even part of such a population for revenue. State rulers had few means of quashing rural unrest short of the policies of forced migration pursued by pre-Qajar rulers and Aqa Mohammad Shah, which drained state resources and caused new problems. Hence, they turned, as on the tax issue, to one person who was held responsible for the group. Exactly how one individual was able to perform successfully in these matters is not known for the nineteenth century, but in succeeding chapters I demonstrate how it functioned in the twentieth century.

State rulers, in desperate need of armed forces to combat external threats and internal unrest, found their best candidates in mobile, armed, organized groups. Those individuals responsible for assembling troops for the state armies drew from the people with whom they already had administrative and military ties and from those they relocated in their territories. In the process, more concrete identities were given to the people from which each of these levies was drawn.

The creation of the Khamseh confederacy, by a stroke of the pen, turned both Khamseh and Qashqa'i confederacies into equivalent political/military units. The act defined more precisely the purpose of a tribal confederacy (military activity) and the function of its leader (a state official), who assumed greater power. Although Naser ed-Din Shah and other powers intended, through the formation of the Khamseh confederacy, to establish a balance of power in Fars and thus neutralize the Qashqa'i (Oberling 1974:65), the Qashqa'i confederacy also became more organized in order to rival what these powers had created in the Khamseh. By the end of the nineteenth century, state rulers were not concerned with Qashqa'i revenue but rather with its political/military role; the confederacy was both a threat to the state and a state weapon.

After the 1850s the British, in objectifying the Qashqa'i as their enemy, gave more concreteness to what had previously been primarily a unit of taxation and a military force. They complained to the shah about the Qashqa'i, with threats if remedies were not forthcoming. State officials, in order to respond to British demands, were also forced to interact with the Qashqa'i as an entity. State access to the Qashqa'i was, however, only by way of the ilkhani, who was, as a result, reinforced in his position.

Finally, prominent Shahilu leaders, occupying a mediatory, brokerage position between the affiliated people and the state, defined each for the other. They especially defined the group for the state, given that the group and its organization were not completely known or accessible entities. From the middle of the eighteenth century to the middle of the nineteenth, state authorities enabled the Shahilu to define who and what was tribal; after 1861 they enabled them to define who and what was Qashqa'i. The Shahilu often used their position opportunistically, by defining people as tribal at one point and not at another. They could and did threaten the state and the British with the military potential of thousands of affiliated warriors, but they could also claim lack of responsibility and control when state authorities demanded taxes. They were in a unique and superior position where no other person or power had information on and access to the large tribal group and high-level state officials simultaneously. Both state and tribe depended on this mediation, which further enhanced the Shahilu position. The Shahilu were among the few prominent figures in provincial politics whose families were long-term residents of Fars, in contrast to the externally appointed, imported Governors, viziers, and other officials who served for brief periods before being dismissed from their posts. Such outside figures depended on the Shahilu and then fought with them when conflicts of interest developed.

Relationships between the Shahilu and state authorities were generally favorable in the nineteenth century (especially as compared with the twentieth), a feature attributable to the government's reliance on indirect rule and delegated authority, the shahs' awareness of their own limitations, and the effectiveness of Shahilu leadership and mediation. In contrast, state authorities often perceived the other large tribal groups in the region (Mamassani, Boir Ahmad, Tangistani, Baharlu) as menaces and conducted military campaigns against them. These other groups lacked the strong centralized leadership of the Qashqa'i, and as a result their members were freer to act autonomously of any wider authority. They also lacked the privileged economic position of the Qashqa'i and may therefore have been more dependent on raiding and robbery. But most importantly, the interests of the Shahilu coincided with those of state authorities; these khans were, in fact, agents of the state, unlike many of the leaders of other groups in the region.

A striking feature of Qashqa'i history during the nineteenth century is that no evidence indicates that the Qashqa'i people as a whole acted in their own interests or pursued their own military goals qua Qashqa'i. Nor is there evidence that the Shahilu utilized Qashqa'i forces for territorial expansion or other political purposes relating to the Qashqa'i as an entity or for specifically Qashqa'i interests. (Shahilu interests were another matter.) The Qashqa'i people appear to have been used only as a pawn in the strategies of other powers. There *were* no collective Qashqa'i interests at this point, despite Western beliefs to the contrary; specifically Qashqa'i interests did not become articulated until Reza Shah. This issue becomes more apparent in the next chapter on the early twentieth century, a time when the British and the Germans intruded into south Iran. The actions of both groups were based on the assumption that the Qashqa'i were a united polity organized to pursue their own interests and hence were viewed as a threat and a means of threatening others.

5

The Foreign Presence

etween 1906 and 1911 the Qajar dynasty was challenged by the constitutional revolution in Iran and during World War I by foreign powers engaging in their own national struggies on Iranian soil. National government was weak during these periods, and local powers exercised considerable autonomy. The effective end of the Qajar dynasty, continued foreign interference, and a decentralized state figure significantly in the changes occurring in Qashqa'i leadership and the tribal confederacy during the first two decades of the twentieth century.

ISMA'IL KHAN SOULAT ED-DOULEH

Isma'il Khan[1] began his political career with modest means. His father, Darab Khan, had left a small patrimony to be divided among his five sons and several daughters. Between the time Darab Khan first began to serve as ilbegi (1876) and the time Isma'il Khan became ilkhani (1904), four other members of the Shahilu family had been ilkhani, and Shahilu wealth was under their control. In 1898, when Isma'il Khan was appointed ilbegi (along with Bahador Khan), he owned only six camels, two mules, and one village (Ab-e Garm in the

---

1. British and Iranian sources usually refer to him by his state-bestowed title only, Soulat ed-Douleh. In this discussion I use his personal name and the tribal title of khan, Isma'il Khan.

district of Qir-o Karzin). He was forced to sell the rent of his village (seven hundred tumans a year) to pay his debts, and he bought a horse on loan for one hundred tumans. With this meager property he traveled to summer pastures to begin his leadership functions. As joint ilbegi with Bahador Khan, he was supposed to share the confederacy's administrative tasks, including tax collection, but he refused to do so until Bahador threatened to inform the ilkhani. Isma'il Khan relented by giving him authority over the Shish Boluki, Bollu, and Gallehzan tribes (Christian 1919:54, *Who's Who in Persia* 1923:135).

In 1900 a new Governor of Fars was appointed who named Isma'il Khan as sole ilbegi and bestowed upon him the title of Soulat ed-Douleh (Authority of the State). In 1902 the ilkhani, Abdollah Khan, growing uneasy about Isma'il Khan's rise in power, availed himself of the appointment of yet another new Governor to have Isma'il Khan deposed. The new Governor assigned Isma'il Khan the governorship of Behbahan, with jurisdiction over the wider Kuhgiluyeh region, in order to remove him from the scene (Christian 1919:54). Although the Governor's secretary refused to give Isma'il Khan written authorization of the appointment, Isma'il Khan left for Behbahan with a hundred supporters and bluffed the citizens of the district of Zaidun into paying him their tax arrears. This income provided him the necessary means to launch his political career.[2] Behbahan, the economic and political center of the Kuhgiluyeh, occupied a strategic location on the boundary of Fars and Khuzistan and on the main road from Shiraz to Khuzistan and Mesopotamia. Isma'il Khan was the third of Darab Khan's sons, after Abdollah Khan and Ahmad Khan, to serve as governor of the Kuhgiluyeh. In the nineteenth century the central government had maintained a sizable military garrison there, but at the turn of the century, being unable to maintain control, it assigned responsibility to prominent tribal leaders from neighboring areas. After these three Qashqa'i governors, one Arab Mohaysen and six Bakhtiyari governors served in the region (Baver 1945:37).

In 1902 the Governor of Fars was displeased with Abdollah Khan and for a short time replaced him as ilkhani with Isma'il Khan. In 1904 Isma'il Khan intrigued to receive the official appointment. First he allied with the Qavam ol-Molk and the Qavam's son against the Governor and asked Abdollah Khan to join. Then he revealed the plot to the Governor, who ordered the Qavam assassinated, the ilkhani thrown

2. Houman Qashqa'i, personal interview, 5 September 1979, Tehran.

into chains (and later poisoned), and Isma'il Khan reappointed as il-begi. The next Governor appointed Isma'il Khan as ilkhani, who promptly seized the former ilkhani's property, including many villages in the districts of Semirom, Firuzabad, and Qir-o Karzin (Christian 1919:54, *Who's Who in Persia* 1923:135–36). In contrast to the four previous ilkhanis, Isma'il Khan was a strong political force in the confederacy. Abdollah Khan had been indifferent to the payment of taxes and the management of the component tribes, and lower-level Qashqa'i leaders had gained considerable independence (Chick 1916:33–34). Isma'il Khan insisted on the full payment of tribal taxes, removed khans who worked against his interests, and appointed ones in his favor. He drew into the confederacy many independent tribal groups in Fars, increased Qashqa'i pastures and his own private property by purchase and seizure, and greatly expanded the tribal body (the Amaleh) serving as his personal retinue and standing army (*Gazetteer of Persia* 1918:801, 812). The Qashqa'i confederacy as it was known in the twentieth century was in large part due to Isma'il Khan's role as ilkhani. He held the title of ilkhani for most of the period between 1904 and 1933; he exercised active leadership until Reza Shah detained him in Tehran in 1925, and no real rivals to his position as paramount leader emerged, despite many British-instigated attempts to have his title removed and to appoint others.

Isma'il Khan's activities during the first two decades of the twentieth century occurred within a broader struggle involving British incursions and interference, British-Russian-German rivalry, the constitutional movement against Qajar rule, a weak central government having no influence in Fars, and the rising national power of the Bakhtiyari. His importance rested on his position as paramount tribal leader (with the accruing political and economic benefits), his ability to play diverse roles in many arenas, and his personal shrewdness. The Qashqa'i people were probably not much concerned at this time with the constitution and related issues concerning nationalism and secularism, or with the extent of foreign interference in Iran's internal affairs against which the constitutional revolution was addressed. That the people did affect provincial affairs and were viewed as a threat by powers in Tehran and by the British were largely Isma'il Khan's accomplishment. He was an advocate of the constitution and favored ridding Iran of foreign interference and the despotic shah, but he also understood that acting in the name of nationalism provided him with the means of relating to other local communities—dissident merchants, religious authorities, landowners, urbanites, and the intelligentsia—

with whom he needed ties in order to secure and maintain regional (as compared with the more narrow tribal) power. Isma'il Khan favored an Iranian nationalism that would incorporate considerable regional autonomy, and he supported the kind of central government that would delegate regional power to him. His antiforeign sentiments were inspired by personal experience with British intervention in south Iran and in his tribal and regional leadership. British officials described him as a tyrant who would oppose any force interfering with his tribal and regional power, which demonstrated their own perceptions of the threat he posed to their interests.

In the nineteenth century, state rulers delegated to the Qashqa'i ilkhani certain responsibilities for Qashqa'i, tribal, and regional affairs, including taxation and law and order, and rewarded him with governorships, land, money, arms, and certain rights and privileges. From 1902 to 1920, however, state rulers were too weak to comply with their obligations on Isma'il Khan's behalf, and other powers interfered with his traditional obligations toward the state. These changes undercut his authority among the Qashqa'i and in the region and engendered rival leaders and intratribal dissension. Despite these circumstances, Isma'il Khan continued to negotiate tribal and nontribal affairs and mediate between tribal and nontribal forces. His intertribal connections were extensive, as witnessed by his ability to acquire non-Qashqa'i tribal support in his military and political actions and by his alliance in 1910 with Shaikh Khaz'al and Gholam Reza Khan, two major tribal leaders of the south. He was a governmental official, wealthy landholder, and prominent member of the regional and national elite. His links with other elite, including the constitutionalist Sayyid Lari, for example, were broad, and he supported revolutionary clubs in Shiraz during the constitutional revolution. His contacts with Muslim clergy in Shiraz and Najaf (Iraq) were part of his wide-ranging political activities, as were his relations with foreign and Iranian commercial agents (Muslims and non-Muslims) concerning the political conditions of trade in south Iran. Although he professed hatred for British and other foreign interference, he often entertained British visitors in his camps and urban residences, visited the British consulate in Shiraz, and associated with the German agent Wassmuss. Out of shared anti-British sentiments, he harbored the Indian agitator Amba Parshad.

Fears about and hopes in Isma'il Khan and the Qashqa'i during this period were often based on stereotyped, false images. Iranian and foreign powers viewed tribal confederacies as tightly knit units whose members acted in concert. Isma'il Khan cleverly manipulated these fears and hopes to his advantage, but he also fell victim to the policies and actions of those who held these same fears and hopes. Regional, national, and foreign powers assumed that he possessed the ability to mobilize the Qashqa'i people toward the causes he supported, while he in turn threatened to use Qashqa'i armies to support his interests. As a result, he carried greater weight than the situation among the Qashqa'i people actually warranted, and other powers treated him with caution or severity, depending on their military strength at the time. When the government or other powers allocated responsibility to him, however, he could not easily procure more than three or four thousand gunmen or engage them continuously. The British especially expected leadership from him, and when, for example, they were able to bribe someone in his family to act in British interests, they took this as an expression of opposition to him and a loss of his power and support.

Outsiders never seemed to understand the limitations of tribal leadership, which centered simultaneously on sometimes precarious relations with state authorities and other powers and on a large, seasonally mobile population spread over great distances, occupied with economic pursuits, and based on small, relatively independent political units. That thousands of Qashqa'i would or would not rally to a call for a seige of Shiraz, for example, is not totally explained by the extent of loyalty to the ilkhani. The Bakhtiyari march on Tehran in support of the constitution in 1909 gave great psychological advantage to Isma'il Khan, because anticonstitutionalists and others feared that the Qashqa'i and other tribal forces could and would do the same. The Bakhtiyari situation, however, was unique on the Iranian scene (Garthwaite 1983).

THE CONSTITUTIONAL REVOLUTION, 1906–1911

In 1906–11 a national movement for a constitutional government challenged the despotic Qajar dynasty, which had come increasingly to depend on foreign powers. The British and Russians continued to interfere in the internal affairs of Iran despite this movement, and as a result competition among national and regional powers increased. The central government exerted little influence in the provinces, especially in Fars, which became embroiled in conflict over power. Bakhtiyari khans and tribesmen emerged as powers on the national scene, and other regional powers and tribal confederacies exerted force on national events.

In 1906 alone, state officials made four attempts to nominate an ilkhani other than Isma'il Khan, a direct reflection of administrative instability and the machinations of other powers. And the first known cases of major conflict among the Qashqa'i tribes, provoked by the attempted manipulations of the ilkhani position, were reported. In 1906 the Qavam ol-Molk, serving as acting Governor of Fars and opposing the constitutionalists, dismissed Isma'il Khan as ilkhani on the grounds that he had failed to pay tribal taxes. Before the newly constituted provincial parliament could successfully intervene on Isma'il Khan's behalf, the Qavam had appointed Ahmad Khan (brother of Isma'il Khan) as ilkhani, who assembled a force of Qashqa'i and Boir Ahmad supporters and set out to challenge Isma'il Khan's supporters. Hundreds died in battle, and a defeated Ahmad Khan fled to Boir Ahmad territory. Isma'il Khan then brought Qashqa'i supporters to Shiraz to support a constitutionalist demonstration against the Qavams. The new Governor, a Qavam ally, appointed Soltan Ibrahim (third cousin of Isma'il Khan and formerly ilkhani in 1896–98) as ilkhani, an act that was generally disregarded. Isma'il Khan offered military and financial aid to a popular political party supporting the constitution and once again fought with Ahmad Khan. Under these and other pressures, the Governor resigned and the Qavam left town (Chick 1916:34, Wilson 1916:22–23).

In 1907 the Anglo-Russian Convention divided Iran into spheres of influence, with Fars part of the neutral zone. The British formally agreed to restrict their activities in the province but did not do so. The same year a new law in Iran gave responsibility for maintaining law and order in the provinces to Governors, who were granted the right to organize private armies and collect special taxes. Governors were sent to Fars in rapid succession but none was able to establish control. Qashqa'i forces, supporters of the Sayyid Lari (of the district of Lar), and contingents from Jahrom demonstrated in Shiraz in 1907 in support of the national parliament and were opposed by Khamseh groups led by Qavam supporters. The fall migration to winter pastures stopped a major confrontation between them.[3] In 1908 a member of a

---

3. Letter from Sayyid Abdolhosain Lari to Isma'il Khan asking for his support in opposing the satanic British; *Nameh Nur* 4 (1979): 163–64. Wilson (1916:22); Great Britain, Parliament: Sessional Papers, cd. 4581, p. 72.

religious faction (no Qashqa'i were involved) assassinated the Qavam, and conflict was renewed. A new Governor punished members of the Qavam faction, appointed his own son as administrator of the Khamseh confederacy, and entrusted this confederacy's finances to a Qavam enemy. With the coup of Mohammad Ali Shah in 1908 and his betrayal of the constitutionalists, the Qavams regained some power in Fars and pro-British elements were again in the ascendancy. Another new Governor sent the new Qavam ol-Molk to capture the Sayyid Lari and restore order in the Khamseh (Wilson 1916:22, 24). Muslim clergy in Najaf wrote to Isma'il Khan requesting that he mobilize the Qashqa'i people against the regime of the shah, expel the Governor from Shiraz, and establish a revolutionary club.[4] The Qavam sent people to attack Shiraz's Jewish quarter and attempted to implicate Isma'il Khan and his allies in order to discredit him in the eyes of the British.[5]

In 1909 armies from the north and the Bakhtiyari confederacy marched on Tehran and forced the anticonstitutionalist shah to flee the country. Bakhtiyari khans assumed responsibility for law and order in Iran and acquired tax revenues for their own use, including those collected from their territories. Bakhtiyari tribesmen provided the military backing of the new regime. The ascendancy of the Bakhtiyaris in national government and their alliance with the Qavams caused difficulties for the Shahilu. The British created another source of tension among the various parties by adopting a pro-Bakhtiyari policy because of their new oil interests in Bakhtiyari territory. The major tribal confederacies (Shahsevan, Turkmen, Bakhtiyari, Qashqa'i, Khamseh) were represented in the newly convened national parliament; a Kashkuli khan was the Qashqa'i representative (Demorgny 1913a:97). In the south, Isma'il Khan, backed by Sayyid Lari and a Qashqa'i force, successfully challenged the appointment of yet another new Governor who was pro-Qavam by proposing to set up a new provincial parliament; Muslim clergy in Najaf urged his restraint (Fraser 1910:150).

Travel on the Bushire-Shiraz-Isfahan route continued to be unsafe, especially for European commercial interests, and trade depending on

4. Letter from Muslim clergy in Najaf to Isma'il Khan, 1908; *Nameh Nur* 4 (1979): 121–22.

5. Shiraz Jews who lived through these attacks reported that the apostate Qavam family had organized them. "The Qawam brothers, who led the Khamseh confederacy against the Qashqais, were attempting to discredit the latter in the eyes of the British by blaming the pogrom on them" (Loeb 1977:33).

this route virtually ceased. The office of the Governor of Fars still had no real army or police force, and the new incoming Governor assigned responsibility for road safety to the Qavam. No improvement occurred, and the Governor asked Isma'il Khan to take over. In exchange for the task, Isma'il Khan asked for control of the road, governorship of several bordering districts, and independence from provincial government, all of which were denied, so he refused the task. The British continued to blame him for "total anarchy" in Fars and "outrages" on the road, and some Iranians apparently accused him of provoking British intervention, for he stated in a letter to a constitutionalist newspaper that the Qavams were the root of the difficulty (Oberling 1974:92–93). He then announced that he would guarantee travel along the Bushire-Firuzabad-Shiraz route, a plan the British did not support, given no available recourse in the event of robberies, insurance difficulties, and no caravansaries for the protection of trade goods. "By guaranteeing one route the Sowlat implies the right to make any other route a hunting-ground for his braves" (Fraser 1910:265).[6] Shiraz merchants paid Isma'il Khan a monthly stipend to secure the safety of their goods traveling via the Firuzabad route (*Who's Who in Persia* 1923:136).

In 1910 Isma'il Khan allied with two major tribal leaders in the south, Shaikh Khaz'al of the Mohaysen Arabs of Mohammarah and Gholam Reza Khan Sardar-e Ashraf of the Lurs of Luristan, to form the "League of the South." Its purpose was to counter Bakhtiyari power in the nation and the growing British involvement (Wilson 1916:26). The three leaders agreed to support Iran's independence, defend the constitution and parliament, maintain security and facilitate trade, and protect their respective territories against encroachment, and they invited other prominent leaders to join in their agreement.[7] Shaikh Khaz'al, paramount leader of the important Arab Mohaysen tribe, exercised political control over most of Khuzistan and all areas of operation of the Anglo-Persian Oil Company, established in 1909. He was increasingly hostile to Bakhtiyari leaders in Tehran, one of whom, Sardar As'ad, was minister of the interior and in charge of policies concerning the oil company that threatened the shaikh's power. Gholam Reza Khan was an important Lur leader and hereditary governor (*vali*)

6. Note the insulting racist tone, not uncommon in many British sources.
7. League of the South agreement, 1910; *Nameh Nur* 4 (1979): 125–26. See also Garthwaite (1983:120).

of the Posht-e Kuh in Luristan. Muslim clergy hoped that the historical rivalry between the Bakhtiyari and Qashqa'i khans would not interfere with the league's support of the constitution.[8]

Sardar As'ad, concerned about the alliance and fearing Isma'il Khan's role as "de facto ruler of the south," influenced the government to dismiss him as ilkhani and to appoint Ahmad Khan, in hopes that Isma'il Khan would lose power within the confederacy. But, as before, Ahmad Khan was unsuccessful and fled to Bakhtiyari territory. In retaliation, Isma'il Khan sent three hundred Qashqa'i to Isfahan to support dissident Bakhtiyari leaders and telegraphed the government that he was ready to march to Tehran and that clergy in Najaf supported him. Sardar As'ad sent two thousand Bakhtiyari to Isfahan to confront him, but no fight ensued, and after negotiations each group withdrew. Isma'il Khan had proved that the Qashqa'i confederacy was a force in national affairs, while the Bakhtiyari leader had proved his own national power (Oberling 1974:98–99).

The British once again threatened the Iranian government with sanctions if trade continued to be disrupted. "His Majesty's Government will insist on the organisation of a local force under British officers lent by the Government of India to police the Bushire-Isfahan road if order is not restored on that road within a period of three months."[9] The Iranian government offered Isma'il Khan "the choice between opening the road and being treated as a rebel,"[10] promised to award him two districts (to be chosen from among Kazerun, Behbahan, Mamassani, and Kamarej—all outside Qashqa'i territory) and to appoint a Governor who was his ally and an ally of the League of the South, and bestowed upon him the title of Sardar Ashayer (Military Commander of the Tribes). Isma'il Khan accepted the offer and assigned Qashqa'i to police the road. Enjoying the power and authority now bestowed upon him and profiting from the ammunition supplied by the government, he collected tributes from (non-Qashqa'i) khans along the Bushire-Kazerun route, sent Qashqa'i forces to assist the new Governor in punishing rebellious Tangistanis, attempted to exert power in the district

8. "I hope your action has been based on sheer patriotic feelings rather than on political motives"; letter from the Ayatollah Kazemi Khorasani to Isma'il Khan, 1910; *Nameh Nur* 4 (1979): 131–32.

9. Great Britain, India Office Library, Political and Secret Files, 10/163, Sir George Barclay to Iranian government, Tehran, 14 October 1910.

10. Great Britain, India Office Library, Political and Secret Files, 10/163, Memorandum by Major Stokes, 1910.

of Kamarej near the gulf coast, sent Kashkuli forces against the Mamassani suspected of robbing travelers, and assumed protection of caravans using the branch of the Shiraz-Isfahan route passing through Qashqa'i summer pastures (*Gazetteer of Persia* 1918:801–802, 811).

The new Governor, after quarreling with the Qavam over an incident involving the death of Qashqa'i villager, arrested him and ordered him into exile. As the Qavam was being escorted out of Shiraz, Isma'il Khan's forces ambushed him, but he escaped and sought refuge in the British consulate in Shiraz, an act that instigated many months of civil strife there. The protagonists in the Shiraz fighting were the Governor (whose forces included a personal militia, Dashtistanis, and Qashqa'i troops from villages near Shiraz and from the ilkhani's army) and the Qavam (whose forces included Shirazis, villagers, and Khamseh tribesmen). At the national level, Sardar As'ad, who had just been reappointed as minister, resigned, and the ex-shah's attempts to reestablish Qajar rule occupied the attention of the government. When the ex-shah was defeated, the Bakhtiyari-led government attempted to dismiss the Governor of Fars, who refused to resign. Fighting in Shiraz between the Governor and the Qavam continued, with twelve hundred Qashqa'i holding out in the commercial section of town and two to three thousand Khamseh in the Qavam-allied quarters. Isma'il Khan and the Governor eventually abandoned the fight and left town. The government stripped both men of their titles and reappointed Ahmad Khan as ilkhani (Wilson 1916:27, Oberling 1974:101–10). Khans of three of the five major Qashqa'i tribes temporarily withdrew their support from Isma'il Khan on account of grievances concerning taxes, the ambush on the Qavam party, and the diversion of commercial traffic away from Kashkuli territory.[11]

British authorities gave the Qavam, again named acting Governor, five thousand pounds to raise a force capable of ensuring the safety of the roads (Demorgny 1913a:141). Fearing further hostilities, they also strengthened their consular guard in Shiraz with forces sent from India.[12] A British political officer, who viewed Iranian perceptions concerning Britain's partisan stance in the conflict between the Qavam and Isma'il Khan as false, complained about the "widespread belief that the

11. Great Britain, Parliament: Sessional Papers, cd. 6105, p. 142, G. G. Knox to Sir George Barclay, Foreign Office, 7 September 1911; Demorgny (1914:91).
12. Three squadrons of the Central Indian Horse and its infantry escort (Wilson 1916:28–29).

ulterior object of the arrival of British troops was to attack the Qashqa'i and curb the license they had enjoyed for some years" (Wilson 1916:30; also Moore 1914:125–26).

1912–1914

The British regarded their vital interests in south Iran as trade, maintenance of power in the gulf, oil, defense of India, and resistance to further Russian advance in Iran. Although Britain and Russia had declared Fars a neutral zone in 1907, the British continued to justify their increased interference in the area by pointing toward unsafe conditions on the roads. Their commercial interests at this point were minor compared with their expanding strategic interests, but they continued to express concern in terms relating to trade. Although the central government still held the Governor of Fars responsible for provincial law and order, it provided no financial or military assistance, and provincial government was too weak to collect sufficient revenue for the purpose. Therefore, in 1910 the British pressured the Iranian government to form a new, supposedly neutral force, a Swedish-trained, Swedish-officered gendarmerie, which they planned to utilize to police trade routes and collect provincial revenues. A contingent of the new force arrived in Fars in 1912, and disturbances erupted throughout the province. The gendarmerie never proved useful for British interests and in fact impeded them, and its presence encouraged Iranian suspicions that foreign powers were rapidly taking over affairs of the state. The Qavam, as acting Governor, organized an attack against the Qashqa'i with the hope of using the new gendarmes alongside his Khamseh fighters, but the Swedes led their gendarmes into battle prematurely and suffered losses at the hands of a Qashqa'i force under the command of Hasan Khan Kashkuli, brother-in-law of Isma'il Khan.[13]

Isma'il Khan complained to British officials in Shiraz about the activities of the Qavam and the new gendarmerie. Noting that the British were pursuing a policy of annexing south Iran through their financial and political support of the Qavam and the gendarmerie, he volunteered to establish order in Fars. In response, British authorities asked him to restore property stolen from the road and to be an obedi-

---

13. Wilson (1916:31–32); Great Britain, Parliament: Sessional Papers, cd. 6807, p. 262, W. A. Smart to Sir Walter Townley, Foreign Office, 30 October 1912.

ent, submissive Iranian patriot[14]—a notable example of the narrow vision of British officials during this period, especially in the face of what appeared to be a correct assessment by Isma'il Khan of affairs in Fars. As a more substantial response to the gendarmes' defeat, the British gave ten thousand pounds to the Qavam, on behalf of the Iranian government, for paying troops and "financing a forward movement" against Isma'il Khan.[15] Qavam's campaign against the "marauding tribes" was never properly launched. Half the Arab contingent in his army deserted and the rest were undependable, with "many of the tribesmen coming and going according to the requirements of their private affairs."[16] In addition, Ahmad Khan, who supported the Qavam and provided him with Qashqa'i troops, resigned as ilkhani, and as a result the rest of the "government" army dissolved. The British received poor returns on their investment.[17]

As acting Governor, the Qavam awarded responsibility for the Kazerun section of the Bushire-Shiraz road to the Kashkuli khans who had been lending him military support. Control of this road offered considerable profit, and from this position of strength the Kashkulis occupied land along the road previously controlled by "weaker tribes and local grandees" (Chick 1916:37–38) and formed alliances with Kuhgiluyeh Lurs to facilitate policing the road. Economic gain rather than opposition to the ilkhani was their principal motive in these independent moves. The Kashkulis controlled this part of the road for only a short period.

The new Governor of Fars promptly reinstated Isma'il Khan as ilkhani and then allied with him, the governor of Kuhgiluyeh, Bakhtiyari khans, and the Governor of Isfahan in order to combat "dissident" and "refractory" Qashqa'i groups, Boir Ahmadis, and Mamassanis. This alliance demonstrates how complicated the local political scene had become. The Governor abolished road tolls between Kazerun and Shiraz (Demorgny 1914:95, 97) and received eighty thousand pounds in "loans" from the British for road safety and troop payments. The

14. Great Britain, Parliament: Sessional Papers, cd. 6807, pp. 216–17, Isma'il Khan to W. A. Smart, Shiraz, n.d. and 30 August 1912; W. A. Smart to Isma'il Khan, 3 September 1912.

15. Great Britain, India Office Library, Political and Secret Files, 10/197, Sir Edward Grey to Sir Walter Townley, Foreign Office, 7 August 1912.

16. Great Britain, India Office Library, Political and Secret Files, 10/357, W. A. Smart to Sir Walter Townley, Foreign Office, 30 October 1912.

17. Ibid.

Fars section of the gendarmerie was in poor condition given the Iranian government's lack of interest, lack of funds, and the Governor's use of its weapons for his own personal militia, and the British advanced the Iranian government 140,000 pounds for its maintenance. To demonstrate good will, they sent back to India the military force that had been stationed at the British consulate in Shiraz since 1911, when the Qavam had taken refuge there (O'Connor 1931:197–98, 201).

In 1913 and 1914 the gendarmerie, expanded through British financing, was dispatched on many military campaigns. Battles involved "government" troops (now consisting of Swedish-officered gendarmes and some Qashqa'i) against Tangistani leaders, "bandits," Boir Ahmad "rebels," Arabs, "brigands," supporters of the kalantar of Kazerun, and "dissident Baharlu raiders" (Oberling 1974:120–23). Isma'il Khan is not mentioned in any of these engagements. A British diplomat in Iran advised one of the Swedish officers that if a tribal leader surrendered to him after battle he should be court martialed and handed over to local authorities, but that "it would be much better that he should be made to fight for his life and lose it on the field of battle, as a warning to others." When someone warned the diplomat that the death of a leader is a signal for the whole tribe to rise and avenge him, he remarked, "it would hardly appear that the tribesmen of today are imbued with any deep feelings of affection and fealty for their leaders."[18]

Although British financing obviously caused the escalation of fighting in Fars, the British were steadfast in proclaiming that they were only quelling preexisting disturbances. This incorrect analysis created further complications, for competition over the British largess and the many resulting armed groups in the region made it increasingly difficult for the British to identify those who supported or opposed their interests. Since the arrival of the new gendarme force in 1912, the Qavam had used it as a personal force against his enemies. His roles as acting Governor and private figure with personal interests to enhance were practically indistinguishable, which added to the animosity of Isma'il Khan and others. The limited extent of his authority over the Khamseh tribes at this time is indicated by his many punitive expeditions against them.

By 1914 the position of Governor of Fars was virtually nonfunctional; it had been weakened by frequent change in personnel, by the

18. Great Britain, India Office Library, Political and Secret Files, 10/357, Sir Walter Townley to Sir Edward Grey, Tehran, 17 March 1913.

British assuming control of provincial finances and claiming to represent the Tehran government in the region, and by many foreign administrators (American and French military advisors, Belgian financial experts, and Swedish gendarme officers) assigned to advise the Governor. At the national level, Bakhtiyari leaders who had functioned in government since 1909 lost their positions. In 1913 the new gendarmerie defeated the Bakhtiyari military contingent in Tehran, which ended its domination there (Garthwaite 1983:121–25, Sykes 1930:430).

WORLD WAR I, 1915–1918

In 1915 the British and Russians agreed that Britain could operate in its own interests in the neutral zone, and the 1907 agreement between them was effectively canceled. In the period that followed, local political struggles in Fars became submerged in the worldwide struggle between the Central and Entente powers. German expansionism, particularly in strategic, commercial, and industrial interests in Iran (and Turkey) since 1900, presented an imperialist and colonial competition to Great Britain and figured in Britain's major commitment of financial resources, personnel, and equipment to Fars. The British stationed troops at Bushire, created a new military force to protect their interests, and continued to supply money and military equipment to their supporters, while a German agent practically singlehandedly organized anti-British activities in Fars. Conflict escalated once again in Fars; few local powers were able to escape being drawn into the wider British-German rivalry. Battles were fought and many lost their lives. The British, and to a lesser extent the Germans, were the only effective authorities in Fars during this period. Each power, manipulating an odd collection of erstwhile allies, operated in its national interests with impunity, without the distracting presence of a central government. Their choices of Governor, ilkhani, and Khamseh administrator were not opposed by Tehran, in large part because the appointments of officials there as well were controlled by foreign powers (Britain and Russia).

The Germans were represented in south Iran by Wilhelm Wassmuss, who, as German consul in Bushire in previous years, was acquainted with the area's leading political figures, which facilitated his maneuvers during the war. He returned to Iran in 1915 to serve as German consul in Shiraz, a post he abandoned within several months because it interfered with his specific charge, the instigation of anti-British actions in the region. Wassmuss, who came to be known as the "German Law-rence," attempted to form an alliance among the anti-British elements in both urban and rural Fars (Sykes 1936). By focusing on the tribes and other populations along the Bushire-Shiraz road, he furthered the process of political consolidation in the area. One reason for his success in organizing local groups and leaders, in addition to the fact that anti-British sentiment was so prevalent in the region and that Germany was viewed as a friend against a mutual enemy, is that he lived with these groups, adopted local dress and customs, and posed as a Muslim (O'Connor 1931:250–51). Wassmuss failed to draw Isma'il Khan's support until the last year of the war, when the British directed their new military force against the Qashqa'i. The degree of his influence on Isma'il Khan and the Qashqa'i is, however, controversial. Wassmuss was unable to organize a mass uprising against the British, but he and his supporters nevertheless conducted a variety of subversive activi-ties proving to be a minor but constant irritant to them (Oberling 1974:128).

Within a few months of Wassmuss's arrival, Swedish-officered gen-darmes proclaimed their anti-British, pro-German sentiments, and lo-cal forces prepared to attack the British. The first of many battles oc-curred in mid-1915, when Dashtistanis and Tangistanis, with the promise from Wassmuss of money and supplies (never delivered), at-tacked British troops near Bushire and attempted to lay seige on the city. In response the British bombed a coastal town and sent Indian soldiers to cut down the area's palm trees, the basis of local subsistence (Oberling 1974:132–33). Isma'il Khan complained to British author-ities about their attack and requested that they withdraw their troops. When he received an unsatisfactory reply, he allied with a Tangistani leader and notified the Tehran government that if it did not prevent British militarism in the south, others in the area (that is, Qashqa'i and Tangistani forces) would be forced to assume responsibility.[19]

The British forced the dismissal of the Governor of Fars, who held anti-British sentiments and was a Qashqa'i ally, and the Qavam became acting Governor again. When the new German consul learned that the British consul was adding forces to his consular guard, he employed

19. Letter from the British consul in Shiraz to Isma'il Khan, May 1915; letter from Major Trevor, British Consulate in Bushire, to Isma'il Khan, 1915; letter from Khazar Khan to Isma'il Khan, 1915; telegram from Isma'il Khan to the Tehran government, 1915; *Nameh Nur* 4 (1979): 138–57.

Swedish-officered gendarmes to arrest the British consul and other members of the British colony and entrusted the prisoners to Wassmuss and a Tangistani leader in Borazjan. He failed to capture the Qavam. The British offered Isma'il Khan money if he would secure the prisoners' release but he refused the task.[20] Several months later Isma'il Khan approached British authorities to suggest that he could maintain order in Fars and take action against Wassmuss if they would guarantee his "person, honor, and property." The British minister in Tehran was enthusiastic and noted that, "these chiefs [Isma'il Khan and the Qavam ol-Molk] exercise influence over thousands of armed men and scores of smaller khans and over very large tracts of country and they may in fact be said practically to rule south Persia. . . . If we now make a satisfactory agreement with them our position in Fars would become comparatively secure. If we allow the opportunity to slip, we must expect that the Germans will take advantage of our failure and the situation in the inland of Fars would become impossible."[21]

The British then assigned the Qavam, acting Governor, together with Isma'il Khan, who they named governor of Dashtistan and Dashti, responsibility for keeping order in Fars, and supported them with a subsidy of fifty thousand pounds (Safiri 1976:65). Galvanized into action by the captivity of their subjects, they also increased their payments of money and matériel to the Qavam's private army and expedited plans for their own military force. Wassmuss had appointed a khan of the Arab tribe, who was pro-German, as leader of the Khamseh confederacy, but the Qavam defeated him. Khamseh forces, expecting greater rewards in serving the British than the Germans, joined the Qavam army, which defeated the pro-German gendarmes at Lar and headed for Shiraz. Meanwhile, a Swedish instructor of the gendarmerie engineered the arrest of the pro-German Swedish and Iranian officers of the corps, and a newly constituted gendarme force, under the command of the Qavam's son, entered Shiraz and established pro-British rule. The Qavam had died in an accident en route, and his son assumed his title and was named acting Governor (Oberling 1974:133–36). Isma'il Khan, having been refused the ilkhani appointment by the newly

20. Great Britain, India Office Library, Political and Secret Files, 10/582, File 334, 1916, Sir C. Marling to Foreign Office, 10 June 1916; O'Connor (1931:231–49).

21. Great Britain, India Office Library, Political and Secret Files, 10/489, File 3516, 1914, Part 13, Sir C. Marling to Foreign Office, 18 September 1915, 21 September 1915, 23 September 1915, 7 October 1915.

appointed (but not yet resident) Governor of Fars because he (Isma'il Khan) was unwilling to pay the requested fee of fifty thousand tumans, formed a short-lived alliance with the Qavam in order to prevent the Governor from assuming his post (Sykes 1930:466).

In 1916 the South Persia Rifles (SPR) under the command of Brigadier General Sir Percy Sykes entered Shiraz, along with the new pro-British Governor. The SPR, a partially Iranian force of six thousand men, was financed by the British government, led by British officers, and supported by British-trained, well-disciplined Indian troops. Its purpose was to support British strategic and commercial interests in Fars, restore British prestige, establish the authority of the central government, counterbalance the Russian presence in the north, and counter pro-German forces, including the Swedish-officered gendarmes (Sykes 1930:452–517; Safiri 1976:87, 153, 156). Its immediate task was "the restoration and maintenance of law and order in the country by the reduction of the robber tribes and the prevention of rebellion."[22] The British, in effect, created a second military force to fight the one they had earlier pressured into creation and financed.

Sykes recruited soldiers for the SPR from Shiraz and the surrounding countryside, often by providing funds to city ward and tribal leaders, who then supplied men. He also gradually assumed control of remnants of the Swedish-trained gendarmes of Fars, without government authorization. By 1918 half the recruited force consisted of men from local nomadic tribes, and the rest were the incorporated forces (who were mostly nonlocal) and the unemployed from the towns and countryside (crop failures and famine contributing to the supply of men). A large portion of the men from nomadic tribes came from the Khamseh tribes, while others were Lurs, Arabs, Baluch, Tangistanis, Dashtis, tribesmen from Kerman province, and, after 1918, Mamassanis. No Qashqa'i are known to have served as soldiers in the SPR. Those who joined the force joined for money and fringe benefits, not for the purpose of supporting the British campaign to restore order in Fars. Officers identified the "enemy" for these recruits: Germans (and their Iranian, Austrian, Indian, Turkish, and Swedish associates), "roaming robber tribes," bandits, political agitators, and Russophiles.[23]

22. Great Britain, India Office Library, Political and Secret Files, 10/579, Viceroy to Foreign Office, 7 August 1916.

23. Information in Floreeda Safiri (1976:111–27), as well as kindly provided by her (personal communication, 28 October 1983).

The arrival of the SPR prompted Isma'il Khan to sign an agreement with the gendarmes to oppose the British. The Tehran government, although holding inconsistent attitudes, frequently refused to recognize the SPR's legitimacy and in effect supported Isma'il Khan. The SPR held an "uncertain status as a nominal Persian force, controlled and maintained by the British Government, operating in a neutral country whose Government was invariably unwilling to recognise its legitimacy" (Safiri 1976:174).

The first military engagement of the SPR was in Kazerun, where anti-British forces forced the SPR to withdraw, and by the end of 1916 anti-British forces controlled the entire Bushire-Shiraz route, except for the section near Shiraz. In 1917 Sykes requested a meeting with Isma'il Khan, who stated that he would support the central government, "restrain" his tribesmen, and keep order in Kazerun in exchange for British recognition of him as ilkhani and a subsidy of thirty thousand pounds. The two men agreed to limit the activities of the SPR to the east and north of Shiraz and to hold Isma'il Khan responsible for the west and south (Safiri 1976:245). The British took advantage of this alliance and the "order" that ensued to consolidate their position in Fars by organizing the SPR more effectively, improving communications, and providing support to the Qavam to enable him to control Shiraz. Then, provoked by a minor but controversial incident over the questionable theft of two donkeys by some Darrehshuri,[24] they sent SPR forces into Qashqa'i territory to "defeat and crush" Isma'il Khan, who, in outrage, issued an anti-British proclamation: "I give notice to all that the army of the South Persia Rifles, that is unauthorized by the Persian Government, has caused all the Kashgais, the inhabitants of Kazerun, the Dashtis, Dashtistanis, and others to take action for the defense of Islam in accordance with the orders of the Persian Government" (Sykes 1930:502n.).

In 1917 and 1918 battles between the SPR and what were now locally (even nationally) considered the ilkhani's "government" forces (Qashqa'i, Kazerunis, Dashtis, Dashtistanis, gendarmes) took place near Shiraz on the Bushire road and in Firuzabad and Shiraz, with

24. SPR officers accused ten Darrehshuri households of stealing two donkeys belonging to the force. The officers apparently arrested the men and women suspected of being involved and later attacked a Darrehshuri group in which women and children were killed. Their bodies were taken to Isma'il Khan's camp, where Bibi Khanom, his wife, "took an oath that she would divorce him unless he took up arms to avenge the death of these women and children" (Safiri 1976:250–51).

much loss of life on both sides. Sayyid Lari, although not formally in a position to do so, declared a *jihad* (holy war), and Muslim clergy in Shiraz announced that it was lawful to attack and kill anyone with active British connections,[25] which added legitimacy to the actions of Isma'il Khan and his forces. Local clergy accompanied troops into battle in order to incite them against British forces. Sykes pressured the new pro-British Governor to appoint Ahmad Khan as ilkhani in place of Isma'il Khan and established an SPR contingent at Firuzabad to maintain the new ilkhani in office. The Qavam and his Khamseh troops joined the battle in Shiraz and, allied with Isma'il Khan's half brother and a Kashkuli khan who had joined the SPR and were receiving British pay, forced Isma'il Khan and his troops to seek sanctuary near Firuzabad. Qashqa'i loyal to Isma'il Khan, under the command of his full brother and another relative, attacked the SPR in Abadeh. A successful British attack on Isma'il Khan in Firuzabad followed; "this sudden blow ended the struggle with the Kashgais" (Sykes 1930:514). The weakening of Isma'il Khan's forces and his defeat are attributed to British-created dissensions among Qashqa'i leaders; British support of the Qavam; effects of famine, cholera, and influenza in Fars; news of reinforcements for the SPR; military activity from the direction of Bushire; the fall of the cabinet in Tehran; and the Allied victory (Safiri 1976:263–65). The British captured Wassmuss in 1919.

Great Britain, aided by the Anglo-Iranian Treaty of 1919 under which she assumed administrative and economic control of Iran, continued to dominate affairs there after the war, despite widespread popular resistance. The SPR remained in Fars until 1921, when the new government of Sayyid Zia and Reza Khan repudiated the treaty. The presence of the SPR had gradually brought about the dissolution of all previously existing government forces in Fars, and British authorities on the scene had pressed for its continuance, in opposition to the British Foreign Office, which wanted its speedy withdrawal.[26] One British official noted, "I anticipate trouble in Fars after our troops leave, but we cannot maintain peace all over the world indefinitely."[27]

25. Great Britain, India Office Library, Military Files, 17/15/33, P. M. Sykes, "Notes on Fars, 1916–1918, With Special Reference to Hostilities with the Qashqais," p. 91.

26. The dispute is an example of the conflict between the British Foreign Office (London) and the Government of India, under whose authority the SPR and some British officials in Fars primarily fell.

27. Great Britain, India Office Library, Political and Secret Files, 10/728, File 299, 1918, Part II, Minute Paper (E. G. D.), 6 May 1920.

The Iranian government reinstated Isma'il Khan as ilkhani after the war. The end of local hostilities also meant the end of active dissidence and rivalry for the position, and Isma'il Khan was once again undisputed leader of the confederacy. British authorities, however, who continued to act in the place of the Iranian government, decided to punish Isma'il Khan for his role during the war and tied negotiations on this matter to those concerning their own troop reductions. They nullified the ilkhani appointment and suggested that Isma'il Khan surrender himself to government authorities in Tehran, who would exile him to Kerbala (a Shi'i Muslim religious center in Iraq) for a period of purgation, followed by an educational tour of Basra and Baghdad. "If he returns in a contrite spirit, if his tribe in the meantime behaves itself and in particular cooperates in maintaining order on the road, he will be restored as ilkhani should the tribe still wish to have him." They proposed that Ahmad Khan remain with the Qashqa'i as Isma'il Khan's deputy during his probationary absence. They debated the merits of having Isma'il Khan exiled permanently but feared that the resulting "disorder" in the province would be more than they could handle, especially given their interest in reducing the great expense entailed in their continuing military presence. "It is to our interest that the ilkhaniship of the Qashqa'i should be in the hands of the man most capable of keeping the tribes in order, provided he is not hostile to us. He undoubtedly fulfills the first of these conditions." They commented that the "puppet ilkhani" (Ahmad Khan) they had nominated and tried to fortify had proved useless. When the British consul in Shiraz informed Isma'il Khan of the plans to exile him, he responded that he had followed orders issued by the Iranian government and by prominent religious leaders and did not understand why he should be punished.[28] Later, at British instigation, he agreed to place ten thousand pounds on deposit in a Shiraz bank, leave one of his sons as a government hostage in Shiraz, and retire to Firuzabad in "voluntary" exile, in exchange for his reinstatement as ilkhani after an unspecified period of "chastisement."[29]

In 1920 Mohammad Mosaddeq returned to Iran from Europe via Bushire and stopped for a few days in Shiraz on his way to Tehran. There he was notified by the Tehran government that he was to serve

28. Great Britain, India Office Library, Political and Secret Files, 10/728, Viceroy to Foreign Office, 10 January 1919, 7 March 1919, 10 April 1919.

29. Great Britain, India Office Library, Political and Secret Files, 10/728, File 299, 1918, Part II, Minute Paper (J. S.), 21 May 1919; Governor of Fars to Isma'il Khan, 1919, *Nameh Nur* 4 (1979):158–59.

as Governor of Fars. When dignitaries of Fars came to offer their congratulations, Mosaddeq noticed a young man present and asked who he was and why he was there. Mosaddeq was told that he was Naser, son of Isma'il Khan, the Qashqa'i ilkhani, and that he was hostage in the government's hands because his family had fought against the British. An astonished Mosaddeq said, "You're *punishing* someone who fought the British?? Let him go!" And the two men were close friends from that time.[30]

Ali Khan, youngest brother of Isma'il Khan, refused to accept the restrictions placed upon the Qashqa'i leadership and in 1920–21 organized a tribal force against the British, supported in part by a subsidy paid by the Governor of Fars and the Qavam. Ali Khan's military attack against the British in 1922 failed, and he became a fugitive (*Who's Who in Persia* 1923:14).

Several general points about events during World War I and their continuing importance during the reign of Reza Shah can be made. First, the British and German presences were markedly asymmetrical. Wassmuss conducted German affairs in Fars more or less singlehandedly and lacked money, military equipment, and foreign military personnel, while the British brought to the area hundreds of government officials and military officers, vast amounts of money and matériel, and as many troops as could be spared from India and Mesopotamia. The British were also closely allied with the Qavam, who controlled a private army, Khamseh forces, and other supporters. Wassmuss was, however, more successful in working with local groups and leaders than were the British because of widespread anti-British sentiment and because he established grass roots support and avoided the machinations of Shiraz politics.

A second point concerns the brutal policies of Reza Shah to pacify the Qashqa'i and other tribes in the decades following World War I. Although he aimed to modernize and unify Iran through these policies, they also stemmed from his fear of a continuing collaboration between tribes and foreign powers, a fear justified by events during the previous decade. A major consequence of foreign interference in Fars during World War I was to bring down the wrath of Reza Shah upon the tribes. Given the possibility that the British helped to establish him in power, it is also possible that, in part, he was carrying out their wishes in his relationships with the Qashqa'i and other tribes.

30. Mohammad Hosain Khan, personal communication, 29 July 1979, London.

And third, the material on the Qashqa'i found in European accounts of Fars during World War I contains what have been taken as definitive descriptions of Qashqa'i political organization and leadership. But these were unusual times, and the accounts are not representative; foreign powers interested in Fars after World War I were misinformed by them.

COMMENTARY

The Qashqa'i confederacy was a different entity in the first two decades of the twentieth century from what it had been in the nineteenth, not because of changes occurring within the confederacy, but because of a rapidly changing context and new external pressures and perceptions. The absence of an effective Iranian government and the presence of rival foreign powers altered formerly key attributes of the confederacy. The ilkhani exercised less control on the regional level, for foreign powers dominated in Fars and drew regional powers into conflict. The central government was unable to curtail foreign interference, and the ilkhani lacked a viable Iranian center with which to interact. Although he was no match for the combined British interests in the area and was unable to control the expressions of the British-German struggle that appeared there, the British, despite an enormous military and financial commitment, were unable to control the ilkhani, his supporters, and the many anti-British elements in Fars.

A nonfunctioning Iranian state raises the question of who and what Qashqa'i forces or any other local power were fighting for or against between 1915 and 1919. Each commander and force undoubtedly considered the immediate local benefits (enhanced power, military supplies, and, for some, territorial control) to be gained through conflict, and probably few of these related at all to British or German goals. Although British officials proclaimed that the various parties were indeed pro-British or pro-German, this did not reflect reality, and British and possibly German misunderstanding contributed to local confusion. Ambiguity in these issues helps to explain the ambiguous outcome, for although the Germans lost the world war in 1918, who won and who lost in south Iran? The Qavam ol-Molk was possibly the only figure in south Iran who fought specifically for British interests as well as his own. Isma'il Khan seems to have had little choice but to oppose the British, given their interference in his rule and their military attacks against him. Wassmuss exploited this opportunity in 1918, the only time he apparently drew a positive response from the ilkhani, and converted it into a fight for German interests, which, although relevant to the ilkhani because of the common anti-British, anti-Qavam stance, were irrelevant to Qashqa'i fighters.

A nonfunctioning Iranian state also altered the ilkhani's role as mediator. Isma'il Khan was faced with the choice of either interacting with the power (Britain) that had assumed state authority or withdrawing from mediatory activities. His choice was complicated in 1915 by the presence of an additional foreign power. He could not easily align with both, although he appears to have tried. The presence of two rival superpowers, each promising rewards, presented the opportunity for rival Qashqa'i leadership. Isma'il Khan's initial, rather reluctant role as a neutral (neither pro-German nor pro-British) confederacy leader in 1915 allowed competitors and recalcitrant tribal leaders to seek out these alliances for themselves; once he allied with Wassmuss, his competitors allied openly with the Qavam and the British. The British complained about Isma'il Khan's fluctuating political stance, but they had armed the Qavam, formed a military force (SPR) to fight against the Qashqa'i, and encouraged rivals and defections from his authority. The Qavam, who had other affairs to attend to, was not enough of an enemy of Isma'il Khan to satisfy British interests, and hence they sought competitors from within Isma'il Khan's family and from khans of the component Qashqa'i tribes, whom they rewarded as rival ilkhanis and dissident khans. The British were, however, surprised that family members and political supporters of Isma'il Khan could be manipulated so easily, and their judgments of Qashqa'i leaders in general became increasingly negative.

A single opposing force can unite a powerful family and a tribal leadership. Two opposing forces, the British and Germans, prepared the way for at least two competing Qashqa'i units. The emerging competition within the Shahilu lineage and among Qashqa'i leaders should not simply be analyzed as a trait inherent to lineage and tribal systems; instead, it was an epiphenomenon as well as a reflection of the broader political struggle. Because tribal leaders, exercising their primary role, mediated with powers outside the tribe, conflicting external powers created the potential for competing mediation. The British and Germans took advantage of internal tribal rivalries in the same ways contenders for state rule had done in the past; just as factions competing over state rule had related to rival factions within the Shahilu family, so did the British and Germans.

During much of the eighteenth and nineteenth centuries, the il-khani (or his equivalent) dealt directly with state rulers, who legitimized his power and authority. By going directly to the center, he could supersede local officials in Fars, which offered him political advantages, especially over less-well-connected, more vulnerable figures. With the demise of the power of shahs and the concomitant decline of state power, such as they were, this aspect of the ilkhani's role also changed. The center was caught up in opposition movements against Qajar rule and ongoing attempts by Qajar rulers and their supporters to reestablish it, but the ilkhani was primarily involved with the local, often indirect expressions of these struggles in Fars. Because much of his power derived from contacts with the political center, when the center's strength waned so did his. A prime base of support and key point of reference was gone. From a "maker of kings" he became a pawn in the international struggle. The rising power of Bakhtiyari khans in Tehran between 1909 and 1913 also inhibited the establishment of ties between the ilkhani and the center.

The British, as the effective local power, did not depend on the il-khani in the ways that state rulers had done in previous centuries, and both the British and the Germans utilized agents who gathered intelligence on Fars according to the needs of their own national interests. The ilkhani was undermined as a source of information and interpreter of politics, and he lost the political advantage he had held, which rendered him vulnerable to political rivals within the confederacy. The ilkhani continued to seek out ties with European powers, however, because he understood the ways they used intelligence data and knew they could cause him political and military harm. In contrast, Iranian officials had often lacked information about the organization and leadership of tribes and depended on the ilkhani and other high-ranking tribal leaders for it. Consequently, the Qashqa'i were more vulnerable when foreign powers were present.

In the nineteenth century, the ilkhani had defined for the state who and what was tribal and Qashqa'i. By collecting and paying taxes, establishing law and order, assembling military forces, and threatening other powers with his armies, the ilkhani manipulated the categories, groups, and individuals within his administrative and political domains for his own purposes. Good relations with the state meant beneficial results for the state; without the ilkhani, or when relations were poor, the state lacked access to or influence over the Qashqa'i. No other equivalent person occupied this advantageous position or played this role. Between 1906 and 1921, however, the ilkhani was often unable to function this way. The British entered south Iran believing they knew what a tribe was and how it could be used or destroyed, for they had years of colonial experience with indigenous peoples and leaders elsewhere. They arrived with definitions of tribes as military forces and as threats to their interests. "Outrages" on trade routes were "tribal" outrages, and the British applied punitive measures to subdue suspected people. In battles, "tribes" were those who fought against British interests or were paid to fight for such interests.

The definition of the Qashqa'i confederacy in the nineteenth century as a taxable and administrative unit within the state, a military force, a rival to the Khamseh confederacy, and an enemy of British interests had changed in the first two decades of the twentieth century. Taxation and other forms of administration were functions of the state, which was powerless—even irrelevant. The state collected few or no taxes from the Qashqa'i during this period, and local forces determined law and order.[31] Local government, represented by the Governor, exerted little influence in the province, especially where people were supported by their own political organizations. Officials were incapable of assigning governorships, but by this time the Shahilu were already well established in their vast territories and had numerous, armed, organized supporters. They did not rely on the state for land. Territory under the use of Qashqa'i leaders and tribespeople expanded during this period, and both gained in power, wealth, and property (Wilson 1916:51, *Gazetteer of Persia* 1918:812). With the restraining presence of the state gone, local forces could, depending on their power, secure their own rights over land. People already part of strong polities, such as the Qashqa'i, held an advantage in this regard.

In the nineteenth century the state used the Qashqa'i confederacy for military purposes and identified it as a military force. In the process, the confederacy also became a potential anti-state force. In response, the state created a rival military force, another tribal confederacy, which increased the chances that the Qashqa'i confederacy would be militarily involved. Between 1912 and 1921, foreign powers in Iran created yet additional military forces in order to end the "anarchy" they

31. Between 1907 and 1911 Isma'il Khan paid no tribal or district taxes, and in 1911 was said to owe the government 250,000 tumans. By 1912 he owed the government 71,000 tumans annually, including the Qashqa'i tax, some district taxes, and additional unspecified sums (*Gazetteer of Persia* 1918:812–13).

blamed on tribal militarism, but which was in large part brought about by their own regional and tribal involvements. Tribes and confederacies in south Iran became pawns in the larger British-German competition, which enhanced their identities as military forces. Foreign powers fostered and sometimes created the conditions of competition over tribal and confederacy leadership, and then utilized the results in their own interests. Qashqa'i who served as superior military commanders could be recognized by external authorities as Qashqa'i leaders. The British provided incentives by plying rivals and potential rivals with money, arms, and other rewards. Those who commanded Qashqa'i or Qashqa'i-allied troops not directly under the ilkhani's authority could develop their own supporters and acquire arms and booty through their successes. Non-Qashqa'i forces in the vicinity, many of whom had served others' military purposes in the past, offered ready-made groups of supporters to potential rivals of the ilkhani. Sheer numbers of warriors, which had not been as important before, became crucial as the British calculated the number of Swedish instructors, Indian troops, and British officers available. How many Qashqa'i and others joined Isma'il Khan in battle and how many Qashqa'i supported his rivals assumed prominence. The role of the ilkhani was transformed in the process, for he now needed to concentrate on acquiring, rewarding, and retaining loyal warriors.

Only at this time was the ilkhani's power based more directly on the Qashqa'i people than on the state and government. He needed to cultivate ties within the confederacy because of pressure from rival military forces and the competition they offered. He needed men on the battlefield to defend his interests and fortify his commitments to other powers. Possibly for the first time in the history of the Shahilu, the ilkhani began to reside regularly in encampments in the seasonal pastures of Qashqa'i nomads and assume a life-style similar to his Qashqa'i supporters. Escalating political competition in Shiraz and the presence there of the British-backed government of the Qavam were also factors in his location.

Isma'il Khan's power in the early twentieth century also derived from alliances with other regional groups. His prominence in the region was facilitated by his role as governor of districts outside Qashqa'i territory (Kazerun, Behbahan, Mamassani, Kamarej, Dashtistan, Tangistan, Dashti). British authorities, who instrumented these assignments, required a strong governor of these crucial districts but then found that Isma'il Khan, in exploiting these posts for his own benefit, became a more formidable power in the region. The League of the South, although undertaking little in the way of specific political action, did serve as an effective warning to the British and to the Bakhtiyari khans then in power in Tehran that its members were not, individually or collectively, forces to ignore. The ilkhani also allied in these two decades with Kazerunis, Dashtistanis, Tangistanis, Dashtis, Boir Ahmadis, Sorkhis, and Baharlus. His use of military contingents from these groups was a key factor in his power, and the British were well aware of the threatening potential in these and possibly expanding alliances. The ilkhani's alliances with Kazerunis and people inhabiting the gulf coast were mutually beneficial, for together they could control the entire Bushire-Shiraz-Isfahan road and organize effective sieges against the road's cities and towns (for strategic purposes, not for occupation or long-term control). None of these people had a leader comparable to Isma'il Khan. He helped them to secure their own interests, and he gained from them regular and backup military forces, which balanced the dissensions occurring within his own confederacy. British plans were disrupted when, after considerable effort, they managed to acquire Qashqa'i support against Isma'il Khan, only to discover that he could easily find additional leaders and supporters from among allied non-Qashqa'i groups.

The Qashqa'i had also been viewed as an enemy of British commerce by the turn of the century, a perception persisting as long as the British worried about the safety of trade routes. But faced with German expansionism in the world, the arrival of Wassmuss in Fars, and the escalation of anti-British activities in the province, the British turned their attention to these affairs and ceased to be much concerned about profitable commerce. Isma'il Khan's refusal to ally with Wassmuss (until the war's end) and his agreement with Sykes also contributed to changed British perceptions of the Qashqa'i. They still mistrusted him, however, and sent troops against his supporters. The Bushire-Shiraz-Isfahan road continued to hold British attention between 1915 and 1921 because they depended on it for the movement of troops and matériel inland from the gulf and to battle locations. Many local powers along the route intercepted and threatened the traffic, but the British blamed Wassmuss for inciting them. Until 1915 they had been certain that Isma'il Khan was behind every robbery. In this regard, the presence of Wassmuss diverted British attention and probably saved Isma'il Khan from being more of a target for British aggression than he already was.

The involvement of Bakhtiyaris on the national scene during this period changed the perceptions of state officials and foreign powers about tribes and confederacies and influenced their policy decisions. The march of Bakhtiyari tribesmen on Tehran, their role in defending the constitutional movement, the assumption of national leadership by Bakhtiyari khans, and the role of Bakhtiyari forces in the state military led all powers to assume that the Qashqa'i confederacy and individual Qashqa'i leaders could be similarly involved.

Astute observations by an early-twentieth-century European traveler and by an Iranian official suggest several concluding comments. "Besides the larger tribal bands, Fars is full of masterless men who have cast off, or never had, any tribal allegiance, and live by plunder" (Moore 1914:122). Referring to conditions in 1921, Arfa (1965:449) notes that Fars had become the haunt of robbers and highwaymen, mostly outcasts from their tribes, former road guards, and dismissed gendarmes. As foreign interests in south Iran expanded at the end of the nineteenth and into the twentieth centuries, as state institutions became unable to ensure local law and order, and as economic conditions worsened, Europeans complained increasingly about banditry, lawlessness, and anarchy in rural areas, especially along trade routes. These phenomena were interrelated, but few at the time understood this. The spread of capitalism in south Iran had transformed social conditions, and certain segments of society were deprived of viable livelihoods and were socially alienated. At the same time, the British increased their trade with Iran, an activity offering instant economic rewards to those daring, desperate, or organized enough to intercept its passage. Theft on the trade routes, thus, was not a "tribal" problem; rather, it was related to social dislocations brought about by capitalist expansion and foreign interference and worsened by famine and outbreaks of cholera and influenza.

The collapse of the state combined with foreign encroachment, and the resulting social transformations, did not create ideal conditions for the formation of tribal confederacies. Instead, they set loose in the province many "masterless men" (Moore 1914:122). Why British officials did not understand the circumstances is somewhat puzzling until one realizes that it served the immediate interests of the British to conceive of their nemesis as bandit tribes led by brigand chiefs. This belief gave them specific objects to oppose. Then, it was merely a matter of assembling a military force to crush them. Even had the British understood that they were often separated from their goods by men unconnected with tribes and that banditry was directly connected to conditions of economic dislocation, they would not have been able to devise solutions to the problems they themselves had helped to create. British descriptions of "tribal" anarchy were inaccurate; the absence of an effective state also meant that tribal leaders lacked control over local people. It is ironic that anarchy resulted from European interference, not from tribal life per se.

The historical evidence demonstrates that, at least for the eighteenth, nineteenth, and early twentieth centuries and during a period of capitalist penetration, the process of state centralization tended to produce tribal consolidation. Centralization of political authority, the primary mechanism of tribal consolidation, requires predictable ties with a stable political center. When the political center loses control of the tribal periphery, fragmentation and decentralization of tribal authority often result. As central power in Iran—such as it was—declined, the "anarchy" that resulted derived less from "tradition" than from the immediate realities of social and economic alienation. In the nineteenth century, individual state authorities might have come and gone, but the regimes they represented remained relatively similar, which facilitated the continued process of tribal consolidation and centralization of political authority in the ilkhani position. Constitutional crises and World War I, however, weakened the state as well as the position of the ilkhani and created competition for leadership and dissension among leaders and groups. What happened when a very different kind of regime was formed in the next decade is the subject of the next chapter.

6

Reza Shah Pahlavi
and the Qashqa'i

$\mathcal{R}$eza Shah's harshest policies against the tribal, nomadic, and non-Persian people of Iran came in the 1930s, but his first steps were taken in the middle and late 1920s. Beginning carefully, in the knowledge that his army was inadequate to accomplish his aims and in fear of generating massive uprisings, he implemented a set of policies aimed against the Qashqa'i, and in response Qashqa'i leaders organized a rebellion against his anti-tribe, anti-ethnic-minority, anti-Qashqa'i policies. Reza Shah imposed military governors, conscription, and dress codes and held leaders under arrest in Tehran, and later followed with other repressive policies. He viewed these policies, which undermined local and tribal formations, as essential for the achievement of his image of modern statehood. Qashqa'i leaders and tribespeople, along with others subjected to the same policies, reacted against them in order to protect their interests.

Isma'il Khan had supported Reza Khan when he became minister of war in 1921. An account of one of their meetings illustrates Isma'il Khan's assessment of the evolving political situation. In 1923 a large party of state and local dignitaries went to Famur (on the road between Shiraz and Bushire) to bid a ceremonial farewell to Ahmad Shah (the last Qajar shah), who was on his way to Europe. The party included Reza Khan (who at this time was prime minister) and Isma'il Khan, with a Qashqa'i escort of some five thousand horsemen. While talking privately with Ahmad Shah, Isma'il Khan noticed that the shah seemed agitated and nervous. Ahmad Shah then pulled Isma'il Khan away from the assembled gathering, and they walked together to the top of a nearby hillock, still in sight of the encampment. But Ahmad Shah continued to speak in whispers and to act uneasy, and Isma'il Khan realized that the fear and concern centered on Reza Khan and that he was a power worth taking more seriously. Isma'il Khan also realized, with a sinking feeling, that he ought not to have brought such a large armed escort with him, for it demonstrated to this rising power the nature of his strength and it unnecessarily overplayed his political hand at a time when such a show of strength was uncalled for.[1]

Qashqa'i ilkhanis have historically formed close personal ties with state rulers, a situation again true in the early 1920s. Until this time in Isma'il Khan's life, no strong state ruler had existed, but Reza Khan clearly was a change, and the two men became close collaborators, even friends. Their relationship at this time appears similar to that of Karim Khan Zand and the earlier Isma'il Khan. Isma'il Khan was influential in Reza Khan's early decisions about the nation's future and his own: whether Iran should continue as a monarchy or become a republic like that in neighboring Turkey, and whether Reza Khan should become shah, remain as prime minister, or become republic president. Exactly which situation Isma'il Khan favored is disputed, but it is clear that he preferred a ruler who would rely on him to perform certain state functions in south Iran and who could prevent foreign and local powers from challenging or impinging upon these rights and privileges. Whether Iran continued as a monarchy or became a republic was not important to Isma'il Khan because the conditions he desired could be maintained under either state form. His concern was for the leadership and personal characteristics of the central state figure, with whom he would have direct contact.[2] The British regarded the "unholy alliance" between Reza Khan and Isma'il Khan with suspicion.[3]

In 1921 the Anglo-Persian Oil Company agreed to pay annual subsidies to five Kashkuli khans for use of land in Kashkuli territory (in the Bidkarz area) and for the provision of guards. Isma'il Khan, with

1. Mohammad Hosain Khan, personal communication, 29 July 1979, London.

2. Bahmanbegi's comment that Isma'il Khan sympathized with Reza Khan's patriotism, recognized tribal systems to be archaic, and urged the Qashqa'i to surrender their arms reflects Bahmanbegi's political stance, not Isma'il Khan's (1945–46:62).

3. Great Britain, India Office Library, Political and Secret Files, 10/730, File 299, 1918, H. G. Chick to Sir Percy Loraine, Tehran, 23 September 1923.

support from Reza Khan, had this agreement canceled and signed a new one for himself. He also removed several of the khans from the post of kalantar and appointed ones more to his liking. In 1923 the new kalantars apparently incited an attack on APOC officials, and the oil company canceled its agreement with Isma'il Khan (Magee 1948:79, 91), which ended official connections between the Qashqa'i and the APOC, although informal security arrangements continued to be made.

In 1923 Reza Khan began to alter his relationship with Isma'il Khan. When Isma'il Khan went to Tehran to pay his respects, Reza Khan wanted to detain him in the capital but feared the consequences in Fars. Instead, he engineered his election to parliament (as representative of Jahrom) and in this way enticed him to Tehran and kept him there. In 1925 Reza Khan began to disarm the Qashqa'i along with the Khamseh and placed the Qashqa'i under military governorship in efforts to establish greater government control in Fars and with the "ultimate object of destroying the Qashqa'i as an independent power" (Magee 1948:1). Isma'il Khan, a virtual prisoner in Tehran, was unable to challenge these moves. Iranian and British official correspondence ceased to refer to him as Soulat ed-Douleh, which reflected his change in status. Naser Khan, nominal ilkhani since 1920, was again ordered to reside in Shiraz, while his brothers and other family members were forced to remain at Firuzabad. Under these circumstances, khans of the component Qashqa'i tribes handled tribal administration.

Isma'il Khan was encouraged to participate in Reza Shah's coronation celebrations in 1926 and arranged for some Qashqa'i to attend, in what turned out to be the next to last tribal function that Isma'il Khan was allowed to fulfill, and it therefore has an ironic element. A new parliament was convened in 1926 and Isma'il Khan and Naser Khan became deputies. Once they were installed, however, Reza Shah ordered them, along with Isma'il Khan's other three sons, to reside in Tehran and prohibited them from leaving the city, and he demanded help in disarming the Qashqa'i. By special legislation in 1927, the parliamentary immunity of both khans was removed and they were arrested (Gashgai 1954:6).

In 1925 Reza Shah had assigned a military governor (*hokumat-e ni-zameh*) named Brigadier Yaver Parvin to the Qashqa'i, who, along with his assistant, Captain Soltan Abbas Moayer, and thirty to forty army soldiers and horsemen, set up headquarters in Farrashband (winter quarters) and Semirom (summer quarters) and migrated with the

Qashqa'i. Government tax agents accompanied the governor on his rounds of tribal territory and attempted to collect the taxes that had not been paid for years. Although the governor's specific assignment was the Amaleh tribe, supporting body to the paramount leadership and now the largest Qashqa'i tribe, he exercised general jurisdiction over other Qashqa'i as well, in much the same fashion as had the il-khani, and regularly summoned leaders of the other tribes for orders. For the first time, with the possible exception of the earliest Shahilu figures, a non-Qashqa'i state official held authority over the Qashqa'i people, an event of momentous consequence, for it changed the nature of tribe-state relations, altered the role of tribal leaders, and marked the end of one kind of Qashqa'i confederacy and the beginning of another. Previously, state officials had lacked direct access to the Qashqa'i, but now the new military governor, as an arm of the state military and bureaucracy, seized more direct contact. As was true of many officials, Parvin and his subordinates were corrupt, cruel, and predatory and overstepped the bounds of their assigned duties. They were particularly noted for theft of tribal taxes. Captain Moayer ordered Qashqa'i women to feed his puppies with their breast milk (Douglas 1951:141), an outrage which came to symbolize the nature of military governorship. The presence and repressive policies of the military officers were major factors in the 1929 rebellion.[4]

Reza Shah's conscription policy was another reason for rebellion. He began rule facing a problem that had always been troublesome to the Iranian state—the army—and one of his most important legacies was the creation of a modern, mechanized, standing army, including related improvements in communications, especially roads and airports, and the elimination of tribal levies and tribal detachments. With a vengeance he conscripted, along with members of the urban lower classes and the peasantry, tribal youth, who were dispersed throughout Iran, forbidden to serve in their home regions, and placed under primarily urban Persian officers. Qashqa'i soldiers had previously always performed military service together, under Qashqa'i commanders. The shah's new policy—in addition to strengthening centralized rule— severed potential fighters from their sociopolitical groups, placed them

---

4. "One of the results of the reign of Reza Shah and his policy of centralization was for the countryside to be invaded by a horde of government officials, most of whom are inadequately paid. At best they live on the country and at worst look upon office as an opportunity to grow wealthy" (Lambton 1953:385).

in a heterogeneous Iranian society, taught them Persian, and began to press on them the values of Iranian nationalism and patriotism—all in direct challenge to indigenous cultural systems.

Another of Reza Shah's well-known policies was the dress code enforced to eliminate ethnic and tribal dress and modernize as well as unify Iranian society.[5] As Ataturk had in Turkey, Reza Shah required Iranians to wear European-style clothes and headgear. For Qashqa'i men, this meant the abandonment of long cloaks, cummerbunds, wide-legged pants, and felt hats (see Goldsmid 1874b:576) and the assumption of dress that equated them with the Persian villagers and city folk they despised. In addition, government attempts to disarm them threatened to remove a major part of the dress and identity of Qashqa'i men: their rifles and ammunition belts slung across their backs and chests.[6] For Qashqa'i women, the ban on veiling had little effect because they had never been veiled, and for the most part they remained in customary dress, which included multilayered skirts, long tunics, short jackets, and headscarves. Qashqa'i of both sexes who chose not to alter their dress stayed away from cities and gendarme outposts and hid when government agents made the rounds of Qashqa'i territory. The dress of nonelite Qashqa'i in the nineteenth and early twentieth centuries was similar to that of other rural, often tribal, people in this area, who were mostly Lurs and Persians. (The more distinctive Qashqa'i dress seen after World War II, including the hat, is a recent development.) Although Persian chauvinism had been developing within Iran from the late nineteenth century, it had little impact on most Qashqa'i until the reign of Reza Shah and his attempted creation of a modern nation-state, largely because of the insulating effects of Qashqa'i leadership. But the military, political, and economic changes he introduced meant that the Qashqa'i lost previous protections, and they became increasingly vulnerable as his reign proceeded. Imposed Persian chauvinism was to remain for many decades a major basis of Qashqa'i opposition to the Iranian state.

5. Parliament outlawed ethnic dress in 1928 and banned veiling in 1936.

6. The nomads seen migrating west of Shiraz in 1821 by Fraser (1825:91–93) were probably Qashqa'i, although he did not identify them by name. "Their dress consists of a coarse blue shirt and trowsers, with heavy cloaks of felt, thrown over the shoulders, the sleeves being left unoccupied; a conical cap of white or grey felt, with flaps for the ears, covers their heads: they usually carry one, and sometimes two guns slung at the back, and a large knife or dagger at the girdle; a sword or a clubbed stick completes their equipment" (Fraser 1825:93).

While these four issues—military governors, conscription, dress, and leaders held in Tehran—were the proximate causes of the 1929 rebellion, the Qashqa'i were more concerned about what they perceived as Reza Shah's ultimate goals. He intended to destroy the Qashqa'i as a military, political, social, and cultural unit, and although this policy was not as clear in 1929 as it became a few years later, the steps taken in this direction had already resulted in the loss of the relative autonomy the people had previously always enjoyed. In the long run, Reza Shah's action against the Qashqa'i served to unify them, and a new dimension of the confederacy emerged. The Qashqa'i rebellion of 1929 was the first time in history that Qashqa'i people fought on behalf of collectively perceived interests, conceptualized initially when Reza Shah implemented explicitly repressive policies against them.

In the spring of 1929 Reza Shah sent his minister of finance to Fars to investigate complaints brought by khans of the component Qashqa'i tribes against the state-imposed military governor. Upon hearing that the complaints were justified, the shah dismissed him and some corrupt army officers. The military governor bribed the new Governor of Fars to reinstate him and then sought revenge against those who had urged his dismissal,[7] which may have been one of the last times that a Governor of Fars could be manipulated by local powers to reverse a shah's decision. Masih Khan, leader of the Farsi Madan tribe and initial organizer of the Qashqa'i resistance, warned the military governor to leave Qashqa'i territory, secured political support from Ali Khan (Isma'il Khan's brother), and formed an alliance with two other Qashqa'i tribes. These activities worried the Governor of Fars, who sent leaders of the remaining major Qashqa'i tribes to Masih Khan to dissuade him from military action. They joined Masih Khan instead, as did many Qashqa'i cultivators, led by Mahdi Sorkhi, head of the small independent Sorkhi tribe of Fars. This action allied all major Qashqa'i tribes and groups. Then leaders of all other major groups in the region joined the resistance, including the Boir Ahmad, Mamassani, Khamseh, Dashtistanis, Tangistanis, and Dashtis, plus small independent tribes and many non-Qashqa'i peasants. For the first time in the known history of Fars, these various groups were politically and militarily allied and comprised a single interest group responding to increasingly re-

7. Great Britain, India Office Library, Political and Secret Files, 10/730, File 299, 1918, "Summary of Events and Conditions in Fars during the Year Ended 31 March 1930" (anonymous).

pressive state policies—not because of any innate truculence, as some writers would have it. They demanded the return of practices enjoyed before Reza Shah: tribal autonomy, reinstatement of leaders, recognition of Isma'il Khan or a son as ilkhani, release of leaders from prison and exile, cessation of imposed European dress, permission to hold arms, abolition of military governors, tax reduction, tax collection by khans rather than government agents, and cessation of compulsory conscription. They also demanded an end to the government's restrictive monopoly on the sale (by producers and to consumers) of sugar, tea, tobacco, and opium and, for the peasants involved in the rebellion, an end to the tyranny of landlords.[8] All these demands represented causes of the alienation accompanying the transformations of the late nineteenth and early twentieth centuries.

At the first sign of military preparation in Fars, Reza Shah, who had become increasingly angered that the Qashqa'i were slow to surrender their arms, imprisoned Isma'il Khan and Naser Khan and urgently requested the British to supply him with airplanes so that he could meet any opposition.[9] General Shahbakhti in Fars sent for Malek Mansur Khan (detained in Tehran with his father and brother) in order to force his help in quelling the resistance. On arrival, Malek Mansur Khan escaped from government control, took over leadership of the resistance movement from Masih Khan and Ali Khan, and became field commander. In their first military action, the allied forces seized the Shiraz-Bushire road (except for the town of Kazerun), and much of the Shiraz-Abadeh road, and captured gendarme posts. A group led by Mahdi Sorkhi destroyed planes at Shiraz airport and sent forces into the city outskirts. As a result, Reza Shah recalled to Tehran the military governor and the head of the gendarmerie in Fars, and there they were arrested, along with the minister of finance, on suspicion of engaging in treasonable conduct. Major General Shaibani, placed in charge of civil and military affairs in Fars and in command of a force of twenty thousand men, fought several battles with the Qashqa'i and sent forces against the Boir Ahmad and the Mamassani. Malek Mansur Khan urged Bakhtiyari leaders who opposed Reza Shah's policies to join the resistance.[10]

8. Ibid.; Sir Robert Clive to Foreign Office, 24 May 1929 and 12 July 1929. See also *The Times* (London), 11 June 1929, p. 15.

9. Great Britain, India Office Library, Political and Secret Files, 10/730, File 299, 1918, Sir Robert Clive to Foreign Office, 27 May 1929.

10. Great Britain, India Office Library, Political and Secret Files, 10/730, File

The government, whose troops were still poorly trained and equipped at this point, quickly sought a negotiated settlement, partly out of concern that the rebellion would spread to the cities and win the support of Muslim clergy, who were also subject to Reza Shah's centralizing policies. Isma'il Khan was released from prison and flown to Shiraz to assist in the negotiations. Several days later he was sent back to Tehran, where he met with Reza Shah. He was then returned to Fars where, in his final representation of the Qashqa'i to the state, he oversaw the fall migration and collected government taxes.[11] During the peace negotiations the government recognized Malek Mansur Khan as ilkhani,[12] the last official state recognition of a Qashqa'i ilkhani.

Fighting continued both in Fars, where Ali Khan served as field commander, and in Bakhtiyari territory. Reza Shah sent his minister of war, the Bakhtiyari Sardar As'ad (son of Sardar As'ad who participated in national government between 1909 and 1913), to negotiate. Baharlu, Inalu, Arab, Afshar, and Buchaqchi (of Kerman province) tribesmen engaged in local battles, organized by their own leaders and uncoordinated with Qashqa'i activities. Malek Mansur Khan called a meeting of Qashqa'i leaders in Semirom after Reza Shah offered him a general amnesty if the Qashqa'i would stop fighting. The assembled group agreed to the proposal if the shah would sign the amnesty proclamation and distribute it to all leaders, drop it by plane throughout Fars, and post it in towns and villages. They were not willing to stand on his word alone. The shah accepted these conditions, and fighting in Fars, Isfahan, and Kerman provinces temporarily ceased. The conditions of settlement included the end of military governors for the Qashqa'i, reinstatement of Isma'il Khan and Naser Khan as parliamentary deputies, and cessation of government efforts to disarm the tribes.

299, 1918, "Summary of Events and Conditions in Fars during the Year Ended 31 March 1930" (anonymous). See also *The Times* (London), 25 June 1929, p. 15.

11. Great Britain, India Office Library, Political and Secret Files, 10/730, File 299, 1918, "Summary of Events and Conditions in Fars during the Year Ended 31 March 1930" (anonymous); Sir Robert Clive to Foreign Office, 12 July 1929.

12. Malek Mansur Khan, personal communication, 5 September 1979, Tehran. The appointment was announced in a Tehran newspaper at the end of September 1929; Great Britain, India Office Library, Political and Secret Files, 10/730, File 299, 1918, Sir Robert Clive to A. Henderson, 20 October 1929; Sir Robert Clive to Sir Austen Chamberlain, 1 November 1929.

Limited disturbances in the region persisted; each rebellious group had its own organization, leaders, and scores to settle. A mullah in Boir Ahmad territory staged a local rebellion, and Mahdi Sorkhi continued his attacks against the military. Parts of the Khamseh and the gulf coast tribes were also active. In 1930 Shaibani organized a campaign against the Boir Ahmad and Mamassani and ordered Naser Khan and Malek Mansur Khan to enlist Qashqa'i levies to assist government troops. Some Qashqa'i joined forces with the two Lur tribes to protest against this action. Shaibani was defeated, court-martialed, and dismissed from the army.[13] Malek Mansur Khan received permission to leave Iran in 1931 in order to study in Europe (not to return until 1943). No one was named ilkhani after his departure. In 1932 Ali Khan, serving as de facto ilkhani, led another Qashqa'i rebellion against government troops to express Qashqa'i complaints that the government had not abided by the 1929 armistice terms. A new but similar armistice was signed.

By 1933 Reza Shah had wearied of the piecemeal attempts to "pacify" the nation's tribes and began to enact harsher measures against them, aided by the rapidly changing nature of warfare brought about by new roads and an increasingly mechanized army of tanks, armored cars, and aircraft. He conducted military campaigns against the Qashqa'i including aerial bombing of migrations, imprisoned and executed leaders, forcibly curtailed seasonal migrations, and forced nomads to settle in inhospitable areas offering no means of subsistence. He rearrested, imprisoned, and then in 1933 executed Isma'il Khan with a lethal injection or a poisonous dose of "Pahlavi coffee." Isma'il Khan's children insist that the British forced Reza Shah's hand in this matter and offer as evidence the message the shah sent to Isma'il Khan's widow that "it was not my doing." Isma'il Khan, who had been in good health, wrote an extensive will the day before he died, which also indicates that his death was not natural or accidental. Government authorities would not allow the body to be taken to Fars for burial for fear of political disturbances. "They didn't want the Qashqa'i name in Fars," reports his son.[14] This was "a pathetic and anti-climatic end for

13. Great Britain, India Office Library, Political and Secret Files, 10/730, File 299, 1918, "Summary of Events and Conditions in Fars from 1 April 1930 to 31 March 1931" (A. C. Trott); A. C. Trott to British Legation, Tehran, 5 September 1930; A. W. Davis to Sir Robert Clive, Shiraz, 19 July 1930.

14. Malek Mansur Khan, personal communication, 5 September 1979, Tehran.

a tribal chief who, for many years, had ruled an area as big as Bulgaria and had been referred to by no less an authority than Sir Percy Sykes as 'the Crownless King'" (Oberling 1974:165).

Naser Khan had been imprisoned with his father, and Mohammad Hosain Khan, Khosrow Khan, and Ali Khan—two other sons and a brother—were forced to live in Tehran under close surveillance by the secret police. Later Mohammad Hosain Khan was allowed to go abroad to study. In an attempt to sever the Shahilu family's ties with Fars, Reza Shah confiscated its land and exchanged it in part for land in Khorasan belonging to leaders of the Hazara tribe.

In 1933 parliament enacted a law merging the major tribal groups (Shahsevan, Turkmen, Bakhtiyari, Qashqa'i, Khamseh) of Iran into a single confederacy and appropriated necessary funds, but implementation did not follow. In 1934 tribal representation in parliament and tribal constituencies were legally abolished (Avery 1965:379).

The Qavam ol-Molk, whose power declined when the South Persia Rifles was disbanded, played a minor role in the politics of Fars under Reza Shah and did not participate in military engagements between government forces and the province's tribes, including the Khamseh. The governorship of the Khamseh confederacy no longer served him much purpose, especially because he had exercised little control over its tribes and derived minimal economic rewards from it. Initially the Qavam enjoyed cordial relations with Reza Khan and served as parliamentary deputy, but in 1929 Reza Shah abolished his hereditary governorships of eastern Fars and the Khamseh and appointed a military governor. He also abolished the post of kalantar, held since 1811 by the five successive holders of the title of Qavam ol-Molk. The Qavam, who avoided imprisonment in exchange for a promise never to return to Fars, received permission to leave Iran. The state confiscated his extensive landholdings in Shiraz and rural Fars in 1932 in exchange for government properties in other parts of Iran and stripped him of his title.[15]

The reign of Reza Shah had transformed the Qashqa'i confederacy. Reza Shah attempted to impose his image of a modern nation-state on all Iranian society, which abruptly changed the nature of tribe-state

15. Great Britain, India Office Library, Political and Secret Files, 10/730, File 299, 1918, "Summary of Events and Conditions in Fars during the Year Ended 31 March 1930" (anonymous). See also Royce (1981:292–96). .

relations, tribal leadership, and political consciousness and action on the part of the Qashqa'i people. The new state required the political subordination of all citizens and the abolition of competing political loyalties, and to effect these ends Reza Shah executed, imprisoned, and exiled Qashqa'i leaders, disarmed and militarily subjugated the Qashqa'i people, forcibly stopped seasonal migrations and ordered nomads to be sedentary, and imposed military governors, conscription, and dress codes. Qashqa'i people suffered from these oppressive measures as much, if not more, than other tribal people in Iran because of the perceived military power and political authority of Isma'il Khan and his family, the success enjoyed by foreign powers in the previous decade in manipulating Qashqa'i leaders and supporters for their own national interests, the well developed and hence potentially threatening polity, and the vulnerable migration routes.

Isma'il Khan was one of the primary military and political figures with tribal affiliations in Iran, along with Shaikh Khaz'al and several Bakhtiyari khans. Reza Shah viewed them all as competitors with powerful backing and proceeded to eliminate them. He also feared foreign interference in Iran, especially in regions where politically organized people such as the Qashqa'i could threaten his attempted monopoly on power. Strategic features contributing to the confederacy's formation also elicited Reza Shah's concern: distance from Tehran; proximity to Shiraz, rich agricultural lands, the gulf, and vital communication routes; and inaccessible mountain pastures separated by heavily settled areas. State forces could gain access to and harm the Qashqa'i because their leaders were prominent and their migration routes uniquely vulnerable. With his new mechanized army of tanks and surveillance aircraft, Reza Shah blocked migration routes at critical places, which, combined with forced sedentarization, meant economic disaster for Qashqa'i nomadic pastoralists, who lost most of their herd and pack animals during the 1930s.[16]

Reza Shah perceived the large Qashqa'i confederacy with its strong leadership as a threat to his efforts to form what he considered a modern, politically unified nation-state. How much truth there was behind this perception is not known with certainty, for he could have continued his initially cooperative relations with Isma'il Khan. Instead, he

16. Many animals died because of severe climatic conditions experienced in year-round settlement and lack of adequate food and water, while others were sold for a fraction of their worth to profiteers (Taheri 1976, Garrod 1946b:298–99).

embarked on brutal policies of pacification and sedentarization; he did not offer the Qashqa'i (or other tribal and ethnic people) a chance to become integrated into the new nation-state. The principal attributes of the confederacy during this period must, therefore, be seen in terms of Reza Shah's policies to eliminate it as a political and cultural entity. The rebellions of 1929 and 1932 were the first occasions in Qashqa'i history in which the people fought for specifically Qashqa'i interests. The attacks of Reza Shah demonstrated who the Qashqa'i were and where they were the most vulnerable; he defined the interests they found the need to defend. Thus the Qashqa'i confederacy emerged under Reza Shah as an entity having specific interests and vulnerabilities, to which confederacy and tribal politics became oriented and from which confederacy and tribal cohesion sprang.

With the ilkhani and his sons and brother arrested, imprisoned, executed, or exiled, lower levels of the Qashqa'i leadership hierarchy—the ruling khans of the component Qashqa'i tribes and the headmen and elders under them—began to assert greater power and assume greater importance, which appears to be new and which reversed (temporarily—until 1941) the process of centralization and confederacy-building that had been developing since the late eighteenth century. In the process, however, something definable as Qashqa'i consciousness emerged and was not destroyed by the elimination of the paramount khans. Lower-level leaders had served as military commanders during World War I but now found common cause and reason to become more politically active. Reza Shah imprisoned and executed some for opposing his policies, including Hosain Khan Darrehshuri, that tribe's most prominent leader.

Conditions under Reza Shah generated a decentralized confederacy whose leaders held common political goals and pursued them in the name of the confederacy. No significant political dissension within the Shahilu lineage or among the khans of the component tribes emerged during Reza Shah's rule; a single external enemy reduced that possibility, and dissension became a luxury that few leaders could afford. For the Qashqa'i as a political and cultural unit to endure, local-level leadership that did not attract the shah's attention or threaten him was essential. For the first time, the Qashqa'i people perceived the confederacy as a united polity and sought to express that perception through resistance to Reza Shah. By contrast, in the nineteenth century the confederacy had functioned only in limited situations, for primarily external administrative and military purposes.

Another new attribute of the confederacy resulted from Reza Shah's Persian chauvinistic, anti-ethnic-minority policies and from the processes of nation-state formation and capitalist expansion. The emerging Iranian state took on a decidedly Persian character, and many of those being integrated into the state either assimilated culturally toward national values or developed their own national identity. In response to the fact that Reza Shah's attack on the Qashqa'i was partly based on the negative connotations he gave to non-Persian languages and cultures, the Qashqa'i defended their own linguistic and cultural traditions, and in the process both people and culture become politicized. Qashqa'i leaders accentuated those customs and behaviors distinguishing them from Persians who controlled Iran's political and economic life. Because other culturally diverse groups in Fars were reacting similarly, local cultural systems in the region gradually became more highlighted and differentiated than they had been before. Notions of Persian/Iranian nationalism and patriotism had been developing since the late nineteenth century, but "national minorities" and accompanying sentiments among Iran's many non-Persians emerged because of Reza Shah's attempts to create his image of a modern nation-state and because of the repressions he conducted to effect this transformation.

The final major attribute of the Qashqa'i confederacy under Reza Shah was that it provided a focus and vehicle for regional alliances initiated during World War I. The rebellion of 1929 involved all major and some minor tribal groups in Fars as well as nontribal peasants and expressed common goals and demands, an unprecedented phenomenon. Many small tribes affiliated with the Qashqa'i during the rebellion in order to oppose the government, and some were incorporated into the confederacy. The Qashqa'i confederacy and its leaders were politically and strategically placed to draw other groups into alliance. State and local officials had previously employed some of these groups as military forces, and some had been pawns in the British-German rivalry in Fars, but the threat posed by Reza Shah and expanding state control was a new problem experienced by all groups. Never before had they collectively experienced a single external threat: together they attempted to move against it.

The Qashqa'i confederacy under Reza Shah lacked many characteristics it had possessed in previous periods. Some nineteenth-century traits disappeared or became irrelevant in the first two decades of the twentieth century because of the absence of state authority and the presence of competing foreign interests. Reza Shah established an unprecedented degree of state control, but the conditions created under previous state rulers did not reemerge, due to changed circumstances caused by his policies to end tribal, nomadic, non-Persian ways of life and to form a homogeneous modern society. Also, his removal of the ilkhani and all possible successors eliminated the previously essential attribute of the confederacy, that of centralized mediation on behalf of the state and the affiliated people. The confederacy as a taxable and administrative unit still existed, but this aspect receded into the background under the state's military oppressions; administration meant pacification and forced sedentarization. As a military force, the confederacy was still powerful at the beginning of Reza Shah's tenure; several of his military campaigns even used Qashqa'i support. Within a few years, however, he had virtually eliminated the confederacy's military capabilities. Because the Khamseh confederacy had ceased to exist as a pawn of the Qavam ol-Molk and the British and as a rival to the Qashqa'i confederacy, these elements in the definition of the confederacy also disappeared. The Qavam ol-Molk, who along with his predecessors had rivaled the ilkhani for over a century, was exiled from Fars and temporarily faded from the political scene there. Finally, the British no longer perceived the Qashqa'i confederacy as a threat to their commercial interests. The nature of British commerce had changed, and trade routes from the gulf were superseded by other forms and routes of communication. The British withdrew their military forces from Fars and concentrated their attention on the Khuzistan oil fields to the north. Events during World War II, however, did reengage their military influence in Fars.

7

The Resurgence of the
Qashqa'i Confederacy

WORLD WAR II

Reza Shah was forced to abdicate when the British and Soviets occupied Iran in 1941, which provided Naser Khan and Khosrow Khan the opportunity to leave Tehran, where they had been held under house arrest, and quickly return to Qashqa'i territory. Malek Mansur Khan and Mohammad Hosain Khan remained in Germany during the war years, where they served as Middle East experts in the German army. Within a year of Reza Shah's abdication, Fars was again the scene of British-German competition, and the Shahilu were once again involved.

The Qashqa'i were caught in similar circumstances during World Wars I and II. The Iranian government, now under the young and inexperienced son of Reza Shah, Mohammad Reza Shah, was unable to control the interference of foreign powers in the nation, and Great Britain, the Soviet Union, and Germany were once again involved. In 1942 the United States joined them. The Qashqa'i people and their leaders, having suffered under Reza Shah, intended to resist any regime that would continue his type of oppression. Qashqa'i leaders opposed the British military occupation of south Iran during World War II because of past British backing for Reza Shah's repressive policies, continuing British influence in the new Pahlavi regime, and opposition to foreign

143

interference in the affairs of south Iran, which these leaders considered their domain.

Naser Khan, eldest son of Isma'il Khan, took over the position of ilkhani upon his father's death in 1933 and was called by that title, but the conditions of arrest made it impossible for him to engage in Qashqa'i politics directly. Official state appointments of ilkhani and ilbegi had ceased by this time. Upon Naser Khan's arrival in Fars in 1941, he set about assisting the Qashqa'i people to return to nomadism and productive pastoralism. Many Qashqa'i had responded to Reza Shah's abdication by burning or simply abandoning their houses, and within a few months they had once again become heavily armed and militarily organized. Qashqa'i men bought new weapons, captured them from the rapidly disintegrating army and gendarmerie, and took them with them when they deserted state military service.[1] Reza Shah had declared that land used by the Qashqa'i for pastoralism and cultivation was government land, but Naser Khan reclaimed it in the name of the Qashqa'i confederacy and, with the assistance of lower-level tribal leaders, reallocated it to the Qashqa'i tribes and subtribes. He redistributed agricultural and pastoral land formerly controlled by or belonging to his family to thousands of Qashqa'i families, without payment or with minimal payments dispersed over fifteen years. He implemented an animal redistribution program to aid those many Qashqa'i who had become impoverished under Reza Shah, and for several years he subsidized the pastoral and agricultural activities of the poorest Qashqa'i.[2] On Naser Khan's initiative a school and hospital were built in Firuzabad. He also kept government tax collectors out of Qashqa'i territory, refused to allow the army to conscript Qashqa'i youth, and opposed the government's plans to build roads in and through Qashqa'i territory in order to prevent government intrusions. He brought into the confederacy, particularly into the Amaleh tribe, previously independent tribal groups in Fars, who, because of their lack of wider affiliations, had suffered greatly under Reza Shah. Naser Khan created, on the basis of earlier models, a distinctive tan (or grey) felt hat characterized by two raised flaps which Qashqa'i men quickly

1. Great Britain, Public Record Office, Foreign Office 371/Persia 1944/6844-155, British consul in Shiraz to the Foreign Office, "Report on Tribal Areas."

2. Naser Khan asked Qashqa'i households to contribute 1 percent of their herds and a portion of their pack animals (essential for migrations) to a pool assembled by lower-level leaders, who redistributed the property to impoverished families. For a slightly exaggerated account, see Douglas (1951:142–43).

adopted in symbolic recognition of their newfound freedom. Other self-defined groups in Iran also utilized hats as political symbols. Previously Qashqa'i men had worn a round felt hat similar to those worn in rural Fars by Lurs and others.[3] Naser Khan's economic programs, which helped to build political support, were soon overshadowed by British and German activities in Fars.

As during World War I, the British and Germans were not equally matched in Fars in terms of personnel, equipment, and funds, but the Germans were again able to harass the British through the activities of a single dedicated agent and despite the now fairly active cooperation of Iranian military forces with the British. The goals of the German effort in Iran during World War II were, as during the previous war, to organize the tribes so that they would rebel against the Iranian government and the occupying forces (Great Britain, the Soviet Union) and to protect or disrupt communications, this time the Trans-Iranian railroad and the supply of the Soviet Union from the gulf. The Germans sent agents to Iran to arm and train "dissident" tribes such as the Qashqa'i and to organize a pro-German, anti-Allies, Iranian nationalist movement (Melliyun-e Iran). Berthold Schulze-Holthus, who went to Fars in 1942, served as a military advisor to Naser Khan and the Qashqa'i tribes for the duration of the war. He promised Naser Khan heavy armaments, which would be flown in and dropped by parachute, and Naser Khan prepared landing strips at Farrashband, Firuzabad, and the Dashti frontier for deliveries of arms and as preparation for a German invasion (Schulze-Holthus 1954:188). Few arms ever materialized, which contributed to Naser Khan's growing dissatisfaction with his foreign guest.

3. Some called the new hat "Naser Khan's hat" (*Naser Khan berk* in Turkic, *kolah-ye Naser Khan* in Persian). For striking photographs taken in 1946, see Duncan (1982). In 1808 peasants near Abadeh were said to wear "a little scull-cap, slit on each side, called *dogoosheh*" (Morier 1816:155). While *do gushi* ("two-eared") is what the Qashqa'i call their own hat today, the style of the 1808 hat, especially the "slits," is not adequately clear in Morier's description. The hats worn by nomads migrating west of Shiraz in 1821 had "flaps for the ears" (Fraser 1825:93), but the wearers are not identified as Qashqa'i and the position of the flaps is not indicated. The hats worn by Qashqa'i in 1871 were conical and lacked flaps (see Goldsmid 1874b:576). In 1912 Qashqa'i wore flared hats made of black felt (Demorgny 1913a:93), and in 1920 they wore short black or beige hats that were rounded and rather flat on top (see Oberling 1974:249), which contrast with the tall, black, conical hats worn by Qashqa'i khans since the time of Jani Aqa in the early 1700s (see Oberling 1974:242, 244–48).

The goals of the British, and then the Americans after 1942, were to protect the Khuzistan oil fields, ensure the flow of war matériel through Iran to the Soviet Union, curtail disruptive German activities, and strengthen the Iranian government. The British maintained regular military patrols along the Bushire-Shiraz-Isfahan road to prevent hostilities from disrupting these cities and to threaten Qashqa'i who could be trapped on either side of the road. The British had experienced their own vulnerabilities on this road during previous decades and did not hesitate to protect their interests this time. The Americans, who leased arms to "friendly" tribes in Khuzistan and Luristan during the war, were not active in Fars. The head of the American army force in Iran (Persian Gulf Command) did, however, commandeer Naser Khan's house in Tehran as his private residence (Lencowski 1949:273).

The British were as concerned about Schulze-Holthus as they had been about Wassmuss, the German agent who had organized anti-British activities during World War I, from whom they had learned another hard lesson. Through an official of the Anglo-Iranian Oil Company, they promptly offered Naser Khan five million tumans and "the recognition of the autonomy of the Qashgai zone by the Teheran Government, guaranteed by Great Britain" in exchange for the German (Schulze-Holthus 1954:167). Naser Khan rejected the offer. In 1942, in a move against the German effort in Iran, the British captured General Zahedi, the key figure in the nationalist movement against the British occupation and a military commander who secretly organized tribal leaders. In response, Naser Khan called a meeting in Firuzabad of Qashqa'i leaders and shaikhs from Dashti and Tangistan to discuss their possible military role. He also renewed his ties with Abdollah Zarghampur, paramount leader of the Boir Ahmad, with whom he had been detained under Reza Shah. In 1941, upon their release, they had created a defensive alliance in which their two groups were united to resist government encroachment (Magee 1948:3, 12). Naser Khan lacked the arms for a successful effort against the British and sought sources other than the Germans, who had still not delivered on their promises. He hoped to capture arms from gendarme posts and purchase them from Arab traders along the gulf and from Indian troops stationed in the Khuzistan oil fields. In the meantime, six German agents parachuted into Iran but failed to bring promised supplies (Schulze-Holthus 1954:175, 191, 195–98, 212).

In 1943 Major General Shahbakhti, who had fought Qashqa'i forces in 1929 on behalf of Reza Shah, took over military command in the south and offered Naser Khan twenty million tumans if he would surrender Schulze-Holthus. When Naser Khan refused, Shahbakhti's British-financed troops attacked the Qashqa'i in both winter and summer pastures and bombed Qashqa'i forces from the air. The British-allied Qavam ol-Molk once again led Khamseh troops against the Qashqa'i. Despite these moves, Qashqa'i forces defeated government troops in the major battles, including a crucial one at Semirom where they fought alongside Boir Ahmad forces, and captured quantities of military equipment. Only then did German personnel and some equipment for the Qashqa'i finally arrive, but they were now of no use and proved to be a liability. The 1943 peace treaty between the government and Qashqa'i leaders, in which the British participated, stated that the Qashqa'i could retain their autonomy and their weapons but had to submit to military garrisons in Firuzabad, Farrashband, and Ghaleh Parian. After the treaty was signed, Naser Khan sent Schulze-Holthus and the new agents to a secluded haven in Boir Ahmad territory. By radio Schulze-Holthus urged Berlin to hold Malek Mansur Khan and Mohammad Hosain Khan as hostages, but they had already fled Germany and were shortly thereafter arrested by British authorities in Turkey. The British warned Naser Khan that if Schulze-Holthus and the other agents were not turned over to them, his two brothers would be shot (Schulze-Holthus 1954:245, 265–69, 279, 283). As an additional incentive, they gave Naser Khan a "letter of indemnity for anything he might have done against British interests in the past."[4] After they captured the agents, the British released the brothers from jail in Cairo and allowed them to return to Fars.[5]

Turkish authorities, expressing sympathy about the Shahilu family's plight under Reza Shah, invited the Qashqa'i tribes to settle in Turkey south of Lake Van near the Iraq-Syria frontier, possibly in an effort to counterbalance the Kurds in the area. In 1941 or 1942 Malek Mansur Khan, who was taken to see the location, declined the offer; he felt the Qashqa'i people would not have wanted to move there.[6]

4. Great Britain, India Office Library, Political and Secret Files, 12/3546, R. W. Bullard to British Embassy, Tehran, 17 May 1945. Also, Malek Mansur Khan, personal communication, 5 September 1979, Tehran.

5. G. M. Wickens, who participated in the arrest of the German agents, comments that "the Germans shrewdly placed several of their agents where they could hope to do the most damage to the central authority and the Allies—among restive tribal elements. . . . From the point of view of a centralised autocracy the Iranian tribes have long been a 'source of trouble'"; personal communication, 22 February 1979.

6. Malek Mansur Khan, personal communication, 5 September 1979, Tehran.

In 1943 the Shahilu and the Qavam ol-Molk competed in parliamentary elections, in what was to be their last major struggle. After the battle of Semirom, the government appointed the Qavam as Governor of Fars and provided him with arms for the Khamseh and Mamassani tribes. With support from gunmen from both groups, he removed ballot boxes from Qashqa'i and Boir Ahmad areas, and three of the five parliament seats went to his supporters. The only Qashqa'i candidate to win was Khosrow Khan (as representative of Abadeh); Naser Khan lost the election in Shiraz. Eleven deputies formed a "tribal group" in the newly convened parliament in 1944; having suffered under Reza Shah, they were anxious to protect their personal and tribal interests, receive compensation for hardships undergone, preserve advantages gained since 1941, secure confiscated lands and the right to bear arms and migrate, and place supporters in provincial administration (Abrahamian 1982:196–97, 200–201).

In 1945 Naser Khan, although holding no government appointment, was officially responsible as Head of Security (*rais-e entezamat*) for Qashqa'i territory. The government appointed governors for four towns in Qashqa'i areas (Firuzabad, Eqlid, Ardekan, Semirom) who were responsible for financial administration, health, education, and the distribution of government monopoly goods (including tea and sugar); Khosrow Khan held the government appointment in Firuzabad but was reported never to be at his post. Gendarmes were also posted at these towns, and the army placed small garrisons at Firuzabad, Baiza, Ardekan, and Semirom, and on the main roads skirting tribal territory. Beyond this, the government did not interfere in Qashqa'i territory (Magee 1948:9, 12). "Instead, to save face, to lighten their own burden, and to make a feeble gesture for law and order, the Government charges certain leading khans with the security of their tribal areas and, frequently, of additional territory as well," a situation much like that occurring in the nineteenth century. The government did not provide khans with arms or ammunition but did replace cartridges "discharged in the preservation of law and order" (Magee 1948:13). No government taxes were collected from the Qashqa'i during this period.

THE "REBELLION" OF 1946

In 1946 the confluence of Soviet occupation in north Iran, British interference in the south, and a communist-influenced central government brought Qashqa'i leaders and supporters again to national and international prominence. Prime Minister Qavam (no relation to the Qavam ol-Molk) attempted to instigate an "anticommunist tribal uprising" throughout the nation in order to force the British and Americans into an anti-Soviet stance and to force the Soviets to cease their interference in the nation, and he sought Naser Khan's assistance. A few years earlier Naser Khan had attempted to undermine the new Pahlavi regime, particularly because of its reliance on Britain, but now he was seen as an ardent nationalist defending Iran from Soviet incursion. American officials suggested that the tribes of Fars could be utilized against a possible Soviet invasion. The British, who also wanted to force the Soviets out, allied with the Qashqa'i and probably provided them some assistance, a reversal of their previous relationship. Although this role was minor, the Soviets accused the British of instigating the rebellion (Lenczowski 1949:305, Arfa 1965:337–38).

Early in 1946 Soviet troops still occupied north Iran pursuant to wartime agreements that had lapsed. The Tudeh (communist) party, a threat to entrenched interests during this period, was growing in strength (Abrahamian 1982), and new governments in Iranian Azerbaijan and Kurdistan had declared their autonomy. The British supported the move of Shaikh Khaz'al in Khuzistan to organize an Arab separatist movement and sent troops to Basra, just across the Iranian border (Lenczowski 1949:304). Prime Minister Qavam, who at times outwardly maintained a pro-Soviet stance, met secretly with Khosrow Khan and other tribal leaders to organize an anticommunist rebellion. The government established a telegraphic code in order to communicate directly with tribal leaders in the field and prohibited its military from attacking tribal forces. Qavam named Major General Zahedi, an ally of Naser Khan during World War II, as commander of government forces in the south. The paramount Qashqa'i khans regarded the uprising as an anti-Soviet, anti-Tudeh maneuver rather than a rebellion against Qavam's government (Oberling 1974:184–85, Fatemi 1980: 154–55).

The rebellion of 1946 began and ended in a week's time, brought to rapid conclusion by government concession to demands. Naser Khan began by convening a meeting of major tribal and religious leaders of Fars. They formed a national movement called Sa'dun and issued Prime Minister Qavam an ultimatum demanding the resignation of the cabinet (except for Qavam), dismissal of officials who had exploited the tribes, release of imprisoned Bakhtiyari leaders, greater autonomy for Fars, formation of provincial councils that would appoint local officials, allocation of Fars taxes to Fars, new roads, and programs of education and health. The demands expressed basic grievances concerning political and economic conditions in Fars, mirrored many privileges currently enjoyed in Azerbaijan, and did not specifically oppose communism in Iran. (At this same meeting, tribal leaders under Naser Khan's leadership drafted a letter to the United Nations asking for autonomy on the grounds that they considered themselves a minority entitled to UN protection—Arfa 1965:359.) Qavam's government rejected the group's ultimatum, and, according to plan, fighting commenced throughout south Iran. Tribal forces captured government-stronghold cities, including Bushire, Kazerun, and Abadeh. The government quickly dispatched a negotiating team to Fars to meet with tribal and religious leaders. Zahedi and Naser Khan reached an agreement, which was approved by Qavam; provisions included demands made by the Sa'dun movement, amnesty for the participants in the rebellion, and continuation of the national movement with prime ministerial support. Qavam formed a new cabinet from which Tudeh ministers were excluded. In December 1946, after Qavam successfully negotiated the Soviet troop withdrawal, the government's army occupied Azerbaijan and Kurdistan without Soviet interference, and the new parliament refused to give the Soviets an earlier promised oil concession. Through action of the deputies forming the "tribal group" and reflecting in part the role of tribes in recent events, tribal representation in parliament (previously abolished in 1934) was reinstated.[7]

The paramount Qashqa'i khans, responding to the threat to their interests posed by Soviet influence in Iran and by the Tudeh party, had attempted to improve conditions for themselves and the Qashqa'i people. They had vested interests in joining a national and international struggle over the fate of the government in power, and much could be gained; Naser Khan could increase his power, once again play a key role in Fars, and possibly become a national leader.[8] They had been anxious to resume political action after many years of imprisonment and exile, if only to prevent state oppression against them. They also had opposed foreign interference in Iran and realized the futility of

7. Arfa (1965:358–59, 373–75); Douglas (1951:134–37); Fatemi (1980:146–55); Oberling (1974:186–90); *The New York Times*, 24 September 1946, p. 22; ibid., 26 September 1946, p. 4; ibid., 27 September 1946, p. 13; ibid., 29 September 1946, p. 38; *The Middle East Journal* 1 (1947): 91–92; Avery (1965:378–401).

8. Arfa states that the paramount khans intended to disrupt Iran by creating a South Persia state or confederacy with a Qashqa'i at its head (1965:338).

cooperating with foreign powers that claimed to have the interests of Iran and the Qashqa'i at heart when instead they ruthlessly operated in their own.

The activities of Qashqa'i leaders and supporters in the 1940s and early 1950s belied the notion held by state authorities and foreign powers that tribes and tribal chiefs would run rampant if not controlled by a wider authority, even if this one brief (but preplanned and government-approved) encounter in 1946 with the government is included. From the time of Reza Shah's ouster to the early 1950s, the paramount Qashqa'i khans, Naser Khan in particular, demonstrated restrained, competent leadership despite political and economic reverses suffered under Reza Shah in the previous decades. Left to handle their own tribal concerns, without the intrusion of either oppressive state policies or manipulative foreign powers, these khans exercised leadership benefiting the Qashqa'i people without simultaneously posing direct threats to either state or settled society (the events of 1946 excluded).

The Qashqa'i confederacy, under the leadership of Naser Khan and his three brothers, was relatively autonomous between 1941 and 1953. The government issued no policies against Qashqa'i leaders and tribespeople, and, except for Naser Khan and Khosrow Khan who were parliamentary deputies, the khans maintained their distance from state officials of all levels. For one of possibly only two periods in Qashqa'i history, the paramount khans did not seek ties with the state ruler, a decision reflecting Mohammad Reza Shah's lack of power. The gendarmerie and army made little attempt to intrude into or enforce state rule in Qashqa'i territory, and military officials held the khans, Naser Khan in particular, in respect. Although a token military force was in Firuzabad in 1949, responsibility for law and order in Qashqa'i territory rested with Qashqa'i leaders (Lambton 1953:286). A Congress of Tribes met in Tehran in 1948 to discuss the possible collaboration of tribal and military forces in national defense (Monteil 1966:21); participation by the paramount Qashqa'i khans was likely but is not documented.

The success of Qashqa'i leaders in helping their supporters regain economic viability and in limiting government activities in the region contributed to the increasing prosperity of the tribespeople. When the paramount khans returned to Fars on Reza Shah's abdication, they reclaimed some of the properties the shah had confiscated (without always giving up those they had received in exchange—Lambton 1953:289). They quickly reasserted their right to allocate pastures to the Qashqa'i tribes, a process that khans of the component tribes had handled but in altered form because of the forced sedentarization of most Qashqa'i nomads. The paramount khans, in reclaiming Qashqa'i pastures from government control and resuming responsibility over them, reorganized people who had been dispossessed and dislocated and returned them to a nomadic life. They also incorporated previously independent tribal groups into the confederacy. These activities accompanied a reassertion of Qashqa'i power in the region.

As a result of the paramount khans' return, the Qashqa'i confederacy reemerged as the political integration of the various components that had operated under local leaders during the 1930s.[9] Some khans of the component tribes had assumed prominence in this interval, but they accepted the implications of Naser Khan's return and no conflict was reported. To handle the situation he sought their advice, delegated responsibility, shared favors accompanying the reassertion of confederacy power, and showed respect for them in front of tribespeople and others. That the four Shahilu brothers exercised leadership of the confederacy jointly, informally dividing among themselves various duties, aided this process. Each brother formed his own personal links with tribal khans and headmen and created his own political network. Naser Khan and Malek Mansur Khan functioned primarily as tribal leaders in Fars and in Qashqa'i territory, but both maintained urban and wider political contacts. Malek Mansur Khan cultivated ties with American officials and entertained the growing number of foreign journalists and travelers who visited the Qashqa'i,[10] while Mohammad Hosain Khan and Khosrow Khan cultivated political networks in Tehran.

THE MOSADDEQ ERA AND ITS AFTERMATH

In the early 1950s yet another crisis drew the paramount Qashqa'i khans into national politics, with ultimately disastrous results. They supported Prime Minister Mosaddeq and threatened military action when he was deposed, actions in keeping with their involvements dur-

---

9. A resurgence of the Boir Ahmad tribal system also occurred during this same period (Loeffler 1978:164).

10. William O. Douglas visited the paramount khans in 1950 (1951). His expressed fascination with the Qashqa'i inspired many journalists and social scientists, and the images he was led to see were perpetuated in other observers' accounts and in the khans' own future attempts to influence impressions made. See also Shor and Shor (1952), Coon (1955), and Ullens de Schooten (1956).

ing times of competition over state rulership in the previous two centuries. The khans seemed not to understand the extent to which Mohammad Reza Shah's new patron—the United States—would support the regime it had been propping up and arming over the past decade. Once again they were victims of foreign interference, and, as on some previous occasions, a shah and a foreign power collaborated in their punishment.

Qashqa'i support for Mohammad Mosaddeq also had a personal basis. Mosaddeq served as Governor of Fars in 1920, and Isma'il Khan and his sons established excellent rapport with him lasting their lifetimes. The four Shahilu brothers were active in Mosaddeq's National Front political party, and Khosrow Khan and Naser Khan served as members of parliament under him. Along with other members of the National Front, they sought to limit the shah's power, curtail foreign interference in the nation, and nationalize Iran's oil industry,[11] but they also personally distrusted the shah because he perpetuated Pahlavi rule, depended on a foreign power, developed sophisticated military and police apparatus that could be employed against them, and pursued Persian chauvinistic policies (although less harshly than his father). They believed that a Mosaddeq government would establish mutually productive relations with them and that it would not use military force against them or the Qashqa'i people.

Between 1951 and 1953 the United States enhanced its support of the shah and strove to defeat Mosaddeq. American officials, having an exaggerated sense of Qashqa'i power in the nation (see Roosevelt 1979), attempted to draw support from the paramount Qashqa'i khans and invited Mohammad Hosain Khan and Khosrow Khan to visit the United States in 1951 as guests of the American government. Later, American officials offered the khans five million dollars (at one point bringing a suitcase full of cash to tempt them) and posts as cabinet ministers in the shah's government if they would support the shah instead of Mosaddeq. They rejected the offer. As the CIA-directed move against Mosaddeq accelerated, American officials promised the four khans a period of exile limited to three years and their property left intact if Qashqa'i forces would not attack Shiraz when a coup was attempted. They also promised to place the khans' friend General Zahedi

---

11. Mohammad Mosaddeq wrote to the paramount khans in 1952 thanking them for support in the legislation nationalizing the oil industry and in forming a new government; *Nameh Nur* 4(1979): 160–61.

in charge of the Qashqa'i people while the khans were in exile if the khans would agree to disband their military forces and not act against the shah. The khans approved the notion of Zahedi but were unwilling to support the shah in any way; they rejected all offers.[12]

On the morning of the CIA-directed coup, 19 August 1953, the paramount Qashqa'i khans invited Mosaddeq to join their forces in Fars to continue the struggle against the Pahlavi regime from the south; he declined.[13] Later he escaped and then gave himself up and was imprisoned. Mohammed Reza Shah, who had sought a hasty exile, returned to Iran. Armed Qashqa'i forces led by Khosrow Khan approached Shiraz to force Mosaddeq's release from prison, and hundreds of unarmed Qashqa'i quietly infiltrated the city. The government responded by declaring martial law, sending additional troops, and appointing a new Governor to negotiate with Naser Khan. Supporters of Mosaddeq in the Iranian air force disabled most of the aircraft that had conducted surveillance on Qashqa'i movements. Given added American and British support to the shah, however, the chance of a Qashqa'i move on Shiraz succeeding seemed increasingly unlikely, and no further military activity occurred. Qashqa'i forces withdrew, ending direct Qashqa'i involvement in the Mosaddeq affair.[14]

For a short time after Mosaddeq's ouster, the paramount Qashqa'i khans continued to participate in Iranian politics. Naser Khan served as a senator and Mohammad Hosain Khan and Khosrow Khan were deputies in parliament, positions requiring the shah's support or approval. Abdollah, Naser Khan's son, interpreted the purpose of parliamentary service as an effort "to maintain a correct relation with the Iranian government so that the Army would have no excuse for another attack" (Gashgai 1954:7). Parliamentary service kept the khans closely abreast of political change and cognizant of policies detrimental to them or the Qashqa'i people and enabled them possibly to influence some decisions made, but it also enabled the shah to hold them under

12. Information from members of the Shahilu family. Miles Copeland, a CIA operative in Iran in 1953, provided corroboration; personal interview, July 1979, London. See also statements about the paramount khans by Kermit Roosevelt, another CIA operative in Iran in 1953 (1979).

13. Letter from Mohammad Mosaddeq to the paramount khans in 1962; *Nameh Nur* 4(1979): 171–72.

14. *The New York Times*, 26 September 1953, p. 2; ibid., 28 September 1953, p. 8; Ullens de Schooten (1956).

surveillance and prevent them from organizing political resistance in Fars.

Several months after Mosaddeq's forced ouster, Mohammad Reza Shah, as part of his new efforts to strengthen the government's repressive apparatus, formed a Superior Council of Tribes, composed of the paramount leaders of Iran's major tribes (Monteil 1966:21), in order to exercise power over them. Having met (with considerable help) one challenge to his rule, he prepared to restrict or curtail the power of others impeding him, including the Shahilu family. He received assistance from the United States, whose officials advised him to exile the paramount khans as well as settle the Qashqa'i people in villages and towns and integrate them into the fabric of Iranian (Persian) society. American officials were convinced that this "tribal chiefdom" was an anachronism in a soon-to-be modern Iran, and that Iran's ability to support United States interests would be impeded if the Qashqa'i (and other groups) remained in a primitive and hostile state. The images and realities of capitalist development denied the perpetuation of communal structures unless they could be integrated into basic productive and political systems. American officials had failed to bribe the paramount Qashqa'i khans to support the shah rather than Mosaddeq, but they now retooled the rewards. As the shah planned the khans' exile, American officials offered them permanent residency status in the United States.

In 1954 the shah exiled Naser Khan and his family from Iran. They settled in the United States as permanent residents. Khosrow Khan was not as easily pressured into leaving. He ignored the shah's order for his exile, and in response the shah sent extra troops to Shiraz. The Governor of Fars, who had been wounded while fighting Khosrow Khan in 1943, described him as "anti-Shah, an adventurer and intriguer" and threatened him with the military.[15] Malek Mansur Khan commented:

"If the Government sends troops against us, we will have to face them. The Government is not sure of its men. We know more about the condition of the army in Fars than they do. We know . . . how many of the pilots are for us. If they use tanks, they may take Firuzabad . . . , but we will be in the mountains. If we accede to this demand [that Khosrow leave Iran], there will

15. *The New York Times*, 3 October 1954, p. 3.

be no end to demands. Why should we be put under pressure because of a personal grudge of the Shah? A Government attack on us will set off a conflagration. The other tribes are our friends and the people in the cities and other provinces look to us, but who likes this Government? . . . American blunders are creating a miniature China in Iran. Americans are paying money but they are only buying dissatisfaction and resentment because they have identified themselves with a decayed and corrupt regime.[16]

Khosrow Khan eventually left for Italy and later settled in West Germany. In 1956 Malek Mansur Khan was exiled, and after a stay in Switzerland traveled to Washington, D.C., in hopes of creating better understanding among American officials about the role of his family in Iranian politics. Given United States pressure on the shah to force their exile, he hoped to change American attitudes but was unsuccessful. The four brothers were offered American citizenship, which they rejected. Mohammad Hosain Khan, ordered to stay out of Fars, left Iran also, but not under the formal conditions of exile as was the case with his brothers. He resided in Great Britain and the United States.

The shah abolished the titles of ilkhani and ilbegi between 1955 and 1957. Reza Shah had also abolished them, and it is not clear if the government had formally reinstated them after his abdication. The government's formal interactions with Naser Khan and other Qashqa'i leaders during World War II and the crises in 1946 and 1953 served as de facto recognition of the titles. The issue is somewhat academic, however, as Naser Khan and Malek Mansur Khan did not recognize either Pahlavi shah. They were not interested in receiving titles from what they took to be illegitimate regimes.

Next, the state (once again) confiscated the Shahilu family's land, and special legislation passed by parliament in 1958 entitled it to be sold to agriculturalists or Qashqa'i who desired to settle. Much of the land ended in the hands of other wealthy landholders in Fars, including military officers, government officials, and some khans of the component Qashqa'i tribes, and only some of the land was deeded over to settling Qashqa'i or to agriculturalists who had worked the land on sharecropping or rental arrangements. Subtracted from the amount to be paid the family were back taxes and indemnity for sugar that had

16. Ibid.

disappeared from storehouses in Bushire in 1946.[17] Government officials self-servingly figured these two amounts. Some money was paid to family members within a year or so, and Naser Khan and Khosrow Khan received some payment in installments during their many years of exile. The family was forbidden to buy land from either the state or Iranian citizens in the future. These stipulations were much harsher than those enacted by Reza Shah. The process of confiscation was not completed by the time of Iran's comprehensive land reform of 1962–72, when special legal provisions subjected the family to further restrictions. The family was completely dispossessed; the state confiscated all its cultivated lands, pastures, and villages for the purpose of redistribution, and the exclusions and exemptions offered to all other landholders by these and subsequent laws and amendments were denied them (Lambton 1969:69, Oberling 1974:200–01).

In 1956 the shah had established a program to settle the Qashqa'i over a five-year period. A commission, set up in Shiraz, was to buy land for resale (through loans) to the nomads, but corruption and insufficient funds prevented all but a few of the targeted groups from settling.

The government assigned military officers to the leading khans of the major Qashqa'i tribes and placed the Amaleh tribe, whose khans were the men now in exile, under direct military control. Smaller Qashqa'i tribes and sections were included administratively with the major tribes. The military officers were to allot seasonal pastures, supervise migrations, and establish the state's law and order, but their more basic purposes were military pacification and political surveillance, which the state had difficulty accomplishing with the paramount khans present. The officers were notably unsuccessful in performing the specific functions of regulating pastures, migrations, and law and order, and they had little success in disarming the Qashqa'i. They represented unwanted state intrusion, tribespeople disregarded them, and lower levels of the leadership hierarchy continued to function. They were somewhat more successful in military pacification and political surveillance because their military presence demonstrated state power

17. The government claimed thousands of rifles, many machine guns, millions of rounds of ammunition, and twenty million dollars' worth of other property (mostly sugar) had been stolen from custom houses in Bushire and other locations in 1946 and held the Shahilu personally responsible (Douglas 1951:136).

in the area. Not until the next decade, however, did this almost symbolic presence have a substantial base.

The Khamseh tribes had suffered greatly under Reza Shah and never returned to the economic and political position they had enjoyed earlier.[18] Almost all Khamseh nomads had been disarmed and forced to settle in inhospitable areas in the 1930s, and many remained settled after Reza Shah's abdication. The military governorship established over the Khamseh continued to function in the early 1940s; its officials amassed wealth but permitted the component tribes to exercise autonomy. In 1944 a relative of the Qavam ol-Molk was named as civil governor of the Khamseh, to replace the military one, and in 1945 Lotfali Qavam, Qavam's nephew, was appointed supervisor (*sarparast*) of the Khamseh, an appointment superseding that of the civil governor. The army provided Lotfali Qavam with an armed bodyguard and transport for his tribal functions. As one condition of his assuming the post, he received full control of the Iranian military and gendarmerie in the area in order to prevent these forces from interfering in his tribal administration. He was also appointed governor of Fasa, and his relatives served as governors of other districts in the area (Magee 1948:108–13). In 1949 the government returned the Khamseh tribes to military governorship, and the Qavam family lost some of the power, authority, and wealth it had regained after the fall of Reza Shah. During World War II the Qavam had engaged several hundred Khamseh troops in the defense of British interests, but he was apparently not involved in the 1946 crisis or in the threatened Qashqa'i move against Shiraz during the Mosaddeq crisis in 1953.[19]

The period from 1941 to 1953 was critical to the Qashqa'i confederacy's consolidation. During this time the conception of the Qashqa'i as a united polity emerging out of Reza Shah's repressions was actualized. And in the years to follow, particularly in the aftermath of the paramount khans' banishment and then upon their triumphant return in 1979, the Qashqa'i evoked this period when they sought to remember their past and as they made plans to reconstitute the confederacy.

18. See Garrod (1946a:44). The group studied by Barth (1961) served as retainers to the Basseri khans and was relatively prosperous; its economic standing was not at all typical of other Basseri groups or other Khamseh tribes.

19. The Qavam family, consisting of three main branches, was able to maintain and enhance its wealth, social status, and political standing in Tehran as well as Shiraz until at least 1979 (Royce 1981:292–96).

All Qashqa'i talked nostalgically about the 1940s and the resurgence of Qashqa'i power occurring then. Outsiders during this period, in depicting Qashqa'i culture and society in written and photographic forms, distorted history by projecting these images back in time. The government out of weakness did not manipulate the levels of leadership in the 1940s, and the confederacy took an unprecedented cohesive and elaborated form. The repressions of Reza Shah were some of the worst that Qashqa'i leaders and tribespeople have suffered, and the exuberance expressed in tribal reassertion and reorganization following his forced departure reflected accumulated sentiments. Qashqa'i tribespeople perceived the resumption of military control in the 1950s after the paramount khans' forced exile as a return of oppressive Pahlavi rule against them, and many despaired. The Qashqa'i confederacy had lost part of its hierarchical structure; the fate of the remaining parts was to depend upon conditions brought about by a rapidly consolidating Pahlavi state.

PART III

The Social Anthropology
of the Tribal Confederacy

Musician playing drums at a wedding

8

Qashqa'i Sociopolitical
Organization

*M*y effort in this book so far has been to present and analyze historical information relating to the Qashqa'i tribal confederacy. A detailed discussion of Qashqa'i sociopolitical organization and leadership—the focus of this and the next chapter—cannot be easily fitted into this historical framework. The actual processes of paramount leadership within the confederacy, the forms taken by the ilkhani's authority and power there, and his relationships with other Qashqa'i leaders and the Qashqa'i people are not documented until the mid-twentieth century, when foreign observers offer glimpses into these domains. Even these recent accounts are severely limited, given the short stays of the observers, their limited access to political arenas other than the ilkhani's camp, their antitribal and romantic biases, and the ilkhani's often successful attempts to influence impressions made. Many aspects of paramount leadership known for the period of 1941 to 1956 were presumably present before then, but how much further back in time is unknown, given lack of evidence.

Nevertheless, it can be said that part of the Qashqa'i political system exhibited considerable stability throughout much of the nineteenth and twentieth centuries. The institution of paramount leadership defined the state and the tribe for each other while simultaneously drawing its vital sources of power and authority from both. It remained, apparently virtually uncontested, in a single patrilineage for at least

163

two centuries and was firmly based in land, other forms of wealth, military power, and political authority for the entire period. The leadership hierarchy was institutionalized and often exhibited resilience despite changes in Iran as a whole. Lower-level leaders functioned continuously, regardless of the ability of higher-level leaders to perform political functions.

Previous chapters stressed historical continuity and change in the form, function, and perception of the Qashqa'i confederacy and its paramount leadership. They focused on the ilkhani's relationships with the Iranian state, foreign powers, and regional political groups. In this and following chapters, I turn to an examination of the Qashqa'i polity from closer range. This discussion refers primarily to periods when leaders actively fulfilled their political functions. For the ilkhani, this includes the period up to 1956; for khans, the period into the early 1960s. Khans and headmen assumed new roles after the early 1960s, and in 1979 the ilkhani attempted to resume leadership; these periods are discussed in chapters 11 and 12. The past tense used in these chapters reflects the historical dimensions involved in sociopolitical organization and leadership. Many of the features discussed, however, continue to be important to the present day. Also, many sociopolitical characteristics existing until the 1960s but disappearing thereafter reappeared during the 1978–79 revolution and persisted under the Islamic Republic of Iran.

THE SOCIOPOLITICAL HIERARCHY: AN
INTRODUCTORY OUTLINE

The Qashqa'i people were organized in a hierarchy of sociopolitical groups, each represented by one or more leaders. At the base was the household (*oba*), whose head represented it in most domains beyond the encampment or village. For the vast majority of Qashqa'i who were nomadic, the encampment was a flexible, temporary association of households; the oldest, most respected men made some decisions concerning this coresident group, but households exercised considerable independence. The pasture group, a collection of encampments in a geographically defined area, was also a flexible arrangement of tents and camps. A coresident group, whether an encampment, pasture section, village section, or village, was often called an oba. A subtribe (*tireh*), consisting of a number of pasture groups in winter and summer quarters and sometimes some villages and village sections as well, was a political group defined largely by kinship ties and affiliation to a headman (*kadkhuda*). A tribe (*tayefeh*) was a collection of subtribes headed by a family of khans, one of whom often held the title of kalantar and the role of providing liaison with the ilkhani. The khan families (*khavanin*) were a small, distinct socioeconomic group with dynastic, aristocratic features. Finally, the confederacy (*il*), a collection of tribes and other sociopolitical units, was headed by a male member of the ruling Shahilu lineage, who was usually titled ilkhani. The chain of political authority extended from household head to elder, headman, khan, kalantar, and ilkhani, and it paralleled a functional hierarchy of groups formally recognized by having spokesmen. Each tribe had its own winter and summer pastures, and khans allocated usufructuary rights to their associated subtribes, via headmen, who in turn allocated pasture rights to member households. All leaders coordinated the long seasonal migrations, especially under conditions of political instability in the region. Khans, often through headmen, handled general tribal affairs; they designated local leaders, administered tribal law and justice, resolved intratribal and intertribal disputes, negotiated with sedentary authorities, collected taxes, coordinated economic redistribution, and organized defensive and offensive activities.

THE ECOLOGICAL SETTING AND THE ECONOMIC BASES OF ELITE FORMATION AND POLITICAL CENTRALIZATION

The specific setting in which a Qashqa'i elite and a centralized political system developed contains many features that help explain their character. The setting was especially favorable for the emergence of particular economic and political formations. It is noteworthy that the major tribal groups immediately to the northwest and southeast of the Qashqa'i, the Lur tribes of the Kuhgiluyeh and the Khamseh tribes, who resided in different settings, developed different political systems at the higher levels. Important aspects of the setting are the local ecology and the strategic proximity of Shiraz and trade routes, while other essential aspects, examined in the following section, include the strategic distance of national borders and the national capital, inaccessible and isolated seasonal pastures, long and vulnerable migration routes through non-Qashqa'i territory, the population's wide geographical distribution, and the dominant, surrounding Persian society.

The Qashqa'i people occupied territory that was ecologically varied and rich in natural resources. The local ecology contributed to the emergence of socioeconomic stratification and a wealthy ruling elite and facilitated surplus production. Fars was not a marginal desert region with greatly fluctuating pastoral resources, as was the territory of tribes to the east, for example. While parts of the province were suitable only for seasonal occupancy, given constraints of climate, water, and natural vegetation and fuels, others were permanently occupied, and population density was relatively high. Nomadic pastoralism in the relatively lush Zagros Mountains is somewhat surprising because the physical environment seemed to favor a settled agricultural way of life (de Planhol 1968:409–10). Throughout history, pastoralists (tribal and nontribal), agriculturalists, village and urban settlers, and collectors of natural resources have competed for access to and control over this land.[1]

A centralized political system was essential for any people's sustained use and control of this land because of its multiple attractions (see also Barth 1961:127–30). Such a system allowed Qashqa'i pastoralists and agriculturalists to produce at maximum levels with relative freedom from predatory incursions, and it facilitated the ability of elite and nonelite Qashqa'i to control access to resources and to extract surpluses from others, practices augmenting their economies, especially during times of drought and regional political instability. Both maximum production and the ability to extract surpluses contributed to the overall, long-term political strength of the Qashqa'i. Regional and national elites, including those controlling the state, were attracted to this territory because of ecological and strategic features. They sought to control the ecologically rich area and the economic surpluses made possible by the environment and generated by the region's inhabitants. They were challenged by a political system that protected Qashqa'i rights in these matters, and they were threatened by the ability of the Qashqa'i to raid neighbors and travelers and to thwart foreign interests. In turn, the demands of regional and national elites created the need for (further) political centralization.

1. Competition over land in the Qashqa'i area increased greatly in the 1960s and 1970s. Land reform and pasture nationalization changed the basis of land tenure; agricultural expansion, economic development, and government programs for pasture protection and hunting preserves brought many new competitors into the area (see chap. 11).

The Qashqa'i elite consisted of two socially distinct parts: the Shah-ilu lineage and the ruling lineages of the component Qashqa'i tribes; this discussion refers to both. The relationships of these khans with the region's rural, nonelite people fell into two categories; their ties with the predominantly pastoral nomadic Qashqa'i lacked an exploitative character, while their ties with non-Qashqa'i settled agriculturalists were exploitative and typical of landlord-peasant relationships in Iran in general (see Lambton 1953).

Individuals and groups affiliating with the Qashqa'i polity recognized the khans as political leaders with the right to collect taxes in exchange for pasture allocation and mediation with external powers. Qashqa'i households and subtribes, as members of tribes and the confederacy, owed certain economic and political obligations. Khans occasionally collected an animal tax to support their office, and the il-khani levied an additional tax when state authorities demanded taxes or he needed revenue for warfare. Neither extraction was exploitative; khans did not appropriate a significant portion of the surplus production. The tax was collected only occasionally, was not burdensome, and at any rate was a small proportion of a form of household property that had the potential of reproducing regularly. Household economies, based on pastoralism, agriculture, and weaving, were not controlled by tribal leaders, except that access to pastures derived from tribal ties and obligations. Matters of animal ownership, allocation of labor, production, and exchange were solely in the hands of individual households. Impoverished Qashqa'i were exempt from the tax, as were those who performed regular services for tribal leaders, such as headmen and gunmen. Khans redistributed part of the tax they collected to those in economic need.

Khans did not derive their primary means of wealth from tribal supporters. They depended on other, more profitable and dependable sources of wealth and avoided heavy extractions from the Qashqa'i, which would have undermined and weakened their support. A similar pattern existed for the Qajar khans of the eighteenth century. "While the Qajar khans collected personal income and property as provincial governors, there is no evidence to indicate that they obtained any significant income from the surplus of tribal wealth. On the contrary, because the Qajar khans relied on their tribe for military support both locally and to pursue their broader political and military aims, they maintained and attempted to strengthen tribal ties" (Helfgott 1977: 53). Qashqa'i khans did retain the best pastures and garden locations for themselves, and their ability to acquire wealth in nontribal domains was based in part on the existence of political and military ties with the Qashqa'i people.

Qashqa'i khans derived most of their wealth from land and the proceeds of agricultural and pastoral production. They accumulated land through inheritance, government service, investment, and confiscation. They owned, controlled, and rented villages and large tracts of land throughout the region, within and outside Qashqa'i territory. Those who worked these lands tended to be non-Qashqa'i, both Lurs and Persians. Tenant farmers paid yearly rents to khans, and sharecroppers paid set portions of the harvests, according to patterns customary in the region, although Qashqa'i tenants and sharecroppers, who provided other services to khans, almost always paid less than non-Qashqa'i ones. The jobs of overseers and headmen were often given to loyal Qashqa'i supporters. Non-Qashqa'i landowners and villagers within Qashqa'i territory, on its peripheries, and along migration routes paid tribute to and bought protection from khans. The ability to secure such payments was connected with the balance of power in the region. Those paying could expect some security from raiding and other exactions by Qashqa'i and non-Qashqa'i. The state's long-term practice of bestowing governorships on the paramount Qashqa'i khans enabled them to acquire wealth through holding back taxes, converting lands to private use, and extracting tribute in exchange for protection. Ilkhanis received land and cash payments from the state for their administrative functions and, until the 1930s, for assembling tribal armies. Foreign powers also paid them and other khans, including dissident ones, to protect trade routes and conduct military campaigns, and merchants paid tributes to ensure the safe passage of commercial traffic. Khans, who sometimes sanctioned raids, received a share of the wealth captured by supporters.

Wealth and a position facilitating its acquisition were inherited, and hence many of these sources of wealth were cumulative. Because the Shahilu family was virtually unchallenged in its elite position for at least two centuries, the potential for wealth accumulation and retention was great. Until the 1950s family members still lived off the proceeds of property and other wealth accumulated over the years. The khan families of the component tribes, who were also unchallenged in their elite positions, acknowledged somewhat shorter histories, but the same patterns also held for them.

The strategic proximity of Shiraz and trade routes also contributed to the khans' economic and political ascendancy. Shiraz, the major city in southwest Iran and a center of Qashqa'i political and economic affairs, lies between Qashqa'i winter and summer pastures, which were south and north of the city, and most Qashqa'i migrated past it twice annually. Khans established residences and extensive networks in the city, which, combined with their tribal backing and wealth, made them major figures in local politics. Tribal, urban, and regional (as well as national and even international) politics often overlapped. The paramount khans and others exploited their position in the region as a basis for national prominence. Much economic activity in Shiraz was geared toward and supported by production in its hinterland, an important part of which was Qashqa'i territory. Khans, controlling large tracts of agricultural land and owning many herds, formed close ties with the market and were among the regional economic elite. Urban merchants and commercial brokers competed for their business and negotiated contracts for the production of animals, lambskins, grain, fruit, wool, carpets, opium, and gum tragacanth, some of which were intended for international trade. Capitalist expansion in Qashqa'i territory, facilitated by these activities, enhanced the wealth and power of khans and helped them compete in political arenas. The household economies of the Qashqa'i people were also closely tied with this market center and, through it, were integrated into regional, national, and international economic systems. While these household economies were independent of the khans' control, the overall economic prosperity of the Qashqa'i in general did relate directly to the khans' political position, because prosperity was facilitated by the exclusion of most competitors from the land in use.

Important trade and travel routes linked Shiraz and its hinterland with national and international markets. It was especially the link between Shiraz and the Persian Gulf port of Bushire that drew the attention of the state and foreign powers and figured prominently in the struggles among these powers and regional ones (local governments, tribes, merchants). Some Qashqa'i, including khans, used the routes to economic advantage by selling protection to commercial transport, collecting road taxes, and raiding.

THE STRATEGIC LOCATION

Other aspects of the setting also figure in the emergence of centralized political authority among the Qashqa'i. Qashqa'i territory did not touch or overlap with Iran's borders, unlike the territories of many other tribal and non-Persian groups in Iran. The state never employed the Qashqa'i to defend its borders, except possibly in the eighteenth century when Nader Shah forcibly moved some tribespeople from Fars to Khorasan, and the Qashqa'i were free from pressures that might have been applied by neighboring states and by fellow tribespeople across borders. Tribal groups divided by borders notably lacked much commitment to states and often encouraged efforts to unify them that threatened one or more states. Kurdish struggles for autonomy, for example, caused difficulties for Iran, Iraq, and Turkey in the twentieth century. Borders did provide escape routes for tribal people resisting state pressure, as with the Turkmen (Irons 1974, 1975), Kurds, and Baluch (Harrison 1981), and facilitated outside military support, but such groups were often victims of competition among other powers and could be decimated in ensuing conflicts (Perry 1975). Leaders of border tribes could manipulate two or more, often competing, states (Ahmed 1980a), but they were also vulnerable to internal political rivalries that could play into the hands of rival states (van Bruinessen 1983, Yapp 1983). The Shahsevan in northwest Iran historically lacked political unity and a leadership system that could establish Shahsevan power, partly because of their vulnerable location—their proximity to a predatory northern neighbor (Tapper 1971:358).[2] The Qashqa'i escaped many of these problems. Distance from state borders was conducive to Qashqa'i autonomy and prosperity in the long run, and the absence of competition over the Qashqa'i by bordering states helped the Shahilu lineage to retain leadership over a long period. The Qashqa'i were, however, encircled by Iranian territory, and they constituted a minority enclave within a strategic part of Iran; hence their integrative, protective political system provided borders of another sort. Iran's border and nonborder tribes developed different strategies to cope with their respective geopolitical settings; the Qashqa'i tribal confederacy was one emergent form.

Proximity to the Zand capital at Shiraz was a factor in the early development of the Qashqa'i confederacy. With the fall of the Zand dynasty in the 1790s and the rise of the Qajars, the central government moved to Tehran, where it has remained. This move allowed the confederacy, after the important formative years under the Zands, a high degree of autonomy from state control and interference, especially during the early Qajar period when the state exerted little power outside

2. "A borderland position, not to speak of actual partition between modern states, is not enviable for an ethnic group" (McCagg and Silver 1979a:xviii–xix).

the areas near Tehran (Abrahamian 1975, 1982). Proximity to the capital could bring influence in national affairs, but it could also sever tribal leaders from their tribal base; both occurred to the Bakhtiyari (Garthwaite 1983). Except for a brief period during the constitutional era (1906–11), state rulers did not view the Qashqa'i as a military threat to the capital. Before Reza Shah, Qashqa'i leaders did not seriously pursue national leadership; most used their Tehran connections to serve their class and tribal interests in Fars. Beginning with Reza Shah's reign, they attempted to strengthen their position in the state, and a few sought national leadership. The Qashqa'i people were too distant from the capital to be much involved in their leaders' quests for national leadership, except when the state brought sanctions against them in order to punish these leaders.

Qashqa'i winter and summer pastures, covering thousands of square miles of often otherwise uninhabited or sparsely inhabited and often rugged terrain,[3] were isolated and virtually inaccessible to outsiders, and their mountain pastures were particularly defensible. Before the advent of Reza Shah's improved roads and mechanized army, state forces could attack the Qashqa'i in their pastures or directly threaten their lands only with difficulty. In the modern age of aircraft, paved roads, and tanks, military forces have had enhanced abilities to assault the dispersed, mobile people. Major military operations were, however, infrequently undertaken in Qashqa'i territory against Qashqa'i pastoralists. It can be argued that no need for defense of Qashqa'i pastures arose because people were thinly dispersed over them, and no resources existed, short of flocks, that could be easily expropriated. When military forces did attack, they usually sought khans and their armed supporters in specific locations rather than Qashqa'i pastoralists in their seasonal pastures. Attacks by the South Persia Rifles during World War I and the British-suppported Iranian army during World War II, and aerial bombings by Reza Shah and Mohammad Reza Shah, did inflict great suffering upon the Qashqa'i people; these were also intended to defeat Qashqa'i leaders.[4] Other regional powers, including neighbor-

3. 40,000 square kilometers (15,444 square miles) (Kortum 1979a:32).

4. Elsewhere state and imperial forces have successfully conducted military operations against nomadic pastoralists. The Iraqi army developed effective military units, including tanks, for mountain fighting against the Kurds in the 1950s and thereafter; the Pakistani military brutally assaulted the Baluch from the air in 1973–77; and the Italians in Libya captured bedouin in battles and imprisoned them in concentration camps during World War I.

ing tribes and confederacies, never seriously threatened Qashqa'i occupancy of pastures; the borders between tribes were, however, often contested and therefore variable. In some regards, the mountains used by the Qashqa'i were virtually impenetrable by outsiders unfamiliar with the terrain. In the 1960s, some Qashqa'i who were fugitives from Pahlavi (in)justice successfully hid in mountain strongholds, and during its first three years, the Islamic Republic failed to impose its authority over the mountain camps of the paramount khans and their supporters, despite repeated attacks by zealous Revolutionary Guards. As an additional strategic feature, winter pastures offered unimpeded access to the gulf and its arms traffic.

The strategic isolation of Qashqa'i seasonal pastures contrasts with their vulnerable migration routes. Because Qashqa'i pastoralism depended for ecological reasons on the seasonal movement of herds between low-altitude and high-altitude pastures separated by as much as 350 miles, these routes have been their Achilles' heel. Nomadism was not a political adaptation for the Qashqa'i, as compared, for example, to the Turkmen, who, situated on the frontier of the Iranian and Russian states, exploited their mobility for military and political ends (Irons 1974). Migration routes took the Qashqa'i past Shiraz and through heavily settled, nontribal agricultural areas. Regional, state, and foreign armies attempted, sometimes successfully, to block migration routes, thus threatening Qashqa'i economic survival. The British government's *Military Report on Fars* even lists precise locations where the migrations of each Qashqa'i tribe can be blocked: "The best places for military operations against the Kashkuli would be . . ." (1922: 124–26). The Qashqa'i were also vulnerable to raids and attacks by non-Qashqa'i during their migrations. Because Qashqa'i leaders played important roles in coordinating movement, this factor also promoted the development of centralized leadership. Under peaceful conditions, the Qashqa'i were relatively free to migrate when and where they chose, uncontrolled by leaders, especially after the migration had begun. A dozen major routes and many more minor ones existed, and migrating groups were independently able to alter their paths quickly if congestion or poor conditions were reported to lie ahead.

The geographical distribution of the Qashqa'i in vast, widely separated seasonal pastures, which caused problems for state administration, facilitated coordination through both centralized and locally based Qashqa'i leaders, among whom a hierarchy or effective chain of communication was necessary. Qashqa'i nomads used winter pastures all along the Persian Gulf littoral covering an area approximately twice as large as that of summer pastures; the northernmost and southernmost of winter pastures were farther apart than most winter and summer pastures. As a result, while some of Iran's major tribal groups resided and migrated within single provinces and could be administratively contained within a single jurisdiction, the Qashqa'i were found in five areas (concentrated in Fars but also in Isfahan, Kuhgiluyeh-Boir Ahmad, Khuzistan, and the gulf coast) and fell under different provincial governments. Many resided in two or more jurisdictions during the year. The government's administration of the Qashqa'i was almost always indirect, even during periods of strong, centralized state rule, and government policy was by necessity relayed from state officials through the hierarchy of tribal mediators and hence was vague and usually unimplemented. Centralized leadership on the tribal level helped to coordinate pasture use and migrations across this broad area, but it could not be heavy-handed, and wide geographical dispersion also meant that the paramount leaders never exercised extensive control over the majority of the people.

The final element in the strategic setting as it relates to centralization is the minority status of the Qashqa'i in the dominant Persian society of the region and nation. Tribal leadership and confederacy organization protected and coordinated Qashqa'i activities and served as political, military, and cultural counterforces to intrusions and to expanding Persian control of nearby centers of power and wealth—the state apparatus, the bazaars, and the religious institutions. Although of diverse linguistic, cultural, and tribal origins, the Qashqa'i expressed their common identity as Turks, affirming group solidarity and creating boundaries between themselves and members of the surrounding society, who were predominantly Persians (Tajiks) and Lurs (often called Tajiks by the Qashqa'i).[5] Qashqa'i leaders shared this Turkic cultural identity and used its associated symbols and institutions to support their leadership.

SOCIOPOLITICAL ORGANIZATION

The Qashqa'i were organized into three types of groups: residential, kinship, and political. While it was likely that any two people sharing residence also shared kinship and affinal ties and membership in the

---

5. *Tajik,* or its pejorative form *Tat,* indicated any non-Turk.

same political group, it was not so easy to determine which members of a political or even a kinship group would share residence. In addition, some people shared residence who did not share kinship, and a smaller number shared residence who were not members of the same political group.

Three levels of socioterritorial grouping existed for nomadic Qashqa'i: encampments, pasture sections, and migration units. An *encampment* was a small, task-oriented, and cooperative unit, with membership based on ties of kinship, marriage, friendship, and contract. Its size, membership, and location varied over time. A *pasture section* was composed of a number of encampments and was often a relatively fixed (but seasonal) territorial unit. Access was determined by membership in one or more patrilineages, affinal ties, and links with the unit's elders. A *migration unit* was a large group of fluctuating size and membership that moved the long distances between winter and summer pastures. Members of encampments and pasture sections usually migrated together and were joined by others. The migrations offered opportunities for those who did not camp together to enjoy some sustained interaction.

Three levels of sociopolitical organization existed for all nomadic and many settled Qashqa'i, especially those in villages: *subtribes* (tireh), *tribes* (tayefeh), and the *confederacy* (il). Use of these terms, although in some contexts interchangeable, follows general patterns of Qashqa'i expression. Membership in each was defined by allegiance to political leaders. One expression of political affiliation was the sharing of territory, and political units were to some extent also territorial units. The Qashqa'i used a segmentary system as a conceptual model to describe their political organization, even though one was not necessarily followed in practice. The political units of subtribe, tribe, and confederacy were each represented by a leader or unit of leaders, and the political system consisted of the linkages among them (table 2).

A Qashqa'i *subtribe* was the smallest political unit with a formal leader and the largest unit below the tribe recognized for formal political and bureaucratic purposes by khans, the state, and other powers. The headman (kadkhuda) of a subtribe, who served as mediator between group members and others, was chosen by group consensus and verified in his position by khans of the tribe of which it was a part. A subtribe was composed of two or more patrilineages (*bunku, boluk*) that sometimes claimed common ancestry. Individuals and groups forming

TABLE 2. Qashqa'i Sociopolitical Organization (1960)

	Total Number	Range	Average Size
Tribes	14	1,000–50,000 people	15,200 people
Major tribes	5	20,000–50,000 people	35,000 people
Minor tribes	9	1,000–10,000 people	4,300 people
Other Units	ca. 20	50–2,000 people	
Subtribes		4–60 per tribe	20 per tribe
Lineages		2–9 per subtribe	5 per subtribe
Households		30–250 per subtribe	100 per subtribe
		15–50 per lineage	30 per lineage
Individuals			5–6 per household

territorial and political ties with a subtribe became in time identified with it and were incorporated genealogically. Equally, individuals and groups severing territorial and political ties with a subtribe became in time lost to it and were eventually omitted from the genealogies. A subtribe was a named group, usually having a descriptive rather than a personal title, unlike the subtribe's composite lineages. Members of a subtribe, who emphasized the unique origin and history of their group, shared a common identity and a sense of group honor and reputation. A subtribe was also the most endogamous unit in the society; most marriages occurred between group members.

Members of a subtribe received rights to use land by virtue of group membership. A subtribe was partly a territorial group in that many of its members shared pasture space. Much of the unity of residence and action among group members centered on the headman, because pasture rights and migration schedules derived from him. Not all members always occupied the same territory, however, partly because of land shortage and conflict over land and other issues, and most subtribes utilized territory in several or more, sometimes contiguous, locations. Territorial separation was part of a process of segmentation and was one way that new subtribes were formed.

A short history of a subtribe within the Darrehshuri tribe illustrates these points. Qermezi ("The Red Ones") subtribe was said to have originated at some unknown time with three brothers, said to be lowly shepherds, who asked to share pastures with members of what is considered to be the "original" Qermezi lineage. Their progeny increased and other families joined them in sharing pastures and migrating. They fought in battles on behalf of khans of the Darrehshuri tribe, attracted their attention ("who are those brave red-faced ones?"),[6] and were rewarded with choice grazing lands, which earned them membership in the Darrehshuri tribe and, by extension, the Qashqa'i confederacy. In the 1940s, when Qashqa'i and others resuming nomadism competed over pasture space, members of Qermezi subtribe, now large in size, divided according to lineage distinctions and began to occupy separate pastures with the help of rival Darrehshuri khans who were feuding. Political unity vis-à-vis these khans was maintained, however, and all members of the subtribe still fell under the authority of a single headman. His authority was strongest over those who were closest to him in descent and residence. In the 1960s, continued use of separate pastures and internal disputes aided and encouraged the development of rival leadership, but no rival successfully secured land for supporters, either from khans whose power in these matters was diminishing or independently in the confusion of the national land reform, and the process of formal political division was slowed. In the 1970s the main rival failed to secure government recognition of his leadership; the subtribe would have formally divided had this occurred.

A *tribe* (tayefeh) was the political group headed by a family of khans who regulated its affairs vis-à-vis the ilkhani and other powers. It was composed of many subtribes of equivalent rank, each structurally equidistant from the khans' leadership, which stood separate from them. A tribe was also partly a territorial group because most of its subtribes occupied contiguous pastures in winter and summer areas. Such proximity was a function of tribal leadership, for khans allocated land in nearby locations to loyal groups and served those groups within their territorial domain. Just as individuals and groups affiliated to a subtribe and became incorporated in it, so did subtribes affiliate to khans and become tribal members. In this way a tribe was able to expand territorially. Subtribes remained attached to a tribe through acts of political allegiance to its leaders. A tribe's component subtribes were diverse in putative origins, of which their names provide possible but not indisputable evidence. Members of each subtribe asserted a unique origin and identity, a means by which their group maintained a separate

6. Qermezi detractors are fond of noting that the khans said, "who are those red butts?" instead.

identity within the tribe. A tribe also provided a source of identification for its members through common leaders, territorial contiguity, and certain cultural criteria. It was the wider endogamous unit; people who did not marry fellow subtribal members usually married fellow tribal members.

The Qashqa'i *confederacy* (il-e Qashqa'i) was a political amalgamation of groups brought into being in the eighteenth, nineteenth, and twentieth centuries through the coordinating offices of ilkhanis and their predecessors, the pressures of the state, and (after the 1850s) the presence of foreign powers. Nomadic pastoralists in Fars during this period formed sociopolitical attachments to tribes and tribal confederacies because of competition over choice land and the need for leaders to negotiate land rights and protect them from intrusive forces. The Iranian state during this same period organized many of its nomadic pastoralists into administrative and military units. And local elites sought people who could put land into production, generate revenue, and protect land from encroachment. These three processes worked together to form the Qashqa'i confederacy and other similar groups. The success of both levels of Qashqa'i khans in securing and defending pastoral and agricultural land and creating effective ties with other powers helps to explain the preeminence of the Qashqa'i confederacy in the region.[7]

The Qashqa'i confederacy emerged precisely because of the intensifying interaction of tribally organized nomadic pastoralists in Fars and the surrounding sedentary, state-organized society. The Shahilu assumed an intermediary position; indeed, in the absence of state intrusion, the Shahilu would have had few functions to perform. The ecological, strategic, and geopolitical factors present in Fars simply contributed to an intensity of interaction that was unusual for nomadic pastoralists.

Two processes served to unify the Qashqa'i as a political confederacy: active relationships between the ilkhani and khans or other leaders of the constituent sociopolitical units and treatment of it by external powers as a single administrative, military, political, and cultural entity. As one of its primary functions, the confederacy produced coordinated political and military action; it was an administrative unit and ideological framework in which political and military alliances were arranged.

7. For contrasting statements about tribal confederacies in southwest Asia, see Sahlins (1968:45–46) and de Planhol (1972:109). For an insightful analysis of the Brahui tribal confederacy in Pakistani Baluchistan, see Swidler (1969).

This did not imply, however, unified action on the part of all constituent units. The tribes of the confederacy were not hierarchically ranked, although one tribe was attached to the ilkhani and both benefited and suffered from this association, and each exercised considerable autonomy.

Groups were defined more distinctly and precisely when they joined the confederacy because they became more institutionalized and occupied a definite position in the hierarchy of groups, and because they thus assumed structures and statuses identical with groups already part of the confederacy. In some cases, tribes were initially formed when groups affiliated to the confederacy. The process of confederacy formation, in other words, could lead to additional tribal formation. The confederacy as the political expression of a number of tribes could strengthen itself by incorporating other tribes as well as other groups that then assumed tribal status and tribal structures. Tribal formation was therefore a process occurring from the top down as well as from the bottom up. Individuals and groups could not ordinarily be members of the confederacy without also being members of a tribe, a situation also true for the components of tribes, for subtribes were formed when groups affiliated to khans of a tribe.

These different processes, which were ongoing, help to explain the confusion in historical records and the literature concerning the exact composition of the Qashqa'i confederacy, for its tribes and other sociopolitical components have varied through history. The initial heterogeneity of the groups coaffiliating with the Shahilu facilitated additions of groups of heterogeneous origins and the movement of groups within the confederacy as well as into and out of it (in many cases leaving and joining other tribal groups in the region). From the mid-nineteenth century, state agencies, foreign powers, and scholars have diligently attempted to record the names and sizes of the confederacy components, which most assumed were fixed entities, and as a result all their lists and figures vary considerably.[8] Ambiguities in local expression and state and foreign usage of the terms *tireh, tayefeh,* and *il,* which in some contexts were interchangeable, add to the confusion. In addition, groups with identical names were found among the Qashqa'i tribes, subtribes, and affiliated groups, as well as throughout Fars, the Zagros

8. Fasa'i (1895–96b), *Gazetteer of Persia* (1918:805–09), Christian (1919), Kayhan (1932–33), Field (1939), Bahmanbegi (1945–46), Magee (1948:16), Hand (1963), Oberling (1960, 1974), Peiman (1968), Bani Hashimi et al. (1977).

Mountains, and even Iran and the wider region. In some cases identically named groups may indicate common origins and the process of group fission, but this association should not be assumed. Government figures on the Qashqa'i, always grossly inaccurate, have usually included only nomads, while Qashqa'i leaders, who included settled Qashqa'i, compiled their figures opportunistically according to political circumstances. In the 1940s Naser Khan quoted a figure of 80,000 to army officials interested in conscription and 400,000 to officials responsible for the distribution of government monopoly goods (Magee 1948:15).

The first known list of the confederacy's components, published in 1865, includes eleven names: three were major Qashqa'i tribes of the twentieth century, three others minor tribes, and five unknown today (Pelly 1865a:182). A second, more carefully assembled list refers to 1875. It includes twenty names, the first four of which were the major Qashqa'i tribes of the twentieth century and the last five the supporting bodies to the ilkhani and khans (Curzon 1892:114).[9] Another list refers to 1890 and distinguishes between fourteen nomadic and four settled tribes, and again the main tribes of the twentieth century are listed first (Curzon 1892:114). A much longer list of the confederacy's components was recorded a few years later by Fasa'i, who includes sixty-five groups but apparently does not differentiate between large groups (tribes) with khan leadership and their component smaller groups (subtribes) (1895–96b). Almost all the names he lists are found today among the tribes, subtribes, and other components of the confederacy. In the twentieth century and apparently before, the Qashqa'i confederacy consisted of five large major tribes (together constituting approximately 75 percent of the total Qashqa'i population), a number of smaller ones, and other sociopolitical units. While the five tribes were fairly well established entities in this period, given the presence in each

9. Morier does not include the Qashqa'i in his list of the sixteen principal tribes of Iran (1837:321–36), nor does he mention them in his other works (1816, 1818), which may indicate that, as of the very early nineteenth century when he gathered most of his information, the group was not yet coalesced or prominent, a suggestion corresponding with the historical analysis presented earlier in this work. Dupré mentions the Qashqa'i ("Kachkai") at the end of a list, arranged apparently according to importance, of the thirty-nine Turkic-speaking tribes of Iran (1819:456). J. Sheil, who published a long list of the tribes of Iran for 1856, unfortunately left out the Qashqa'i. He commented, "enumeration of the . . . branches of the Kashkai . . . is omitted as being tedious" (1856:399).

of a ruling khan family and associated institutional supports, the smaller tribes and other units were not.

The *Amaleh* tribe ("Workers"), associated with the ilkhani and the Shahilu lineage, constituted the group of personal retainers and others drawn to the paramount leaders because of their activities and the benefits they offered. Through the nineteeth century the Amaleh was a relatively small group compared with the other major Qashqa'i tribes, and contained the ilkhani's retainers, bodyguards, military force, and close supporters. During periods when the ilbegi was a power in his own right and maintained encampments separate from those of the ilkhani, the ilkhani's Amaleh and the ilbegi's Amaleh were considered separate units. Upon seizing control of the confederacy in 1904, following a succession of weak ilkhanis, Isma'il Khan incorporated many small, previously independent groups in Fars and the region into the Amaleh in order to build his strength, a process he continued as the khans of the other Qashqa'i tribes grew in power, facilitated by British and German manipulations during World War I. Under Reza Shah and in the absence of the paramount leaders, many small Qashqa'i tribes were isolated from the main body of the confederacy and were more vulnerable than the large tribes to the army's efforts to annihilate the Qashqa'i as a coherent group (Magee 1948:71). Naser Khan, upon his return to Fars in 1941, incorporated many of these groups into the Amaleh. In the twentieth century and possibly before, members of the Amaleh had the most diverse ethnolinguistic and tribal origins of the confederacy. The tribe consisted of two parts: a nucleus called *dour-e khaneh* ("those around the house") or *dourebar* ("entourage"), containing approximately five hundred households serving the khans as a personal retinue, and the rest of the Amaleh, who were not retainers but sought affiliation with the khans in order to receive necessary services. In the 1960s the Amaleh contained forty to sixty subtribes and approximately 45,000 people.[10] Its garmsir (winter pastures) was near Firuzabad and its sarhad (summer pastures) near Khosrow Shirin, both centrally located vis-à-vis other Qashqa'i.

The *Darrehshuri* tribe derived its name from Darreh Shur ("Salty Valley"), a place near Semirom in northern Fars. Darrehshuri khans claim

10. The figures included in this and following paragraphs are approximations based upon information provided to me by many Qashqa'i leaders, including Jehangir Khan Darrehshuri (personal interviews, August 1973, Amherst, Massachusetts), and on the sources cited in Oberling (1960:179–89) and Kortum (1979a:31). Kortum (1979b:79) lists the Amaleh tirehs and their population figures.

their ancestors forced the Shahilu family and the other Qashqa'i tribes to leave the area in the early nineteenth century and then monopolized it for themselves. A variant pronunciation of the name is Darrehshuli, which can possibly be connected with the Shul, a Turkic tribe that came to Fars from Luristan in the thirteenth century (Minorsky 1934b:391–92). Some Qashqa'i believe the Darrehshuri descend from the *qizilbash,* a religious military order composed of Turkic tribesmen during Safavid times. An ancestor of today's Darrehshuri khans, Min-bash Haidar (or Haidar Minbashi), was said to have been a qizilbash leader and a subordinate of Sir Robert Sherley, an Englishman serving as military advisor in the court of Shah Abbas (1587–1628). *Minbashi,* "Master of a Thousand Men," is one of the Turkic titles applied to offi-cers in the Safavid armies. Shah Abbas is believed to have awarded the Vardasht region near Semirom to Minbash Haidar. He and his followers settled there, and their descendants joined the Qashqa'i confederacy during the reign of Karim Khan Zand. Another version of Darrehshuri origins is that Jani Aqa (no relation to the Shahilu), who was Nader Shah's head groom, fled Khorasan in 1747 when Nader Shah was killed. He traveled to Mahur-e Milati in Fars with fifteen hundred horses, which he sold in order to buy land in the area; he established himself as leader (*kikha*) there and acquired retainers (a mark of leaders).

A popular legend told by many Darrehshuri concerns the origin of their ruling khan lineage and its founder, Allahqoli (Minbash Haidar's grandfather). Allahqoli, a dark-skinned ("black"), ugly Bakhtiyari, was a retainer of the leader of the Naderlu in the plain of Darreh Shur.[11] One day it began to rain heavily and everyone in the encampment, including the leader's daughter, with whom Allohqoli had a secret and pure relationship, rushed to pound in the tent stakes more securely. Allahqoli went to cover her up with a felt cape to keep her from getting wet. Her father, sitting in his tent, became annoyed when he saw them talking and told his son to stop their conversation ("cut their speech"). The son, who thought he said "cut her head," cut her throat. Allahqoli, afraid he would be blamed, fled. He sought sanctuary with khans in the region, soon proved himself to be strong and capable, and was eventually appointed a headman. He then returned to the Naderlu camp with many followers, took over as group leader, and gradually

11. Naderlu was a branch of the Dadekai tribe of the Oghuz, present in northern Fars before the arrival of the Shahilu family; Malek Mansur Khan, personal interview, 28 August 1979, Tehran.

drew others into his political domain. Out of this, the Darrehshuri tribe was born. His descendants have monopolized Darrehshuri leadership since that time, and today Naderlu is one of the tribe's many subtribes. Naderlu tribespeople regard themselves as the social equals, if not superiors, of the Darrehshuri khans and refuse to address them by the term *khan,* on the grounds that, according to history, the Naderlu were once tribal leaders and the ancestors of today's khans, their retainers.

In the 1960s Darrehshuri contained forty-four subtribes and approximately 45,000 people. Its garmsir was near Dogonbadan and its sarhad near Semirom, both politically significant locations. Dogonbadan is northwest of Shiraz, far from the winter pastures of the ilkhani and most other Qashqa'i tribes, and Semirom and its territories are the northernmost of Qashqa'i summer pastures, close to Bakhtiyari territory and political refuge with the Bakhtiyari khans.[12]

Kashkuli Bozorg derived its name from *kashkul,* a bowl or hollowed-out gourd carried by itinerant sufis. The Kashkuli tribe is believed to have originated in the Kalhor tribe, brought by Karim Khan Zand from the Kermanshah area of western Iran to Fars. Today's Kashkuli disagree as to whether the Kalhor tribe was composed of Lurs or Kurds, but all agree that its members became Turks after they settled in Fars. One day, it is believed, Jani Khan, the ilkhani, was traveling through the area where Karim Khan had settled the Kalhor and saw a beautiful young woman named Nazli rescue a calf (or ram) from drowning in a raging river. He wanted her as a wife and sought permission from her brothers Hasan and Mohammad, who agreed to the marriage. Later Jani Khan appointed them leaders of their group, which became the Kashkuli tribe, and gave them the title of aqa. Kashkuli forces under Qasem, son of Hasan Aqa, fought in the Anglo-Persian war of 1856, and the central government rewarded him the title of khan. Later Isma'il Khan nominated three men of the leading lineage as khans, who, because of disputes with him over taxes and the exploitation of the Bushire-Shiraz road, disagreed among themselves and formed separate tribes: Kashkuli Bozorg ("Greater Kashkuli"), Kashkuli Kuchek

12. In the 1870s the Bakhtiyari ilkhani provided refuge and pastures for dissident Darrehshuri groups as well as other Qashqa'i and helped to mediate their conflicts. Bakhtiyari tribespeople have sought refuge in Qashqa'i territory as well (Garthwaite 1983:89, 148, 159).

("Lesser Kashkuli"), and Qarachahi. They are separate tribes today, each with its own family of khans.

Another version of the origin of the Kashkuli is that Hasan and Mohammad (the same two brothers) deserted Nader Shah's army after his conquest of India in the 1730s and went or returned to Fars along with other Turks. The two brothers, members of the Dadekai tribe, affiliated with the Shish Boluki (below) and became farmers, carpenters, and itinerant merchants. One year in winter pastures, Jani Khan, the ilkhani, happened upon their sister, Nazli, while she was tending sheep and soon took her as his wife. He appointed her brothers as leaders and they formed the Kashkuli tribe. A third version, which ascribes Zand origins to the Kashkuli khans, states that Jani Khan married the sister of Qasem Khan Zand, a collateral descendant of Karim Khan Zand, and offered him the leadership of the Kashkuli tribe. In his rise to power, Qasem forced Mamassani Lurs out of choice pastures and claimed the areas for the Kashkuli, where today many still reside. A significant portion of the Kashkuli trace Mamassani origins. In the 1960s Kashkuli Bozorg contained from forty to fifty subtribes and approximately 25,000 people. Its garmsir was near Mahur-e Milati and its sarhad near Ardekan.

The *Shish Boluki* tribe ("Six Regions" or "Six Family Groups") possibly derived its name from the six regions from which early members came or stands for six tribal sections. Some say the group has Khalaj origins and was present in Fars before the arrival of the Shahilu family, and others say it accompanied Chengiz Khan when the Mongols entered Iran. *Boluk* is a variation of the term *bunku* (patrilineal group). In the 1960s the tribe contained twenty large and twenty small subtribes and 35,000 people. Its garmsir was near Farrashband and its sarhad near Eqlid.

Farsi Madan, "Those Who Do Not Know Persian," is said to have once had less contact with Persian-speakers than other Qashqa'i tribes. It also claims Khalaj origins, and its ancestors are reputed to have come to the Kuhgiluyeh region near Behbahan from the Tehran area in late Safavid times and then farther south into Fars, where they joined other Turkic groups, before the time of Jani Aqa and prior to the arrival of Karim Khan Zand. A Farsi Madan leader who held the title of beg fought with the Governor of Fars in a rebellion against Shah Abbas in 1590 (Fasa'i 1895–96b:124). In the nineteenth century, Farsi Madan leaders purchased a large tract of summer pastures at Padena from a

Basseri leader who had been granted the area by the central government. In the 1960s, Farsi Madan khans who had inherited this land sold it to members of their subtribes to avoid the confiscations of land reform. The tribe contained twenty-one large and small subtribes in the 1960s (Marsden 1978:7) and 20,000 people. Its garmsir was Jereh and its sarhad Padena.

Smaller tribes were also part of the confederacy. Some of them, and some of their component subtribes, originated from the larger tribes. The smaller tribes varied in their political affiliations and degrees of political autonomy. Qarachahi and Kashkuli Kuchek, considered as politically autonomous units, had their own families of ruling khans, who were more independent than the leaders of the other small tribes. The leaders of Safi Khani and Namadi adhered more closely to the ilkhani's leadership, and these tribes were sometimes considered part of the Amaleh. One or several subtribes of a tribe could separate and establish autonomy. Some of these new groups continued to express loyalty to khans of their original tribe, while others sought new khans and tribes. Still others gave their loyalty to the ilkhani and avoided the secondary level of khans, a mechanism by which groups dissatisfied with these khans were still afforded protection and land rights. As a result, Qashqa'i groups unattached to the five major Qashqa'i tribes, or to Qarachahi or Kashkuli Kuchek, were often considered to be part of Amaleh.

Qarachahi, or "Black Well," was once part of the Kashkuli tribe, and its khan family traces descent from an ancestor shared with the khan families of Kashkuli Bozorg and Kashkuli Kuchek. Some Qashqa'i believe that Qarachahi was the first of the many Turkic groups to emigrate to Fars from central Asia. Qarachahi leaders were said to be allied with Safavid shahs, and the group affiliated with the Shahilu family at the end of the Safavid dynasty (Christian 1919:50). The tribespeople of Qarachahi were more territorially dispersed than those of other tribes. In the 1960s it contained eight subtribes and 3,000 to 10,000 people. Its garmsir was near Mahur-e Milati and its sarhad near Padena.

Kashkuli Kuchek was also once part of the larger Kashkuli tribe. Of its thirteen subtribes, only one (Nafar) was said to be Turkic by origin, while the rest were said to have Bakhtiyari, Kurd, Lak, Mamassani, and Boir Ahmad origins. Such heterogeneity of origin, whether actual or reputed, is typical of tribal groups in Fars. For example, members of the twelve subtribes of the Basseri tribe of the Khamseh confederacy claimed origins from Persian nomads indigenous to the area, Turks from Khorasan, Arabs from the Arabian peninsula, Qarachahi Qashqa'i, Nafar Turks, and former villagers from Sarvistan (Barth 1961:52–53, passim). The Aqa Jari, considered a Kuhgiluyeh Lur tribe, is an amalgamation of Turkic, Persian, and Lur elements (Oberling 1964:172–80). Kashkuli Kuchek's population was 4,300 (Salzer 1974:79–91). Its garmsir was near Hengam and its sarhad near Kakan.

Safi Khani, or "Those of Safi Khan" (perhaps an early leader), is said to have come from Luristan. It contained ten subtribes and 4,000 people. Its garmsir was near Farrashband and its sarhad near Khosrow Shirin. *Namadi,* or "Felt Rug," contained four subtribes and 7,000 people. Its garmsir was near Farrashband and its sarhad near Asopas. Other smaller tribes include *Igdir, Jafarbeglu, Rahimi, Bollu,* and *Gallehzan* ("Robbers of Flocks").[13]

Settled Qashqa'i were part of the confederacy as well. Some Qashqa'i living in villages maintained active political contacts with subtribes and tribes of the confederacy and are to be considered as part of these groups. Other Qashqa'i settled in villages exercised their affiliations more passively yet could also occasionally be drawn into political expression. Many Qashqa'i living in towns and cities in the region and in the oil fields after 1908 retained their Qashqa'i identity and worked, resided, and intermarried with members of their lineages, subtribes, and tribes. Many Qashqa'i in Abadan, Behbahan, and Gachsaran (major oil areas), as well as in Shiraz, lived as tribal groups in shantytowns, town quarters, and even apartment buildings. Some reports from the nineteenth and twentieth centuries estimate that as many as half of the Qashqa'i were settled. Regardless of the accuracy of these estimates, settled Qashqa'i should not be excluded from the confederacy, for many of them continued to associate in terms of lineages, subtribes, and often tribes, and many of their leaders were part of the Qashqa'i political hierarchy. Also, the processes of sedentarization and nomadization were (and are) ongoing, and a change in mobility did not necessarily alter political affiliations and loyalties.

The largest single settled Qashqa'i group with a specific identity is the *Abivardi* (*Bolvardi* represents a more informal usage). The Abivardi originated in Khorasan and is Turkic by origin, possibly Afshar. Mem-

13. Igdir was one of the twenty-four original Oghuz tribes, while Rahimi was once one of the most powerful, warlike Qashqa'i tribes (Oberling 1960:179, 189).

bers of the group today believe that Nader Shah sent their ancestors to Fars in the early eighteenth century to oppose the Shahilu; instead, the two groups allied. Abivardi consisted of a settled component (Abivardi Khaki, "Abivardi of the Earth") and a nomadic one (Abivardi Badi, "Abivardi of the Wind"). Abivardi Khaki settled in several villages near Shiraz (one is named Bolvardi) and in Shiraz, where there is a Bolvardi quarter. A number of village Abivardi were itinerant merchants serving Qashqa'i and surrounding territory. Wealthy Abivardi were also merchants, and the most prominent ones served Qashqa'i ilkhanis as scribes and were the Shahilu family's most trusted commercial agents in Shiraz.[14] Bolvardi subtribes having both settled and nomadic components are also found in the major Qashqa'i tribes.

Fairly well-defined and bounded groups that specialized in music (Usa, Asheq), blacksmithing (Ahangar, Largar, Gorbat), craft production, camel herding (Korosh, Jadd), livestock trading (Gavbaz), and peddling provided vital services to the Qashqa'i as well as others in the region and were also part of the Qashqa'i confederacy. Partly because of their patterns of mobility and subsistence, which differed from those of most other Qashqa'i, members of these groups were not as politically active in the confederacy as those of the groups considered above. Real or perceived cultural differences also served to set some of these groups apart from other Qashqa'i; some were considered to be gypsies while the Korosh traced Baluch origins and spoke Baluchi.

Another category of sociopolitical groups attached to the Qashqa'i confederacy includes those who were ordinarily politically independent. They chose their own leaders and handled their own internal affairs without interference from Qashqa'i leaders, and if they paid state taxes they did so directly or through district governors. They found their own seasonal pastures, sometimes renting them, and developed economic and political ties with landowners and headmen to protect their use of land. On specific occasions, however, they allied with the ilkhani or khans when some benefits were likely. Some of these groups had never formally been part of the Qashqa'i confederacy, while others had cut their ties and become independent. An example of a group in this category is the *Sorkhi* tribe. Its leader has been labeled an "outlaw" (Oberling 1974:156), but his distinctive characteristic was political independence. In the 1940s Shahbaz Sorkhi bought land southwest of Shiraz from Persian landowners and enhanced his power by bringing

14. Bahman Abdollahi, personal interview, 6 November 1982, Philadelphia.

Qashqa'i (members of the Safi Khani tribe and the Alikurdlu subtribe) as well as Sorkhis to cultivate it. Sorkhi leaders have exercised power in the twentieth century, and the government has either executed them or killed them in battle. The subtribes of Sorkhi trace origins from western and eastern Fars (Dashtistan and Fasa); they combined under Lur leadership, and the group today is considered both Lur and Qashqa'i. In the twentieth century most of its members were settled.

A further category includes groups once part of the Qashqa'i confederacy who remained independent or who sought or were assigned other affiliations. The efforts of the two Pahlavi shahs to pacify and sedentarize the Qashqa'i people and depose their highest leaders, combined with the effects of economic decline, aided the process by which groups became independent. The *Kordshuli* tribe was part of the Qashqa'i confederacy in the nineteenth and early twentieth centuries (Curzon 1892:114, Peiman 1968:224), an affiliation enabling its members to maintain access to resources in a region competed over by others. In the 1930s, because of the ravages of Reza Shah, it no longer fell under the administration of Qashqa'i leaders, and it remained independent until 1943, when the government, in an attempt to dilute Qashqa'i power, placed it under Khamseh administration. Kordshuli winter and summer pastures are located between Qashqa'i and Khamseh territories, which facilitated the administrative change. In the 1940s and early 1950s the Kordshuli professed Qashqa'i "nationality" but took orders from and accepted Khamseh administrators (Magee 1948:102). In the 1970s many Kordshuli considered themselves Khamseh and not Qashqa'i, but their unity was more a function of spatial proximity than of political integration (Swee 1981:48–49, 169). Qashqa'i khans consider the Kordshuli a purely Qashqa'i tribe and cite its Turkic origin. Kordshuli themselves believe that both their core section and chiefly dynasty have Bakhtiyari origins, and their other sections trace Baharlu (Turkic), Qashqa'i, and Mamassani Lur origins (Swee 1981:78). Most Kordshuli today speak Luri as their primary language.

Finally, non-Qashqa'i agriculturalists who worked land owned or controlled by Qashqa'i khans were called *ra'iyat-e Qashqa'i* and often fell under the confederacy's political protection. Khans collected their taxes and provided some mediatory services. Some villagers provided paramilitary support to Qashqa'i fighters during conflicts and reported on government and other troop movements and in return were protected from raids and some government incursions. In the early twentieth century, one hundred thousand villagers in Fars fell under the

Qashqa'i khans' control (Sykes 1930:478). Peasants sometimes attached themselves politically, and to some degree socially, to the Qashqa'i subtribes frequenting their districts, and their villages were often selected by Qashqa'i nomads who settled. Intermarriage helped to solidify the bonds between them.

The existence of these many sociopolitical categories, combined with ambiguities in local and official expression of terms, the movement of groups into and out of the confederacy, the varying degrees of confederacy cohesion, and the presence of many identically named groups within and outside the confederacy and Qashqa'i territory, explains why outsiders had difficulty ascertaining the precise composition of the Qashqa'i confederacy at any given time. Many of the individuals and groups were difficult to locate temporally and spatially. In addition, outsiders could not always identify individual Qashqa'i and distinguish them from others in the region. Wilson states that it was "extremely difficult to separate the nomad families from the sedentary peasants and cultivators of those districts in which the Qashqai have properties, or encamp, or from the deserters and refugees from other tribes of Fars" and notes the complicating presence of the protégés, allies, tenants, and cultivators of the Qashqa'i (1916:51–52).

When the government exiled the paramount Qashqa'i leaders in the 1950s, the component tribes of the confederacy became independent. When the government restricted the power and authority of the khans of the tribes in the 1960s, many subtribes and subtribal sections became more politically independent. Between the 1960s and 1978, some Qashqa'i maintained few active political links to khans, tribes, or in some cases subtribes. State officials, however, consistently dealt with nomadic Qashqa'i in terms of these tribal and subtribal identities, which served to maintain them as politically significant units, if sometimes only on administrative and conceptual levels. Before the 1960s, tribes and subtribes had been flexible, changing sociopolitical and socioterritorial groups, but government action in the period that followed dealt with them as fixed entities and hence solidified them.

THE PARAMOUNT RULING LINEAGE

The paramount leaders of the Qashqa'i have always been members of a single patrilineage; they trace descent from Amir Ghazi Shahilu and his direct descendant six generations later, Jani Aqa, considered the founder of the confederacy. The longevity of this family's rule and that of the Qashqa'i as a polity in Iran are vitally connected. While some of Iran's nontribal, urban-based elite families are as historically prominent as the Shahilu family, and have been equally or more wealthy, they have not enjoyed the long-term political support behind them that the Shahilu has enjoyed, nor did they attract as much attention from state rulers and foreign powers. The Shahilu family as a unit represented a political bloc in Iran, whereas other elite families tended to produce single individuals who exercised power and/or authority at specific times.

Another distinguishing feature of the Shahilu family is the charisma attached to its individual members, especially male leaders. Charisma is defined here both in the specific Weberian sense of special contact with the sacred and in the generic sense of perceived worthiness to lead. The quality was based on features centering on notions of "holiness," which many believed descended by blood from the earliest known ancestor, Amir Ghazi Shahilu, who was possibly a sufi and who assisted his reputed relative, Shah Isma'il, in establishing Shi'i Islam as the state religion in the early sixteenth century. Some believed that Amir Ghazi's descendants, including those living today, inherited by blood a special "presence" or "essence," which was exhibited, for example, in the rendering of just decisions, settling of disputes, and curing.[15] I was present when an educated urban Persian, a former member of parliament, visited a Shahilu khan in order to borrow a shirt, "preferably old, recently worn, and unwashed," which he would wear in order to cure himself of a lingering chest ailment. The Qashqa'i regarded former campsites and hearths of the ilkhanis as sacred places where even today they seek cures, swear oaths, and settle disputes. The lines of stones marking ancient tent sites were sacrosanct and undisturbed. Dust from ancient hearths was carried away and stored for future cures, and people would often swear "by the ashes of Jani Aqa's hearth." Many Qashqa'i believed that misfortune would befall the families of those who acted against the Shahilu and often told stories of those so stricken. Some Shahilu family members identified themselves and their ancestors as sufis and stressed the associated inner spiritual qualities, which, long

15. The notion of the khans' charisma (a gift from God) also extends to such behavior as superlative hunting skills. Malek Mansur Khan once said, "the khan must be able to shoot, with a single bullet, a falcon from his horse in full gallop, but he must never be seen target practicing" (Reinhold Loeffler, personal communication, 2 February 1982). The Arabic concept of *baraka,* or supernatural grace, is comparable. The Qashqa'i did not use this term or, to my knowledge, any equivalent one.

before the establishment of rule by Muslim clergy in Iran, they considered far superior to qualities associated with such clergy.

For many Qashqa'i and other Iranians, Shahilu charisma was also based on more contemporary traits, particularly those associated with the khans' consistent opposition to the Pahlavi regimes and to despotic state rulers and regimes in general. Their long-term stand against the Pahlavi shahs and their association with opposition leaders such as Mosaddeq, Bazargan, Bani Sadr, and Khomeini (only as long as he was in opposition) placed them unequivocally in the ranks of those who struggled against tyranny and despotism.

The Shahilu lineage, a small family group and separate sociopolitical unit since at least the time of Jani Aqa, did not derive from a Qashqa'i tribe, as far as is known. It was never a "tribe" in the way that the kin groups of many other tribal leaders in Iran, including those who became state rulers, were perceived to have been. Paramount leaders and followers maintained no belief in or fiction of common descent or common blood, as is reported to be the case with many other politically centralized tribal groups in the Middle East. Both sides, however, believed that they were jointly and equivalently Qashqa'i, that they shared a history to which both contributed, and that they were different as a unit from all other Iranians. Neither claimed a "purer" Qashqa'i identity or background, although each pointed to certain Qashqa'i segments with reputed non-Qashqa'i origins (which, as has been indicated, applies to *all* Qashqa'i). In the twentieth century, if not before, members of the Shahilu family consciously maintained close ties with the Qashqa'i people. They did not employ cultural grounds to set themselves apart from them nor did they seek their primary identity with Iran's upper class, despite their own membership in it. This process of identification was closely tied to the politics of the relationship between the Qashqa'i and the state.

Family ties within the Shahilu lineage were often close, despite the policies of government officials and foreign agents to create rivalries among its members in order to divide and rule them. The few reported incidents of serious conflict occurred in 1846 among the sons of the ilkhani and ilbegi, who were then detained as hostages in Tehran, and during World War I, when competing foreign and local forces in Fars offered rewards to those within Isma'il Khan's family to oppose him. No murders within the lineage occurred, in contrast with acts occurring within the leadership families of the other major tribes and confederacies in the area—the Bakhtiyari (Garthwaite 1983), Mamassani, Arabs of Khuzistan, possibly Basseri (Barth 1961:84), and Boir Ahmad. Of the twenty-one men in the leading dynasty of the Boir Ahmad tribe who became khan or were close pretenders, nineteen died violent deaths and the twentieth chose to be blinded rather than killed (Loeffler 1978:158; also Fazel 1979:39, 43, 44). Oberling (1974:78) and Garthwaite (1983:38) attribute the lack of internal family violence among the Shahilu to the infrequency of polygyny, a practice that can cause disputes over succession and create competition and hostility among the sons of cowives.

The sociopolitical separation of the Shahilu lineage from other Qashqa'i components gave it considerable autonomy through time. The lineage was not socially or structurally bolstered or constrained by patrilineal links with other Qashqa'i sections. It maintained this separation and created a high degree of exclusivity through marriage restrictions. The lineage's small size at any given time meant that the ideal of endogamy was difficult to practice, but it was applied consistently to women of the family. Those who were not members of the family were rarely allowed to marry its women. The lineage did, however, ally with prominent Iranian families through the marriages of its men. Men, enjoying a potentially wide range of marriage partners, married within the core of the lineage or with collateral kin (the most common patterns), or they married with a few select khan families of the component Qashqa'i tribes (Kashkuli Bozorg in particular), with other tribal elites such as the Bakhtiyari khans, or with nontribal regional and national elite, including provincial and national rulers. All of these marriages created different kinds of political alliances.

Women of the Shahilu family lacked this range of possible marriage partners because more control was exercised over their marriages. Some women never married, partly because of the sexual imbalance resulting from men's more frequent marriage outside the family; the reason often given was that suitable men of comparable or higher status did not exist.[16] The fact that women inherited property, including land, was a major reason for not allowing them to marry outside the lineage, because husbands would assume a degree of control over the property and it would eventually be inherited by children who traced descent from their fathers. Marriage would also move these women away from their natal families, given patrilocal and virilocal residence after marriage, and, in addition, it would deprive them of much of their power and

16. The efforts of mediators on behalf of Mohammad Reza Shah, who sought a Shahilu woman to marry, were rebuffed. Shahilu family members commented that their women marry only persons of equivalent or higher status.

influence within and outside the family. Therefore, some women chose to remain unmarried, sometimes over the objections of family members. The title of *bibi* was used for the family's married and unmarried women, the title of *khan* for all its men.

The wife and mother of the ilkhani, and sometimes his older female kin such as sisters and father's sisters, played important political roles, both in a tribal context and in the many extratribal relationships he established. They acted in his absence, which was frequent, and they had their own seals, with which they formalized documents. They usually remained with the primary residence, which in the twentieth century was a mountain encampment or a house in Firuzabad, Shiraz, Tehran (house arrest), or abroad (exile). Khadijeh Khanom (Bibi Khanom) was the "admirable wife" of Isma'il Khan, "whose subtle understanding of all that was going on about her, her encouragement to all those near to her, and her tenacity and strength of character, equipped her well for the difficult position of Il-Khan's wife." She urged him to take military action against the British in 1918 after their forces had killed Darrehshuri women and children (Safiri 1976:150, 251). Bibi Mehrafruz, Isma'il Khan's sister, who was known as Bibi Qashqa'i, assisted the Swedish officers of the gendarmes in 1912 in order to facilitate her family's influence in Tehran, joined the struggle against foreign usurpers who were violating Iran's neutrality during World War I, and assisted in government efforts to establish order in the Firuzabad area under Reza Shah at a time when her father and brothers were in prison or under house arrest. She owned land and a village, was described as being always armed and on horseback, and never married (Lindberg 1955:143–45). In the middle and late 1950s Farrokh Bibi, Naser Khan's sister, represented the family in Iran and acted on its behalf, and in the 1970s Homa Bibi, Naser Khan's daughter, performed in similar fashion. The shah's restrictions on residence in Iran and travel to Fars for men of the family did not extend to women, who moved about freely and were the major conduits of information among those in exile, other Qashqa'i leaders, and the Qashqa'i people. Other than a few comments by Lindberg (1955), Ullens de Schooten (1956), and Safiri (1976), observers have taken virtually no notice of Shahilu women as political figures, but few discussions with Shahilu men and women on general topics relating to Qashqa'i politics omit them.[17]

17. One Shahilu khan, after reading a published account of Qashqa'i leadership in which I mentioned the prominent role of Shahilu women (Beck 1980c), objected

The Shahilu family was part of Iran's upper class and its national elite. Tribal khans in Iran approximate a hereditary aristocracy, according to Lambton (1967:47). Although she seems to overstate this point and rely too heavily on Malcolm (1829:412), she may be using the term in the European sense of a feudal nobility. Iran did have prominent, wealthy, nontribal families rooted in land, the bureaucracy, and often religious institutions that spanned centuries; several examples include the Qavams (Royce 1981) and Moqaddams (Good 1981). Lambton may have based her notions about Iran's (tribal) hereditary aristocracy in part on her knowledge of the paramount Qashqa'i khans.[18] "Repeated conquest and the inheritance laws of Islam effectively prevented the emergence of such a class [a landed aristocracy]. . . . The only other class, which had, perhaps, some claim to be regarded as hereditary aristocracy was that of the tribal leaders. So far as they constituted such a class, their authority was essentially personal, and derived from their possession of the flocks and tribal followers, not from the possession of land (though tribal leaders often acquired land)" (Lambton 1967:47). The authority of the paramount Qashqa'i khans did not derive from flocks, however, and followers provided only a partial basis. The primary basis of authority was the crucial mediatory position they occupied between other powers and the Qashqa'i people, a position somewhat independent of either, yet drawing power and resources from both. Land was important also, but the family's political fortune did not depend primarily on possession of land, as was the case with many nontribal elite families. The paramount khans remained figures of authority and power decades after Mohammad Reza Shah had confiscated all their land. Islamic inheritance laws did not prevent the emergence of a landed aristocracy in the case of the Bakhtiyari khans, who broke such laws in order to ensure the dominance of one son in the family's aristocratic rule (Garthwaite 1975).

---

strongly. Yet, in our following discussion of the plight of the Shahilu under the Khomeini regime, he talked as much about the politics of women as of men in his family. Vincent Cronin, in a semifictionalized account of the Qashqa'i ("Falqani"), states that the ilkhani's mother held the tribe together and was feared and respected even by the army (1957:34).

18. Lambton visited the camps of the Qashqa'i ilkhani and khans and was said to have traversed a major section of Qashqa'i territory by foot (Mohammad Hosain Khan, personal communication, 29 July 1979, London). Her work on land tenure contains more information on Qashqa'i leaders than on any other tribal leaders in Iran (1953, 1969).

In the twentieth century, the paramount Qashqa'i khans identified less with other members of the upper class than they did with other Qashqa'i, but it is not known if this was also true in the nineteenth century or earlier. In the eighteenth and nineteenth centuries and possibly before, these khans and their ancestors may have been oriented toward urban life and the life-style of the urban elite of the time, but, toward the end of the nineteenth and beginning of the twentieth centuries, they increasingly sought links and an identity with the Qashqa'i people. This contact may have saved them from the fate of many other elites when the regimes they formed or supported fell.[19] The paramount Qashqa'i khans were not associated with ruling regimes to the point that they became tainted by them, as was the case with many other elite families.[20]

Members of the Shahilu family, however, did not live according to standards commonly found among the Qashqa'i people. They established elaborate urban residences and large tent encampments in winter and summer pastures. Their wealth was extensive, and they drew retainers and workers from the Amaleh. Wealth in the form of hospitality, gifts, and favors was lavished on loyal supporters, visitors, and political contacts. This life-style offered to Iranian and foreign observers an image of unlimited wealth and prosperity. In the minds of many urban Persians, such wealth could have been generated only through extortion and theft, and they never understood the bases of its accumulation or the reasons for its redistribution.[21]

But in many ways, members of the Shahilu family often lived quite frugally. They rarely indulged in conspicuous consumption in the form practiced by Iran's upper class. Most lived on a daily basis well below their means, which was intentional and can be seen as a form of inconspicuous consumption. They frequently adopted simple manners of

19. That some of Iran's elite families have survived changes in ruling regimes may be explained in part by the diverse political associations found in each family. A member of the upper class commented to me, with some accuracy, that whenever a regime in Iran fell, half the members of his extended family were released from prison and took top government posts, while the other half that had held top government posts were imprisoned.

20. The relationship between Isma'il Khan and Karim Khan Zand may be one exception, because the next state ruler, Aqa Mohammad Shah Qajar, punished the Shahilu family for its role in holding him hostage in Karim Khan's court.

21. For a discussion of redistribution in chiefdoms that illustrates basic principles probably also operating in nineteenth- and early twentieth-century Qashqa'i society, see Sahlins (1963, 1972).

dress, food, housing, transportation, and entertainment. Naser Khan commented, with only slight exaggeration, that even the most prominent khan should never dress in clothes that the poorest of Qashqa'i men could not afford, and he recounted how he used to walk through the bazaars of Tehran without being recognized as anyone other than an ordinary Iranian.[22]

THE RULING LINEAGES OF THE COMPONENT QASHQA'I TRIBES

Each Qashqa'i tribe was ruled by a family of khans, who both cooperated and competed with one another for the privileges and benefits of active leadership positions. The khans of each tribe were members of a ruling lineage separated from the tribe's subtribes. Khans of the Kashkuli Bozorg, Kashkuli Kuchek, and Qarachahi tribes formed separate lineages but traced common descent, while the other ruling lineages were unrelated by descent. Each family was highly endogamous, and the patterns discussed above for the Shahilu lineage also pertain here, including marriage with people of comparable or higher status. The khans did not establish kinship links through marriage with members of their tribes. Only rarely did men of these families marry nonelite women, and women of these families almost never married nonelite men. One difference with the Shahilu lineage is that almost all women of these khan families married.

Each khan family consisted of two components: men (and their immediate families) who played active political roles and men (and their immediate families) who were marginally involved in or aloof from politics. Those who were marginally political inherited wealth and social position from men who had played roles in Qashqa'i politics in the past. At any given time these tended to be members of the collateral branches of the ruling lineages. Each generation a few of these politically inactive families became even more peripheral, and their high status gradually disappeared. Members of today's ruling families, men more than women, have lost touch with and lack information about some people in collateral branches of their own lineages. The leadership core of each family retained its small, exclusive nature by this sloughing-off process, which relates to the process of political centralization. At the same time as the ilkhani, the state, and other powers

22. Naser Khan, personal interview, 29 August 1979, Tehran.

were seeking out single Qashqa'i leaders with whom to deal, internal social mechanisms were thinning out the number of possible contenders and concentrating power and status in only a few.

Men in both categories were referred to as khan, but in the case of men with little or no political position the title was only honorific and indicated the status of the wider group of which they were a part; in other words, khan was used for all men when they reached the age to function as leaders, but for some, the title was formal and indicated active leadership, while for others it was only a gesture of respect if they did not function as leaders. Young males were sometimes called khan by tribespeople out of respect but not by their own family members, except in jest. Members of the Shahilu lineage did not use the title of khan for any Qashqa'i outside their own family. They sometimes used the title of kalantar when speaking about the second level of leaders, but they usually referred to individuals at this level by their personal names, sometimes with tribal names attached (for example, Ayaz Darrehshuri).[23] The general principle involved in these usages is that people used the titles of khan and bibi for those of equivalent or higher social status than themselves.

Married women of the families were called bibis, as were a few women from non-khan families who had married khans. In one case, a Darrehshuri khan married the daughter of a Persian military general from Tehran; they had met in Tehran at a shooting contest, a skill at which she was proficient. Tribespeople used the title bibi for her as a gesture of respect, while members of the khan's family were always slightly condescending and called her *khanom* (Persian for "lady"). It might be added that she became fluent in Turkic and adopted a more authentic Qashqa'i life-style than that practiced by any of the women in her husband's family. She moved into the summer tent earlier in the season and remained in it longer than any other khan family, and she was the only wife of a Darrehshuri khan to migrate overland with the tribe in the 1960s and 1970s and to spend winters in a tent in winter pastures. Also, she refused to install electricity in the summer tent, unlike other Darrehshuri bibis. As with bibis of the Shahilu lineage, bibis of the khan families played political roles in Qashqa'i contexts, especially when the khans were absent and in matters concerning their

23. Shahilu family members sometimes corrected me when I used the title of khan for members of the second level of leaders.

own and other khan families, but they tended not to play the wider political role that Shahilu women played.

This second level of Qashqa'i khans shared many features of wealth and social position with the paramount khans. Missing were the charismatic qualities and, during the time the paramount khans still lived in Iran, the international connections. After the paramount khans were exiled in the 1950s, the political and economic position of many khans at the secondary level was enhanced. These khans were also members of the national political elite because of the roles they played in regional and occasionally national affairs, the tribal support available to them, and their wealth. Combining the two levels of khans, Qashqa'i khans held at least fourteen seats in parliament (seven different deputies) and one senate seat before the early 1970s (Bill 1975:34), and several seats since then. As large landowners, they were provincial elites and played roles in local, town, and regional affairs. Their wealth was considerable, with a dual base of land and flocks.

I conclude with a short discussion of the khan family of the Darrehshuri tribe with special reference to sociopolitical organization. Leading Darrehshuri figures in the nineteenth and early twentieth centuries carried the title of kikha, functionally equivalent to khan but considered by some other Qashqa'i to be inferior. When Darrehshuri leaders assumed the title of khan, the title of kikha was relegated to their less prominent male relatives. The leadership of the Darrehshuri tribe passed by patrilineal descent through thirteen generations. The length of the genealogy, in comparison with the shorter ones of nonelite Qashqa'i, served to legitimate the lineage's rule. Ten generations ago a lineage member along with some supporters established autonomy from the larger group of which they were a part. As his family expanded, a core segment developed and peripheral segments were sloughed off, which were called *kikhali* (equivalent to "little kikhas") and played a negligible role in tribal politics. Members of the present generation of khans are married to women in peripheral segments of the lineage, but in the 1970s their children were intermarrying, and marriage with peripheral segments was increasingly considered to amount to a loss in status and to be undesirable.

In the twentieth century, the Darrehshuri ruling lineage consisted of four major branches tracing descent from Haj Ali Pana Kikha, a prominent Darrehshuri leader of the nineteenth century. The core

branch, called Ayazkikhali, consisted of the descendants of Ayaz
Kikha, Haj Ali Pana Kikha's grandson. This branch assumed responsibility for the majority of Darrehshuri subtribes and contained almost
all the functioning high-level leaders of the tribe. The second branch
was Aqakikhali, consisting of the descendants of Aqa Kikha, brother
of Ayaz Kikha's father. Ayaz Kikha's father expanded the tribe's size
and power, and, after his death, his son and brother competed for control. In the 1970s the schism between Ayazkikhali and Aqakikhali was
still being expressed in hostility between the two groups, and open,
sometimes violent and bloody, conflict erupted at weddings and other
occasions when members of both were present. Frequent intermarriage
of the two did not stem the flow of blood and often seemed to exacer-
bate the conflict. The khans of Aqakikhali served as leaders for a small
portion of Darrehshuri; only a few Darrehshuri subtribes and sections
of subtribes gave support to this branch. The third and fourth branches
of the ruling family were composed of other descendants of Haj Ali
Pana Kikha. Some of its men were called khan, others kikha. Those
individuals whose ascendants were active in tribal leadership played
minor leadership roles and had only a few followers, while those individuals whose ascendants were peripheral to tribal leadership played no
role in wider tribal affairs.

Of the sixteen living married men in Ayazkikhali in the 1970s, nine
were formally titled khan. They resided together, each in a large tent
encampment, in summer pastures, the location of their major landholdings, and their winters were divided between residences in winter
pastures and cities. Their positions of authority and power varied. Six
were functioning tribal leaders, and the other three were their less active brothers or sons. Of the seven who were not formally given the
title, four had left Iran at young ages during times of government
repression and resided permanently in the United States; one was educated in Italy and returned to Iran as an architect; one was a lawyer in
Isfahan; and one returned to Iran as a university professor with a doc-
torate from an American university.

The ruling lineage, the khans and kikhas, contained the leadership
of the entire Darrehshuri tribe and was regarded by the tribespeople as
their leaders. Through time and tribal expansion, subtribes aligned
themselves with and expressed loyalty to specific khans. Groups could
switch from one khan to another, and fissioning subtribes previously
under one khan's authority sometimes divided their loyalties as an
expression of separation. But for most tribal sections, adherence to a

khan and his direct descendants was carried through several generations. Most subtribes have been traditionally connected with either Ayazkikhali or Aqakikhali, an adherence strengthened by the feuding between these two branches. Ayazkikhali and Aqakikhali occupied opposite ends of Darrehshuri summer pastures and utilized separate winter pastures, and those subtribes loyal to one were located near its territory and separated from the other. Dissatisfied subtribes or groups fleeing to the other branch were often rewarded with grazing space.

Young woman on the migration

Herds assembled for a river crossing during the migration

Shepherd carrying a newborn lamb and leading sheep during the migration

Woman weaving a carpet

Winter tent being dismantled in preparation for the migration to
summer pastures

Women churning butter in a goatskin bag

Girl spinning goat hair into yarn to be woven into tent-strips

Watering horses at a water hole in winter pastures

Bagh-e Eram, the ilkhani's main estate in Shiraz. Confiscated by Mohammad
Reza Shah's government in the 1950s and utilized as a museum and public
garden, it was seized by Revolutionary Guards in 1979

Mother braiding her daughter's hair

A family during the migration

People gathered by a bridal tent in readiness for the bride's arrival

Jehangir Khan Darrehshuri, one of the Darrehshuri tribal khans, with his
granddaughter Maral

Sara Bibi Darrehshuri, with her daughters and daughter-in-law

Bridal tent prepared for the bride and, in the background, the ritualized chase
of the bride on her arrival at the groom's encampment

Elderly man and daughter-in-law at a river crossing during the
spring migration

Musicians performing at a wedding

Man preparing tea for guests

Camel herder using a water pipe to smoke tobacco

Threshing winter wheat harvested in summer pastures

Camel herder feeding camels supplementary grain during a harsh winter

Shepherd washing a sheep in preparation for shearing the wool

Musician playing a reed horn at a wedding

Mehr-e gerd, a Darrehshuri village near Semirom in northern Fars

Iranian army moving families from their winter pastures to a location chosen by
the government for their settlement, 1964

Children approaching their school

Schoolchildren

A circle dance at a small wedding in summer pastures

Drawing by Qashqa'i artist Bijan Kashkuli illustrating a wedding celebration

Young man in Qashqa'i hat, cloak, and cummerbund

9

Qashqa'i Leadership

$\mathcal{L}$eaders at all levels of the Qashqa'i political hierarchy dealt with wider authorities and external forces on behalf of the tribespeople and communicated information to higher and lower levels in the system. They possessed extensive political, economic, and social networks in the wider tribal system and in sedentary society which most other tribespeople did not, and they provided services for them in these realms. Tribespeople, who were members of political groups by virtue of their allegiance to leaders, were obliged to reciprocate these favors by paying taxes and providing other services. From the perspective of the Qashqa'i people, tribal and confederacy membership brought benefits that the region's non-Qashqa'i peasants and pastoral nomads lacked. They gained relatively secure and protected access to pastures, which facilitated pastoral and agricultural production, and leaders assisted them in times of economic need. Relations with external powers were mediated for them, and, in their interactions with non-Qashqa'i, they profited from the military power and political authority of their leaders.

No leader exercised absolute power, and each depended on the goodwill of the people under his authority. Tribespeople who were discontented could effectively deny support to leaders, ultimately by severing ties and joining other units or forming their own. Much of the history of the Qashqa'i people is characterized by such activities, and popular

200

legends recount the process by which individuals changed leaders, groups, and territories. Leaders, too, had mechanisms to gain support. Because they were the source of the most crucial pastoral resource—land—as well as essential mediatory services, they were in a position to apply sanctions and punishments, including denial of land and favors, allocation of poor pastures, and temporary imposition of high taxes. Advisors, overseers, tax collectors, and gunmen who served leaders enforced their policies and administered tribal law. Denial of pasture rights was the strongest sanction, although those denied by one leader could obtain land from another who was anxious to increase his following. Ilkhanis and khans never used government forces against tribal members to enforce their rule, as has sometimes occurred elsewhere in Iran.

An example of the connections between leaders and supporters concerns conscription. Since Reza Shah, most nomads have lacked the means and the networks necessary to prevent their sons from being drafted into the Iranian army, but their leaders have possessed urban and official contacts, the literacy required for government business, the necessary eloquence in the Persian language, and the financial means to bring the issue to a successful result. Personal ties, such as those created between families with sons liable for conscription and leaders who could prevent conscription, were an essential part of the Qashqa'i political system. Their relationships were often those of patrons and clients.

Leadership itself combined both ascribed and achieved characteristics. Ilkhanis and khans were members of noble lineages and inherited their positions through patrilineal descent, at which point personal qualities were considered relevant. A principle of primogeniture was generally followed, with latitude allowing for ability and interest. Headmen, however, achieved their positions primarily through recognized abilities, and rules of descent and primogeniture were less relevant. From a young age, a leader's oldest son participated in his father's political activities, first as a silent observer and then increasingly as a person of responsibility. As a youth he carried messages for his father and by early adulthood discussed tribal affairs with visitors in his father's absence. Leadership qualities were said to be observable at an early age. If the eldest son did not demonstrate ability or interest, a younger son might, and would gradually assume leadership responsibilities. Occasionally a man succeeded his brother, particularly when the brother's sons were still young. Leadership later reverted to the brother's line or continued in the new one, according to demonstrated qualities and interests and to the internal selection process. In this way, a leader's family functioned as a reservoir of talent, and leadership emerged in part through opportunity. In only one known case was a woman a formal, titled leader; she succeeded her deceased brother.[1] Tribespeople did not support leaders unacceptable to them but shifted their allegiance to others. If a serious divergence of opinion within a group occurred, it could divide. In less serious cases, delegations of elders or spokesmen on behalf of leaders visited recalcitrant individuals, and harmony, often expressed through idioms of agnatic solidarity, was stressed. Those who were still unconvinced could join other groups or take passive roles in tribal affairs rather than fight majority opinion.

While few Qashqa'i were polygynous, leaders, almost all of whom were monogamous, were more apt to take additional wives than nonleaders. Leaders needed adequate domestic support to fulfill the responsibilities of hospitality, and additional sons were helpful to the office, as well as indicating status and honor. Leaders at the level of ilkhani and khan possessed the wealth to support large families. In polygynous households no rule governed the hierarchy of sons; no political or economic distinctions were necessarily made between the children of cowives. The eldest son of any wife was most likely to succeed his father. If he did not demonstrate ability, the next younger son might. Subtle political and social distinctions *were* made between the children of cowives if one wife was non-Qashqa'i. Although marriage with non-Qashqa'i was rare, men were more apt to marry outsiders than women, and male leaders (especially at the higher levels) were more apt to marry in politically opportune directions outside the tribe, with families of leaders of other tribes or with nontribal elites, than other Qashqa'i males. The sons of a prominent Qashqa'i father and a non-Qashqa'i mother, especially if she were Persian, were politically impeded. Nonendogamous marriages conducted in the past, even many generations ago, were believed to leave perceptible marks on descendants and were offered as partial explanations for questionable political behavior. A khan whose grandmother was a Mamassani Lur, for example, was said to lean in a particular direction because of his "weak" Qashqa'i blood,

1. In the 1960s, Maryam Shokuhi, known as Bibi Kalantar, succeeded her late brother as leader of the Qora'i tribe, and the headmen of seventy-two Qora'i villages came under her authority. The shah and empress received her in audience and apparently formalized her position; *Kayhan*, 27 July 1969.

while the quick temper of another khan was attributed to the blood of his great-grandmother, who came from a Sunni Muslim family near Bushire. And a khan who chose a non-Qashqa'i wife more than twenty years earlier was watched closely in 1979 for signs of disloyalty to the cause of resurgent Qashqa'i politics. Such beliefs indicate the importance placed on endogamy and lineage exclusivity.

The lineages of the ilkhani and khans accommodated various political needs and were usually large enough to produce leaders of varying personalities and abilities. The men of ruling lineages worked in concert; but they were motivated by competitive self-interest as well as by collective and cooperative joint interest. Some individuals were more skilled or effective in certain aspects of leadership than others. One would be proficient in warfare, another in diplomacy and dispute settlement, and a third in contacts with sedentary society. The first perhaps thrived on pleasures in the chiefly encampment, the second on trips to encampments of nomads, and the third on luxuries in the city. A fourth individual might have demonstrated no interest in leadership and spent his life pursuing private interests, such as tending apple orchards and hunting. In practical terms, the men of ruling lineages formed quasi corporations or pools of talent, which was the basis of their leadership status and their aristocracy.

CULTURE AND SYMBOLS

Cultural and symbolic factors offer insights into the nature of leadership, demonstrate dynamic aspects of the interaction of leaders and supporters, and help to explain continuity as well as change in the power and authority vested in leaders. An essential unifying factor of the Qashqa'i political system has been its association with the cultural system of the Qashqa'i people. Qashqa'i leaders, drawing legitimacy and identity from this cultural system and contributing to its maintenance and perpetuation, also helped to create certain key Qashqa'i symbols and utilized them in their leadership—thereby blending together the symbols, their leadership, and the identity of the Qashqa'i people in ways that distinguished this unit from all other units in Iran.

Seeing the Qashqa'i as part of the Iranian state, not as an isolated "tribe" or as explainable only in its own terms, helps to place these cultural factors in broader context. The Qashqa'i, one of many culturally distinct peoples in Iran, are not distinct simply because of the survival of ancient customs and beliefs. Rather, they emerge from a historical context in which people chose as an adaptive strategy to affiliate with leaders who helped to protect them from oppressive state institutions and from other, more exploitative ruling elites, and who, in the process, articulated and reinforced a distinctive cultural system. Astute leaders utilized various symbols, some of which they drew from the affiliated people and others of which they formed themselves, to give coherence and continuity to their role. Such connections gave them a competitive edge in regional and national politics over those who lacked similarly enduring, meaningful ties with supporters, including the men holding the title of Qavam ol-Molk who maintained an urban, upper-class, Persian life-style and who did not attempt— and possibly were unable—to link themselves with members of the Khamseh tribes. For the Qashqa'i, and presumably other groups as well, the nature and quality of the bonds between leaders and supporters helped to structure the bases of these leaders' relationships with other powers. That the Qashqa'i have a cultural system different from those of other people in Iran is not merely of passing interest, an exotic but otherwise unimportant detail. Rather, it has proven to be crucial in their political adaptations and their survival as a polity.

The Qashqa'i people were not and are not culturally homogeneous. They did not have a single place or group of origin or an identity with a single cultural system. They consisted, instead, of people of diverse origins, identities, and languages who affiliated with leaders who were part of the Qashqa'i political hierarchy. "Qashqa'i" and "Turk," which are virtually synonymous in Fars, referred more to a sociopolitical than an ethnolinguistic unit. The people politically affiliating had prior, in some cases vaguely articulated, identities as Turks, Lurs, Laks, Kurds, Arabs, Persians, gypsies, and Baluch. Language was the main criterion of these labels but other cultural features were also relevant. At least by the 1930s, however, the vast majority of the Qashqa'i people held many cultural features in common, and their common identity was based upon more than their ties of political affiliation.

Cultural features associated with the Qashqa'i, influenced by historical and political circumstances, were and are continually changing. The cultural system existing today was formed by a process based in part on the Shahilu lineage, which traces descent from Oghuz Turks who at one time resided in central Asia and possibly the Caucasus. Turkic groups may have accompanied lineage members on their move from the Caucasus through Azerbaijan and other areas of Turkic concentration and during their association with the Turkic Aqquyunlu dynasty and empire. Once in Fars, members of the Shahilu lineage extended their authority over Turkic and other groups already present in the area as well as over other newcomers. Holding a distinctive Turkic language, history, and cultural heritage, they became the focal point of peoples in the region. Turks who affiliated with them retained their language and culture (as compared with some other Turks in the region who were gradually Persianized). Non-Turks, a significant portion of the confederacy in the nineteenth century, gradually adopted many linguistic and cultural traits associated with the dominant lineage and its Turkic supporters. The power and cohesion of the dominant lineage and these supporters explains the primary flow of cultural assimilation. Non-Turks also contributed traits from their own backgrounds to the society, and they retained traits in variable degrees depending on their political and geographical proximity to high-level leaders. Cultural diversity as well as assimilation were seen most prominently in the Amaleh tribe. Its members originated from all other Qashqa'i tribes and from other populations in south Iran and elsewhere, but they supported the ilkhani and fell under his cultural influence more than other Qashqa'i. Those who were closest to him molded themselves in the particular Qashqa'i image he most admired.

The primary basis of identity for the Qashqa'i, at least by the twentieth century, was allegiance to political leaders and affiliation to political groups (subtribes, tribes, and the confederacy). Identity also came with residence in Qashqa'i territory and the assumption of associated rights and duties of control and defense. Cultural features such as (western Oghuz) Turkic speech, dress, and custom were also important and, although not uniform among the people, were sufficiently recognizable to distinguish most Qashqa'i from most non-Qashqa'i in the region. The identifying labels of Qashqa'i and Turk marked these affiliations. The definition of a "true Qashqa'i nomad," according to Magee (1948:15), is probably not far off the mark: someone with Turkic ancestry or long-standing connections with Turkic tribes in Iran who migrates (or who has some family members who migrate) and who acknowledges Qashqa'i nationality and the authority of the ilkhani.

Uniformity in culture among the Qashqa'i increased in proportion to the efforts of leaders to oppose state and foreign domination and to consolidate their rule vis-à-vis non-Qashqa'i, while greater cultural diversity resulted from decreased external pressure and increased internal political competition. Under certain historical conditions, uniform cultural features were deliberately emphasized and often became highly politicized. For example, when Naser Khan resumed active leadership as the new ilkhani upon the abdication of Reza Shah in 1941, he introduced a distinctive hat for men, which in a few years was worn by practically all Qashqa'i men and became the most prominent symbol of the Qashqa'i people. The hat symbolized political autonomy and ethnic distinctiveness at a historical period immediately following state-directed attempts to erase the Qashqa'i as a unique people in Iran. In the 1960s many Iranians and foreigners assumed that this hat had existed for centuries as part of Qashqa'i "tradition," in the same way they assumed carpet motifs and tent styles were age-old Qashqa'i symbols. As another example, when Mohammad Reza Shah attacked the confederacy's political institutions and eradicated the offices of the ilkhani and khans, the Qashqa'i people elaborated and politicized their only remaining large gatherings (wedding celebrations and school examinations) and celebrated their unity. Under other historical conditions, cultural diversity was emphasized. These differences were not necessarily the residues of older cultural systems, for some were fairly recent phenomena brought about by competition among Qashqa'i leaders and groups for power. For example, after the exile of the paramount leaders, khans of the component tribes competed for recognition as the primary Qashqa'i power. The lineage of the Darrehshuri khans, who have always maintained a political distance from other Qashqa'i khans, was the most endogamous of the ruling lineages, and its members proudly stressed this trait when comparing its group with others. Members of each tribe prided themselves on their own unique cultural traits, which they held superior to those found among other Qashqa'i. The Kashkuli considered themselves the most skilled weavers and claimed to accord their women high status and to subject them to few restrictions, while the Farsi Madan considered themselves the best dancers and the most beautifully dressed.

CONFEDERACY LEADERSHIP: THE ILKHANI

The ability of the Qashqa'i confederacy to act as a quasi-independent polity rested on the coordinating and mediating efforts of its leader. The ilkhani's main functions derived from other powers, especially the state; the historical course of the development of this process is traced in chapters 3–7. The ilkhani exercised leadership of the confederacy during times of political struggle in south Iran. His efforts were usually directed outward and did not always affect the political activities of the component tribes and subtribes. His importance derived largely from the use of his leadership by the state and other powers as their point of articulation with the Qashqa'i and other people, and his power and authority stemmed partly from this contact. Through the ilkhani, the Iranian government had indirect access to the many Qashqa'i people dispersed throughout southwest Iran in small groups. It lacked other means of exerting control, short of violence, forced sedentarization, and relocation, each of which had its own costs. Most internal Qashqa'i affairs were handled in the political group in which they occurred by the group's respective leaders. Only when issues could not be settled at this or a higher level was the ilkhani involved. The separation of Qashqa'i politics into these two domains—extratribal issues under the ilkhani and intratribal issues under the khans and headmen of the component units and only occasionally under the ilkhani—helps to explain why few internal Qashqa'i affairs ever reached the historical record.

The ilkhani and his ruling lineage held an elevated social and political position by right of birth and history, which no other khan lineage challenged, not even during the 1954–78 period when the ilkhani was in exile. Most Qashqa'i continued to regard Naser Khan as ilkhani, and in fact maintained his "presence" with frequent, respectful mention of his name and evocation of past events, and did not consider themselves politically consolidated until he or a patrilineal kinsman was able to function as leader.

Institutional aspects of paramount leadership, including the hierarchy of political offices, the ilkhani's assistants, two groups of workers, and ritual specialists, supported and maintained the office and provided it with stability and continuity. Centralized leadership through the office of ilkhani favored the development or enhancement of other political offices and supporting personnel, and they in turn supported paramount leadership. The ilkhani was assisted in his duties by an ilbegi, who often served as his lieutenant and who was a member of the Shahilu lineage and a close relative, often a brother. The ilbegi was responsible for some internal affairs of the confederacy, including collection of taxes, and when the ilkhani was absent or under arrest, the ilbegi or another close relative acted as de facto ilkhani. Other close relatives also performed leadership functions, which were usually informally divided according to personal skills and interests. The political hierarchy consisted of offices ranked in hierarchical order and authority, each being responsible to the office in the next ascending level. The ilkhani traditionally appointed one or several khans of each of the member tribes of the confederacy as kalantar, chief khan of the khans, whose primary duties were to represent his tribe to the ilkhani and government officials and to collect his tribe's taxes for the ilkhani. He was usually the most prominent and respected khan of his tribe, and the ilkhani's recognition of him was usually pro forma. The ilkhani depended on the support and loyalty of tribal khans and subtribal headmen, and they often depended on and profited from his wider leadership functions. That he could and did act without their consent or knowledge, however, was his prerogative, based upon his superior social and political standing, mediatory position, participation in provincial and national politics, and foreign contacts.

Khans or equivalent political figures were lacking among many tribal and nomadic pastoral groups in Iran. Among the Qashqa'i and other similar groups, the position was directly connected with the centralizing process, unlike lower-level leadership positions. The degree of power and authority held by khans was partly correlated with the degree of centralization. Khans mediated between tribespeople and the ilkhani and drew sources of power and legitimacy from these connections, but they also formed their own independent relationships with supporters, and they escaped many of the pressures acting upon the ilkhani. After the ilkhani was exiled, khans were almost as vulnerable as he had been, because state officials held them responsible for activities in the region. Their office was a scaled-down replica of paramount leadership's and held the same type of institutional supports and self-sustaining characteristics.

The lowest levels of the political hierarchy, headmen and elders, were found among almost all tribal and nomadic pastoral groups in Iran and the larger geographical area, regardless of the extent of political centralization. Under a centralized system, however, these two roles and positions were enhanced in power and authority, given their importance in the hierarchy. The ilkhani, despite his prominence with shahs, Governors, and foreign agents, exercised little actual power or authority over households and small lineage-based socioterritorial groups, which had the ability, often with impunity, to change political affiliations and move to new locations. The ilkhani relied on the support of tribal khans, who in turn relied on subtribal headmen, for the continuing support of individual tribespeople, many of whom had little understanding of or interest in his wide-ranging political activities.

The ilkhani's assistants and retainers, also part of the institution of paramount leadership, were drawn from the Amaleh tribe or soon became attached to it. Some were permanently in his service and others provided services as needed. Of greatest importance were personal secretaries and advisors, men of unquestioned loyalty who handled many of the practical matters of leadership. These individuals often held the honorific title of aqa and were sometimes members of small lineages having historical traditions of serving paramount leaders. They were literate, educated men, and the ilkhani invoked their abilities in decision-making and dispute settlement. They also served as scribes, accountants, tax recorders, and teachers. They handled his economic affairs within and outside of tribal territory and dealt with his non-Qashqa'i commercial agents in Shiraz and elsewhere. They were usually present in his tents and urban residences, sometimes accompanied him on trips, and were sent to settle disputes. For instance, if the ilkhani heard of a dispute between two khans of a component tribe, he sent an advisor, who acted on his authority, to investigate. The advisor could assemble a more unbiased account than the disputants would be able to provide if summoned before the ilkhani, and he suggested possible resolutions. Drawing from their wide experiences, secretaries and advisors were often good storytellers, and the ilkhani enjoyed their company and relied on their impressions and opinions. The persons holding these posts were not full-time nomadic pastoralists. They entrusted the care of their flocks and fields to relatives and hired workers. They camped near the ilkhani and owned or rented houses and gardens in Qashqa'i territory and sometimes also in Shiraz. Their service earned them economic rewards and privileges. They were part of the small group of wealthy, nonelite Qashqa'i.

Isma'il Khan's principal secretaries were Mohin Daftar and Qavam Daftar of the settled portion of Abivardi/Bolvardi, the Turkic group Nader Shah sent to Fars from Khorasan in the early eighteenth century and whose prominent members have served ilkhanis and their predecessors since then. They coordinated affairs with Isma'il Khan's main commercial agents in Shiraz, Hesam Daftar and Mushir Daftar, urban Persians known by the last name of Dabiri after Reza Shah. Mohin Daftar was arrested with Isma'il Khan in the 1920s and then served Naser Khan on his release, and his nephew assisted the Qashqa'i insurgents in 1980–82. Nimtaj Khanom, Isma'il Khan's political agent in Shiraz in 1905–14 and his secretary in 1913–14, negotiated on his behalf with the British minister in Tehran and assisted in his schemes to gain power over the Qavam ol-Molk. She was the daughter of a nonprominent Persian Shirazi, was educated in Tehran, adopted European dress, and in her youth traveled to Europe with a daughter of Mozaffar ed-Din Shah (*Who's Who in Persia* 1923:112).

The ilkhani's personal bodyguards and gunmen (*tofangchi*), the embodiment of his power, were nonelite Qashqa'i from the Amaleh tribe who were proven in military skills and personal loyalty. They camped with him and he took them on political visits, hunting, and into battle. He also sent them alone or with advisors and secretaries to settle disputes, punish dissenters, and collect fines. The ilkhani provided them with mounts and arms, paid them wages, and offered them favors. The Amaleh tribe, consisting of those who had over the years sought the ilkhani's support and offered him their service, was regarded as his standing army in case he needed a large military force. When he planned military action he notified Amaleh headmen, who selected gunmen and horsemen from their respective groups. The ilkhani drew military forces from other Qashqa'i tribes as well, sometimes more as a statement of authority than out of the need for extra forces, and he also went outside the confederacy. Other Qashqa'i khans, and occasionally other tribal leaders in Fars, sent small armed forces to serve the ilkhani for short periods as a sign of support.

The ilkhani's household retainers and workers, also drawn from the Amaleh tribe, cared for his many guests and visitors, tended to his personal needs, cooked, prepared tea and directed the meal service, established and broke camp, groomed his and his guests' horses, and served as messengers. Household workers, although often performing work that was servile in appearance, enjoyed fairly high social status as a result of their serving the ilkhani and had opportunity for economic and social mobility. They received food, clothes, supplies, and some animals in exchange for their work.

Workers whose tasks were part of the duties of paramount leadership can be analytically separated from workers who produced and tended the ilkhani's wealth, although some overlap in function and personnel occurred. This second group included shepherds, tenant farmers, sharecroppers, gardeners, and weavers. Those who tended his sheep, served in his homes, and wove his goods were always Qashqa'i, not only because their skills in these activities were regarded as superior to those of non-Qashqa'i, but also because their presence in his camp was not an intrusion or a political threat. Those who worked his land, especially outside or on the periphery of Qashqa'i territory, were usually

Lurs and Persians, and their relationships were similar to those of land-owners and peasants elsewhere in rural south Iran. Utilizing non-Qashqa'i rather than Qashqa'i to serve in economically subordinate positions, especially in agriculture, was deliberate, for the ilkhani could exert greater control over them, including physical force, and extract a larger surplus than he could from Qashqa'i. Also, the agricultural population in the region consisted largely of Lurs and Persians, who thus constituted the available work force. Lurs and Persians were believed to be much more suited, mentally and physically, to tedious, dulling agricultural work than were Qashqa'i, an ideological justification for the resulting inequality. Distinctions made among these workers are important, given Iranian officials' often negative statements about the Qashqa'i khans as "feudal lords." The ilkhani and other khans employed peasants, as did the nontribal landed elite, but they also formed less exploitative relationships with their own Qashqa'i workers, who had opportunities for economic and social mobility that non-Qashqa'i workers usually did not, at least within the Qashqa'i socioeconomic system.

Overseers, foremen, and village headmen served the ilkhani in capacities relating to his personal wealth by supervising his tenants, sharecroppers, and shepherds and overseeing the process of wealth accumulation. Their payment was usually a percentage of production.

Ritual specialists who performed music and other services at wedding celebrations and other festive occasions staged performances for the ilkhani, as they did for all Qashqa'i. Their importance with regard to paramount leadership derives from the ilkhani's role in setting the cultural forms used by the Qashqa'i people. No religious practitioners or religiously trained individuals were attached to the ilkhani's service. No "saints" or sayyids performed mediation or other tasks for him, as they did for leaders of some other centrally organized nomadic pastoralists (Evans-Pritchard 1949, Gellner 1969). Qashqa'i ritual specialists asserted no special connections with Islam, nor did they utilize its symbols.

The long seasonal migrations through non-Qashqa'i, heavily settled territory and the wide geographical dispersion of the Qashqa'i tribespeople in seasonal pastures were major factors in the centralization of Qashqa'i political authority. The ilkhani's leadership here, though often symbolic and ceremonial, was crucial, and it linked him with other levels of the political hierarchy. Because of ecological and strategic factors, coordination of the complicated move of hundreds of thousands of people and millions of animals was a function of all Qashqa'i leaders. They acted primarily in unusual circumstances and under conditions of political instability, however, and Barth exaggerates the extent to which Khamseh and Qashqa'i leaders controlled migrations in the region (1959, 1961). Migratory patterns and routes were well known by individual Qashqa'i, who needed no advice about them; what was needed, however, was strategy in case of hostile moves against them. The Qashqa'i have historically been vulnerable to raids and attacks during their migrations, and forces capable of blocking migration routes threatened their economic survival. The external links of the ilkhani and khans offered crucial sources of information for Qashqa'i pastoralists on these matters.

The spring migration was ordinarily more regulated than the fall one (except during times of military threat) because of ecological conditions. Herds depended on new spring grass, and some coordination of people with regard to access was essential to the pastoral livelihood. Winter was a time of hardship, often with little for animals to eat, and pastoralists were anxious to gain access to freshly growing vegetation along migration routes and in summer pastures. In the fall, however, no new grass was available for herds, and movement did not need much, if any, regulation. On the spring equinox, the beginning of the Iranian New Year, khans and prominent headmen traveled to the ilkhani's camp near Firuzabad to receive instructions concerning the order in which their groups could leave winter pastures. Under ordinary circumstances, no group left without first receiving such permission. No change was usually made in the order in which groups departed, and hence receiving such permission was pro forma. Those who had fallen into the ilkhani's disfavor, however, were moved to last place, which meant that most new grass would already be gone by the time of their passage. Khans and headmen were held responsible for the movements of their affiliated groups, and the ilkhani could bring sanctions against them. A common punishment was to require a recalcitrant group to return to a given location, where it could then resume the migration. The ilkhani used this New Year's gathering to assert his authority, judge individual and group loyalty, and reward and punish. It was also an occasion for general discussion and for relaying information about Iranian politics to which only he had access. Khans, headmen, and others, some of whom saw the ilkhani only at this time of year, sought favors and advice and offered information about local conditions. The ilkhani set the amount of the animal tax during this visit (in the years when it was levied), and it was delivered to him during the spring migration.

Symbols of paramount leadership, at least during the twentieth century, centered on the sociopolitical context of leadership itself: the il-khani's camp, the body of supporters who resided close to him, his hospitality to visitors and political contacts, and his life-style. In many regards these represented the residences and customs found among the Qashqa'i people. Qashqa'i who visited the ilkhani's camp found there a more elaborate replica of their own tents and camps. The ilkhani strove to reproduce the life-style of his supporters, yet he also set an example for those same supporters to emulate. He made a conscious effort to identify with them and separate himself from settled Persians. It was not necessarily political opportunism that motivated him to be in a tent in riding clothes instead of in a house in formal attire. Despite the time he needed to spend in Shiraz, he still preferred his mountain camps. It must be added that his leadership was more acceptable in a form familiar to those being led than, for example, in the forms established among Persian landowners in the area. Qashqa'i who visited the ilkhani received a concrete image of the Qashqa'i life-style as (re)created in his camp and in his person, an image they carried away with them and applied according to their economic means and personal tastes. The Qashqa'i, a political and cultural minority in a predominantly Persian society, derived their sense of uniqueness partly from their leaders, especially the ilkhani, who encapsulated and condensed those features they most admired. Clearly reciprocal borrowing took place, for the ilkhani, despite his wealth and prominence, modeled part of his life-style on that of the average Qashqa'i nomadic pastoralist, while the average nomad followed the model presented by the ilkhani.[2]

This evidence concerning symbols of paramount leadership comes from interviews, oral histories, photographs, foreigners' accounts, and my own observations of the leadership styles of khans of the component tribes who lived in tent encampments and participated in tribal politics in the 1960s and 1970s, despite the Pahlavi regime's attempted disruptions, and who styled their residences and life-styles after those of the ilkhani. Both before and after the ilkhani's exile, they competed with one another through their elaborate camps and residences, supporters,

2. Similar examples are found elsewhere. The Sha'alan shaikhs of the Ruwallah bedouin in Jordan and Saudi Arabia are multimillionaires yet continue to reside in tent encampments year around (Lancaster 1981).

and visible wealth. Their encampments and expressed modes of leadership were less elaborate versions of what occurred at the paramount level, until after the exile, when they equalled and in several cases surpassed them.

The ilkhani's large encampments in winter and summer pastures were the center of paramount leadership. He migrated seasonally between these areas, as did nomadic Qashqa'i. The winter camp was near Firuzabad or Farrashband, and the summer one at Khosrow Shirin or near Semirom. Amaleh tribespeople were assigned pastures in these areas, which were some of the choicest lands under Qashqa'i use. These winter and summer sites were centrally located vis-à-vis the seasonal pastures of most of the Qashqa'i people, a fact facilitating political contact and influence. Khosrow Shirin was located within a day's ride of most other summer pastures. Being surrounded by the Amaleh and then by other Qashqa'i groups, the ilkhani was well protected from outside incursions. The centralized nature of tribal authority, as represented in these camps, enabled state officials and foreign agents to deal with the ilkhani without having much contact with the Qashqa'i people, which simultaneously served to enhance his power and to protect these people. (This centrality enabled Mohammad Reza Shah to abolish paramount leadership without disrupting political organization at lower levels.)

The center of the ilkhani's encampment was the large black tent used for receiving guests and holding meetings. The tent, rectangular in shape, was identical in manufacture and form to the tents of nonelite Qashqa'i but was much larger and more elaborately furnished. It was constructed of strips of woven goat hair sewn as well as fastened together with sharpened wooden pins. Wooden poles of equivalent height supported the four corners and sides, and braided guy ropes connected the pole tops to stakes in the ground. Tassles were fixed to the ropes, and decorative woven strips ran from pole to pole inside the tent. A long open side served as an entrance, and along the other long side, in the tent's rear, possessions were stacked to a height of five or six feet on a foundation of stones and arranged aesthetically to display attractive storage bags, weavings, and bedding. Along the top was a row of pillows. The ground was covered with pile carpets. Qashqa'i weavers and craftspeople constructed the tent and furnishings. Visitors and guests entered the tent and greeted the ilkhani or awaited his arrival, then sat down on the carpets in a semiformalized order roughly reflecting prominence and seniority. Members of the ilkhani's family or his secretaries pulled pillows off the baggage pile and tossed them to some guests for comfort in sitting and leaning. Retainers promptly served tea in small glasses on saucers, and melon or other fruit sometimes followed. At mealtimes often hundreds were fed; everyone present, regardless of status or purpose of visit, joined in the meals. The kind of food prepared and the service offered depended on the status of visitors.

The ilkhani sometimes slept in a small, often canvas, tent where he kept personal possessions such as official papers, guns, and clothes, but otherwise the main tent served these purposes. His wife and children used the main tent as well as other tents when many guests were present. Some of his relatives pitched their own tents nearby in the same encampment or as separate encampments a short distance away. Tents were available for guests who stayed overnight, although they sometimes slept in the main tent, and bedding was always provided. Other tents, often British-made and of canvas, served as sleeping, kitchen, and food storage tents. The actual cooking of food, virtually a continuous process, was conducted over open fires in shallow pits outside the kitchen tents, and hearths were also located within these tents for tea preparation and cooking in inclement weather. One tent was often used as a school, in which children of the ilkhani, his relatives, and other members of the encampment were instructed by his secretaries or occasionally by hired non-Qashqa'i teachers.

The tents of many retainers and workers were part of his encampment and ringed its periphery, partly for protection. They were identical in size and function to those of other nonelite Qashqa'i, although their interiors and immediate surroundings tended to be neater and cleaner, out of respect for the ilkhani and his guests and to create a good impression. The animals of these households were tended by relatives in other locations. The men, women, and older children of these tents performed specific chores and functions for the ilkhani; they were not full-time pastoralists. They handled personal affairs on days when few or no guests were present but came without delay or summons when guests appeared in the camp. Those Qashqa'i who tended the ilkhani's herds and cultivated his fields and orchards usually pitched their tents elsewhere, although they reported to him regularly. A small herd, source of meat and milk products for guests and camp members, was kept close to his camp, and animals brought as gifts sometimes went into it. Weavers often lived in this camp and produced goods to outfit the ilkhani's household and to be given as gifts to guests and supporters. Those who provided the ilkhani protection and military support in case of attack and who were used for small offensive and defensive actions resided in his camp or nearby. These were usually Amaleh households but could be from other tribes as well. And those who were seeking political asylum from government authorities, other khans (Qashqa'i and other groups), tribal disputes, or oppressive landlords found shelter in the ilkhani's camp, where he was obliged to protect them from harm or revenge. In some cases they stayed only until the dispute in question was resolved, while in others they joined his service and were eventually incorporated politically and socially into the Amaleh.

The ilkhani's power and authority in a Qashqa'i context, expressed in part by the number of tents in his camp and the size of the group migrating with him, could be seen in the number of people attached to his service and providing support. The camp contracted and expanded depending on political circumstances, his activities, and the absence or presence of his kin. During some periods, especially when the ilbegi was a power in his own right, the ilkhani and ilbegi maintained separate encampments, where each presided. Some British reports noted the complicating existence of these separate "capitals." The ilkhani's residences in Shiraz and other cities also included a full complement of assistants and retainers.

The size of the military force the ilkhani generated demonstrated his power. State officials, the Qavam ol-Molk, and foreign powers, often seriously misjudging this, feared the size of the fighting force represented in the total Qashqa'i population and acted accordingly, either by avoiding a confrontation or by sending a large force against him. Or they took at face value the actual number he brought into battle or to confrontations, which might be a small portion of the total number of loyal, able-bodied Qashqa'i men who owned horses and guns, and they mistakenly assumed that he had lost support within the confederacy.

The ilkhani's power, authority, and leadership abilities were also demonstrated by the numbers and kinds of people who visited him. Qashqa'i returning from a visit to the ilkhani or his camp were asked: "Who were his guests? What business did they have? What news did they bring?" Information gleaned in this fashion was essential to local-level decision-making because of the territorial dispersion of the Qashqa'i. The size of the encampment, elegance of the receiving tent, number of guests and attendants, and generosity of hospitality all symbolized the ilkhani's position. Visiting patterns indicated the nature of his political ties; the presence of guests in his camp was a function of his outside contacts. The ilkhani's ties with government officials, often not apparent to the Qashqa'i people because of their urban context, were indicated when officials visited him in his encampment.[3] Qashqa'i from beyond the camp, aware of the sometimes precarious position the ilkhani held with officials, came to assist and demonstrate support when they heard of the arrival of officials or other dignitaries. Special care was taken for these visitors, who often left with highly exaggerated notions of the ilkhani's power, authority, and wealth. They never knew that his camp was ordinarily less crowded.

Foreign visitors, especially those on political missions, generated the most attention and were the most hospitably received. Through the nineteenth and twentieth centuries, foreign visitors represented potential military and political benefits for the ilkhani. Their nations were determining influences behind Iranian politics, it was believed, and the ilkhani regarded such visitors opportunistically. The Qashqa'i and Iranians in general thought that even foreign tourists and scholars influenced Iranian politics and the foreign powers who were manipulating Iranian affairs. From the 1940s on, foreigners—primarily Americans—also represented networks that could assist in visas, medical treatment and education abroad, and publicity about the plight of the Qashqa'i under the Pahlavis. The ilkhani (and khans after 1956) used foreign visitors to advantage in his relationships with government officials and other Iranians, because foreigners actively sought him out to the exclusion of others. Part of the ilkhani's hospitality (and later that of the khans) was manipulation aimed at ensuring positive responses and resultant reports and publications by foreigners, which raised his and his family's status in the eyes of other Iranians who, perhaps more than the ilkhani himself, valued Western contact and desired Western approval. The ilkhani knew what appealed to foreign visitors and exploited it to his benefit in political competition.

The ilkhani sometimes met government officials and foreign agents outside Shiraz to avoid potentially threatening encounters in the city. On these occasions he erected canvas tents and established temporary camps guarded by gunmen (see Sykes 1930:478). His hospitality also

3. A marked change of the 1960s and 1970s over the pre-1956 period was the increased frequency with which government officials visited Qashqa'i leaders in their encampments for purposes of demonstrating state power and extorting hospitality and gifts.

extended beyond his camps and urban residences. He often escorted the newly appointed Governor of Fars from Tehran or Bushire to Shiraz (and acquired his support along the way), and he traveled outside Shiraz to greet and escort dignitaries, including shahs, coming to visit the city. Isma'il Khan once laid a long stretch of carpets on the road a shah was to travel. In 1923 Isma'il Khan and Reza Khan escorted Ahmad Shah, the last Qajar shah, from Shiraz to Bushire. In 1979 thousands of Qashqa'i and others made Naser Khan the beneficiary of this gesture by traveling as far as Isfahan and Tehran in order to escort him back to Fars after many years of exile.

A primary feature of the ilkhani's style of leadership, which reflected political processes among the Qashqa'i in general, was the large open gathering in the reception tent, where he presided but did not explicitly dominate the discussion. The process Barth (1961:43–46) describes for the Basseri, in which men talk most of the evening about the possibility of migrating the next morning, and in which a consensus slowly emerges without any single individual's having made the decision unilaterally, is similar to a process found among the Qashqa'i. The ilkhani possessed information, especially about the state and foreign powers, that others present did not, but he tended to introduce it in general conversation to allow others to consider and discuss it. When he required or sought the presence of other Qashqa'i leaders, he called large tribal gatherings and war councils (*ordu*s). Otherwise, he kept no regular schedule of meetings or political gatherings. Those with issues to discuss or disputes to settle simply went to his encampment (or sought him elsewhere). If the ilkhani were absent or occupied with other pressing business or guests, another visit would be made later. In these cases, visitors stayed awhile in the camp and joined others gathered there; they were always hospitably received and something of political note undoubtedly occurred. The ilkhani's tent was usually filled with people who might or might not have a chance to discuss their concerns. Meetings and discussions were usually public, and those attending prepared their statements carefully because of the scrutiny of others. All present had the right and opportunity to add opinions and details, although not all did so, rank, age, and sex being the primary determinants of who spoke and how often. Overall, the nature of the gathering was relatively egalitarian, and the decision-making process was often informal. People presented their problems in this open forum, presided over by the ilkhani and his advisors, and decisions could be reached in the course of group discussion without the ilkhani's having made any kind of a definitive statement.

During the ilkhani's absence, much the same kind of process oc-curred. His brothers or other close relatives acted in his place, and his personal secretaries and advisors also exercised authority. The ilkhani's mother, wife, and sisters contributed to political discussions, especially in his absence, when people often told them what they would have told him. These women could pass along, reword, or ignore these conver-sations. Qashqa'i with problems often came to them first in order to get their opinion. The ilkhani's mother and wife frequently partici-pated in his discussions with others and hence knew the likely course of his opinions as well as having their own. They could be of great assistance to others, especially those who felt insecure in front of the ilkhani or in the large gathering, such as women who might hesitate to speak to the ilkhani but who were assured of assistance from the bibis.

The ilkhani also exercised leadership in a ritualized, nonpublic way, which mirrored a style of interaction found among the Qashqa'i in gen-eral. He invited someone to accompany him on a stroll away from the tent and assembled visitors, often to the top of a hill or to "check on his horses." Others respected the privacy they created. Individuals could also approach the ilkhani alone, on the assurance that no one else would join them. In 1923 Isma'il Khan and Ahmad Shah conferred about Reza Khan's growing power during a private stroll.

Hunting was a favorite form of relaxation and sport for all Qashqa'i men, and it was closely identified with the ilkhani (and other leaders) and his style of leadership. Hunting combined skills and qualities val-ued in Qashqa'i men: horsemanship, shooting, ability to maneuver in difficult mountainous terrain, and spartan living. By participating in hunting, the ilkhani, who was required to spend time in the city with urban folk, asserted himself as a hardy mountain warrior and demon-strated the skills necessary to a successful fighter. He enjoyed making trips with skillful hunters with whom he could compete. He some-times invited along government officials and foreign guests in order to demonstrate his military prowess. Hunting was also a time when the ilkhani could escape the often crowded tent and limit the number of people engaging in discussions. He kept falcons, and trained falconers were among his retainers.

Wedding celebrations for all Qashqa'i were occasions for large gath-erings of clan and tribe and were major political and social events. For a people who were otherwise widely dispersed in territory, attendance at weddings affirmed their social solidarity. Under the tutelage of the ilkhani (and khans), elaborate wedding celebrations emerged as politi-

cal and cultural events expressive of centralized political authority and
were vehicles for developing and maintaining a distinctive Qashqa'i
identity. By virtue of his wealth and position and the numbers of supporters and guests he drew, the ilkhani was able to stage more elaborate
weddings than anyone else, these being symbolic of his power.

Limits were placed on the power of the ilkhani and the activity of
the confederacy. All tribal leaders, especially the ilkhani, were restricted by the fact that their political activities held consequences for,
and generated reactions from, other powers. As part of the state, the
Qashqa'i were always vulnerable to its instabilities, internal power
struggles, and foreign intrigue. When the ilkhani engaged in regional
and national politics, and when other powers attempted to engage the
Qashqa'i as a political or military unit, he functioned as confederacy
leader, consulting other Qashqa'i leaders and planning joint action in
large tribal gatherings. But he never controlled the other tribes of the
confederacy or their khans, and the confederacy itself never acted as a
totally united political or military force. The most concerted military
effort by the Qashqa'i involved, at most, five thousand horsemen (at a
time when the total population approached four hundred thousand),
and these were drawn primarily from the Amaleh tribe. Some tribal
activities were always independent of the ilkhani's leadership, and
many continued uninterrupted when he was removed from the scene,
as was the case during much of Pahlavi history. Also, khans could act
independently, and some, including members of his own family,
overtly opposed him.

Khans sought to benefit from the ilkhani's political strategies, but
they were often unwilling to subordinate their interests to his, especially when the advisability of his schemes was in question, as, for example, when Naser Khan harbored the German spy Schulze-Holthus.
Some khans avoided him when it could possibly harm them vis-à-vis
potentially stronger forces in Iran, as, for example, in Isma'il Khan's
confrontations with Great Britain and the South Persia Rifles and in
Khosrow Khan's challenge to Khomeini's Revolutionary Guards. Powerful khans, whose interests were competitive with the ilkhani's, such
as in the exploitation of trade routes, could defy him and remain aloof
"in a sort of sullen hostility" (*Gazetteer of Persia* 1918:812). Lack of
direct interaction, possibly confrontation, aided their attempts to remain autonomous and uncommitted to his policies. At times khans
avoided even casual contact with the ilkhani, because this too could
entail reciprocal obligations. The desire for autonomy was seen in the
high rates of endogamy in each ruling khan lineage.

Darrehshuri khans, more than the others, maintained independence from the ilkhani and other khans. Darrehshuri winter and summer pastures were far from the areas used by the ilkhani and most other tribes, which some say was deliberate. Darrehshuri khans claim their ancestors displaced the ilkhani and other Qashqa'i groups from the area they once all shared (Darreh Shur), and their migration to winter pastures took them in a direction different from that of most Qashqa'i. They often migrated through Boir Ahmad territory, and they formed marriage and other alliances with Boir Ahmad khans. Some of their pastures were more contiguous with Lur and Bakhtiyari pastures than with those of other Qashqa'i tribes. The ilkhani always feared the Darrehshuri might join their neighbors, especially the Bakhtiyari, if too much pressure was applied, and so he too maintained some distance. The Khamseh confederacy to the east brought him difficulties and he did not desire an expanded Bakhtiyari confederacy to the north. Darrehshuri khans used the threat of flight to the protection of Bakhtiyari khans as a weapon against pressure from the ilkhani and to ensure their own autonomy.

TRIBAL LEADERSHIP: THE KHANS

As was the case with the ilkhani, many individuals and groups supported the leadership and life-style of the khans, but in a less elaborate fashion. Most of the information here on tribal leadership is also applicable to the ilkhani, who, as khan of the Amaleh tribe, functioned in similar ways. Separate subtribes called Amaleh but having no connection with the Amaleh tribe contributed the khans' retainers and workers.[4] Originating from all subtribes, their members were a cross section of each tribe and were from other tribes as well. Those who came to work for khans usually did so as a result of poverty or political disputes. The khan they served provided them food, clothing, animals, and money in times of need, such as illness and marriage. Khans rewarded retainers who performed faithfully and offered the most favored ones the rights to the products of particular gardens and agricultural lands. Amaleh subtribes expanded and contracted as individuals and families joined and left the khans' service. A few retainers of some khans were said to descend from black Africans brought to the Persian Gulf ports as slaves during the nineteenth century. The descendants, called *kaka*

---

4. Separate Amaleh sections were attached to the two major, often feuding, branches of the khan family of the Darrehshuri tribe.

siah or "black brothers," had negroid physical features and darker skin than most Qashqa'i. They usually intermarried with low-status Qashqa'i.[5]

Included in a khan's entourage of retainers were shepherds (*chupon*), garden workers (*baqbon*), and field workers, as well as household retainers who included, in order of importance: bodyguards (*tofangchi, noukarbob*) who were provided mounts and arms; a personal retainer (*pishkhedmat*) who made tea, set the meals, and was in charge of supplies; camp retainers (*farrash*) who put up tents, loaded camels, and meted out punishment; grooms (*mehtar;* the head of the stable was called *mirakhor*); camel drivers (*darqa*); cooks (*ashpaz, nazer*); weavers; and general servants (*noukar* for men, *kolfat* for women). Six to eight personal bodyguards accompanied each khan on migrations, on political trips, hunting, and in battle, and he sent them to settle disputes, issue punishment, and collect fines. Women of the khan families, who were proficient weavers, wove jointly with Amaleh women residing in the camp.

In the Darrehshuri tribe two small families traditionally assisted the khans in their most essential political functions. The Zahedis of the Urujlu family, Turks by origin, had been the advisors and confidants of khans for generations and considered themselves ministers of court. The family's men held the honorific title of aqa and a social position between khan and commoner, which aided them in their role of settling disputes. The second family, the mirzas of the Musavi family, originated from Boir Ahmad Lurs and joined the service of the Darrehshuri khans in the 1870s, where they specialized as teachers (*moalem, munshi*), scribes (*nevisandeh-ye khan*), accountants, and tax recorders. They derived from a special lineage whose men held the title *mirza* (secretary) and served as secretaries to Boir Ahmad khans (Loeffler 1978:154–55). Mirzas of the same lineage, also found among the Kashkuli and Bakhtiyari and in cities where they worked in offices, were respected throughout southwest Iran for their secretarial abilities.

Khans owned many herds of sheep and goats (ten to twenty or more herds, three hundred animals per herd) tended by shepherds who were

5. Ten to thirty such households were part of Kashkuli Bozorg, while five to ten were in Darrehshuri. The fourth wife of the founder of the lineage of the Kashkuli Kuchek khans was a black slave purchased from a gulf port (Salzer 1974:138). In 1833 a black slave was killed as he attempted to protect the Qashqa'i ilbegi from attack (Busse 1972:224). The descendants of black African slaves were the trusted retainers of local chiefs in other parts of south and southwest Iran as well (Wilson 1932:33–34).

dispersed in seasonal pastures. Each khan appointed from one of his subtribes an overseer of shepherds (*mukhtabod, rais-e chupon*) on the basis of previous service and proven honesty, whose tasks were to visit these shepherds every spring to count newborn animals and brand them with the khan's brand, attend shearings, and supervise migrations. In exchange, the overseer was entitled to 1 percent of each herd and its products, paid in lambs, oil, and cheese. The position was prestigious, involved little effort, and entailed personal contact with the khan.

A group of musicians, circumcisers, dentists, and barbers, often called *usa* and *asheq,* was associated with every tribe, and some members regularly offered services to khans. No religious practitioners or religiously trained individuals were connected with khans. Bibis utilized itinerant non-Qashqa'i mullahs, darvishes, and sayyids for cures and Islamic ritual paraphernalia such as written prayers and amulets, but most khans publicly shunned and even ridiculed them.

Qashqa'i khans exercised power and authority over land use and migrations, internal tribal affairs, and relationships between tribal members and others. They owned or controlled villages and large tracts of pastoral and agricultural land throughout the southern Zagros Mountains in both winter and summer areas and along migration routes. Their villages were occupied by Persian, Lurs, and sedentary Qashqa'i who worked the land for khans. Historically, khans controlled some non-Qashqa'i-owned villages by exacting tribute in exchange for protection. Their power and authority extended into other areas through the occupation of pastoral and agricultural land by their subtribes. A khan extended his control over a region by sending members of a subtribe to occupy and defend the territory. After several seasons of occupation, use of the land became the right of the subtribe (and tribe) occupying it. If the subtribe later fell into disfavor with the khan, he could assign the land to another subtribe. Competition between the two main branches of the Darrehshuri khan family often took the form of struggles over pastures and subtribes. Ayazkikhali khans sent their own subtribes into Aqakikhali's territory as a challenge, and in response Aqakikhali khans enhanced the military strengh of the subtribes originally occupying the land or encouraged the incoming subtribes to switch affiliations. Each spring and fall, shortly before or during the migration, khans assigned seasonal pastures to their subtribes according to historical patterns of usage and services rendered the previous season. Headmen were obliged on a semiyearly basis to seek permission to use pastures, despite the fact that most subtribes occupied the same seasonal pastures year after year.

Khans occasionally rented agricultural land to, or sharecropped with, Qashqa'i rather than Persians or Lurs, especially in strategic areas along trade routes and borders with other tribes. Qashqa'i cultivators guarded the land and in exchange paid a lower rent or a smaller share of the harvest than was charged by non-Qashqa'i landowners in the region. These cultivators tended to retain active political affiliations, which was not always the case with settled agricultural Qashqa'i, and so benefited the khans. Khans also solidified relationships with supporters by rewarding loyalty and bravery in battle with rights to collect taxes and tributes from the villages and agricultural and pastoral lands they controlled.

Khans assigned migratory routes and schedules to their subtribes, particularly during times of political instability in the province. As one of his regular tribal functions, the ilkhani provided a place for the discussion of routes and schedules among khans and their headmen and offered mediation. Khans hoped to arrange good routes and schedules for their subtribes. They oversaw migrations and assisted at a time when hundreds of thousands of nomadic pastoralists, Qashqa'i and others, moved between seasonal patures. A few funneling areas along migration routes became crowded, and khans often camped nearby to coordinate movement.

Khans mediated and settled intratribal disputes involving members of one or more subtribes. Although elders and headmen settled most conflicts within subtribes before khans learned of them, aggrieved parties, together or separately, could also present their cases to a khan. The headman, who formed a working relationship with the khan, often provided background information. The disadvantage of carrying a case to this higher level was that the khan, regarded as final judge of intratribal conflict, possessed the power to punish and fine either or both parties, knowledge of which provided an incentive for a resolution before involving him. Khans were generally known for fairness of judgment, and a genuinely aggrieved party could put its faith in them. If a tribesperson brought a case against someone known to be in the khan's favor, such as a headman, however, the khan was likely to act in the latter's interest. Those who sought the khan's mediation accompanied their requests with gifts.

Conflicts concerning the abuse of women, including forced marriage and cruelty by husbands, which could not be settled within families and local kinship groups, were brought by the women's families to bibis, who decided the merits of the cases and brought them to the khans' attention. Of the disputes over marital arrangements, the most frequent cases involved women who resisted marrying the spouses chosen for them and who sought support from bibis and khans. The khan asked all parties, including the future bride and groom, to come before him to present their cases publicly. He was often known to side with the woman, he might express admiration for her courage in resisting an undesired marriage, and he would occasionally agree to her marriage with someone she desired if the potential groom and his family agreed. Men who were refused the hand of a woman could also appeal to bibis and khans.

Eloping couples sought refuge with khans, who offered sanctuary, ensured that they were properly married, and provided them with a livelihood. Romantic love was highly valued by the Qashqa'i, and protection for couples who placed love before family ties and thus risked losing their inheritance was often readily offered. If khans were unaware of the circumstances surrounding eloping couples who appeared at their tents, they offered temporary shelter, ensured that they slept separately, and summoned their parents. Elopement was not a common pattern of marriage, however (cf. Bates 1974).

Khans punished crimes and misdemeanors such as murder, theft of animals, and destruction of pastures. In the case of murder, they arranged for the payment of blood money or the transfer of a woman to the victim's family, and in lesser offenses they summoned the violator or sent a representative (*ma'mur*) to mete out punishment, which was usually a fine (*jurm, jarimi*) or a beating either on the bare back or feet. Corporal punishment was often halted by advisors soon after it began, with unspoken approval, which saved the khans from appearing too lenient; khans were known to delay punishment until such an advisor was present. Khans also held sanctioning power over tribespeople by denying pasture rights or economic or political aid. They assisted families who had lost animals or other property due to raids by attempting to retrieve the goods and punishing the thieves (especially if they were members of the same tribe as the victims) or by replacing the goods themselves.

Khans tried to prevent news of crimes and disputes from reaching the government's attention, in order to avert its interference in tribal affairs and avoid repressive, often violent, forms of state justice. If one Qashqa'i killed another, settlement was attempted through traditional means. If state authorities heard of the death, an investigation would occur, and the killer, if found, be imprisoned, usually for life, or executed. Khans tried to conceal knowledge of the death or attribute it to accidental or natural causes, in addition to settling the case for the involved parties. In the case of violent conflict between subtribes, khans interceded so that the government would not be tempted to deploy military force. Khans offered protection to both Qashqa'i and non-Qashqa'i fugitives. Qashqa'i fugitives often fled to a khan who was a rival of their pursuers' khan, and his tent was regarded as hallowed space where no retribution or revengeful killing could occur. Khans and their advisors provided mediation. If khans were under government surveillance and unable to provide sanctuary in their own tents for fugitives from extratribal forms of justice, they could send fugitives to others, such as headmen, and profess ignorance if state authorities sought help in capturing them. Khans also provided refuge for groups seeking sanctuary; the arrival of refugees, especially from other tribes, attested to the reputation of particular khans and tribes and expanded their numbers. Providing sanctuary was part of the process of tribal formation and helps to explain the diverse composition of tribes and the confederacy.

Khans also supported lower-level political processes. They recognized the title of headman for men chosen by their own groups. Although khans could not appoint a headman against group wishes, they could tip the balance when two men in a subtribe were vying for the position. Such a struggle was sometimes symptomatic of an impending schism of the group. The strategy of the rival leader was to solicit recognition from a khan other than the one to whom the group was affiliated and be appointed by him, which caused the group to split. Also, a headman in trouble with his group might be supported by his khan to regain group confidence. Because the subtribe was dependent on the khan, his decision to support one leader and not a rival carried considerable weight. Khans rewarded distinction and faithful service by bestowing the honorific titles of aqa and beg. Those receiving such titles were usually headmen or other prominent individuals at the subtribal level. No specific rights or privileges accrued to the possessors, but they gained prestige and public recognition.

Khans, who were wealthy landowners, regional and occasionally national elites, occasional residents of urban centers, and knowledgeable about sedentary society, represented Qashqa'i groups and individuals in non-Qashqa'i contexts. They possessed wide political, economic, and social networks which they used for personal benefit as well as parlayed into benefits for their supporters. Most tribespeople lacked direct contact with the government, and disputes, conscription, and legal problems were handled through the office of khan. Association with a khan provided the entree of many tribespeople to sedentary society. Khans also assisted supporters accused of crimes by state authorities with whom they often had long-standing relationships. They interceded for imprisoned tribesmen and worked to secure their release with minimal bribery. If relatives of an imprisoned man knew how much and whom to bribe, they might secure his release, but it cost persons unknown to the authorities long delays and much money. After relatives of a jailed Darrehshuri man appealed to a Darrehshuri khan who was slow to provide assistance, they successfully appealed to a Kashkuli khan. When the Darrehshuri khan heard of this, he hastened to intercede, for he was embarrassed about rumors that Darrehshuri khans did not help their own supporters.

Certain obligatory acts expressed the ties of tribal members to khans of their tribe. Although both khans and tribal members sometimes claimed that their respective duties toward the other far surpassed reciprocal acts, and complained of the others' demands, they often did so somewhat good-naturedly, for they each held the option of severing ties. Both sides required regular services for the relationship's continuance, but a foundation of historical events often placed one or the other in debt. For example, Darrehshuri khans continuously supported the headman of a Darrehshuri subtribe against rivals, because his father (who had been headman at the time) was killed fighting government troops. This act of sacrifice, the extreme expression of tribal loyalty, indebted the khans to the sons of the dead warrior and served as a basis of their long-standing close ties. But the sons were unwilling to exploit this debt to an extreme that would have nullified the appearance of honorable conduct they were attempting to present, and they continued to reciprocate in customary ways. If individuals or tribal sections discontinued obligatory acts, khans applied pressure for their resumption or ceased giving favors.

Gallehbegireh ("taking flocks") was the main obligatory act owed khans by tribespeople. Khans collected this animal tax once every several years from their subtribes and viewed it as just payment for services rendered during previous years and as income that helped defray the expenses of leadership. Tribespeople viewed the tax as an unwelcome obligatory act that increased the khans' already large herds and allowed them to live in an extravagant fashion. In the spring, as tribal sections approached a funneling point on the migration route, khans, who were also migrating and who assisted in migrations and allotted summer pastures on this occasion, set up camp and were not easily avoided. Each subtribe was affiliated with specific khans who collected their taxes; competition among khans for supporters was partly based on this revenue. Most subtribes, except for small ones, were divided in loyalty and hence divided their animal tax between several khans.[6]

The tax, levied as a percentage of the sheep and goats owned by every independent household, was usually 3 percent; the range ran from 1 to 6 percent, depending on the khans' claims concerning economic need, the ilkhani's levy, and the government's power to demand taxes. When the ilkhani taxed the tribes, occasionally on behalf of the government, khans and kalantars handled the collection, and the percentage was increased, sometimes to 6 percent.[7] The animals taken were sometimes rams and fat ewes, which were household capital, so the value of the tax could be higher than the stated percent. As tribespeople approached the collection point, headmen consulted household heads, computed taxes, collected animals (taking a percentage for themselves as payment for their own leadership services), and delivered them to the khans' encampment. Headmen, who hoped to pay as small a tax as possible, often in their reports bemoaned the difficult winter that had caused reductions in herds. They were exempt from the tax, as were khans' shepherds, families of men killed in battle, the impoverished, and, occasionally, families with more than three unmarried daughters or sons with expensive marriage costs in the offing. The last time the ilkhani collected the tax was in 1953, when he needed aid in supporting the military force assembled to pressure the government during the Mosaddeq crisis, and he had collected it twice in the years between 1941 and 1951. The last time khans formally collected their own tax was between 1959 and 1962, when the government abolished the title of khan, which, from the state's perspective, was an act officially ending the nomads' responsibility to pay taxes. Some nomads continued

6. For particular affiliations between subtribes (and their sections) and khans pertaining to the 1940s and 1960s, see Magee (1948) and Hand (1963).

7. On at least one occasion, Isma'il Khan set the tax at 10 percent for three consecutive years for members of an Amaleh subtribe who were paying much larger bridewealth payments than was commonly accepted among the Qashqa'i. He opposed large marriage payments (both bridewealth and dowry) and stated that if families could afford them, they could also handle a large tax.

to pay beyond this point or substituted other payments in order to maintain customary ties with khans.

Khans called on their subtribes for armed horsemen, and subtribes were obliged to supply them, which was a hardship as well as a privilege. Service disrupted pastoral and agricultural activities, but it also held the promise of reward. Khans maintained no large, permanent, armed force in their camps, as it was not generally necessary, but on occasion a contingent larger than the coresident unit of bodyguards and retainers was needed. They required gunmen to protect territory from incursions, acquire and hold land, battle government forces and foreign armies, fight other tribes and other khans, punish recalcitrant subtribes, and raid villages and trade routes. They sent gunmen on missions alone or took them on tours of the territory in order to settle land claims along the way and to present a show of strength to other khans and tribes. When khans needed gunmen, they summoned armed, mounted contingents of ten to twenty men from several or many subtribes by issuing orders, often written, to headmen who, in selecting the strongest, most courageous men, were careful not to deplete any household of adult males. In poor subtribes only the few rifle-owners served. Selection appears not to have been difficult, for men were eager for adventure and the possibility of reward. Part of the property captured in battles and raids went to the gunmen, the amounts varying according to the property, inclination of the khan, and the number of gunmen, but often the khan and the gunmen divided it equally. All captured arms were the khans' property, but they distributed guns and ammunition to the bravest fighters. Khans offered sheep, land, and the privilege of collecting their rents and tributes to exemplary fighters. Popular stories featured ordinary tribesmen who served khans bravely as gunmen in battle, were rewarded by khans with special favors (possibly even their daughters in marriage), and later became leaders themselves. When khans were in defensive postures and needed protection, they summoned gunmen to bring their households and encircle their encampments. Tribespeople disliked this service because it disrupted the pastoral cycle, herds had to be portioned out to relatives who remained in seasonal pastures, and no adventure or captured property was likely. Members of one subtribe often told the story of several households who for six months, along with fifty from other subtribes, surrounded the camp of a khan who feared an attack by a rival khan.

Finally, some optional acts and services contributed to good relationships with khans. Men with sons ready to marry presented the khan with a ram or other large animal and asked his permission for the marriage to occur. The khan almost always consented; the gift "sweetened" the decision. On the day of the wedding they sent another gift, and the khan in turn presented a gift to the new couple. Tribespeople also sought permission for divorce (which was rare). Tribesmen who were closely associated with khans gave yearly gifts, such as young camels, rams, or white lambs, often on New Year's Day. When the khans' sheep were branded or sheared, headmen in the vicinity sent several men to assist, and when khans prepared new gardens, headmen sent laborers. Because tribespeople required services which only khans could provide, and because khans depended on the military support of the tribespeople within their political domain, the "gifts" of each side helped to ensure response in times of need.[8]

SUBTRIBAL LEADERSHIP: THE HEADMEN

The position of headman (kadkhuda) among the Qashqa'i has been present at least from the eighteenth century, and it was also found throughout rural Iran. Reza Shah legally recognized the position as part of his centralizing policies; a headman functioned as an agent at the local level for the execution of government laws and in villages represented the landowner and guarded his interests. His duties were to oversee agricultural production in accordance with the landowner's orders, decide on minor cases, prevent and settle disputes through conciliation, prevent the flight of accused persons and the destruction of evidence, and report his actions to a gendarmerie post or governor (Lambton 1953:190). Among the Qashqa'i, the headman functioned on behalf of his group and in relation to khans and local authorities.

Leadership of a subtribe (tireh) rested in the hands of the headman and the elders, or "white beards" (*aq saqal* in Turkic, *rish safid* in Persian). The boundaries of a subtribe included all those who expressed loyalty to one headman. The installation of another indicated group fission. The headman, whose position constituted a permanent office, held power and authority in the subtribe and was primarily responsible for external affairs, while elders were the force of popular opinion behind him and oversaw many internal affairs. Elders represented subtri-

---

8. Bourdieu (1977) discusses why the "voluntary" nature of such gift-giving is necessary to maintain political organization in the absence of autonomous state institutions.

bal sections, were influential in formulating day-to-day decisions, and advised the headman. Their activities distributed the decision-making process, and many matters were settled without involving him. Elders, consisting of most elderly men, were usually older than the headman and sometimes were more knowledgeable and experienced than he; a few were former headmen. A headman could not remain in office without their support.

The subtribe acted as an independent social, political, and, occasionally, resource-utilizing unit, responsible for its own political survival, and the headman's duties were essential to these ends. Because subtribes were autonomous and equal with respect to the leadership of khans, no formal ties bound a tribe's headmen with one another. Headmen emerged by consensus from the subtribe's lineages, not by descent from ruling lineages as with ilkhanis and khans. Whereas khans by their lineage, nobility, and wealth were set apart from the rest of the tribe, the headman was often indistinguishable from many other members of his subtribe. The wealthiest man of the subtribe was not necessarily the headman, nor did the office necessarily allow the occupant to become wealthy by it, but the headman could not be a poor man because his expenses were larger than those of other group members. He usually hired outside labor because his own time and effort were focused on political affairs rather than on the immediacies of household production.

If the majority of the subtribe did not approve the headman's actions, it could hold an assembly and select a new headman. If a minority segment did not support him, it could choose a leader and form its own subtribe or join another one. Khans who competed for supporters contributed to this process by supporting rival leaders. Through political processes often phrased and symbolized in terms of lineage segmentation, subtribes expanded and contracted, and leadership passed from one segment to another. In the history of Qermezi, a Darrehshuri subtribe, the position of headman passed through four of its five lineages (bunkus). Kacheli lineage, constituting the "original" subtribe, produced three headmen. Three brothers who are regarded as founders of three new lineages joined Kacheli, and in time one lineage (Imamverdilu) gained in strength and provided a powerful leader. Shortly thereafter leadership was taken over by another lineage (Aqa Mohammadlu), where it remained through the 1970s. This tenure was once interrupted briefly when the headman was restrained in chains and held captive during a battle by a khan who rivaled the one he supported and who installed another headman for the subtribe from a fourth lineage (Qasemlu).

The headman mediated between group members and the khan and served as their spokesman. The khan passed instructions concerning land use and migration schedules to the subtribe via the headman, who collected the animal tax for him and assembled men to serve him as gunmen, sheep shearers and branders, and garden workers. These tasks brought rewards to the men chosen, and the headman distributed these privileges to those who had served him. When someone asked permission of the khan for marriage, divorce, or assistance, the headman, who was articulate and familiar with the khan, often presented the case.

The headman, to whom the khan allotted winter and summer pastures, used his own networks of kinship, marriage, and politics to distribute land. He favored those who performed favors for him and neglected those who were socially distant, unresponsive, or disloyal. This power was used carefully, however, because everyone had inherent rights to their subtribe's pastures and could complain to the khan. The headman maintained political contacts with neighboring headmen and landowners, and when members of his group required pastoral or agricultural land beyond the areas allotted to the subtribe, he negotiated usufructuary rights. He helped to coordinate migrations, even though all households exercised considerable independence of movement. Because movement through foreign territory presented risks and dangers, most nomads migrated in groups. Those traveling with the headman positioned themselves around him; their numbers indicated his status and the extent of his authority.

The headman maintained order with the assistance of elders. He held the power to punish violators of tribal custom through corporal punishment, loss of pasture rights, allotment of poor patures, and refusal of favors. He settled disputes before other powers, such as khans and state authorities, heard of them and intervened. Parents sought his permission for the marriages of their children, which was usually pro forma, but he could and did refuse permission and prohibit marriages if he and the elders objected, particularly in cases involving women whose fathers wanted to marry them to outsiders. The headman might on the occasion of the veto offer an alternative match, but he had no power to force a union the parents did not desire. A headman, obligated to protect and shelter fugitives and other newcomers, could also increase the strength of his subtribe by giving land and protection and by taking or offering women in marriage to receptive outsiders. He sought to prevent subtribal members from joining other groups. The headman organized military units in the event of war, raid, and retaliation and sent group members on peace delegations. He was expected to be a model of honor because his actions reflected on the subtribe, and he tried to ensure that group members behaved honorably and to conceal incidents dishonorable to the group. The headman represented the subtribe to other sections of the tribe, other tribes, and settled society. He organized and handled the affairs of the subtribe and its members with the gendarmerie, army, courts, and government offices. He assisted in the financial transactions of tribesmen with merchants and moneylenders and protected them from chicanery.

As agent for the khan, the headman was rewarded by a percentage of the khan's animal tax, 3 percent of the grain harvested by subtribal members on the khan's land, a percentage of the property resulting from khan-directed raids, a lamb whenever members of his group assisted in shearing and branding, and various gifts accruing from the job. Subtribal members were obliged to reciprocate the headman's services. He exercised the right to request labor from group members at any time; those on whom he called were usually unmarried or newly married men. On occasion he collected money from each household for land utilized or services rendered, an amount varying according to herd size, which reflected the size of land used. Every year all households were obliged to give the headman a lamb or a kid and, for those who were most dependent, to slaughter an animal and prepare him a formal meal, and every spring each household gave him two days' production of butter. Fathers of grooms gave him animals when marriages occurred. He restricted his own services if these "voluntary" gestures did not occur regularly. A headman could simply take an animal from the herd of a group member if it had been some time since he had been voluntarily given one.

The headman did not accumulate much of this income, for the office required considerable expense and elaborate hospitality. Much of his time was spent away from home, and travel and urban visits were expensive. Hardly a day passed without guests to feed. Important visitors in the vicinity went at once to his tent, and animals were usually slaughtered for the meals. His tent served as a gathering place for all group members, who were automatically fed at mealtimes. The headman was expected to provide animals or monetary assistance for group members who suffered hardships and to encourage others in the group to be generous. He was an honored guest at weddings, but he was also expected to assist economically the groom's parents who hosted the event. As representative of the subtribe he was invited to weddings in other groups, where he was also expected to give generously. He hosted the newly married daughters of the subtribe at ceremonial meals, for which an animal was killed, and he gave them the obligatory bridal gift of a live animal.

The positions of ilkhani, khan, and headman were thus for the most part functionally indistinguishable, their activities differing only in scale. Qashqa'i tribespeople could acquire identical services from all three leaders (although most did not). This interchangeability of leaders was a control on their actions and lessened the likelihood that they would use coercive force. Not only could Qashqa'i change affiliation from one headman to another (and switch subtribes) or from one khan to another (which could mean switching tribes), but also they could seek from khans or even from the ilkhani services ordinarily performed by lower-level leaders, especially if they were dissatisfied with them. Leaders lost status and potential supporters when it was known that people supposedly under their authority sought services elsewhere, an act explicitly critical of their leadership. The functional interchangeability of leaders also relates to the devolution of leadership. The general process of government penetration of this rural social formation, in particular the government's appropriation of many of the linkages previously embodied in the Shahilu leadership, shifted the locus of interaction to lower levels in the political structure. The brokerage remained the same; the central power simply sanctioned different brokers.

10

Qashqa'i Socioeconomic Organization

*T*he Qashqa'i are now and historically have been socioeconomically stratified into a small, wealthy ruling elite, a large category of those having adequate access to the means of production (land, water, animals), and two small categories of those dependent on others for the means of subsistence. Processes of socioeconomic stratification and political centralization were closely and dynamically interrelated, although one does not totally explain the other.

The appearance in history of the Qashqa'i as a distinct polity appears to have coincided with the formation of bonds between members of the Shahilu lineage and people utilizing winter and summer pastures in the southern Zagros Mountains. At first these bonds were apparently based on the state's recognition of selected Shahilu individuals as representatives of these people, with certain rights and obligations to perform on behalf of the state. The Shahilu assumed control over lands utilized by these people and regularly allocated pastures to them. As these functions and the population base expanded, a chain of power and authority formed; leaders of the component tribes emerged as major powers in the process, and lower-level leaders were enhanced in their positions. All Qashqa'i leaders benefited economically from the state's indirect rule of the people and from the developed political system.

The ilkhani and khans acquired for themselves and their supporters the best pastoral and agricultural land in the region. Both drew labor

235

and surplus production from supporters for use in their leadership duties and for their own personal benefit. But it was particularly the non-Qashqa'i domain that provided these khans with their primary source of wealth. As territorial governors with rights of taxation, the ilkhani and ilbegi were able to hold back taxes and acquire property for private use. All khans owned or controlled vast tracts of agricultural land, the key means of production in the region, and through military power and political authority also controlled the means of production of many non-Qashqa'i inhabitants of the region and created exploitative landlord-peasant economic relations for their own personal benefit. Both patterns of relations—administrative and political ties with Qashqa'i nomadic pastoralists and cultivators, and exploitative economic ties with non-Qashqa'i agriculturalists—were the basis of the khans' economic position and had a long history in Fars. The Shahilu khans fitted into preexisting patterns in a way that probably eased the process by which they established local ties. Khans of the component tribes, as their own positions developed, also followed existing patterns.

The vast majority of the Qashqa'i, the second socioeconomic category, received regular use of pastures in exchange for allegiance to leaders. They held an economic advantage over pastoralists in the region who lacked such political ties, for their use of pastures and freedom of movement in the environmentally rich, heavily populated, competed-over region was backed up by the khans' military power, administrative authority, and political influence. For this reason, both levels of khans were successful through history in attracting and retaining political supporters. The third and fourth socioeconomic categories, consisting of those Qashqa'i who depended on others for the means of subsistence, include hired shepherds, camel drivers, field laborers, sharecroppers, retainers, producers of specialized goods and services, and wage laborers.

The Qashqa'i people were more economically diversified and characterized by greater socioeconomic differentiation and stratification than many other nomadic pastoralists in Iran and elsewhere in the Middle East, in large part because of the ecological and strategic setting and the highly developed political system that prevailed in Fars. Both levels of khans were part of Iran's upper class. Although leaders of other Middle Eastern nomadic tribes were usually wealthy, the particularly high class standing of the Qashqa'i khans was atypical. Within the second socioeconomic category, greater socioeconomic differences were present than were ordinarily found among nomadic pastoralists elsewhere. Households short of labor and households short of animals and income were mutually dependent. Poor households could remain in nomadic pastoralism and be integrated into sociopolitical groups, as could wealthy households, a situation differing from that described by Barth (1961) for the Basseri and often assumed to be generally true for nomadic pastoralists, in which the poor and the wealthy settle, "leave the tribe," and assimilate into sedentary society. Neither poor nor wealthy Qashqa'i were compelled to settle or sever sociopolitical ties, and the population had the potential of expansion, in contrast with the demographic equilibrium said to exist among the Basseri (Barth 1961:113–21). Finally, variation in wealth among Qashqa'i households within subtribes and among subtribes within tribes was greater than was generally found among nomadic pastoralists. Close connections between supporters and leaders, along with other political factors, enabled some households and some subtribes to be more prosperous than others.

Although the domestic economies of most Qashqa'i households were similar to those found in Fars among non-Qashqa'i nomadic pastoralists and some agriculturalists, the Qashqa'i tended to be more prosperous than non-Qashqa'i who practiced similar economic activities. The Qashqa'i, who controlled much of the best pastoral and agricultural land in the region, generally enjoyed more secure land use and were better protected from incursions disruptive to productive activities than non-Qashqa'i, and leaders provided herd animals, better pastures, and income-producing work if ecological or economic disaster struck.

Change in the Qashqa'i confederacy did not always necessitate change in the socioeconomic patterns of its members. Nor were economic activities at the household level necessarily affected by the political machinations of the ilkhani and khans. For the vast majority of Qashqa'i, individuals at the household level made their own decisions concerning herd ownership and economic production, consumption, and exchange, with no interference from or control by tribal leaders of any level. The ilkhani and khans controlled only those households in their service, but even these held the options of quitting and assuming other livelihoods. Also, the vast majority of the Qashqa'i had always cultivated and pursued other nonpastoral subsistence activities in addition to pastoralism and therefore could rely on a range of economic strategies in case political events temporarily disrupted nomadic patterns. Some continuity in economic patterns among the Qashqa'i apparently existed in the twentieth century, if not earlier. In the 1880s a "moderate fortune" for a nomad in southwest Iran consisted of one hundred sheep, three to four mares, and ten asses (Bell 1885:82), which, if correct, is remarkably similar to livestock owned by a Qashqa'i family of average wealth in the 1960s.

From the time of their first appearance many millennia ago, nomadic pastoralists in the Middle East have exchanged products and traded with settled agriculturalists and rural and urban merchants and been subject to some of the same regional and broad economic pressures as were villagers and city dwellers (although they were protected from others). Nomadic pastoralists depended on the goods and services of settled society, for which they exchanged their own products; the pressures affecting prices on both sets of goods were felt by both segments of society. In the eighteenth century and thereafter, these patterns of simple commodity exchange in Fars were increasingly overshadowed, in some cases supplanted, by a market monetary economy and eventually by capitalist commercial relations. The expansion of a market monetary economy in and around Shiraz in the eighteenth century established the economic matrix of the emerging Qashqa'i polity and contributed to its growth.

The different levels of the political and socioeconomic systems were not always equivalent; although some correlations between the political hierarchy and socioeconomic position did obviously exist, placement of the Qashqa'i in the sociopolitical system did not always have economic explanations. Some members of the socioeconomic elite also held top positions in the political system, while some members of the lowest socioeconomic groups were only loosely integrated into it. Also, in the second socioeconomic category, those closely affiliating with tribal leaders enjoyed better pastures and other favors and hence tended to be wealthier than those who remained aloof from leaders. Some members of the socioeconomic elite played no role in Qashqa'i politics, however, while some members of the lowest socioeconomic group were the closest associates of the ilkhani and khans, acquired personal prestige, and exercised individual power.

Table 3 depicts the many levels of the Qashqa'i socioeconomic system in the twentieth century before 1962. The units considered in the table are independent households (economically separate from parental households and responsible for decisions concerning production, consumption, and exchange), and the economic activities described are those of adult men and women and the children who worked alongside them. Married adults who lived with parents and unmarried adolescent

TABLE 3. Socioeconomic Distinctions among the Qashqa'i before 1962

Description of Category	Title/Label	Wealth Base	Clients/Workers	Patrons/Employers	Life-style
Wealthy political elite	Khan (functioning leader)	Agricultural production Land (esp. rents) Herds Taxes and tribute State payments Raiding Foreign bribes	Tribespeople Retainers Shepherds Tenant farmers Sharecroppers		Tents in winter and summer Houses in villages and cities
Wealthy elite	Khan (minor or no tribal functions)	Land Herds Agricultural production	Retainers Tenant farmers Shepherds		Tents in winter and summer Houses in cities, towns, or villages
Wealthy commoners holding political office	Kikha Kadkhuda Aqa Beg	Herds Some land Payments from followers Favors from khans Raiding	Shepherds Camel drivers Agricultural workers	Khans	Nomadic or seminomadic
Herd owners (self-sufficient in flocks)	Ra'iyat (commoner)	Herds Some agriculture	Shepherds (possibly)		Nomadic
Landowners (economically self-sufficient; combined agricultural and pastoral economies)	Ra'iyat (commoner)	Agriculture Herds	Shepherds (likely)		Settled or transhumant

Category	Local name	Payment	Employer	Mobility
Hired shepherds	Chupon (shepherd)	A few animals Salary from employer: food, clothes, animals	Herd owner	Nomadic
Camel drivers	Darqa (camel driver)	Salary from employer: food, clothes A few animals	Camel owner	Nomadic
Agricultural laborers Sharecroppers Tenant farmers	Kargar (worker)	Cash or portion of crop Small herds	Landowner	Nomadic between jobs
Retainers Workers	Noukar (male) Kolfat (female)	Maintenance	Khan Wealthy person	Reside with employer/patron
Providers of specialized goods & services; nonpastoral work	Qorbati (gypsy) (only some)	Payment from sale of goods & services		Nomadic Seminomadic
Wage laborers	Kargar (worker)	Payment for work	Employer	Nomadic between jobs

males who were hired shepherds in other households are not considered separately. Four socioeconomic categories can be distinguished on the basis of access to and control over the means of production. Only the first is unambiguously a socioeconomic class, and it must be analyzed in the context of the regional and national class structure rather than isolated at the Qashqa'i or tribal level. Qashqa'i khans exercised class rule in a larger Iranian context and hierarchical rule in a tribal context. Qashqa'i people label those in the other three categories as *ra'iyat* (commoners), in contrast with the elite.[1] Nonelite Qashqa'i, who shared a number of characteristics, did not see themselves nor were they seen by others as separate classes. Impeding the development of class consciousness among these Qashqa'i were their primary identification with their own political groups (each of which was socioeconomically diverse), integrative vertical ties between supporters and leaders and between clients and patrons, shared notions of common Qashqa'i identity among all socioeconomic categories, and opposition to Persian-dominated society and to non-Qashqa'i in general. Abrahamian notes that communal ties in Iran, based on language, tribal lineage, religion, and regional affiliation, cut across socioeconomic lines, fragmented the horizontal strata, and strengthened vertical bonds (1982:5, 1979:388, 1975).

The top level of the Qashqa'i socioeconomic system is a wealthy elite that formed part of Iran's upper class. Already small in size, it was further fragmented into socially separate and clearly distinct khan families. The khan family of the confederacy—the Shahilu—was wealthier and higher in status than the khan families of the component tribes. Wealth derived primarily from control over land, ownership of herds, and sale of agricultural and pastoral products (including woven goods). Qashqa'i tribespeople paid taxes and tributes. Additional income in taxes held back, government grants of land and money, fees from merchants for protection of trade, and foreign bribes accrued when state, mercantile, and foreign powers sought services from this elite. Many retainers, sharecroppers, and tenants performed the actual labor necessary to generate and sustain wealth. The elite had two components: men (and their immediate families) who played active political roles, and men (and their immediate families) who were marginally involved in or aloof from politics. The politically inactive inherited wealth and

1. The distinction made in many nineteenth- and twentieth-century sources between *ra'iyat* (defined as peasants or the lower classes of the countryside) and *ilat* or

social position from men who had played roles in Qashqa'i politics in the past.

The second level of the socioeconomic system consists of the vast majority of Qashqa'i, those of nonelite status who had adequate access to the means of production for their own sustenance. These were predominantly nomadic pastoralists who owned their own flocks, cultivated, and exchanged or sold pastoral products (including woven goods) for needed materials and supplies. They were integrated into the political system through lineage-based, resource-sharing local groups and through subtribes and tribes, and they formed political ties with leaders of these units, from whom they received rights to use pastures. Their local-level ties were defined by combinations of patrilineal descent, intermarriage, coresidence, cooperation, and friendship. Environmental conditions, developmental cycles of domestic groups, political ties, and personal relationships generated flexibility in the composition of local groups. This level can be divided according to type of economic activity, extent of wealth, and degree of political involvement.

Wealthy nonelite Qashqa'i, including some subtribal headmen and many of those holding titles of aqa and beg who served the ilkhani and khans as secretaries and advisors, often played political roles. Wealth accrued from political office, and established leaders were often able to enhance both their wealth and power, but active leaders also required the means to support their posts and the ability to hire or acquire extra-household labor such as shepherds and field laborers. The income of wealthy nonelite Qashqa'i was based on cultivated land, larger-than-average herds, payments and favors offered by the ilkhani or khans, and taxes and gifts paid by followers. Expenditures connected with leadership were high, especially for hospitality, aid to supporters, residence away from camps, bribes to government officials, and payment of extra-household workers. These individuals tended to intermarry with similar figures in other subtribes and tribes, which expanded their political networks laterally and also illustrated that their status was higher than the relatives with whom they lived and upon whom they depended for a political base. They did not marry into the elite.

Nomadic pastoralists who were self-sufficient in flocks and in most cases labor, and who periodically cultivated grain, comprised the majority of all Qashqa'i. During some developmental stages these house-

---

iliat (nomads) incorrectly assumes a tribal organization and identity only for the latter.

holds fell short of shepherding labor, and some hired or acquired out-side labor for limited periods.

Those self-sufficient households that regularly combined nomadic pastoralism with agriculture were often settled for part of the year in villages. In all periods of Qashqa'i history, some nomadic pastoralists have settled for economic or political reasons, and, even if they later resumed full-time nomadism, they often retained a reliance on private land and agricultural production. They experienced more severe labor problems than those who were more dependent on nomadic pastoral-ism, for agricultural and pastoral activities conflicted in space and time, and they were forced to rely on hired or acquired extra-household labor on a regular basis. The political connections of these individuals with subtribes and tribes tended to be weaker than others in this sec-ond socioeconomic level. Settlement or partial settlement was often a sign of political disagreement or disinterest. Some who settled had no pressing economic reason to do so; that is, they were not more impov-erished or more wealthy than others (cf. Barth 1961). Year-round no-madism was symbolically significant for political and cultural identity, and those who settled, especially if they did so for reasons other than poverty or wealth, were often less committed in these respects. The other end of this argument—and the other end of the socioeconomic spectrum as well—includes those who owned few animals and hence had no economic reason to migrate but who continued to do so for political and cultural reasons.

The third and fourth levels of the socioeconomic system consist of those dependent on others for their means of subsistence. Their access to the means of production, extent of exploitation, degree of mobility, and concomitant life-styles varied.

The third level consists of households that hired out their labor as full-time shepherds and camel drivers and as part-time field laborers and sharecroppers. They could not subsist on their small herds, and they lacked other income-producing work, such as agriculture and weaving, to make up the difference. They depended on Qashqa'i with adequate access to pastures, herds, camels, agricultural land, seed, and water. Shepherds and camel drivers contracted their labor to house-holds in need and able to afford payment, which included animals, food, and clothes and provided little more than basic subsistence. Their households joined the camps and migrations of their employers. No marks of socioeconomic differentiation distinguished employers and employed, except that the tents and possessions of shepherds and camel drivers tended to be of poorer quality than those of employers. Shepherds and camel drivers moved from employer to employer and sub-tribe to subtribe, depending on the availability of jobs, and they either lacked rights to pastures initially or lost them because of separation from their subtribes of origin. They tended to be inadequately inte-grated into sociopolitical groups. For these reasons, especially the low pay, some remained in these jobs permanently. During periods when khans and headmen competed for followers and could assign extra pas-tureland, households such as these were given pasture rights and a few animals in exchange for military and political support, in which case economic and social mobility was probable. Shepherds and camel driv-ers, while often politically marginal, could be drawn into active polit-ical participation in this way and were often gradually integrated into new sociopolitical groups.[2]

Part-time field laborers and sharecroppers had fewer opportunities for such economic and social mobility because their work required sea-sonal settlement, which interfered with pastoralism and nomadism. Leaders, for whom mobility was essential for military and political strength, could not depend on followers who were tied to cultivated fields. So field laborers and sharecroppers tended to be politically in-active and subsisted on their combined earnings in agriculture and pas-toralism.

The fourth socioeconomic level, including the khans' retainers and workers, providers of specialized goods and services, and wage laborers in mostly non-Qashqa'i contexts, also consists of those having inade-quate access to the means of production; but their subsistence activities and life-styles separate them from those in the third level and from one another. As a category they did not ordinarily practice nomadic pastor-alism, their migration patterns were attuned to nonpastoral work, and their integration into sociopolitical groups was weak or different from that of most other Qashqa'i.

Retainers and workers were individuals of diverse sociopolitical and ethnolinguistic origins who sought political or economic refuge with the ilkhani or khans. They were paid in food, clothes, supplies, and some animals. Particular families of these workers often served khans through the generations; at any one time, three generations and all individuals over the age of eight or so might be serving in some capac-

2. Further discussion of the socioeconomic and political status of hired shepherds among the Qashqa'i is found in Beck (1980a). The Korosh, a small Baluchi-speaking group of some forty to fifty families who trace Baluch origins, have been employed by some Qashqa'i as camel herders for at least three generations (Mahamedi 1979:277–78).

ity. Deep loyalties were thus created, and khans rewarded their best workers with land, gardens, flocks, and educational opportunities for their children.[3] Retainers and workers lived with or near khans because their work tended to be year-round and permanent. Although distinctions between these workers and members of the khan families were unmistakable in terms of wealth, status, and life-style, the two groups interacted socially with comfort and familiarity, a situation facilitated by the open tents and encampments and everyone's active labor and participation in camp life. These workers were not indentured or bonded; they were free to quit service if they chose. Those who did quit ordinarily joined relatives in the Amaleh sections and took up or resumed nomadic pastoralism. The Amaleh possessed some of the best pastures available as well as other advantages, so workers who quit service with khans had a reasonable chance for economic success as nomadic pastoralists, provided no major disagreements stood between them and their former employers. Some workers periodically moved into and out of the khans' service, especially for seasonal agricultural work. Many Amaleh families had members working for khans as well as engaging in nomadic pastoralism, which facilitated changing patterns of work.

Providers of specialized goods and services were often among the poorest Qashqa'i, but they had no ties of dependency with any particular individuals or classes. They survived by peddling their wares and services for cash, pastoral products, and market goods. They lived in tents and migrated seasonally but owned few if any herds. Some were caste-like groups, including gypsies, and most were the poorest members of subtribes as well as members of the poorest subtribes, with names such as "Ironworkers" and "Shepherds."

Members of the caste-like groups were similar in physical appearance and occupation to those identified elsewhere in Iran as gypsies, but they did not ordinarily admit to such an identity. Gypsies had lower status than any other socioeconomic or ethnic group in this part of Iran and were generally considered to be pariahs. Members of the caste-like groups claimed to have joined the Qashqa'i in the same way that many other groups claimed—as refugees from political repression elsewhere and as seekers of improved economic conditions. Their tents

3. The case of Mohammad Bahmanbegi, discussed in chapter 11, is an example. Some Qashqa'i say his father was Isma'il Khan's groom, while others give him a more elevated social position. The ilkhani supported Bahmanbegi's education, and he became possibly the first Qashqa'i to receive a postgraduate degree.

and clothes, although poor, were identical with those of other Qashqa'i. They did not share territory as a group, unlike many other Qashqa'i holding beliefs in common origins. Rather, they were dispersed throughout Qashqa'i territory and were loosely attached to subtribes and tribes, in which they played little or no political role. Their own social attachments were close, however, and their lineages were highly endogamous. Their specializations included music, circumcision, dentistry, barbering, horseshoeing, and tin and copper smithing—skills that no other Qashqa'i shared. They offered these services primarily to other Qashqa'i and received payment or products in exchange. Skilled musicians often prospered, especially between 1941 and 1979, when Qashqa'i weddings acquired increasing social and political importance, and they accumulated wealth and invested in flocks and land, which their relatives tended.

Other Qashqa'i who also possessed specialized occupations and skills were members of subtribes similar to the majority of Qashqa'i who owed political and economic obligations to tribal leaders. Out of poverty, they tended their small flocks and peddled specialized services (reed caning, wood carving, china repairing, sieve making, livestock trading) and raw and processed products (firewood, charcoal, gum tragacanth, indigenous medicines, dyes for weaving). Their customers were both Qashqa'i and non-Qashqa'i, including villagers and urban merchants, and the economic tie was one of simple commodity exchange, not exploitation or dependency.

Wage laborers were economically and politically marginal. They tended to be impoverished nomadic pastoralists who had no means of economic support short of selling their labor. Others in these circumstances became workers for Qashqa'i khans and hired shepherds for other Qashqa'i, but these individuals sought work in non-Qashqa'i contexts, primarily as agricultural laborers and sometimes as hired shepherds for villagers and commercial stockraisers. In the 1950s and thereafter, many sought work as wage laborers in a variety of low-status jobs in cities and the oil fields. Household by household, they tended to drift away from Qashqa'i territory and from sociopolitical ties and were eventually lost to their tribes of origin and hence to the Qashqa'i confederacy. For this reason and because of their poverty, they are placed at the bottom of the socioeconomic hierarchy.

The exile of the paramount leaders in the 1950s and the end of confederacy-level political activity had little immediate effect on socioeco-

nomic patterns among the Qashqa'i. Significant economic change occurred after 1962, when Qashqa'i pastures were nationalized and land
reform began (discussed in chapter 11). These events coincided with
capitalist expansion throughout Fars, particularly in commercial stock
raising and agriculture, and with massive government-subsidized food
imports. Economic change among the Qashqa'i after 1962 reflected
national pressures more than it did political change at a specifically
Qashqa'i level.

PART IV

The Political and Economic Transformations of the 1960s, 1970s, and Early 1980s

Schoolgirl reading a lesson; note portrait of Mohammad Reza Shah inside
the tent

11

Pahlavi State Formation
and the Qashqa'i

*T*he impact of the ouster of the paramount Qashqa'i khans upon the Qashqa'i people cannot be understood outside the context of the political and economic changes occurring in Iran in the 1960s and 1970s. During these two decades, Mohammad Reza Shah rapidly expanded state institutions and extended power over potentially competitive forces, processes facilitated in Fars by the absence of the paramount Qashqa'i khans. The Qashqa'i people experienced political and economic pressures that the paramount khans could not have effectively challenged even had they been allowed to remain in the country, however, and the khans of the component Qashqa'i tribes eventually acquiesced to national pressures and passively participated in state consolidation. In the 1960s and 1970s new state policies detrimentally affected Qashqa'i nomadic pastoralists and their leaders. The government implemented a national land-reform program, nationalized all pastures, ceased to recognize the authority of khans over tribes, and placed land use and migrations under military control. Because of far-reaching disruptions brought about by scarcity of pastures, government restrictions, undermined tribal institutions, and capitalist expansion, most Qashqa'i found it exceedingly difficult to continue nomadic pastoralism. Their unique adaptation to the physical and social landscape was disappearing as they rapidly adopted settled agriculture and migrant wage labor. Chapter 12, covering the attempted resumption

251

of paramount Qashqa'i leadership in 1979–82, indicates the extent to which the position of the Qashqa'i people had been transformed in the preceding two decades. The current chapter outlines these political and economic transformations and then addresses three issues: the emergence of a tribal education program, the Qashqa'i as a national minority, and the state's exploitation of the Qashqa'i image.

THE IMPACT OF NEW GOVERNMENT POLICIES

Mohammad Reza Shah (and his American advisors) expected that his difficulties with the Qashqa'i would cease if he removed the paramount khans, but their forced exile in 1954–56 did not mean that his government had found the means to rule the Qashqa'i people directly. Military officers assigned to the Qashqa'i tribes proved to be ineffective administrators, and the state instead allocated some responsibility over Qashqa'i affairs to khans of the component tribes and issued them arms and ammunition. Khans within ruling families competed for the benefits resulting from state service, and ruling families competed for recognition, from Qashqa'i and non-Qashqa'i alike, as the leading Qashqa'i family. Darrehshuri khans quickly emerged as the major contenders. Government officials thought that dividing the Qashqa'i would help to decrease further the political and military threat they posed, but they underestimated the enduring qualities of tribal leadership, for khans of the component tribes continued to handle tribal affairs in customary fashion and indicated little interest in facilitating state administration. The shah placed the Amaleh tribe, left without an overarching leadership, under direct military governorship, but its component subtribes often acted without regard for the assigned official.

In 1960 the government, wary of the continuing power of the khans of the component Qashqa'i tribes, abolished the title of khan and the duties and powers associated with it: collection of taxes, allocation of land, supervision of migrations, and settlement of disputes. It increased the duties of military officers, which had in practice been little more than supervisory between 1954 and 1960, so that they could administer the tribes more directly. Several years passed before the officers achieved much success, and in the meantime many tribespeople continue to interact with khans as usual.

The introduction of the national Land Reform Law in January 1962 and its Additional Articles in January 1963 radically changed the state's role from supervision over, to control of, the Qashqa'i. Protests erupting throughout Fars in 1963 were related to land reform but spoke more directly to the government's increasing repressions. The catalyst to the protests was the government's response to the murder of a minor land-reform official near Firuzabad in November 1962. The government interpreted the murder as an act of resistance to land reform, declared martial law in Shiraz, and quickly moved against suspected perpetrators. Hasan Arsanjani, minister of agriculture, blamed the death on Naser Khan, who was in exile, and by inference on his brother Mohammad Hosain Khan, who had not been and was forbidden to be in Fars; "when there is a shot in Fars, the trigger is pulled in Tehran."[1] Qashqa'i sources state that a young Qashqa'i man acting independently killed the official and note that had Qashqa'i leaders wished to protest against land reform at this point they would have organized a resistance rather than killed such a minor official.[2] Arsanjani declared Fars the "acknowledged center of feudalism in Iran" and ordered the immediate implementation of land reform in the province. The shah personally distributed a few land deeds to tribal, presumably Qashqa'i, families in Firuzabad. The government declared "tribes" officially nonexistent and ordered the word deleted from official correspondence.[3] The shah and his government, expecting further resistance to land reform in Fars, set out in 1963 to crush potential resisters before they could organize. They moved to curtail the participation of khans in tribal affairs, fortified military forces in Shiraz, and declared a general disarmament, then dispatched five specially organized military contingents to five tribal areas (including Firuzabad) in order to disarm within two months the Qashqa'i, Mamassani, Boir Ahmad, other Kuhgiluyeh Lur tribes, and the tribes of Dashtistan, Tangistan, and Dashti. The government also sent military forces to destroy poppy fields in Fars, a major source of revenue for many provincial inhabitants, including Qashqa'i.

From March to May 1963 government troops fought small and several large battles with local tribal forces led by local tribal leaders. After the first military encounter, the minister of agriculture an-

---

1. *Ettela'at*, 15 November 1962, pp. 1, 5, 23; *The Tehran Journal*, 22 November 1962, p. 3; *Iran Almanac 1963*, p. 399.

2. In 1964 gendarmes held three "highway bandits" responsible for the slaying; *Kayhan*, 13 August 1964.

3. *The Tehran Journal*, 14 November 1962, p. 8; ibid., 29 December 1962, p. 1; *Iran Almanac 1963*, p. 429.

nounced that the government would immediately confiscate the land of any rebellious tribe and distribute it among those who were more worthy.[4] As the government killed and captured tribal leaders, more supporters joined the resistance and the fighting escalated; many men later killed in battle, executed, or imprisoned were the relatives of those who died at the beginning. By July, the government claimed to have killed or captured all rebel leaders; in 1964 it tried eleven of the captured leaders, then executed six and imprisoned five.[5] Although published accounts often refer to these events as the Qashqa'i rebellion of 1963,[6] few Qashqa'i were involved; the only Qashqa'i the state tried and sentenced were Sohrab Khan Kashkuli, son-in-law of one of the non-Qashqa'i involved, and Mohammad Hosain Khan Qashqa'i, who had not even been in Fars. The resistance, although representing all major tribal groups in Fars, was not coordinated; each group responded to the military presence of the government in its own region.[7] The timing of the resistance corresponded with a national economic recession. Rural producers had not fared well, and land reform seemed to many to be the means by which the government could gain greater control over the countryside. Most poor peasants in Fars were given no opportunity to obtain land, and some supported tribal leaders in their efforts to resist government encroachment.[8]

The timing of the resistance also corresponded with national struggles against the shah and his increasing military and political power. Clergy, leftists, students, workers, and members of the bazaar classes also used the occasion of land reform to protest against the government. The "tribal" problem was the one, however, that the shah and his military could handle most easily. The government blamed the

4. *Kayhan* , 13 August 1964; *The New York Times,* 20 March 1963 and 12 May 1963; *Iran Almanac 1963,* p. 429.

5. The six who were executed were Boir Ahmad, Sorkhi, Mamassani, and Hayat Davoudi men. The five who were imprisoned were Qashqa'i, Mamassani, and Bakhtiyari men (*Kayhan,* 8 August 1964, 11 August 1964, and 6 October 1964).

6. For example, see Halliday (1979:214) and van Bruinessen (1978:150). Katouzian appears to confuse the events in 1963 with those that followed in 1964–66 (1981:306).

7. The resistance movement among Boir Ahmad leaders drew support from the Ayatollah Khomeini (Loeffler 1973:129, 1982:70–71).

8. Although land reform was successfully carried out in one Boir Ahmad area, the holdings of most peasants were too small for adequate subsistence, and they were forced to rely on other economic options, particularly migrant labor (Loeffler 1973, 1982).

rural protest in Fars primarily on the Qashqa'i and attributed it to the resistance to land reform of wealthy landholders, Qashqa'i khans in particular. The severity of the state's punishment of the Qashqa'i people and their leaders after 1963, in contrast to the level of overt protest, demonstrates its intentions. Although very few Qashqa'i had participated in the 1963 protests, the government took the opportunity to undercut Qashqa'i power, particularly the power of landholding khans, and rapidly implement land reform. The shah depended on the quick implementation of land reform to prove the sincerity of his efforts to alter rural land tenure and rural economic structures and would not tolerate opposition. "There have been a number of side effects from land reform, affecting rural life and the country as a whole. The improvement which has occurred in security, notably in certain districts of Fars and other tribal areas, although not the direct result of land reform, is closely connected with it. If . . . real or alleged opposition to the reform had not given the government an excuse for action, the government would probably not have been able to reduce the tribal leaders of Fars as rapidly and successfully as it did" (Lambton 1969:351). The new minister of agriculture, alluding to the Qashqa'i ilkhani, declared, "the days when one man ruled from Shiraz to the Persian Gulf are over" (*Iran Almanac* 1963:400). As a result of government efforts to blame rural protest on the Qashqa'i, the notion of the Qashqa'i as a group opposed to reform and modernization was fortified for state officials and American advisors.

Rural protest involving Qashqa'i and others after 1963 occurred in a similarly uncoordinated, small-scale fashion. Bahman Qashqa'i, the young British-educated son of Farrokh Bibi and nephew of the paramount khans, attempted to activate the Qashqa'i people in armed struggle against the central government and, with a small armed group ranging from only six men to three hundred, attacked gendarme posts in Fars. He was captured and arrested in 1964, deceived concerning his fate, and then executed in 1966. That same year a small armed Qashqa'i group killed some army soldiers in retaliation for Bahman's execution. At least three times in 1967 small groups of Qashqa'i attacked gendarme posts in and near Qashqa'i territory, and their leaders, including Massi (Bolvardi) and Dashti (Gallehzan), were killed in action or later executed. In the late 1960s Iraj and Atta, cousins from the khan family of Kashkuli Bozorg, formed a small armed group of twenty to thirty men and conducted guerrilla raids against gendarme outposts in Fars. They operated independently of traditional Qashqa'i leaders, and the paramount khans advised Qashqa'i not to join them. Regarded as folk heroes by some Qashqa'i and other rural inhabitants, they received protection within Qashqa'i territory for years; state authorities, who regarded them as bandits and fugitives, condemned them to death in absentia. In the 1970s Iraj and Atta were active in leftist movements in Kurdistan, elsewhere in the Middle East, and Europe, and in 1979 they returned to Fars.

The state's growing power in Qashqa'i territory in the early 1960s was indicated by the rapid expansion of the military and secret police, justified officially by the incidences of rural protest. Although no traditional Qashqa'i leaders coordinated or directed the protests, the state nonetheless held them responsible and regularly harassed them. As state control over Qashqa'i territory expanded, Qashqa'i khans, who were steadily increasing their landholdings and capital investments in Qashqa'i territory, publicly claimed innocence concerning the anti-state activities of others and attempted to disassociate themselves, which suggests some growing awareness of or at least a more obvious class stratification.

In 1963 the government transferred authority over the Qashqa'i from military officers to the Rural Security Force (*entezamat*), a gendarme unit created especially for the purpose. Military governorship had been deemed ineffective and, at any rate, would have conflicted with the other new task given the gendarmerie, the enforcement of land reform. The government assigned a gendarme officer (*afsar-e entezamat*) from the Rural Security Force to each major Qashqa'i tribe and established gendarme posts in towns near winter and summer pastures to police Qashqa'i activities. The new force, chiefly responsible for political and military control, also allocated pastures and regulated migrations, tasks formerly supervised by Qashqa'i khans and headmen. The force was not immediately effective, but most tribespeople found it increasingly difficult to use pastures other than those formally assigned to them. Gendarme headquarters set the starting date for each tribe's seasonal migrations, basing its decision on political rather than ecological factors; flocks suffered accordingly, forced to stay too long in winter and summer pastures or to leave prematurely, and denied use of peak-growth pasturage along migration routes. The power of the state, not the needs of pastoralists, was paramount. Once permission for migrations was issued, gendarmes, stationed in camps at passes and bottlenecks along routes, policed movement. During the shah's celebration of twenty-five hundred years of the Iranian monarchy near Shiraz in 1971, gendarmes forced the Qashqa'i to delay departure from their high-altitude summer pastures for six weeks, on the grounds that the movement of tribal people by Persepolis and Shiraz would be a security risk to the government. While the shah, Spiro Agnew, and dozens of other world leaders celebrated, nomads suffered and many animals died, trapped in cold, barren pastures. Gendarmes also forbade nomads to camp longer than forty-eight hours in a single location during the migration. Hostile landowners and villagers notified local authorities when nomads exceeded the time limit, and gendarmes by the jeep-load forced their departure. Clearly, it was not the pastoralists' interests that gendarme control was serving.

Gendarmes, also responsible for disarming the Qashqa'i, had difficulty confiscating guns at first, primarily because they lacked access to individual Qashqa'i, a perennial problem of state administration of nomads. Qashqa'i men entrusted favorite weapons to village friends or urban patrons, gave up worthless or outdated weapons to government officials (receiving in return receipts proving to future authorities that they had already complied), and disassembled weapons, spreading their parts throughout household baggage. In the mid-1960s gendarmes began to require Qashqa'i headmen to collect guns from their subtribes and withheld pasture allocations until a sufficient number were submitted. Those withholding guns risked state punishment. For Qashqa'i men, possession of firearms was closely connected with political autonomy, and hence the state's attempts to remove their weapons altered political and military conditions and evoked deeply felt sentiments.

From the mid-1960s, SAVAK, Iran's repressive secret police established with United States assistance, conducted increasing surveillance over the activities of both elite and nonelite Qashqa'i.[9] SAVAK officials, assigned to towns near Qashqa'i territory, gathered intelligence on the Qashqa'i and generally harassed them. They frequently visited unannounced the residences and encampments of khans and other wealthy Qashqa'i, occasions demanding elaborate hospitality, which was a financial and social burden on their "hosts."[10] Many SAVAK officials conducted their official "business" this way on Fridays and other holidays in order to escape the confines of their assigned towns and offer their families an outing. They also summoned Qashqa'i to their offices,

9. SAVAK, established in 1952, later received Israeli assistance.
10. For a wider discussion of involuntary hosting, see Beck (1982).

where, on any given day, a forlorn group of elite and nonelite Qashqa'i
and other inhabitants of the region sat for hours in outer offices waiting
to be seen. SAVAK officials actively solicited informers and contacts,
and all Qashqa'i, elite and nonelite, held suspicions of collaborating
family members and acquaintances.

The Land Reform Law, Additional Articles, and many amendments
made no provision for the seasonal use of pastures by Iran's nomads,
and the effects of land reform were drastic for them. Only individuals
who occupied land permanently (and who met other requirements)
were considered qualified for land distribution. Some villagers received
deeds to nearby pastures that they had traditionally used (Lambton
1969:235–36, 247), but the Qashqa'i and other nomads did not occupy specific plots of land year-round and hence could not claim land
under the new laws.[11] Even those who did stay in one seasonal pasture
area all year did not remain in a single location and in any case lacked
the necessary verifying documents. Of the Qashqa'i and non-Qashqa'i
who cultivated in winter and summer pastures, usually the settled non-
Qashqa'i were informed about land-reform procedures, first registered
the land in their own names, and received deeds to it. Land-reform
officials often visited land when Qashqa'i users were in other seasonal
pastures or on migration, and again the nomads lost out in land regis-
tration.

Pastoralists elsewhere in Iran in the 1960s had varying success in
retaining land. Some Sangsari in north central Iran, possibly Iran's
largest group of nontribal pastoralists, moved into the traditional pastures of the Chubdari, who had recently settled, and received official
grazing permits to them. "The Chubdari, who were unlettered and had
little knowledge of official procedures, did not contest this process until too late" (Spooner 1976:89). Some Boir Ahmad settled in order to
guard land claims until land titles were registered and then resumed
nomadism (Fazel and Afshar Naderi 1976:39). Some Shahsevan in
northwest Iran hoped to maintain rights to land by dry-farming good
pastures (Tapper 1979:274). In Qashqa'i areas, however, settled non-
Qashqa'i who cultivated pastures and engaged in other land-expropriating techniques received legal title to most of the reallocated
land.

11. The majority of Iran's villagers were not provided for through land reform
either; Lambton (1969), E. Hooglund (1982a), Dillon (1976), Keddie (1972).

The Qashqa'i report that bribery of land-reform officials was prevalent during the early years of reform. Lambton's account of land reform provides some evidence for corruption, but her general view is that most land-reform officials were honest and genuinely concerned with the law's intentions. Her book, however, lacks information on the status of land reform in areas occupied by tribally organized pastoral nomads. She does state that land reform was more difficult to implement in Fars and the south than elsewhere (1969). Qashqa'i khans who had withdrawn or were withdrawing from participation in tribal affairs at this time were usually unable to prevent these abuses and losses of lands.

In the abortive land reform of 1960 many landowners learned forestalling measures which they utilized even after the 1962–63 laws had gone into effect. Owners subdivided landholdings and deeds among family members and predated the times they had planted orchards and gardens, developed woodlands, mechanized cultivation, utilized wage laborers in cultivation, and installed motor pumps, activities exempting the lands involved from land reform. In Qashqa'i areas, many non-Qashqa'i as well as some wealthy Qashqa'i (including khans) plowed pastures that were not theirs even by customary right. All these actions were illegal, but violations were difficult to prove. Because of military control over the Qashqa'i and their nomadism, these land-expropriating techniques often went unnoticed and hence unprevented until the lands in question had already been legally deeded to the perpetrators.

Land reform encouraged the widespread expansion of cultivation at the expense of grazing land in all Qashqa'i areas. Previously uncultivated land outside the range of existing village water supplies was opened for distribution through land reform, and many people received rights to cultivate new land. The availability of new agricultural technology, such as implements, chemical fertilizers, and motorized pumps, facilitated these efforts. The areas with the best soil and moisture conditions for both grazing and crops passed from pastoral to agricultural use, and many Qashqa'i lost their best land and were left with inferior, arid tracts. New cultivation often occurred in areas unsuited to agriculture, and soil erosion, especially after dryland farming was attempted, resulted. In the Boir Ahmad area the most damaging aspect of land reform was the "mindless conversion of valuable pastures to less profitable farm plots" (Fazel 1971:219). The unprofitable dry-

land farming done on pastures by some Shahsevan was intended to secure land rights (Tapper 1979:274). In the Qashqa'i area, many new
cultivators introduced motorized pumps in order to utilize ground
water for irrigation, which lowered the water table and otherwise de-
graded the environment. On land that was plowed but never planted,
wind erosion worked quickly because vegetation and topsoil were
turned under, and natural pasturage was destroyed. The importance
the government placed on a settled agricultural rather than a nomadic
pastoral life is indicated by these new measures and activities. Cultivation of Qashqa'i pastures caused conflict between field owners (generally non-Qashqa'i) and Qashqa'i who owned animals. The Qashqa'i
had difficulty keeping their animals out of fields, which were rarely
walled or protected, and state authorities tended to favor the claims of
agriculturalists over those of nomads.

The effects of land reform were combined with those of the Forest
and Range Nationalization Law to the further detriment of Qashqa'i
pastoralism. These were the first two principles of the "revolution of
the shah and the people" (formerly titled the White Revolution). According to the new law, all natural pastures now belonged to the government. Village pastures, defined as twice the size of a village's cultivated lands, were exempt. Nationalized land, constituting 75 percent
of Iran,[12] included forests, pastures, deserts, mountains, and all uncultivated lands lying outside the service of village water supplies. Almost
all Qashqa'i pastures were included in the nationalization. The government began to collect taxes on herd animals sold to state-run slaughterhouses on the grounds that grazing had been done free on state land.

The Forest and Range Organization of the Ministry of Agriculture,
responsible for allocating and controlling the newly nationalized pastures, was aided by the new (1967) Ministry of Natural Resources
(Iranfar 1970). The government reserved land for programs in range
improvement, livestock feed development, wildlife conservation,
watershed protection, and recreational use, which either restricted livestock numbers and periods of use or totally excluded them from the
areas concerned. The Ministry of Natural Resources employed forest
rangers to enforce prohibitions against grazing, hunting, cutting live
vegetation for firewood, and other newly illegal activities in these protected areas. Qashqa'i areas were affected, notably the Dasht Arjan area
west of Shiraz, established by the shah's brother as a huge hunting

12. Department of the Environment, Tehran (1977:49).

preserve and off limits to traditional users—both villagers and nomads. The Forest and Range Organization did not reopen improved pastures to the pastoralists who had been removed from them because it could not enforce new range-management regulations. Instead, it preferred to allocate large blocks of grazing land to commercial and state-owned corporations on fixed-term contracts and refused to issue grazing permits to pastoralists who did not form corporations (Sandford 1977:6–12).

Land reform and pasture nationalization facilitated state and foreign interests by expropriating land for the rapidly expanding oil industry in southwest Iran. Qashqa'i pastoralists and agriculturalists, along with Arabs, Lurs, Bakhtiyari, and others, lost wide stretches of land in winter quarters in areas where Iranian and foreign oil companies established new oil fields and set aside areas for future exploration and development. [13]

Until the early 1960s, Qashqa'i nomadic pastoralists held and defended land collectively. Although some agricultural land was formally registered in khans' names, control over almost all Qashqa'i territory depended on military and political power rather than written deeds. Khans allocated winter and summer pastures to subtribes on a seasonal or longer-term basis, and individuals and groups secured rights to this land through payment of taxes and other expressions of loyalty to tribal leaders. Well-organized groups with effective leaders were able to increase land and members, while weak groups lost land and members. Groups could change political affiliations and territories, and land beyond the confines of tribal boundaries could also be utilized. Pastoral production as practiced by the Qashqa'i hinged on such flexible patterns of land use. Tribal leaders were essential in the overall system of land use and in negotiating land disputes.

The removal of top tribal leaders, the annexation of Qashqa'i land by non-Qashqa'i cultivators, and the nationalization of pastures all drastically changed these patterns. The government required Qashqa'i nomads to obtain land rights through bureaucratic channels rather than through traditional tribal rights and customs. The government, realizing difficulties in dealing with the vast, dispersed population now

13. The Khomeini regime ordered that many of these new oil wells and prospective sites be abandoned (for the Boir Ahmad area, see Loeffler 1982). For a map indicating the extent of land covered by oil concessions in south Iran in 1975, see Ferrier (1977:92).

that both the ilkhani and khans were divested of authority in these matters, turned to headmen as its mediators, men who were now empowered to negotiate land and migration rights and government relations and become indispensable to their affiliated tribespeople. In recognizing subtribes for administrative purposes, the government caused their boundaries to become firm and stable in the same way that gendarme authority over tribes had fixed their boundaries. Just as the ilkhani had defined for the state who was and who was not a Qashqa'i, tribal khans and subtribal headmen now defined who was and who was not a tribal and a subtribal member, respectively. Qashqa'i nomads who lacked, chose not to have, or were denied tribal or subtribal affiliations during this period had no official status with regard to the government and had extreme difficulty securing land rights and other state services.

By the mid-1960s, headmen received land use and migration schedules for their subtribes from the gendarme officer of the Rural Security Force assigned to their tribe to administer government policies. In most cases the officer recognized customary winter and summer pastures of subtribes. He required headmen to submit the names of land-using households in their sections and then issued deeds for the land in question. These deeds later became the legal basis for land use. The new procedures caused difficulties. The officer fixed the use of one winter and one summer pasture for each Qashqa'i section and prohibited use of alternative pastures, which ran against customary patterns of land use and threatened pastoral production. Qashqa'i had always utilized many pastures before and after using their allotted seasonal ones, and they also needed alternative pastures in case of poor conditions in customary areas. Once resident in seasonal pastures, they had not been restricted to one or several areas but moved from place to place seeking fresh grazing, water, and clean campsites. The officer now required each household to remain in a single demarcated plot for the entire season regardless of conditions and the presence or absence of pasture and water. He also fixed the identity and number of households to use each section, which further disrupted traditionally flexible patterns. Previously, occupants of winter and summer pastures had changed from year to year in response to environmental, economic, political, and social conditions. Although the core groups of a seasonal pasture had been defined patrilineally, those related only by marriage or maternal ties or by political or economic ties had been able to utilize the area according to their ties with the core groups. These customary practices now virtually ended. Headmen added individuals at their own discretion but could not easily subtract them, because those removed could appeal to the gendarmes. Some headmen registered land in only their own or a few relatives' names, which allowed them to exert pressure on dependent households. As an additional problem, the government's procedure for allocating pastures did not allow for normal processes of household division, which put pressure on already limited pastures as the years passed under the new regulations and families grew and divided. Parents were forced either to share their pastures with economically independent children, causing crowding and overgrazing, or to cast them adrift in the regional wage labor market.

In 1975 government officials decided that "tribes" no longer existed and that the overseeing Rural Security Force and its special gendarme units were no longer needed. The 1962 government decree abolishing tribes had apparently not been effective. Henceforth, the government considered the Qashqa'i as any other rural population under regular gendarme authority. Control of migration schedules and routes suddenly ceased, and the Qashqa'i could again move according to pastoral needs instead of government whim, but they did not welcome the other consequences of the abolition of the Rural Security Force. Nomads who had always acquired land through tribal structures were now required to secure individual land-use permits directly from the government. Headmen were suddenly stripped of their recently enhanced authority. The Rural Security Force transferred its records to the urban offices of the Ministries of Agriculture and Natural Resources, which issued permits for seasonal use of pastures to some individuals who requested them.[14] For purposes of control as well as administrative continuity, officials determined rights to particular areas according to the usage established under the Rural Security Force. Many nomads could not secure these new permits because their names and locations had never been officially recorded. Ministry officials, visiting some pastures in order to assign land and record boundaries on the basis of herd size, issued some permits "on the basis of a quick look at the area and common sense" (Sandford 1977:5), but in most cases no officials saw the lands in question. Only "grazing land" (*marta'*), defined as land above water channels, was available for permits. Land below this level, classified as cultivable land (*mazra'eh*), was denied to nomads, even though

14. This licensing system, in theory universal, was said to cover about 40 percent of Iran's pasturelands in 1977 (Sandford 1977:5); the actual percentage was probably much less than this.

they had often grazed and cultivated there. Instead, the government deeded it through land reform to non-Qashqa'i villagers and even townspeople. Officials generally assigned pastures to families on the basis of current flock size, a practice that ignored seasonal fluctuations in herds. In one area officials counted animals and assigned land in late summer when herds were their smallest and did not consider the fact that one month earlier these families were grazing large herds. Officials expelled those nomads present who were not of the location's dominant kinship groups.

Qashqa'i nomads had always been able to build houses, cultivate, plant orchards and gardens, and establish seasonal or permanent residence on tribal land, but the government, through its new grazing permits, now prohibited these activities and allowed only seasonal and pastoral use of land. No houses, protective walls, wells, or other kinds of construction were allowed; no fields could be sown or trees planted. In one area army personnel cut down trees planted by an agriculturalist along a stream running by Qashqa'i pastures while a few miles away they planted trees in a reforestation program. Many Qashqa'i needed to cultivate and construct shelters in order to subsist. Only agriculture with the required land deeds preserved land claims in the face of advancing outside encroachments and met the new demands of the market economy. Houses and animal dwellings were necessary for protection against the severe climate experienced in permanent residence. The government now prohibited the Qashqa'i from engaging in any permanent or nonpastoral activities on lands traditionally theirs for generations and did not permit them to buy these lands.

The new regulations were designed to support government policies to restrict the number of animals using pastures as well as to eliminate nomadic pastoralists and the political systems containing them. Policymakers in Tehran, many of whom had never visited the countryside and were unaware of land-use patterns among pastoral nomads, stated that Iran was rapidly being denuded of vegetation, that deserts were expanding, and that pastoralists were at fault.[15] Programs for pasture use emphasized measures against desertification, not social and economic issues. Had these new programs been successful, they might have dealt with some environmental problems and might have helped some individuals, but they did not address the needs of pastoral groups. "We are in danger of . . . demanding ever more drastic powers

15. Sandford (1977); Department of the Environment, Tehran (1977).

to impose technical solutions . . . which will be of great immediate injury to many pastoralists while of very uncertain long term ecological or economic benefit to anyone other than to those who may be able to recolonise land from which the traditional pastoralists have been excluded; and such beneficiaries will benefit only by grabbing what already existed rather than from any overall increment in output" (Sandford 1977:21–22). The government's nationalization of pastures "may have been a wise policy for the maintenance of their long-term fertility as well as supervision over the use and allocation of this agricultural resource. What in practice happened was not nationalization in that sense, but expropriation and exclusion" (Katouzian 1978:367).

New government policies for handling environmental degradation, especially overgrazing, were particularly misplaced in light of the greatly increased pressure on pastoral resources caused by other government programs: land reform, pasture nationalization, and removal of tribal leaders. Most Qashqa'i, whose ancestors had successfully grazed these lands for generations, had usually practiced careful range management.[16] Under new restrictions, however, those with insufficient land to support their herds put increased pressure on existing resources, overgrazed, and destroyed vegetation previously left relatively undisturbed, such as trees and shrubs. They often cut and dried ungrazed vegetation and carried it away for future use. These practices had immediate and long-term ecological effects. Those nomads receiving land deeds in 1975 attempted to conserve resources, despite the increased herd sizes needed for economic support, while those denied deeds ceased to care much about conservation. To compensate for pasture shortage, some Qashqa'i rented grazing land from other Qashqa'i or from villagers. A 1971 law prohibiting herd-owners from grazing rentals was not enforced. Renters lacked long-term interest in the tracts and tended to misuse them. Some Qashqa'i who received more land than needed, rented land to others, and some who were in the process of settling did not inform authorities so that they could keep their grazing permits, rent their pastures, and retain the option to use them in the future. In a matter of a few years, land rents and new regulations had turned formerly tribal, corporate land into private property with explicit monetary value. Many Qashqa'i became impoverished in this

16. They avoided overgrazing, rotated grazing areas, protected certain kinds of vegetation, restricted camels' foraging, and constructed basins to catch rain in order to improve local grazing.

process, directed as it was more to ruling them than to regulating their activities for other purposes.

Military control over the Qashqa'i opened their lands to non-Qashqa'i herds, further depleting vegetation available to Qashqa'i herds and increasing overgrazing. Commercial stock raisers with large herds were the first to enter Qashqa'i pastures; commercial herding and family economy pastoralism quickly proved to be incompatible. Wealthy merchants and landowners, often new to stock raising, invested in flocks or acquired flocks through default on debts and hired nontribal shepherds to graze them in Qashqa'i pastures. The newcomers entered pastures before Qashqa'i occupancy, leaving little vegetation for Qashqa'i animals, and followed after them, utilizing vegetation that Qashqa'i herders were conserving for the next year. Few Qashqa'i could guard their seasonal pastures all year against such trespassing herders. Disarmed, under military control, and lacking government support as well as effective tribal mediators, the Qashqa'i could not adequately challenge these armed herders. The government did not enforce its 1971 law prohibiting use of nationalized land by herders without grazing permits and with flocks of over two hundred.

Village pastoralists also began using Qashqa'i pastures, reasonably confident now that their flocks would no longer be raided. The Qashqa'i depended on seasonal use of specific areas, but village pastoralists increasingly used these same areas almost all year, so that little vegetation remained for Qashqa'i herds. Villagers traditionally owned a few animals, but as the balance of power in the countryside changed, they increased their production as well as their flocks and became competitors not only for land but also in the marketplace. With larger herds, they sought additional grazing beyond the village periphery, which resulted in further encroachment on Qashqa'i pasturage. Qashqa'i flocks had always depended on grazing the stubble of harvested village fields. With increased village pastoralism, this access was jeopardized, and the Qashqa'i were forced to cultivate and buy fodder, a previously unnecessary effort and expense. Qashqa'i and non-Qashqa'i pastoralists who held no legal land rights also used Qashqa'i pastures surreptitiously; they traveled in small groups and sought temporary grazing wherever possible. These many illegal grazers, especially the large commercial herds, decreased the chances that even Qashqa'i nomads with legal land rights would find adequate pastures, and they were a major factor in the impoverishment of pastoral resources and in the settlement of many Qashqa'i.

Changes in land use brought about by land reform, pasture nationalization, disruption of tribal institutions, and military control—combined with increased capitalist penetration of Qashqa'i economies—
meant the rapid settlement of many Qashqa'i into villages, towns, and
cities and the assumption of new livelihoods and changed relations of
production.[17] Possibly 30 to 40 percent of the Qashqa'i were settled in
the early 1970s, as compared with some 15 percent in the 1960s.[18]
Although government control of migrations ceased in 1975, expanding cultivation, agribusiness ventures, irrigation projects (especially in
the Marv Dasht plain, where the enormous Dariush Kabir dam was
built on the Kur River), and paved roads increasingly blocked migration routes and contributed to the rapid settlement of the Qashqa'i.

Although Mohammad Reza Shah did not forcibly settle Qashqa'i
nomads in the brutal way his father had done in the 1930s, the impact
of the modernizing, centralizing state and economy had similar effects
on them. A top government priority in the 1960s was to "settle the
tribes," a political slogan containing a hysterical note that sounded
much like "wipe out the tribes."[19] An Office of Tribal Settlement,
under the Ministry of Housing and Development, was established in
Shiraz to assist in the settlement process, but its efforts were primarily
directed toward the tribes of the long-disbanded Khamseh confederacy.
Government loans at low interest rates, supposedly available through
this office and the government's Agricultural Bank, were extremely difficult to secure; the process required access to urban networks, years of
bureaucratic effort, and sufficient money for bribes to move documents
through channels. Land for settlement, by law outside Qashqa'i pastures, was available for purchase from the government and from private
owners, but the disruptions brought about by a poorly handled, often
changing land-reform program complicated the process. Land prices
doubled and tripled every few years, making settlement difficult for
the most needy. The Office of Tribal Settlement and other government
agencies were also charged with the responsibility of helping the
Qashqa'i and others establish rural cooperatives and providing them
with assistance in securing loans, but they were ineffective.

17. For accounts of these transformations, see Beck (1980a, 1981a, 1981b).
18. According to the Department of Tribal Education, Ministry of Education
(1972), and Kortum (1979b:75–76). For a map of the regions of Qashqa'i settlement, see Kortum (1979b:77).
19. Gregory Lima, *Kayhan,* 2 February 1964.

In the 1970s the government announced plans to settle half a million of Iran's nomads in fifty centers, one of which was to be connected with the new slaughterhouse and meat-processing plant in Qassemabad in Fars. Two thousand Qashqa'i families, who would provide workers for the plant, were to be settled at the center. This project was not fully realized at the time of the revolution. The government also proposed that Qashqa'i be settled near sugar factories in Fars (particularly in Marv Dasht, Kavar, and the northwest outskirts of Shiraz, where some spontaneous settlement was already occurring), largely because these factories needed seasonal unskilled labor and produced a sugar-beet by-product useful as animal fodder (Kortum 1979a:35–37, 1982:212–13). Projects for water development benefited existing and new settlements, not migratory groups. As is obvious, the government preferred to settle the Qashqa'i than to encourage continued nomadic pastoralism, and its plans fulfilled the wishes of city technocrats, not the Qashqa'i, who were not officially or unofficially consulted. Pahlavi University's Veterinary School did, however, sponsor a veterinary program in the 1970s which experimented among some Qashqa'i nomads, and the United States Agency for International Development supported the creation of several livestock feeding stations for Qashqa'i use.

Increased government manipulation of the national economy, especially with regard to food imports and subsidized food prices, was destructive to Qashqa'i producers, both pastoralists and agriculturalists. Local products (grain, meat, and many dairy products) were increasingly noncompetitive in the government-manipulated market. Many Qashqa'i and others who found it difficult to sell their products discovered that it was often cheaper to buy government imports than to produce these products themselves, but they continued production because they lacked sufficient cash. The government's Meat Organization, established in 1960, fixed the prices of live animals and meat and imposed new taxes on animals sold at government-run slaughterhouses. The government also strictly controlled opium production—an important source of cash for the Qashqa'i and others—by selling the right to grow poppies to wealthy landowners and severely punishing others who were caught cultivating poppy fields. It outlawed charcoal production, another major income-producing activity for some Qashqa'i, and controlled the production of gum tragacanth by requiring permits of, and collecting taxes from, producers and by setting prices. Wide-ranging forest rangers, gendarmes, and army personnel, all of whom held powers of enforcement, supervised these measures.

Conscription increasingly threatened all Qashqa'i families with young males. Government identification cards, required for school, identified males of draft age, and escaping conscription became difficult. Gendarmes periodically toured Qashqa'i territory in order to question draft-age males and seize resisters and deserters. A small number of Qashqa'i who had finished high school served in the Literacy, Health, and Rural Extension Corps, part of the shah's White Revolution, in lieu of army service. Although the Health Corps served some villages, the government offered no medical assistance to nomadic Qashqa'i. Those Qashqa'i desiring modern medical services sought them independently.[20] The government established Houses of Justice, a program for dispute settlement in rural areas, including some Qashqa'i areas, and appointed a few Qashqa'i khans as administrators.

Almost all Qashqa'i viewed government expansion into their territory negatively; for most it meant exploitative encounters with officials who demanded bribes and other favors and who offered little or nothing beneficial in return. Prior to the 1960s, Qashqa'i khans had buffered the people from the incursions of most government officials. After the early 1960s, little prevented officials from having access to most parts of Qashqa'i territory, especially given new roads built by government programs. Those with sanctioning powers, including gendarme officers, SAVAK agents, and forest rangers, found the trips lucrative.

Most government officials held prejudices against rural and especially tribal people that became more virulent as the gap in the rate of change between urban and rural Iran, and between Persians and non-Persians, rapidly increased in the 1960s and 1970s. As Iran modernized, officials viewed with growing scorn the patterns of life in rural Iran, especially those patterns that seemed to present obstacles to rapid development in these areas. Partly because of these attitudes, communication between the government and rural society was abysmal. The Qashqa'i suffered from these attitudes as much as, if not more than, other rural, non-Persian people in Iran, partly because of state-fostered notions that they were bandits and robbers led by feudal chieftains opposed to change.

Khans of the component Qashqa'i tribes carefully assessed the increasing power of the Pahlavi state in the 1960s and 1970s. Many

20. In the 1960s and 1970s some Pahlavi University Medical School teams conducted health surveys on a few Qashqa'i groups and provided on-the-scene cursory examinations and some medicines (Petrosian et al. 1964).

avoided playing formal political roles for the state during this period and, although frequently asked to participate, shunned service in parliament. Seeing that government policies were not likely to be reversed soon and increasingly cut off from functions relating to tribal administration, they adjusted their economic activities. Largely because of pasture nationalization, they divested themselves of almost all their flocks and kept only a herd or two for meat and dairy products. With changes in land tenure underway or anticipated (land reform was not effectively enforced in all locations simultaneously) and technological innovations in agriculture, khans converted pastures to wheat fields and orchards and turned their efforts to commercial grain and fruit production. Land brought under mechanized agriculture and developed for orchards and gardens was exempt from land-reform confiscations and enabled khans to secure legal title to these lands. Qashqa'i and others who were dispossessed lacked official recourse.

Under government pressure to cease tribal functions, most khans in the late 1950s and early 1960s ceased to migrate overland with the tribespeople and concentrated on establishing permanent residences in seasonal pastures and cities. Most abandoned their huge, elaborately decorated tents and encampments in winter and summer pastures, partly in symbolic protest against increasing government exactions. Some used the reed mats that had formed their tent base as part of the roofing in their new houses, an indication that they regarded the change to be permanent. During the renewed emphasis on tribal identity and consciousness in the 1970s (see below), however, many khans reestablished and embellished their encampments in summer pastures and moved back into their tents. Although their contacts with Qashqa'i tribespeople were diminishing, creating less reason for rural residency in the face of increasing urban demands, their expanded agricultural activities kept them rooted in the countryside. Urban demands included more frequent government contacts, commercial ties relating to production, formal education for children, and the obligations and pleasures of their upper-middle-class and upper-class lifestyles. Some khans bought land in cities, not for speculative purposes as did many other Iranian elite, but for residences, while others continued to rent houses wherever they spent their winters (Firuzabad, Kazerun, Shiraz, Shahreza, or Isfahan, depending largely on the location of their interests in winter pastures). Some assisted Qashqa'i supporters by establishing tribal schools, rural cooperatives, and Houses of Justice and by negotiating bank loans, despite government pressure on them to sever such ties, while others chose to be uninvolved.

Headmen of Qashqa'i subtribes, the only mediators now available to most tribespeople, played essential roles in the 1960s and 1970s. The government, having assumed control of land, assigned responsibility to headmen for acquiring documents from various agencies for land rights for their subtribes, a task requiring literacy, money, and finesse in bribing officials. The Rural Security Force required headmen to visit its seasonal headquarters periodically in order to issue orders and migratory schedules. The state, having ordered the confiscation of arms, forced headmen to collect their groups' guns and held them personally responsible for all group members retaining guns illegally. Headmen attempted to settle disputes before the gendarmes or army learned of them, helped men cope with the military draft, and obtained the identification cards required by law for school, army, and marriage. With the increasing dependency of the Qashqa'i on a cash economy, headmen assisted in economic transactions with merchants and moneylenders and helped to secure additional credit for those already heavily in debt. Headmen continued to collect an animal tax, using the income to support their ever-increasing expenses, and they collected cash payments based on herd size when their groups were forced to pay for pasture use and when government officials demanded bribes.

BAHMANBEGI AND THE OFFICE OF TRIBAL EDUCATION

One of the most important single developments affecting the Qashqa'i as a political and cultural entity between 1954 and 1979 was the creation of a tribal education program.[21] For most Qashqa'i during this period, the program's tent schools were the only government service reaching them directly that could be considered beneficial, and the program's director was their only effective, official link to the state.

21. The material in this section derives from many sources, including my own observations of schools and many discussions with Mohammad Bahmanbegi. Dorothy Grant recounted her observations on the education program from her visits in 1963–65. Brad Hanson and Paul Barker (1981) related their experiences as American Peace Corps volunteers with the Office of Tribal Education in the 1970s. See also Bahmanbegi (1945–46, 1971), Gagon (1956), Hendershot (1964), Shafii et al. (1977), and Kortum (1979a).

Mohammad Bahmanbegi, the originator and director general of the tribal education program and a Qashqa'i himself, assumed the role of representative of the Qashqa'i people and was so regarded by the state and other powers. He served, as had the now-absent ilkhani, as broker between the people and the state, and he expanded upon the role to create new linkages with the state and the foreign power (United States) that was then increasing its influence in Iran. Bahmanbegi provided continuity in representation and official recognition in the relationship between the Qashqa'i and the state from 1954 to 1979, despite the state's moves against other parts of Qashqa'i society and despite political and economic transformations in Iran as a whole. He quickly improvised in a rapidly changing political context to fill the position vacated by the ilkhani and to establish contacts of his own with the shah and empress, officials of the Iranian government, and American advisors newly charged with the task of helping the shah to modernize the nation.

Bahmanbegi's education program was part of government efforts to integrate the Qashqa'i into a rapidly changing Iran. The government intended to assimilate Iran's diverse people into the modernizing state through education and other institutions, and the program under Bahmanbegi's leadership was sufficiently oriented in this direction to succeed and expand without much resistance from the state. Traditional tribal leaders could not have performed the same function. Despite the fact that Bahmanbegi's policies were designed to destroy Qashqa'i economic and political systems, they served to assert and enhance Qashqa'i symbols and ideologies. During this period many Qashqa'i people emerged with clearer, more articulate notions of Qashqa'i identity and nationality than ever before in their history, while simultaneously state policies oriented toward the integration of tribal, rural, and non-Persian people into the modernizing nation-state were undermining the bases of their existence. Bahmanbegi and the tribal education program were instruments in both these processes.

In the 1920s Isma'il Khan, the Qashqa'i ilkhani, perceived that Mohammad Bahmanbegi, son of an Amaleh retainer in his camp, was highly intelligent and singled him out for special education, first in the ilkhani camp and later in Tehran when the retainer and his family accompanied Isma'il Khan into exile there. Bahmanbegi went on to receive a law degree from Tehran University; he is the first Qashqa'i known to have acquired a postgraduate degree of any kind. He returned to Qashqa'i territory in his twenties as an entrepreneur in stock raising and as an assistant to Naser Khan, the new ilkhani. Bahmanbegi's literacy and advanced education gave him advantages over other more traditionally trained and oriented advisors, and his command of French, German, and English were assets in Naser Khan's interactions with foreigners. Bahmanbegi translated in Naser Khan's camp for Schulze-Holthus, the German agent assigned to the ilkhani during World War II (Schulze-Holthus 1954:152–53, Monteil 1966:15).

Bahmanbegi's emergence in the early 1950s coincided with Mosaddeq's rise to power and challenge to the shah, Qashqa'i leaders' support of Mosaddeq, and increased American interference. Bahmanbegi, although not a member of the Shahilu lineage, was closely associated with it and was high in achieved status, factors contributing to his quest for power and influence. His long-standing interest in education attracted him to American officials who began work in 1951 in the American government's Point Four Program in Iran and its Educational Division, established to reform the nation's educational system. Together with Glen Gagon of Brigham Young University in Utah, he developed plans for mobile schools for the Qashqa'i. American officials sent Bahmanbegi to Brigham Young University to consult with experts there, and, while on a tour in the American southwest, he was inspired by schools on a Hopi (Native American) reservation. Point Four provided funds for Bahmanbegi's program but would not finance teacher salaries. The Iranian government, initially unenthusiastic about the program, was also unwilling to finance teacher salaries but acquiesced to plans introduced by the American team. Bahmanbegi sought support from khans and other wealthy Qashqa'i, each of whom agreed to pay the salary of one or more teachers.

In August 1953 those Qashqa'i personally chosen by Bahmanbegi to receive teacher training began classes in Shiraz, and in January 1954 seventy-three tent schools opened. These months coincided with Mosaddeq's ouster and the government's moves against the Shahilu family. The same American officials who urged the paramount khans' ouster actively supported Point Four's plans for the tribes of Fars, including Bahmanbegi's education program. The fall of the paramount khans and the rise of Bahmanbegi cannot, thus, be separated or understood outside the context of United States involvement. The initial success of Bahmanbegi's program depended on the support of four powers whose interests did not always coincide—the Iranian government, the American Point Four Program, paramount khans, and secondary khans—and "it is a credit to Bahmanbegi's diplomatic skills that he was able to emerge from the crisis with his embryonic school experiment relatively intact" (Barker 1981:151). Bahmanbegi gradually drew away from the Shahilu family, increasingly under government attack, and toward other, often newly emergent powers outside Qashqa'i society. He enhanced his ties with American officials in Shiraz and Tehran and developed networks in national and local politics, no easy feat given his family's lack of prominence in these domains. He also allied with elements in the Qashqa'i confederacy that had conflicted with the paramount leaders, including some Darrehshuri and Kashkuli Bozorg khans. As the government increasingly restricted the activities of all Qashqa'i khans, they became less inclined to finance teacher salaries, and in 1955 the Ministry of Education began to pay teachers.[22]

In 1957 Bahmanbegi opened a Tribal Teacher Training School in Shiraz, and each year thereafter the numbers of students trained, schools opened, and youngsters educated increased dramatically. Bahmanbegi's initial plans for education concerned only the Qashqa'i, but he gradually added non-Qashqa'i people to his programs, and by the late 1960s his schools and teachers served most major tribal groups in Fars and the Kuhgiluyeh-Boir Ahmad region. Teachers usually served in their own tribes; the common cultural background of students and teachers facilitated learning and was a key reason for the program's success. A boarding school in Shiraz, established in 1967, eventually became the Tribal High School, which by 1979 had two large campuses and over one thousand students. Many considered the school the best educational program in Shiraz and possibly all of Iran; it attracted superior students and entrance was highly competitive. American Peace Corps volunteers served as teachers.

Bahmanbegi also established a Tribal Carpet Weaving School, a Tribal Technical School, and training programs for midwives and paramedics, and he supported the efforts of Pahlavi University's Veterinary School to improve livestock in the province and train tribal youth as paraveterinarians. He attempted to set up traveling stores so that nomads could avoid the extortive practices of bazaar merchants and moneylenders. At the government's urging, he reluctantly helped to

22. As long as the paramount khans "had ruled in relative autonomy, an education system largely sponsored by the tribal elite was a source of pride and a partial justification of their autonomy. . . . With the increasing erosion of Qashqa'i independence, there was little reason for khans to continue assuming financial burdens which they felt belonged to the government" (Barker 1981:151–52).

establish teacher training and tribal school programs for other tribal groups outside of Fars, but they were unsuccessful and were eventually abandoned. He blamed their failure on the lack of involvement of the groups themselves in these programs and noted that the success of the programs in Fars, especially among the Qashqa'i, was due to dedicated local participants.

As a result of Bahmanbegi's efforts, white or orange canvas tent schools became a distinctive feature of the Qashqa'i landscape. These schools offered the only formal education available to most Qashqa'i. Qashqa'i who were already settled in cities, towns, and large, primarily non-Qashqa'i villages usually had access to regular government schools, while recently settled and settling Qashqa'i usually had no schools or schools newly established under the Literacy Corps program. Some settling Qashqa'i received government permission to retain tribal schools in their new villages.[23]

Tent schools were not "migratory," as some accounts described them; rather, they operated in winter and summer when Qashqa'i were fairly stationary in seasonal pastures and they closed during the migrations. Teachers did not migrate overland with their students; they sent their tents and equipment by truck. By 1978 most Qashqa'i subtribes were represented by at least one tent school, and many Qashqa'i children had access to five years of education (table 4). Some youngsters continued their education past the fifth grade in town schools. Those who demonstrated intellectual promise and who could pass stiff entrance examinations could enroll in the Tribal High School and the Tribal Teacher Training School in Shiraz. In the 1960s and 1970s, the brightest, most motivated Qashqa'i youth could plan on jobs as teachers, school inspectors, and assistants in Bahmanbegi's office, and a smaller group could enter university and contemplate professional careers in the wider society if their families could spare their labor and afford the expense of additional education. While both groups constituted a small fraction of all Qashqa'i, tent schools were widespread in Qashqa'i so-

23. The phrase *tribal school* is used in this text as it was used in Fars, meaning schools stemming from the Office of Tribal Education and servicing non-Persian rural people. The tribal schools of Bahmanbegi's program fell into a different administrative category than the schools set up in rural areas through the government's Literacy Corps. Because of the educational superiority of the tribal schools and the lack of prejudice on the part of teachers toward non-Persians, settled and settling Qashqa'i pushed to retain tribal schools for their children.

TABLE 4. Tribal Schools among the Qashqa'i[24]

	Amaleh	Shish Boluki	Darreh-shuri	Kashkuli Bozorg	Farsi Madan	Totals
Nomadic and settled individuals	35,400	21,400	20,300	15,500	10,400	103,000
Subtribes	54	17	41	51	21	184
Tribal schools	72	25	44	44	27	212
Male students	2,047	533	1,170	1,675	689	6,114
Female students	344	137	227	319	120	1,147

ciety, and the role of education in creating new livelihoods did alter many people's views.

The education offered in the tent schools was the standard curriculum found in all Iranian government schools. The government required all students in Iran to read and write exclusively in Persian, a national policy aimed at Persianizing and hence politically integrating the nation's multilingual populations. National education stressed Persian culture and civilization to the neglect of the contributions of non-Persians. History texts glorified the exploits of Persian shahs and ignored the impact of Iran's minorities on Iranian history. These culturally imperialistic policies were intended to erase non-Persian cultures.[25] Teachers in Qashqa'i schools were required to teach in Persian despite the fact that they and their students were Turkic-speakers. Per-

24. Kortum (1979a:13, 1979b:76) provides these statistics for 1967 on Qashqa'i tribal schools. The figures on tribal size are inaccurate. On the basis of a survey conducted in 1973 among 3,000 nomadic Qashqa'i households (whose tribes, subtribes, and locations are not mentioned), Shafii et al. (1977:153) report that although the average literacy rate of the population was over 20 percent (34 percent for males, 5 percent for females), only 1.7 percent of the population had completed elementary school and only 0.3 percent secondary school.

25. For the role national education played in undermining local cultural values among the Lurs and Baluch of Iran, see Amanolahi (1985:69) and Harrison (1981:93–126), respectively.

sian is, of course, a written language, which Qashqa'i Turki is not; the Qashqa'i did not use written forms of other Turkic languages, including the Turkish of modern Turkey. The books used in the tent schools were those used throughout Iran. The pictures and stories in elementary texts were initially copied directly from American texts and then translated into Persian, with boys and girls, fathers and mothers, cats and dogs, enjoying middle-class American lives in suburban tract houses. Later the texts were changed to include pictures of urban and rural Persian families performing activities typically found in Persian Iran. Qashqa'i children did not identify with either set of pictures and stories. In the 1970s Bahmanbegi introduced a few curricular changes and included simple scientific equipment for demonstrations, but essentially the education bore little or no relevance to a nomadic pastoral and rural existence.

Bahmanbegi's image of a new Qashqa'i society contained many components; he directed his education program toward the goals of a progressive and educated citizenry, new occupations and livelihoods reflecting the demands of a modernizing nation-state, eradication of the traditional class structure, elimination of the khans' monopoly on power and wealth, a pacified Qashqa'i polity, and greater opportunities for women. The shah, his American advisors, and Bahmanbegi shared the notion that education was key to the modernization of Iran; the particular success of Bahmanbegi's program rested partly on this commonality of views. They agreed that the inevitable fate of the Qashqa'i was the loss of their traditional subsistence system and their integration into the state and society of (Persian-controlled) Iran, and they praised the education program for making this feasible. Bahmanbegi believed that in the future the Qashqa'i and other tribal peoples in Iran would assimilate into a modern life and that his education program would facilitate the transition process. He was proud that so many Qashqa'i students had completed school and entered new occupations and professions, and he attributed these success stories to the primary education his program offered to them. Bahmanbegi helped to form the image of "the 'new tribal warrior,' whose shield was a book, whose bullets were chalk, and whose enemy was whatever kept the warrior from attaining a dignified position in the emerging Iran" (Barker 1981:154).

Bahmanbegi especially opposed the Qashqa'i class structure, in which khans held great wealth and power while many Qashqa'i lived at what he regarded as subsistence level. He believed that by offering education to worthy students regardless of class, status, or family position, the traditional socioeconomic structure would eventually dissolve. His ideas in this regard coincided with those of the shah concerning rural society in general; both wanted to eliminate rural chiefs and lords. Bahmanbegi also saw education as a means to destroy the Qashqa'i as a polity threatening the state and disrupting law and order; he held the same prejudiced views about the Qashqa'i and especially their higher-level leaders as the shah and other officials.[26] An Iranian military general witnessing the examination of Qashqa'i schoolchildren congratulated Bahmanbegi, adding that he was "amazed that the children of *yaghis* (rebels, highway robbers) could become such outstanding students. Bahmanbegi replied, 'I'll tell you something which will make you even more surprised: I'm the son of a *yaghi* who became a Director General'" (Barker 1981:139).

The shah and his American advisors included notions about increased equality for Iranian women in their modernization plans, with which Bahmanbegi's program was compatible. In an early publication, Bahmanbegi (1945–46) stressed the high position of women in Qashqa'i society and compared it positively with that of other Iranian women. His initial plans to involve Qashqa'i women in the educational process were met with some resistance, both from within and from outside Qashqa'i society, but he eventually succeeded. From the beginning he encouraged girls to attend tent schools, and in 1962 he accepted women as teacher trainees. He often pressured prominent Qashqa'i families to send their daughters to school and teacher training in order that they might serve as examples for others. By the 1970s a significant number of students and teachers in his programs were female, and their presence in these roles was generally accepted throughout Qashqa'i society.[27] Possibly no other program in rural Iran was as successful in introducing the idea of opportunity for women as Bahmanbegi's. Those segments of Iranian society which favored greater

26. On days when the shah visited the Tribal High School in Shiraz, Bahmanbegi would prevent children of the Qashqa'i khans from attending class or participating in the ceremonies, out of fear that they would undertake some anti-shah action.

27. The ratio of male to female students was approximately 5:1 (table 4), according to Kortum (1979a:13, 1979b:76). Shafii et al. (1977:153) report that the literacy rate for Qashqa'i males was seven times greater than that for females. The ratio of male to female teachers in the tribal schools was approximately 20:1.

equality for women praised him, and foreign visitors were impressed with the self-esteem and confidence demonstrated by women in the program.

Qashqa'i teachers, dispersed throughout tribal territory, were some of Bahmanbegi's best supporters on these many issues, and they influenced many Qashqa'i. Those who were leftist or leftist-oriented were more concerned at the time with the shah's excesses than with critically examining the impact of the education program on the lives of their fellow Qashqa'i. They supported the expansion of education and the chance for socioeconomic mobility that literacy and advanced education in Iran sometimes allowed and chose not to examine all the wider consequences of Bahmanbegi's programs. These teachers, who also opposed traditional khan rule, supported the ouster of the paramount leaders and the undermining of the privileged position of all khans. They agreed with Bahmanbegi that education helped to eradicate exploitative class relations.

Before 1979 few Qashqa'i openly criticized Bahmanbegi's education program. Some who did were members of the political elite who were witnessing the erosion of their traditional power base and who saw Bahmanbegi as a usurper. He was rapidly replacing them as figures of power and influence, and he increasingly obtained state favors and services that they lacked. It is wrong, however, to say that they opposed education because they "had a vested interest in maintaining a highly illiterate population over which to rule, a population whose world view and tribal identity were uncompromised by excessive contact with non-tribal peoples and ideas" (Barker 1981:141). The elite did not oppose education per se but rather the techniques used and the role played by Bahmanbegi. They resisted the changing balance of power in Qashqa'i society. But these Qashqa'i, along with others who lacked political interests to defend, also stressed that Qashqa'i youth were indoctrinated through the educational system with the nationalist dogmas of the shah's government (Barker 1981:157) and were prepared by the schools to assimilate into Persian-dominated society. They feared that local linguistic, cultural, and political attachments would weaken, signaling the beginning of the end of the Qashqa'i as a distinctive people in Iran. Bahmanbegi required Qashqa'i schoolchildren to salute the Iranian flag, sing the Iranian national anthem, and act with respect in front of a portrait of the shah. All tent schools prominently displayed symbols of the state; the flag flew from the top of the tent pole, and the shah's

portrait hung from this pole inside the tent. Bahmanbegi often effu-
sively praised the shah in front of schoolchildren, at public gatherings,
and in publications (1971).

The inroads the government made into Qashqa'i society through information supplied by Bahmanbegi as well as that gleaned from the
schools also worried many Qashqa'i. Previously the ilkhani had been
the only person who could provide accurate data on the Qashqa'i people
for the state. No census had ever been attempted, and no government
official knew exactly how many Qashqa'i existed or where they resided.
When tribal schools first opened, the government formally registered
all students and collected information on their families. Shortly thereafter, it required students to have identification cards to attend class,
and these could be obtained only from government offices where information was gathered on the individuals and their families. During this
period, government agencies and armed forces were conducting political surveillance, implementing land reform, and restricting Qashqa'i
use of pastures, and they gathered basic information relating to these
issues, especially for SAVAK and conscription purposes, from the children's parents. Many parents faced the dilemma of wanting their sons
to be educated but not wanting them to be drafted later on. Some
Qashqa'i viewed Bahmanbegi's programs and the shah's efforts to undermine Qashqa'i society as one and the same process, and they identified Bahmanbegi as an agent of the shah. Strong sentiments against
him did not surface openly until the shah's ouster, when angry crowds
drove him and his family out of Shiraz.

Several other dimensions of Bahmanbegi's program did, however,
assert organizations and identities unique to the Qashqa'i, and part of
the strength and resiliency of Qashqa'i affiliations in the 1960s and
1970s was a direct outcome of his policies. Most importantly, he dealt
with—even glorified—the Qashqa'i as a unique people in Iran at a
time when the state was implementing Persianizing policies. Bahmanbegi placed schools in Qashqa'i society according to traditional sociopolitical organizations and responded to traditional lower-level political leaders, and hence the program enforced these boundaries and
enhanced these positions. Tribal schools, set up as they were in subtribes and their sections, came to represent these groups and hence
helped to preserve these structures at a time when other pressures
worked for their destruction. Bahmanbegi often assigned schools at the
request of headmen who took responsibility for liaison between him
and their groups and who sought favors and services from him. For

many Qashqa'i, Bahmanbegi was their only direct link to the state and the apparatus of the central government; he was the only Qashqa'i recognized officially by the government as a link to the Qashqa'i people.[28]

Bahmanbegi held a special regard for the Qashqa'i and insisted that teachers assigned to them be Qashqa'i themselves. The government's plan in 1955 to train Persian/Iranian teachers to instruct Qashqa'i children met with immediate failure; these teachers disliked serving in rural areas with few physical comforts and could not identify with their charges. The government did not interfere in his choice of teachers again. As the program expanded, Bahmanbegi sent Qashqa'i teachers to other tribal areas, which some nationalistic host groups resented, although they preferred Qashqa'i teachers and tribal schools to Persian/Iranian ones. As the program expanded to include Lurs, Kurds, and other ethnic and tribal people as teacher trainees, these individuals were used exclusively in non-Qashqa'i tribal groups. Both practices enhanced Qashqa'i status over that of other non-Persians, and the non-Qashqa'i people associated with his program were often resentful about the attention given to the Qashqa'i. Bahmanbegi expressed pride in his Qashqa'i identity, often positively compared Qashqa'i traits with those of Persians, and favorably demonstrated these traits not only for Qashqa'i but also for Persian and foreign audiences.[29] He did not attempt to model his schools and teachers after those in the Persian/Iranian educational system despite his use of the government curriculum, and he consistently attempted to integrate Qashqa'i features into his own program.

Bahmanbegi urged Qashqa'i men and women to be proud of their culture. He required female Qashqa'i, whether seven-year-old first-graders in tent schools in isolated mountain pastures or eighteen-year-old teacher trainees in Shiraz, to wear customary Qashqa'i clothing in attractive styles and colors and to be neat and well dressed. The dress of non-Persian tribal and rural women in Fars featured many similar elements, but the economic prosperity of the Qashqa'i in comparison to many other tribal and rural people meant that Qashqa'i dress tended to be more expensive and elaborate. Bahmanbegi used the most ornate features of Qashqa'i dress as a model for all tribal women attending his

28. Several Qashqa'i khans were members of parliament in the 1960s and 1970s, but they did not formally represent the Qashqa'i people or serve Qashqa'i interests.

29. Bahmanbegi's article in a National Geographic publication demonstrates his high regard for the Qashqa'i (1971).

schools, and as a result Qashqa'i and non-Qashqa'i women were often indistinguishable.[30] He created an image of an educated tribal woman through his manipulations of dress styles. Bahmanbegi did not allow Qashqa'i male teachers and students to wear traditional Qashqa'i men's dress, however. He expected Qashqa'i men to assimilate fully into Persian/Iranian society, and they became indistinguishable in dress from urban Persians; but he wanted Qashqa'i women to continue to be picturesque.

Bahmanbegi used Qashqa'i dance as entertainment and a media event for national and foreign consumption. He organized women's circle dances at school examinations and on festive occasions at the Shiraz schools and encouraged Iranian dignitaries and foreign guests to attend and photograph the performances. While most non-Persian tribal and rural people in Fars performed similar kinds of circle dances as a traditional form of entertainment at weddings and other festivities, accompanied by similar musical instruments and tunes, the ones Bahmanbegi chose for his school events were associated with the Qashqa'i. He prohibited at school functions the other traditional activity performed at Qashqa'i and other non-Persian weddings, a competitive, choreographed stick fight/game, on the grounds that it encouraged Qashqa'i and other tribal youth to think aggressively in terms of their own parochial tribal groups, when instead they should be thinking of themselves as progressive educated citizens. The harmonious movements of the women's circle dance possibly symbolized to him the non-belligerent nature of an educated citizenry. Because the dance was phrased in terms customary to the Qashqa'i and other tribal people, it contained, in the larger Iranian context of the times, an explicit non-Persian, non-Iranian message.

Bahmanbegi applied the Turkic term *ordu* to the festive summertime school examinations, a term previously used for tribal military gatherings and war councils, in an explicit attempt to demonstrate how far his transformations of basic Qashqa'i institutions had gone. And he promoted a new version of the tribal warrior, one who replaced the gun with the pen. He also encouraged the production of fine Qashqa'i carpets and other handicrafts through the Tribal Weaving School. Al-

30. The young women dancing for public audiences in the central square in Isfahan in 1977 as part of the government's Festival of Popular Traditions were dressed in ornate but typically styled Qashqa'i clothes. They were, however, Mamassani Lur women from the Tribal Teacher Training School in Shiraz. For Nikki Keddie's photograph of this event, see Beck (1981c:27).

though weavers who received training at the school were mostly non-Qashqa'i women, predominantly Lurs, they were taught a limited number of Qashqa'i designs personally favored by Bahmanbegi and associated with the Kashkuli tribe. He hoped to expand the commercial market at home and abroad for Qashqa'i weaving and to integrate the families of weavers more intensively into the national economy.

In weaving as in dress, dance, and other forms of expressive culture, Bahmanbegi propagated Qashqa'i culture at the expense of other non-Persian groups associated with his program. He manipulated Qashqa'i culture according to his own vision of the future by selecting and defining certain key elements. Thus, through his education program he created not only an image of an educated tribal youth but also an image of an ideal non-Persian people, which served to raise the status of the Qashqa'i over other non-Persians and to define further the Qashqa'i cultural system and give it greater coherence and unity. His intended audience in these manipulations went beyond his students, teachers, and their families and groups to other non-Persians, Iranians in general, and foreigners.

While the shah was intent on Persianizing Iranians through universal education, conscription, and modernization, a few other state institutions were exploiting Iran's cultural diversity by encouraging its colorful but nonpolitical expression. Bahmanbegi played a major role in both policies. His most important patron after the shah was the empress, who chose as a special dimension of her official role in Iran to be a proponent of the artistic and creative abilities of Iranians of all cultural backgrounds, and he offered her guidance. The elaborate cultural demonstrations that Bahmanbegi staged for the shah, empress, and foreign and Iranian dignitaries served as models for representatives of other ethnic groups in Iran who also sought favors from the state.

As is apparent, mixed, often contradictory, messages emerged in the tribal education program. It was clearly an instrument of state encroachment on a people who were politically vulnerable because of the loss of their primary leaders and economically at risk because of land reform and pasture nationalization. While some people resented the program, they, along with others, also viewed it as a vehicle for new jobs and opportunities and possible socioeconomic mobility. They welcomed the skills of Persian-language competency and literacy as a means of obtaining the economic rewards then being promised in a rapidly changing Iran. And, because of the success of Bahmanbegi's program, many Qashqa'i had advanced their educational skills over other rural Iranians and were seen as exemplary models of achievement. Many Qashqa'i increasingly valued education, which was equated with economic development and progress. The particular kind of development and progress the shah advocated, however, did not offer many actual improvements in livelihood and socioeconomic status for most Qashqa'i. Rather, most became impoverished because of his other programs. The new educational system taught Qashqa'i children to be proud of literacy and learning; yet, except for those who became teachers themselves, they did not often have the chance to make productive use of such skills. Bahmanbegi's brand of education was applicable to modern, urban, nonpastoral livelihoods, which some welcomed, but at the expense of losing customary economic practices. Simultaneously, the symbols through which education was offered were traditionally Qashqa'i ones, associated with traditional adaptations and livelihoods: the mobile tent, the seasonality of education, a degree of equality between men and women, Qashqa'i dress and dance, other expressions of Qashqa'i identity, and even the teachers themselves. While use of these symbols did serve to ease a largely illiterate people into a formal educational system, the cooptation of these symbols in state-sponsored education was politically manipulative. Bahmanbegi may have intended to preserve some unique Qashqa'i cultural qualities, but in the process he rendered the Qashqa'i more vulnerable to state and outside encroachment because he facilitated their assimilation into Persian/Iranian society.

When modernizing nation-states attempt to foster assimilation, traditional brokerage roles are vulnerable, and the political, economic, social, and cultural discontinuities that brokers profit from bridging are decreased, even broken down. Bahmanbegi's kind of brokerage was predicated on undercutting the bases of brokerage of the traditional tribal elite, a fact of which he was clearly aware, and he was able to establish linkages for himself that the elite were no longer capable of creating and maintaining. Bahmanbegi posed a deliberate, obvious threat to their status. Just as the traditional system produced one type of brokerage, maintained so adeptly by the Shahilu family, so modern nation-building programs generated a new brokerage arrangement.

The efforts of the Qashqa'i ilkhani before 1954 and Bahmanbegi after 1951 to form a cultural entity out of the Qashqa'i people were similar, although the contexts were different. Each was the principal mediator between the Qashqa'i and the state and other powers, and each defined the nature of the group for these powers. Bahmanbegi was more successful at creating an image than any ilkhani had been, not only because the stakes were higher—given that ethnic groups in Iran were increasingly forced to politicize (or face assimilation) in response to state repression, underdevelopment, and neglect—but also because he captured media attention in a way that no ilkhani ever had. (The media were, of course, more prevalent at this period than they had been for earlier Qashqa'i mediators.) Bahmanbegi encouraged outsiders to perceive the Qashqa'i as a progressive and nonthreatening, yet colorful and unique people, and the media regularly disseminated this message to both Iranian and foreign consumers. As the self-appointed and externally recognized spokesman for the Qashqa'i, he especially directed this message to government officials and foreign advisors from whom he sought favors, and to foreign and Iranian journalists, filmmakers, and social scientists who would give him a good press. All seem to have accepted the distorted images he presented and upon which he capitalized.

Bahmanbegi created a niche for himself in a modernizing Iran by forming institutions to meet what he and others regarded as the needs of the Qashqa'i people. He walked a delicate line between a shah and a state that desired rapid transformations and the Qashqa'i people who sought to avoid assimilation and loss of cultural identity while adapting to changing political and economic conditions. That he was able to accomplish this feat, first at a time of political unrest, then over an extended period, is a testimony to his skill and determination.

THE QASHQA'I AS A NATIONAL MINORITY

Some scholars favor the phrase *ethnic group* over the term *tribe* (Southall 1970, Cohen 1969). In some cases this may be appropriate, especially if the political institutions of the people in question are decreasingly able to function because of the increasing power and authority of the state. As the nature of political activity changes, a tribe may be transformed into an ethnic group. But *ethnic group* need not replace the term *tribe* in all contemporary contexts (cf. Southall 1970:48). Some who urge this substitution regard tribes as politically autonomous and ethnic groups as integrated parts of more complex polities, states in particular, and therefore as somehow less political in orientation. Both tribes and ethnic groups, however, emerge out of a particular political context, are maintained through political interaction with other polities, and contain their own integrating political activities (Fried 1975,

Cohen 1969:3–5). Tribes are often ordered differently than ethnic groups, especially in terms of their boundaries. The term *tribe* emerges in reference to some form of sociopolitical organization, while the phrase *ethnic group* emphasizes a culturally defined self-consciousness.[31]

Some scholars substitute the phrase *national minority* for *tribe.* The conditions for the existence of tribes, in their view, are no longer present in the modern world, while modern nation-states generate national minorities among their politically articulate, culturally diverse peoples. *Tribe* and *national minority,* however, can occasionally be used to refer to the same entity. National minorities often combine cultural self-consciousness with sociopolitical organization. In twentieth-century Iran, national-minority consciousness emerged among many non-Persian people in the developing nation-state controlled by Persians, and sufficient differences among these national minorities exist to warrant the continued use of the term *tribe* for some of them, including the Qashqa'i, Turkmen, and Baluch.

I have postponed a discussion of the Qashqa'i as a national minority until now because both the phenomenon itself and the phenomenon of discussing them in such terms are recent ones. The Qashqa'i became particularly conscious of having a distinctive identity during the reign of Reza Shah because of his oppressions. When he abdicated, they reformed the confederacy under Naser Khan's leadership and overtly asserted their tribal and ethnic identity. Outsiders during the Mosaddeq period perceived the Qashqa'i as a political threat to the shah and to American interests in Iran and acted upon these fears by ousting the paramount leaders. Several years later they perceived the Qashqa'i as a group resistant to reform and modernization and so used military forces and SAVAK surveillance to suppress incipient rural protests and pacify the people. By the late 1960s they saw, in what they now considered a depoliticized Qashqa'i people, exotic images that could be parlayed into commercial benefits and public relations for the Pahlavi state. The emergence of a specifically Qashqa'i identity and consciousness was directly related to these perceptions and their consequent developments.

The national-minority issue in Iran is often misunderstood by those who ignore the predominantly Persian character of Iranian nationalism; who underplay the extent of Persian control of the bureaucracy, the military, the economy, and religious institutions; and who overestimate the political strength of the national minorities. Iran's population is

31. For relevant recent discussions of ethnicity and ethnic change, see Enloe (1980), McCagg and Silver (1979b), Wirsing (1981), and Keyes (1981).

culturally diverse, but such diversity does not automatically translate into ethnic groups, national minorities, politically articulated notions of distinctiveness, or demands for political and cultural autonomy. The emergence of national-minority consciousness in any Iranian group is a unique development, yet it also relates directly to an emerging modern nation-state, Iranian (Persian) nationalism, capitalist expansion, economic underdevelopment and neglect of ethnic and minority areas, repressive theocracy, minority movements in adjoining areas, and foreign interference. The processes yet to be understood fully are the ways and means by which Persians acquired and maintained control of the dominant political, military, economic, and religious institutions of the state—at the expense of non-Persians—and the development of national-minority consciousness and demands for rights and possibly autonomy on the part of some non-Persians.

The Qashqa'i live in a state dominated numerically, politically, and economically by Persian-speakers (Persians). Iran's highly heterogeneous population consists of different categories of people defined by language, religion (Shi'i and Sunni Islam and other religions), culture, socioeconomic class, tribal affiliation, and region. Most Iranians consider language the primary distinguishing characteristic of people living in Iran.[32] Persian, the mother tongue of under 45 percent of Iran's population of forty million (1985), is the idiom in which the nation's dominant political, economic, religious, and cultural activities are conducted. Persian language and culture, propagated from urban centers for centuries, dominate the nation. Persians predominate in all urban areas of central Iran and most of the plateau. The majority of the upper class is Persian, and wealth and power are concentrated in their hands. Persians fill most government posts and high-level military positions, are the best educated and professionally trained, and are the most subject to Western influence. Most high-ranking clergy are Persians. Many of Iran's regional peoples who do not speak Persian as a first language are regarded as national minorities. The extent of their consciousness as national minorities varies considerably, for reasons not yet well understood. They include, in approximate order of size: Azerbaijanis (Azeris), Kurds, Baluch, Bakhtiyaris, Lurs, Qashqa'i, Turkmen, Shahsevan, Arabs, and many others. They also include non-Muslims and non-Shi'i Muslims.

32. Many Iranians in the 1980s, for largely political reasons, have increasingly come to view different degrees of religious conservatism as another major distinguishing feature of people in Iran.

Iran's economic, political, cultural, and social divisions are a product of history. Until the late nineteenth and early twentieth centuries, Iran's population was characterized primarily by two socioeconomic and political formations.[33] One consisted largely of Persian-speaking, sedentary, agricultural, and urban populations; the other, largely of non-Persian-speaking, nomadic and seminomadic, pastoral, rural, often tribally organized populations. The Iranian state, with its bureaucracy, military centers, bazaars, and religious centers, was within the first population sector, which it fostered; while the second sector was geographically peripheral, fairly independent politically, and associated infrequently with the state bureaucracy, although from this sector had often come conquerors who established the successive dynasties of Iranian empires and states.

The development of the modern Iranian nation-state in the late nineteenth and early twentieth centuries coincided with foreign involvement in Iran and with the integration of Iran into the world economy. This international contact resulted in the development of national consciousness and patriotism—a nationalism that predictably took a Persian form, given the dominance of Persians as national leaders and in the state bureauracy, politics, military, economy, and religion. Advocates of the new nationalism ignored cultural differences in Iran, and the gap between the dominating Persian and the nondominant non-Persian sectors of the population not only increased but also became invidious. International contact also resulted in the Iranian government's efforts to achieve national integration for purposes of political control and economic benefits. The state apparatus spread to the periphery, which state military forces attempted to pacify. Neither Pahlavi shah did much to develop the periphery economically outside of oil-rich Khuzistan, however, and the gap between the developed and underdeveloped areas in Iran increased. Although underdevelopment and pacification weakened the ability of people on the periphery to resist the center's domination, some were able to express their resistance to the pressures acting upon them. National-minority consciousness developed and expanded as a result. Only when identity comes under pressure, when the objective bases for it no long suffice, does it necessarily become a matter of conscious construction. Hence, it is often the case that objective cultural differences and consciousness of such differences vary inversely. The development of national-minority

33. This and the following paragraph derive partly from Helfgott (1980) and from personal communication with him.

consciousness was and is an on-going process, and was particularly manifest during the formation of the Islamic Republic in 1979. This regime was viewed by most national minorities as one that continued Pahlavi policies of Persian chauvinism while adding the element of restrictive theocracy. The Islamic Republic contributed to the growth of national-minority consciousness in Iran.

The Qashqa'i were and are one of these national minorities. Except for the elite class, they were not part of the society found in the Persian-dominated centers of power, authority, wealth, and religion. Elite and nonelite Qashqa'i held few, if any, sentiments of Iranian nationalism; they perceived few, if any, benefits in Iranian citizenship. Iranian nationalism was couched in Persian form, with which they did not identify, and amounted to cultural imperialism. Their own distinctive culture was not formally recognized by the state, and they did not identify with the Persian cultural system, which many despised and ridiculed. Although Persian shahs in the twentieth century pacified the Qashqa'i in order to place them under government jurisdiction, they offered them virtually no beneficial state services, and state policies further undermined their livelihoods. Although some Qashqa'i did receive educational opportunities, their education was ambiguously presented through Qashqa'i symbols but in terms of modern urban livelihoods. Students did not acquire sentiments of Iranian nationalism through education, as was the intention of those who urged the development of such programs. Some distinctive Qashqa'i features, including weddings, Turkic speech, and the men's hat and cloak, were enhanced in political meaning as the state disrupted the Qashqa'i area economically and subjected the people to the surveillance of SAVAK and other repressive institutions. No Qashqa'i leader emerged between 1954 and 1979 to articulate the people's discontent, however, and most Qashqa'i believed that their inevitable fate was assimilation into Persian/Iranian society at the lowest socioeconomic levels. The Office of Tribal Education became the major vehicle of the articulation of Qashqa'i identity for outsiders in this period, and the state, in exploiting the Qashqa'i image for public relations and commercial purposes, contributed further to the notions of outsiders concerning Qashqa'i identity. It was, however, the Qashqa'i wedding celebration, an elaborate ritual event, that best articulated Qashqa'i sentiments concerning their own identity in the 1960s and 1970s.

Wedding celebrations held in specially constructed encampments, lasting many days, and drawing hundreds of participants were a key expression of Qashqa'i values and gave cultural coherence to their identity. Many young Qashqa'i men wore the cloaks and cummerbunds that all Qashqa'i men had worn before Reza Shah outlawed them in 1928, and females of all ages wore their newest, brightest multilayered skirts, tunics, jackets, and headscarves. Other symbolically laden events had included political gatherings in the ilkhani's elaborate camp—now ended—and the seasonal migrations—now changed because of fewer numbers migrating and military control over movements. As in the past, Qashqa'i khans were the primary sponsors of the largest weddings. For many khans, these events were their only remaining tribal function; for many Qashqa'i, they were their only attachments to khans that could be defined as political. Qashqa'i weddings became highly politicized under Mohammad Reza Shah's repressions, and heightened national-minority consciousness in the participants resulted. Just as the mosque in Iran became the scene for disguised political protest in the 1960s and 1970s, so did Qashqa'i weddings in this period. Plotting against the Pahlavi regime was certainly not a regular feature of wedding celebrations, but they were a place where people who did not otherwise meet could discuss contemporary politics, as was also the case with the mosque. Weddings were direct, conscious statements by their participants of Qashqa'i identity in the face of a state that was attempting to pacify and Persianize them. It is ironic, especially in retrospect, that the Pahlavi regime encouraged the performance of Qashqa'i weddings for elite and foreign consumption and used them in its propaganda concerning Iran's attractions. Weddings contributed an exotic dimension to an otherwise quite nondescript cultural landscape, at least as seen by foreigners and urban Iranians. For the Qashqa'i, however, weddings, as self-conscious statements of political and cultural identity, indicated their rejection of the cultural models offered them by the state through its institutions.

THE STATE'S EXPLOITATION OF THE QASHQA'I IMAGE

Iranian state officials were not very interested in Qashqa'i culture until the mid- to late-1960s, a time that corresponded with Qashqa'i political and military pacification, prevalent notions about a rapidly integrating and modernizing nation-state, and new forms of foreign attention including tourism. One event demonstrates the transition that occurred in the relationship between the Qashqa'i and the state during this period. In 1966 Mohammad Reza Shah invited the king and queen of Belgium for a state visit and inquired about the sights they wished to see. Foremost among their preferences were the Qashqa'i of Fars. National and local officials were horrified by this request, especially given their concern that some Qashqa'i would choose this occasion to seek revenge against the shah for the recent execution of Bahman Qashqa'i. These officials would be responsible for the difficult task of security. They could not comprehend the Belgians' interest in the Qashqa'i, whom they viewed as bandits and outlaws and unworthy of attention. The shah summoned Shahbaz Kashkuli, nephew of the Shahilu khans, to Tehran and ordered him to prepare a festive tribal display. Nomadic Qashqa'i had already migrated past Shiraz on their way to winter pastures, but military authorities ordered their return so that they could move in picturesque fashion by Shiraz at the time of the royal visit. Representatives of various Qashqa'i sections, including khans of the component tribes, were ordered to assemble, and Shahbaz Kashkuli constructed an elaborate tent encampment near Shiraz. Officials, still worried about security, staged a rehearsal visit and invited many Shiraz dignitaries and foreigners. Shahbaz Kashkuli and Mohammad Bahmanbegi offered welcoming addresses to the two royal couples at the Shiraz airport and escorted them to the camp, where the visit went smoothly. After military officials permitted the Qashqa'i migration to resume, a small Qashqa'i force attacked an army unit and killed some soldiers; the event was not reported in the press.[34]

Western powers and interests had long been attracted to the Qashqa'i because of the prominence of their leaders, their strategic location, and the exotic way of life. From the mid-nineteenth century on, foreigners translated their interest into direct interference at Qashqa'i expense, and Iranian rulers and governments periodically punished the Qashqa'i for these contacts. The British blamed the Qashqa'i for disrupting their commercial and political ventures in south Iran, plotted and even waged war against them, and, along with the Germans, utilized the Qashqa'i as instruments of foreign policy. The Americans pressed for the removal of Qashqa'i leaders, urged land reforms and nationalizations, and supported a tribal education program—all to maintain the regime of Mohammad Reza Shah in power and make Iran an "island of stability" in the Middle East for American

34. This account derives from oral reports of people living in Shiraz at the time, including several doctors who performed autopsies on the soldiers, and from Ramage (n.d.:6–7).

interests. The shah, with American assistance, tried to integrate the state politically and socially as a nation and to control and Persianize its culturally diverse peoples through a modern military, secret police, centralized bureaucracy, conscription, rural development programs, and education. He exiled and deposed Qashqa'i leaders and substituted military forces and secret police that inhibited political activity. The military confiscated the guns of most Qashqa'i and restricted the travel of outsiders—particularly foreigners—in Qashqa'i territory. By 1970 the state considered the Qashqa'i pacified, and what Persians had viewed as tribal unrest no longer existed. The Qashqa'i and other non-Persian groups were increasingly regarded as relics of the past, even as curiosities, and the state began to use these groups to advertise at home and abroad the exotic (a "polite euphemism for powerless"—Enloe 1980:48) nature of Iran and to demonstrate the extent of modernization. Only when state officials believed that Iran was well on the road to development did they feel they could afford to show off so publicly its "undeveloped" side.

In the 1970s Western filmmakers, museum and private collectors, journalists, photographers, tourists, and social scientists, all motivated by economic and personal interests, sought access to the Qashqa'i. The state, to increase this attention, officially sponsored and financially backed exhibitions of Qashqa'i ways of life and customs on television and in newspapers, magazines, tourist organization materials, handicraft shops, and international festivals of arts and popular traditions. Iran's state-controlled television provided coverage of Qashqa'i weddings, school examinations, migrations, and visits of government officials to Qashqa'i leaders. Qashqa'i who were chosen to greet the shah and empress at the airport in Isfahan and Shiraz were occasionally featured in newspaper photographs of the arrival; Qashqa'i men were shown to be respectfully humble in the presence of royalty and Qashqa'i women wore festive attire. Posters printed by the government tourist organization featured Qashqa'i women in colorful dress as central figures in collages of Iranian sights. Government handicraft shops, which catered to elite and foreign consumers, displayed and sold Qashqa'i woven goods. The Festival of Popular Traditions in Isfahan in 1977 exhibited the dress, dance, and music of the Qashqa'i and other ethnic minorities. The government also officially sanctioned and heavily financed foreign and Iranian filmmakers, museum collectors, and others who wanted to exploit the Qashqa'i commercially. The film *Caravans,* based on James Michener's novel and filmed partly in Qashqa'i territory in 1977, starred Anthony Quinn as a nomad chief and Jennifer O'Neill as a wayward American gone native and in love with him. The Iranian government contributed five million dollars, personnel, and equipment to the production. The Qashqa'i were featured as the film's "tribe," although the story actually concerned a small group of Afghan nomads. Darrehshuri khans provided liaison between the Hollywood film company and the Qashqa'i used in the production.[35] A David Frost documentary on Iran contained a sequence on the Qashqa'i, and a BBC *Tribal Eye* documentary entitled *Woven Gardens* investigated Qashqa'i weaving. Museum exhibits of Qashqa'i material culture also drew foreign attention.[36]

The image of the Qashqa'i in films, exhibits, publications, and events was one of a primitive but colorful and content people following patterns of life derived from the steppes of central Asia, carried forward from ancient history, and somehow anachronistically surviving in a modern Iran.[37] Literature on the Qashqa'i, produced primarily by foreign journalists, photographers, art historians, rug dealers, and social scientists, implicitly supported government efforts to exploit their appeal. Because the authors received elaborate hospitality on their brief visits to Qashqa'i camps, their publications tended to exaggerate and romanticize Qashqa'i wealth, leisure, livelihood, and proud nobility.

In the 1970s Iranian entrepreneurs joined foreign ones to facilitate the process of marketing the Qashqa'i by financing and supporting handicraft production and assisting journalists and photographers to capture the unique Qashqa'i lifestyle in various media. Until the mid-1970s most of this attention was directed to foreign consumers, but Iranians themselves soon became attracted to the Qashqa'i and other ethnic groups for their own enjoyment and amusement. The attention long given by Westerners to the Qashqa'i had begun to make an impression within Iran. Iranians, mostly Persians of the upwardly mobile

35. The attire of Jennifer O'Neill was an adapted version of Qashqa'i women's dress, the major change being that the bodice was tightly fitted. Elite Qashqa'i women admired this adaptation and seriously considered making it in their own dress.

36. See *The Qashqa'i of Iran,* Whitworth Art Gallery, Manchester (1976).

37. "In the Qashqa'i . . . we witness the survival of an archaic way of life into modern times. They are the living heirs . . . of the pagan Turks of Central and North Eastern Asia . . .[and] of those ancient Iranian peoples, the Scythians and Sarmatians, the first of the mounted nomads." John Boyle in the Whitworth Art Gallery's *The Qashqa'i of Iran* (1976:8).

urban middle class, were fascinated by cultural demonstrations at arts festivals. Soheila Shahshahani, an Iranian anthropologist, comments on the government's 1977 Festival of Popular Traditions: "This was a bazaar of various cultural manifestations, from mystical music to fortune telling, from tribal group dance to. . . . What could one do with all these cultural traits put on the scene, and naturally transformed to fit the scene, but to ridicule them without comprehension or analysis?" At this time she was doing research among the Mamassani and had witnessed the importance of their dance. Recruited for the purpose of performing in public at the festival, young unmarried Mamassani women were heavily made up and had dyed their hair, which she notes was out of place and offensive, and had introduced sexually enticing movements into their "traditional" dance. "This excited the public, and the police had to be called to rescue the popular culture!!"[38] Iranians also enjoyed being served by waiters in restaurants and by doormen at hotels dressed in costumes derived from Iran's ethnic groups. Both these roles demonstrated subservience and low status, confirming the notions held by those being served about the socioeconomic position of non-Persians and also confirming the real-life situations of the people represented by this attire. From bazaars and tourist shops Iranians bought handicrafts of the sorts that foreign tourists had been buying for years and decorated their homes with them. Qashqa'i culture, for many chic, upwardly mobile Iranians, became little more than elements of decor.

Some Iranians were inspired by government and foreign attention to see for themselves living examples of these groups. Internal tourism, supported by new roads and facilities, affordable automobiles, and a burgeoning, partially state-sponsored tourist industry, became a new middle-class pastime. The Qashqa'i were particularly appealing to Iranian tourists because of their unique and colorful life-style and their accessibility. Their migrations and encampments along paved roads and their proximity to cities and towns made them vulnerable to passersby and visitors. Many Qashqa'i reluctantly provided traditional hospitality for these uninvited "guests," who marveled at the exotic sights and privately enjoyed the economic benefits of elaborate meals and gifts of pastoral products and woven goods. For some urbanites, a trip to Qashqa'i camps in mountain pastures recalled what they imag-

38. Soheila Shahshahani, personal communication, 20 April 1985; also Shahshahani (1986). Rumors were widespread in Iran that these dancers were prostitutes from Tehran dressed as Qashqa'i.

ined were the rugged conditions of Iran's past. As a result, Iran's modernization was thrown into more exaggerated relief. For citizens of a society rapidly undergoing modernization, urbanization, and industrialization, the life of nomads was seen as time gone by; it represented a way of life they were certain was soon to be erased from the Iranian landscape.

The government facilitated these exploitations because its efforts to disseminate information on ethnic minorities and to spread propaganda about the unity of the Iranian nation-state created desires among Iranians and foreigners to participate directly in and profit from diverse cultural settings. Its efforts allowed both groups to ignore, and hence to violate, geographical and cultural boundaries. Many Iranians felt entitled to the total national territory and free to exploit its human and natural resources, and few foreigners felt restrictions on their travels and personal pursuits. The existence of a police state ensured that the Qashqa'i and other "colorful" minorities had no effective means of resistance. The Qashqa'i were victims of a state which, in its efforts to modernize, began to romanticize cultural systems believed to be part of a more traditional, more primitive Iran, soon to disappear forever.

12

The Iranian Revolution and
the Islamic Republic of Iran:
The Impact of Changing Regimes

*G*iven the political and economic depredations suffered under Mohammad Reza Shah, one might assume that Qashqa'i leaders and tribespeople would have quickly joined the revolutionary movement against him in 1978. They had benefited little from his regime, and they had a history of opposition to Pahlavi rule. In addition, Iranian tribes in general had historically played important roles in dispatching and establishing central authority. The revolution, however, was coordinated—such coordination as there was—by Muslim clergy and leftist and student groups in cities. Iran's tribal people did not take significant military action against state forces.

From September 1978 until the fall of the Bakhtiar government in February 1979, Qashqa'i people participated in street protests in Shiraz, Isfahan, Ahwaz, and other cities, along with millions of other Iranians. At first these were primarily Qashqa'i who resided in cities and towns for purposes of education and work, and they participated as individuals, along with non-Qashqa'i students and workers. But by January 1979, Qashqa'i men from the countryside were joining city street demonstrations in increasing numbers.[1] Those who protested to-

1. Much information in the rest of this paragraph derives from letters (21 January and 30 March 1981) and conversations with Mary Hegland and Eric Hooglund, who lived in Iran in 1978–79 and observed street demonstrations in Shiraz.

296

gether in marches in Shiraz were conspicuous by their clothes, banners, and Turkic slogans.[2] Qashqa'i men wore their distinctive hats and women their multilayered skirts, tunics, short jackets, and headscarves (with *chadors*—head- and body-covering veils—tied around their waists, in partial conformity to urban custom). One group of Qashqa'i men demonstrated on horseback in the cloaks and cummerbunds worn before Reza Shah outlawed them in 1928. In the 1970s this traditional male dress had become popular among young Qashqa'i men who wore it at weddings, but the attire, assuming new meanings, came to symbolize Qashqa'i participation in revolutionary activities and served to separate the Qashqa'i from the non-Qashqa'i in the demonstrations. Qashqa'i men in the demonstrations carried posters of Khomeini and large reproductions of old photographs of armed Qashqa'i and their leaders. Qashqa'i women formed several groups, and young Qashqa'i and Lur women and men from Shiraz's Tribal High School and Tribal Teacher Training School marched together with alternating Turkic and Luri slogans. Qashqa'i from the Bolvardi quarter of Shiraz also marched together, at first in small groups and later in a large group with a banner identifying their neighborhood. Regarding these urban Qashqa'i, Mary Hegland comments:

> I personally feel that the process of Qashqa'i involvement was much the same as the process of involvement of other Iranians. Once they started to get involved and become less afraid, they participated in small groups—a couple of friends—anonymously, just as did other Iranians. At first, those marching were people who happened to get thrown in together; there were no differences in the composition of groups—except for men and women who marched separately. But by the marches of January seventh and eighth, more people began to announce themselves by groups; people started to carry identifying statements on large pieces of white cloth at the front of their groups, which told who they were and where they were from. Gradually structure emerged; the Qashqa'i were no different and began to march in groups with identifying symbols as well. It was a revolution of

2. Mary Hegland (personal communication, 21 January and 30 March 1981) notes several chants used by the Qashqa'i in their demonstrations in Shiraz. One is translated as follows, "Struggling Muslim brothers, come, for it is the time for war. The answer to the criminal shah is bullets and guns."

marches, demonstrations, and strikes; the Qashqa'i took part in these activities just as did other members of society.[3]

The identifiable presence of Qashqa'i groups and the conspicuous use of their dress and other symbols indicated to all observers that the Qashqa'i were revolutionary participants. Given an estimated Qashqa'i population of three to four hundred thousand, however, the proportion actually participating in revolutionary activities at this stage was quite small. The vast majority of the Qashqa'i and other rural-based tribal groups did not participate in any way in the effort to rid Iran of the shah. The only known political meeting in Iran organized by Qashqa'i and relating to the revolution occurred in Ahwaz among Qashqa'i oil-field workers in the fall of 1978.

As revolutionary action against the Pahlavi regime expanded throughout Iran in late 1978, some Qashqa'i khans and headmen in Fars and the paramount khans in exile began a kind of political partic-ipation that they had avoided for years. Those in Fars hesitated to co-ordinate activities without the participation of the paramount khans, so they telephoned Naser Khan in the United States and Khosrow Khan in West Germany to seek advice. Both cautioned restraint and no call to action was forthcoming. They also telephoned the Ayatollah Khomeini in France to ask if the Qashqa'i should attack government forces, in particular the gendarmerie, but he replied that street dem-onstrations and strikes were more effective. Naser Khan and Khosrow Khan expected that Khomeini would play a significant role in Iran's future, and in December 1978 they paid separate visits to him in France. Neither had met him previously. Khomeini expressed apprecia-tion for the support that this implied and noted that the father of the two men—Isma'il Khan Soulat ed-Douleh—had been the only leader in Iran to organize a military response to the Muslim clergy's call for holy war (jihad) against the British during World War I. He hoped that Naser Khan and Khosrow Khan would be "their father's sons," as equally inclined to respond to the clergy as had been their father. The two brothers, pledging their support, noted that their fifty-five-year battle against the Pahlavi dynasty had cost them their father, home-land, and property; what else did they have to lose?

Also in December, in what was the first organized activity in Fars of any of the paramount khans, Malek Mansur Khan recruited from vari-

3. Mary Hegland, personal communication, 21 January 1981.

ous Qashqa'i sections fifty armed guards to protect an oil field south of Firuzabad, in what the family had always considered its territory. As central authority weakened, he distrusted the ability of the Iranian military to ensure the safety of the field.

In one of the shah's last speeches from Iran, he angrily attacked the paramount Qashqa'i khans by name for continually threatening his regime.[4] One of them remarked that the shah, who had by then lost control over events in the nation and was psychologically disturbed, probably imagined that he saw the two flaps of the Qashqa'i hat poking out from the turbans of Khomeini and the other clergy who were attempting to overthrow his regime. That is, the shah, who had been threatened by the paramount Qashqa'i khans in the past, may have imagined that they were instigators of the national uprising.

In January 1979, shortly before the shah's ouster, Naser Khan returned to Iran. He admitted that he risked imprisonment by doing so but was unable to postpone his return any longer. At the Tehran airport authorities detained him, but after his daughter phoned Prime Minister Shapur Bakhtiar—a friend and fellow National Front member—he was released.[5] Naser Khan's reception, by all accounts, was overwhelming. Hundreds of Qashqa'i and non-Qashqa'i came to greet him, and he enjoyed warm reunions with relatives. Many individuals and groups, tribal and nontribal, urged him to take an active role in national politics, and those forming a new government offered him the ministry or governorship of his choice, including Governor of Fars. But Naser Khan and his family were anxious to leave Tehran, and, two days after the shah's departure on January 16, a caravan of cars escorted Naser Khan south to Fars. Clergy in Isfahan wanted to welcome Naser Khan as he traveled through that city, but he feared the army might use the occasion to attack the gathering and so did not stop. News of his return was widespread, and welcomers from towns and rural areas lined the road from Isfahan to Shiraz. Many stood ready with sheep to be sacrificed ritually as his car passed by. The largest welcome was at Takht-e Jamshid (Persepolis, an ancient capital of the Persian Empire), and from there thousands of people in hundreds of cars escorted him to Shiraz, where he visited Shah Cheragh, the city's major religious

4. I heard a tape-recording of the speech but was unable to discover the date of its original broadcast.

5. Shapur Bakhtiar and Naser Khan came from similar tribal backgrounds, and their fathers had been allied. Reza Shah executed Shapur Bakhtiar's father for his participation in the 1929 rebellion.

shrine.[6] Standing between Shiraz's two most prominent ayatollahs, Dastghaib and Mahallati, and amidst other clergy, Naser Khan told the large audience that he was not back to serve as khan or reclaim land or former privileges but to work along with the citizens of Fars to create a new political order. His speech was published in local newspapers.[7]

Naser Khan and his party then moved south to Hengam, south of Firuzabad, where thousands of Qashqa'i from all parts of Qashqa'i territory and from towns and cities gathered in a tent encampment called by some an *ordu,* a term used in the past for a tribal military gathering.[8] Some feared that the Iranian army or gendarmerie would attack the camp, a notion augmented by supervisory overflights of Iranian air force planes, and members of the camp made military preparations of the sort last made during World War II. Except for one small but hostile civilian incursion, however, the gathering was left undisturbed. Ten days after the shah's departure, Khosrow Khan returned to Iran. Because he had fought against the shah in the 1950s, he ran a greater risk of arrest on arrival than others in the family, and Prime Minister Bakhtiar had warned him to delay his return. A small party went to Tehran to greet him and escort him south. He spent less than a day in the camp and then returned to Shiraz to discuss politics with other former exiles. He also delivered a speech at Shah Cheragh.

On the fall of the Bakhtiar government on February 11, young Qashqa'i men from the camp, regretting what they considered the insignificant participation of the Qashqa'i in the revolution, planned an

6. Shah Cheragh held no particular religious significance for the paramount Qashqa'i khans or their ancestors. The power inherent in the symbolic act of Naser Khan's visit came from the preeminence of the shrine in Shiraz and the region as a place of pilgrimage. Political leaders, including the two Pahlavi shahs, often made ritual visits there when in Shiraz, and the shrine continued to be the major religious site in the city after 1978. Qashqa'i people frequently made pilgrimages to Shah Cheragh when in Shiraz. After the Governor of Fars in 1833 desecrated the graves of the Shahilu family at Bagh-e Eram, its estate in Shiraz, the family often buried its dead at Shah Cheragh in order to protect them from abuse. In 1963, when the Shahilu family was implicated in rural protests, Prime Minister Alam ordered its graves at Shah Cheragh destroyed and its names obliterated.

7. The great attention given by the media in Iran to the paramount Qashqa'i khans from this point on contrasted with the previous twenty-five years, when government-imposed restrictions on media coverage of these khans and political events concerning the Qashqa'i were in effect.

8. Other than several women of the Shahilu family, Qashqa'i women and children did not attend this gathering.

attack against government forces. Naser Khan and Khosrow Khan urged restraint, partly because of Naser Khan's promise to Khomeini to maintain order in Fars, and attempted to prevent military action, but two enthusiastic groups from the camp seized several gendarme posts. They captured caches of arms and later ceremonially distributed one cache to a local ayatollah and returned another to the gendarmes. But the first phase of the revolution, deposition of the shah and his regime, was essentially over, and they felt little sense of victory. On the same day, Homa, Naser Khan's daughter, negotiated the surrender of a gendarme post and ended a false rumor of an imminent Qashqa'i attack on Shiraz's airport by going there personally to announce publicly that there were no Qashqa'i attackers in the vicinity.[9] Also on 11 February, armed Qashqa'i and others attacked the police station and the Zand prison in Shiraz, two holdouts of government forces.[10]

Shortly thereafter, Khosrow Khan traveled to Kazerun, where he spoke to a large audience at the city's major shrine, and then on to Khuzistan through the oil-rich western foothills of the Zagros Mountains, in order to reestablish a Qashqa'i political presence. The region's inhabitants, consisting primarily of Qashqa'i, Lurs, Bakhtiyaris, and Arabic-speakers, lined his route of travel and greeted him with enthusiasm. Settled Qashqa'i oil-field workers, who continued to adhere to their tribal affiliations, told him that they would respond to his call for labor strikes, production cut-off, and sabotage. Other oil-field workers, tribal and nontribal, also responded positively to him.

Naser Khan and his family moved to a favorite winter pasture near Firuzabad, where he continued to receive a steady stream of visitors. Family members turned a building of theirs in Firuzabad, which the government had seized in the 1960s and converted into a gendarme post, into a Qashqa'i political headquarters and appropriated the military equipment stored there. In the spring, Naser Khan traveled through summer pastures, while Malek Mansur Khan and Mohammad Hosain Khan established tent encampments in their former pastures. Naser Khan, stating that he lacked the necessary equipment and financial resources, did not set up a camp; nor did Khosrow Khan, who spent most of the summer in Shiraz and Tehran.

9. On several previous occasions of political unrest in Fars, Qashqa'i forces had attacked the airport and damaged military equipment that was being used against them.

10. Mary Hegland, personal communication, 21 January 1981.

The circumstances from which members of the Shahilu family emerged in January 1979 were diverse (fig. 2). Only people mentioned in the following discussion are included. Naser Khan and his family lived in the United States for twenty-five years and had recently moved seasonally between California and Maine. Abdollah, who held a medical degree from Cornell University, was a general practitioner in Maine and returned to Iran in March 1979.[11] Homa, who returned to Iran in the early 1970s, held a professional job in a Tehran medical clinic. More than any other family member, she prepared the way for her father's return by establishing political contacts. Malek Mansur Khan and his family returned to Iran in 1965, while Mohammad Hosain Khan and his family returned in the late 1950s. The government prohibited both brothers from traveling to Fars and kept them under close surveillance. Nazli, a student in Belgium, returned in 1979. Houman, holding a master's degree from a university in Kentucky, had worked in Iran for several years. Khosrow Khan, who was unmarried and had no children, lived in West Germany for twenty-five years. Farrokh Bibi and Molki Bibi had always lived in Iran, as had Shapur and Manuchehr. The shah had executed Bahman in 1966. Kaveh and Golnar, students in Great Britain, returned to Iran with the revolution.

THE PROCESS OF REESTABLISHING LEADERSHIP
IN 1979

Qashqa'i leaders of all levels, enthusiastic in the spring of 1979 about their potential role in the tribe and the state, became disillusioned by fall. The four paramount khans and their families left tribal territory and settled into residence in Tehran. Naser Khan, fatigued by the intensity of his return to Iran and suffering respiratory difficulties, left in September for medical treatment in the United States, despite personal requests from Khomeini to remain. (He returned to Iran in December 1979.) The attempted reestablishment of Qashqa'i leadership in 1979 after the shah's ouster took many dimensions.

In the past, leaders of the Qashqa'i confederacy had politicized their Shi'i Muslim identity in ways unavailable to Iran's Sunni minorities. From January to March 1979, Naser Khan, Khosrow Khan, and other

11. For many years Abdollah was a party to a legal case concerning his medical practice in Maine. He selected as a lawyer Katherine Douglas, wife of the late Supreme Court Justice William O. Douglas, who had visited the paramount Qashqa'i khans in 1950 and published his observations (1951).

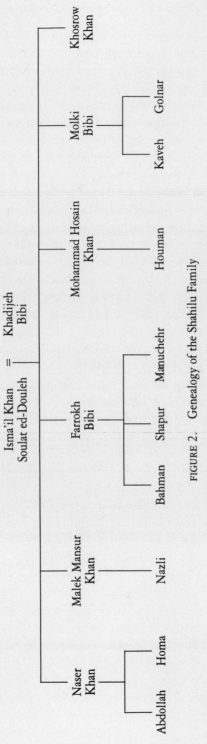

FIGURE 2. Genealogy of the Shahilu Family

Note: Only those individuals mentioned in the text are included here.

men of the family developed ties with clergy in Qom, Shiraz, and Tehran. They visited Khomeini shortly after his arrival in February, delegations of Qom clergy visited the khans on behalf of Khomeini, and both parties kept in contact by telephone. The khans also met with the Ayatollahs Taleqani and Shari'atmadari (an Azerbaijani Turk). Khomeini, who had asked Naser Khan for assistance in maintaining security in Fars, publicly attributed peaceful conditions in that province to the presence of Naser Khan and Khosrow Khan and contrasted it to Kurdistan and Baluchistan where armed resistance to the new regime was emerging. Abdollah, Naser Khan's son, was asked to be Khomeini's official escort for a high-ranking Nicaraguan Sandinistan on a mission to seek the new revolutionary government's support. Abdollah's visits to Khomeini on behalf of the Sandinistan helped to legitimize Qashqa'i relationships with the new government and created new ties for the paramount khans. Historical alliances between the paramount Qashqa'i khans and religious leaders, the persecution which both groups had suffered under Pahlavi rule, and the khans' visits to Khomeini in exile all served to place these khans in a stronger position vis-à-vis the revolutionary government than any other tribal or national-minority leadership in Iran at this time. Qashqa'i relations with the center had probably not been better since the reign of Karim Khan Zand in the eighteenth century.

As the Pahlavi regime weakened and fell, the Qashqa'i people quickly transferred local power to their own hands by heavily rearming, reaffiliating with political leaders, and renewing other political contacts. Understaffed gendarme and army forces were weak and ineffective and did not impede this process.

During its first months, the Islamic Republic of Iran had parallel, often conflicting, governments: Prime Minister Bazargan's provisional government dominated by secular liberals and the Revolutionary Council dominated by clergy and operating locally through Revolutionary Committees (*komitehs*) and Revolutionary Guards (*pasdaran*). From the start, the Qashqa'i did not participate in either Revolutionary Committees or Guards and were unwilling to allow these Persian, usually urban, lower-middle-class, and ostensibly religiously devout groups to enter tribal areas. In early spring, religious figures and their supporters in some Persian-dominated towns in Qashqa'i areas, anxious to establish their own local authority, clashed with the Qashqa'i. In Firuzabad, whose population at the time was about evenly divided between Persians and settled Qashqa'i, some Qashqa'i fought with Revolutionary Guards and Committee members. Four committee members were killed, and a Qashqa'i group forced the guards out of town. [12] The tension between Persians and Qashqa'i in Firuzabad was based on economics as well as politics, for some Persians there viewed the many years of conflict between the government and the Qashqa'i as the cause of government neglect of the town and region. Firuzabad had received few government services in the 1960s and 1970s compared with other towns of comparable size; even the road from Shiraz was still unpaved in 1979. Some Persians in Firuzabad feared that resurgent Qashqa'i politics would create problems for them with the new regime. In Semirom, a Persian-dominated town surrounded by summer pastures, the Qashqa'i and Revolutionary Guards avoided armed conflict by agreeing that if Qashqa'i men would not brandish arms while visiting town, Revolutionary Guards would keep out of the surrounding tribal territory and permit Qashqa'i vehicles to travel through town without being searched. Some Qashqa'i khans carried government-authorized guns in order to escape harassment by Revolutionary Guards.

As in the past, state authorities once again relied on the paramount Qashqa'i khans for some local administration and control, while they simultaneously resorted to divide-and-rule tactics by favoring one khan over another. When guards and committees were unable to settle local disputes, they frequently asked these Qashqa'i leaders to mediate. When the Basseri and Shish Boluki tribes fought over pastures, the government asked Khosrow Khan to settle the dispute; he declined to become involved. The Revolutionary Council and Bazargan's office often sent documents relating to development programs and appointments of officials to serve in Fars to Naser Khan, Khosrow Khan, or Abdollah for approval and signature. The government's dual, often conflicting, nature complicated these relations, for Bazargan sent officials and documents to the khans and often intentionally ignored committees and religious authorities, while the Revolutionary Council took action without consulting Bazargan. In September 1979, when the Revolutionary Council sought Khosrow Khan's assistance in its demand that Fars citizens be immediately disarmed, Bazargan personally informed Khosrow Khan that he did not wish to see the order implemented, and Khosrow Khan took no part in the government's attempted confiscation of arms.

12. Revolutionary Guards did not return to Firuzabad in force until June 1980.

At a time when local governments associated with the Pahlavi regime were being (partially) dismembered and new ones assembled, and
with accusations rampant about alleged SAVAK connections, the paramount Qashqa'i khans were seen as unambiguous authority figures by
a wide spectrum of the Iranian people. Their antagonism to the Pahlavi
regime was unquestioned, and they represented continuity in leadership and authority. Their popularity, and for some their charisma, was
based on their previous leadership, their stand against Pahlavi rule, and
their association with Mosaddeq and Khomeini. Few other political
figures in Iran held such credentials. Leftists attacked the khans for
representing propertied interests, but they were not able to attack
them effectively on these other grounds. Non-Qashqa'i as well as
Qashqa'i sought assistance from the paramount khans, an indication of
the high regard in which they were held. In Fars many appealed to
Khosrow Khan, partly because he resided in Shiraz more frequently
than the other khans. His mother's residence there, where he stayed,
was often filled with people who sought favors.[13]

The Revolutionary Council, Committees, and Guards were, however, puzzled by what they saw as inconsistency in the personal association of the paramount Qashqa'i khans and Khomeini, on the one hand,
and the resistance of these khans, other Qashqa'i leaders, and the
Qashqa'i tribespeople to those who claimed to represent state authority,
on the other. The ruling Islamic Republican party, in an effort to sustain its mass base of support, relied on Revolutionary Guards, mobs of
Hizbollahis (Followers of the Party of God, mostly the urban poor and
unemployed), and village mullahs who worked as grass roots agitators
and supported local Revolutionary Committees (Zabih 1982:69–70).
For the Qashqa'i, interaction with Khomeini did not necessarily require subservience to Revolutionary Guards and mullahs. The tie with
Khomeini was similar to the ties that Qashqa'i ilkhanis and their ancestors had created with virtually every state ruler since Nader Shah in the
mid-eighteenth century and possibly Safavid shahs even earlier: personal, direct, often mutually advantageous, and often unmediated and
uncomplicated by local officials. Despite their own pretentions, Revolutionary Guards and mullahs did not represent Khomeini or the new

13. Dr. Bahram Azadeh, professor of medicine at Shiraz University and former
officer of the Health Corps who had worked among the Qashqa'i, notes that Khosrow
Khan helped him to have the death penalty of an innocent military officer reduced to
life imprisonment and then to a five-year sentence; personal communication, 6 February 1985.

Iranian state, in Qashqa'i eyes, and hence could be ignored or resisted. The Qashqa'i held no sympathy for mullahs, who were attempting to acquire for themselves the legitimacy of the power in Qom, and they had long scorned local religious functionaries; the establishment of the Islamic Republic only increased their anticlerical sentiments. They had never accepted the conservative, dogmatic Shi'i interpretations of society and human behavior, and religious functionaries had regarded them with contempt for laxity in pious expression. Also, for most Qashqa'i, their main regular contact with non-Qashqa'i had been with town and city merchants and moneylenders, who, while masquerading as pious Muslims, extorted high interest rates and otherwise exploited them economically.

The geographical dispersion of the Qashqa'i contributed to ambiguity in expressions of state power and authority on the local level, as during previous historical periods. Abdollah, who was attempting to reestablish a Qashqa'i political presence, complained about having to deal with different government officials and policies whenever he traveled from one Qashqa'i area to another. Under revolutionary conditions, government administration was highly decentralized, and what little national policy existed was vague and unenforced.

For all Qashqa'i the two-eared felt hat was a symbol of Qashqa'i repoliticization and revived identity in 1979. Use of the hat had diminished somewhat under the last two decades of Pahlavi rule, but within a few weeks of Naser Khan's return and coincident with the shah's ouster, almost all Qashqa'i men wore expensive, fine-looking hats, not only in Qashqa'i territory but also in settled areas, especially where Qashqa'i power was reemerging, such as in Persian-dominated towns. Before the revolution, Qashqa'i men in Shiraz were often indistinguishable from men of similar economic status because they usually left their hats behind when they came to town, to avoid harassment, or they cut off the two flaps to avoid being identified as Qashqa'i (creating a plain hat similar to that worn by Persian and Lur villagers), but these disguises were no longer resorted to by February 1979. Some Lurs and other non-Qashqa'i rural people, especially those associated in some way with the Qashqa'i, wore the Qashqa'i hat in order to identify with the group's revived presence. Khans of the Qashqa'i tribes and other wealthy Qashqa'i also wore the hat conspicuously in Shiraz and Isfahan. Under the shah's regime, these same individuals had intentionally blended into the urban, professional, upper and upper-middle class in style and dress and shunned such an obvious display of non-Persian identity. Qashqa'i women, too, of elite and nonelite status, paid greater attention to their dress while in cities and towns and wore more elaborate apparel than before the revolution.

The outpouring of support for Naser Khan from the Qashqa'i people was deeply moving for both sides. Men, women, and children came in large numbers to greet him everywhere he traveled. People marveled at his ability to recognize individuals and recall details of their former association after twenty-five years of separation. Many brought gifts of animals and money. Former supporters and retainers pledged to assist him again, and some who volunteered their services as gunmen were chosen by the khans as their armed escorts and accompanied them everywhere. Lower-level leaders were anxious to reestablish ties, become politically active, and join the khans in reasserting Qashqa'i power. Naser Khan and Khosrow Khan, however, did not agree about the course their leadership should take. They rarely traveled together, were not always in close contact, and seemed to avoid one another. They did not remain long in one location, spent time in distant Tehran, and were often difficult to reach. They did not set a tribal policy, nor did they effectively engage the existing leadership hierarchy. And, except for the armed escorts, they did not utilize the many associates and retainers who had formerly assisted in leadership and implemented policies. Many Qashqa'i, expecting the khans to propose and implement a program of leadership, were puzzled, and some were disappointed.

The Pahlavi regime had removed the collective resource base of the Qashqa'i by nationalizing pastures, deeding tribal land to non-Qashqa'i through land reform, and encouraging agricultural expansion by non-Qashqa'i into Qashqa'i pastures. By 1978 the economies of many Qashqa'i no longer depended on tribally allocated resources. The paramount khans made no plans to collect taxes, which would have supported the expenses connected with leadership, partly because they wished to avoid appearing to be exploiters, as their leftist detractors depicted them. Many Qashqa'i sought the khans' leadership in expectation that tribal land would be returned, existing exploitative economic relations ended,[14] past modes and relations of production resumed, and tribal strength in the region reasserted. Many were anxious to return to nomadic pastoralism, especially those whose lands had been expropriated, who had become impoverished by the shah's eco-

14. With bazaar moneylenders and merchants, capitalist stock raisers, and some urban employers, all of whom were non-Qashqa'i.

nomic policies, and who had been forced to take up low-paying wage labor.

Urban Qashqa'i who were part of the Iranian middle class and integrated into the Iranian state expressed mixed feelings about the paramount khans' resumption of power. They rejoiced in the shah's departure and recognized the khans as victims of Pahlavi rule, but their interests rested in continued participation in middle-class Iran. The khans had not yet spoken to the class interests of these Qashqa'i, who wondered how a resumed "Qashqa'i" leadership would relate to them. Formally educated nonelite Qashqa'i, many of whom had opposed khan rule for years, regarded a possible resumption of paramount leadership with some distaste. The tribal education program had nurtured in many teachers and students strong anti-khan sentiments. Some Qashqa'i in the new wealthy landowning class welcomed the khans' return and expected to gain in regional power. This group had not existed to any degree in the 1950s but was created by land reform, pasture nationalization, agricultural mechanization, and Qashqa'i depoliticization; it had benefited under Pahlavi rule. Some worried that the repoliticization of the Qashqa'i might threaten their wealth and position and feared confrontations involving the government, khans, and Qashqa'i leftists that would jeopardize their interests. In short, political and economic changes during the previous twenty-five years had created a more socioeconomically diverse population, significant parts of which were now urban-based, formally educated, state-oriented, integrated into the national capitalist economy, and politically inactive and unaffiliated. For these Qashqa'i, a resumption of traditional Qashqa'i leadership seemed most unlikely. The paramount khans' understanding of this situation partly explains their own lack of political aggression.

Many Iranians and most Qashqa'i assumed that the paramount khans, Naser Khan and Khosrow Khan in particular, had returned to serve as tribal leaders, restore the Qashqa'i to a powerful place in the nation, and use their local power base to enter national leadership. But, beyond their determination to remain armed, expel non-Qashqa'i pastoralists from Qashqa'i land, and keep Revolutionary Committees and Guards out of Qashqa'i territory, neither khan introduced plans for the Qashqa'i and their place in the Islamic Republic. Neither fully supported for the Qashqa'i the notions of regional autonomy then being expressed by many Iranian Kurds, Baluch, and Turkmen. Given the location of Shiraz and other heavily settled non-Qashqa'i areas between

Qashqa'i winter and summer pastures, and the residence of many Qashqa'i in cities, towns, and predominantly non-Qashqa'i villages, regional autonomy was not seen as feasible for the Qashqa'i as it was for Iran's many border-situated national-minority groups. Leaders of other national-minority and tribal groups, including Kurds from both northwest Iran and Khorasan (Zafaranlu), Baluch, Bakhtiyari, Boir Ahmad, Mamassani, Basseri, Afshar, Buchaqchi, and those of the gulf coast, visited Naser Khan. Newspapers, radio, and television had announced his return from exile, and many groups, especially those with less centralized or nationally linked political systems, sought solutions to their own political difficulties from him. Kurd and Baluch leaders expected that he would, through his superior national connections, aid in their own efforts to obtain regional and ethnic autonomy. They assumed that Qashqa'i leaders held identical aspirations. Naser Khan never implemented his ideas for a Confederacy of Southern Tribes and a Union of Iranian Tribes, although many were enthusiastic.

Naser Khan and Khosrow Khan, like other minority leaders, did support the notion that people should manage their own local concerns, including land, water, and schools. According to Mohammad Hosain Khan, the immediate needs of Qashqa'i pastoralists included money to repay debts, bottled gas to end the burning of natural vegetation, supplies for pasture reseeding, and trucks and tents for those resuming nomadism. He urged bans on unirrigated agriculture in pastures, charcoal production, pasture rental to non-Qashqa'i, and contract herding with non-Qashqa'i commercial stock raisers.[15] Abdollah sent a letter stating Qashqa'i needs as he saw them (wells, pasture reseeding, clinics, and schools) to Khomeini, Bazargan, and other officials, and he circulated copies throughout Fars. The government did not respond, and in frustration he went alone to Firuzabad to begin a medical program. Golnar, niece of the four khans, provided classes in literacy, Islamic law, and health to impoverished Qashqa'i women and children in Shiraz shantytowns and surrounding villages.

In the 1960s and 1970s, most Qashqa'i had suffered hardships because of land scarcity. Land reform had made no provision for the seasonal use of land by nomadic pastoralists, and enforcement of pasture nationalization had placed control of land in government hands. With the shah's ouster, many Qashqa'i joined other Iranians in regarding these land programs as illegitimate and illegal as his regime had been,

15. Mohammad Hosain Khan, personal communication, 29 July 1979, London.

and they sought to establish their own rights over land.[16] The many Qashqa'i resuming nomadism desired unimpeded access to former pastures, and some who had lost cultivable land through land reform, particularly those of the lower and middle economic groups, now seized these lands or threatened to do so. Many Qashqa'i thought Naser Khan ought to establish a Qashqa'i land program, and even non-Qashqa'i came seeking his leadership, but he was unwilling to act forcibly. Those who took matters into their own hands caused heightened tension with local Revolutionary Guards and Committees, who continued to seek the khans' adjudication. In the meantime, Khosrow Khan publicly announced that the only legal use of land was the one in practice in 1953, and that the Qashqa'i should return to the land they or their families had occupied twenty-five years before. He thus denounced the land reform and changes in land tenure put into effect after 1953, but he did not suggest practical steps for changing present tenure, which increased local uncertainty. The khans did publicly support the expulsion from tribal land of nontribal encroachers, including commercial stock raisers and those who had seized land illegally in the confusion of the reforms and nationalizations of the 1960s. The Qashqa'i, who were now heavily armed, easily expelled people from many areas. They told Persians who had developed orchards in tribal territory that they could, for the moment, keep what was within existing walls but could not use agricultural or grazing land beyond. Water disputes arose because orchard developers had encircled springs and wells within garden walls. Although Naser Khan stressed publicly that he had not returned to claim his confiscated lands, uneasy local people were not totally convinced. He told the mostly non-Qashqa'i villagers who occupied what was once his family's land that the shah was to blame, not the villagers, and that he held no personal grudge against them. He made no attempt to reclaim these lands.

Another major problem over land involved the Darrehshuri, who, under the direction of their khans, had seized many Amaleh summer pastures after the exile of the paramount khans. The ilkhani had allocated Amaleh pastures, and the group was vulnerable when he was exiled. Before the 1979 spring migration, the paramount khans told Darrehshuri pastoralists, who made no public protest, that they could not use these summer pastures. Pressure on more southern summer

16. For the situation in one village in Fars, see Mary Hooglund (Hegland) (1980). Also see Eric Hooglund (1982a) and Bakhash (1984:195–216).

pastures utilized by other Qashqa'i groups was increased. The paramount khans struggled with these many land issues throughout the summer of 1979, and when the fall migration commenced they took up residence in Tehran, partly to avoid having to handle the new set of conflicts arising in winter pastures. Disputants in emerging land problems telephoned them constantly, however, introducing a new dimension of tribal communications. The khans, anticipating conflict in the oil-rich area northwest of Shiraz where Qashqa'i, Boir Ahmad, and Mamassani pastures meet, sent armed supporters with Ayaz Khan Darrehshuri to his winter pastures there. Iran's new government in 1979 was unable to enforce either previous or current land tenure or to implement its newly approved land-reform bill, and thus local powers settled land issues independently. The paramount Qashqa'i khans did not effectively establish their authority in this regard, despite the acceptance it would have received in some areas.

Some Qashqa'i who visited Naser Khan sought his reassurance about the extent of their complicity with the Pahlavi regime. Naser Khan stressed publicly that he had not returned to punish collaborators and that he recognized that many Qashqa'i had been forced to accommodate their lives to the regime, but privately he was bitter about those who had acquiesced to Pahlavi rule. He made no specific policy about the treatment of SAVAK informers among the Qashqa'i, partly because a few were found in the other khan families. Revolutionary Guards arrested or sought some of these informers.

The one Qashqa'i whom Naser Khan would not excuse was Mohammad Bahmanbegi, director of the Office of Tribal Education. Many Qashqa'i accused Bahmanbegi of having attempted to destroy the Qashqa'i as a political and cultural entity, and both levels of khans disliked him for having assumed certain aspects of Qashqa'i leadership. Many were also angry about his exploitation of young unmarried Qashqa'i women as performing dancers for the shah and visiting foreign and Iranian dignitaries, which they saw as symbolic of his attempts to exploit the Qashqa'i for his own political purposes and as indicative of his close ties with the regime. By using Qashqa'i women this way, he was said to have jeopardized Qashqa'i honor. Bahmanbegi personally welcomed Naser Khan on his return to Iran but was not hospitably received, and shortly thereafter armed Qashqa'i and zealous nontribal Shirazis anxious to punish state officials close to the shah forcibly drove Bahmanbegi and his family out of Shiraz and into hiding in Tehran. Some Shirazis say he provoked this attack by guarding his home and family with armed Lur tribesmen.[17] In September 1979, Bahmanbegi again sought reassurance from Naser Khan but was summarily dismissed, and Naser Khan noted bitterly that the several months of "exile" spent by a complaining Bahmanbegi were insignificant compared with his own twenty-five years of exile.

Some members of the Shahilu family urged Abdollah to become director of the Office of Tribal Education, which would ensure continuity in the program and in Qashqa'i control of it and would return Qashqa'i leadership, partly usurped by Bahmanbegi, to them. In addition, the program was government financed and owned two hundred vehicles and buildings in Shiraz and elsewhere, resources useful for tribal and personal purposes. The paramount khans, it will be recalled, no longer owned any property in the region. The government would have approved of Abdollah's appointment; he was respected, eminently qualified, and well educated, and state officials had asked him to assume other government positions. In the indecision of the times, however, he did not act aggressively, and the government eventually appointed a Boir Ahmad Lur.

Members of the Shahilu family were acutely aware that competition among them was damaging the attempted resumption of leadership. By early fall 1979, some felt that their moment had already passed, that it was too late to reestablish themselves and the Qashqa'i as major powers. Of the four khans, Khosrow Khan in particular took an independent, unpredictable course and allied with other powers in the area, including leftists who wanted to abolish the khan system. Family members were appalled when he publicly volunteered a thousand Qashqa'i warriors to end Khomeini's problems with the Kurdish insurgency, even when he privately noted that he never would have undertaken such a mission. Later he denied having made the original offer. Khosrow Khan issued under his own and the Qashqa'i name a letter of sympathy in Tehran newspapers at the unexpected death of the Ayatollah Taleqani, an act some said reflected his attempts to assume Qashqa'i leadership unilaterally. Naser Khan played a quietly political, almost ceremonial, role as he traveled throughout tribal territory and did not create the discord that seemed to follow in Khosrow Khan's wake. Several younger members of the family complained that he often resorted to "old" Qashqa'i ways of handling political affairs and did not adequately understand the changes that had occurred to the Qashqa'i

17. Bahmanbegi's wife is a Lur.

people during his long absence. Malek Mansur Khan, an eloquent tribal historian, was also more interested in the ceremonial aspects of Qashqa'i life than in serving as an aggressive political leader. Mohammad Hosain Khan, whose concerns focused on national rather than specifically tribal politics, visited Qashqa'i territory infrequently and continued to be the one who established links at the national level. Men such as Abolhasan Bani Sadr and Rahmatollah Moqaddam-Maraghe'i, an Azerbaijani Turk who at the time was one of the most influential nonclerical members of the Assembly of Experts charged with drafting a new constitution, were his close friends and frequent visitors, and both Mohammad Hosain Khan and Malek Mansur Khan continued to associate with National Front members. Distinctions made between the two brothers who were in exile for twenty-five years (and hence seen as untainted by political accommodation to the Pahlavi regime) and the two who had returned earlier were sources of tension within the family. The latter two brothers had adequate sources of income by now, but the former two were in economic difficulty. Family discussions about rights over Bagh-e Eram, the ilkhani's estate in Shiraz confiscated by Mohammad Reza Shah, served to obscure as well as to air some of these difficulties.[18]

The children of these khans also had opposing interests, and some competed for leadership roles. They were professionals or students educated and enculturated in the West. Because of the state's political repression of their parents, most of the children had never lived in tribal territory, and their ideas of tribal life and leadership were distilled versions of nostalgic stories told over the years, enhanced by romantic accounts published by journalists. Some members of this generation were leftist or leftist-oriented yet seemed to have difficulty applying leftist ideals, which often generalized for all Iran and ignored cultural differences, to their own unique cultural identity and national-minority status. Also, they were aware that elite status and leftist activity were inherently contradictory. One person with Tudeh party (communist) affiliations took no action either for or against the khan system. The older generation valued age and experience and did not

18. Upon their return to Iran, Naser Khan and Khosrow Khan announced publicly that they were donating Bagh-e Eram to the people of Shiraz as a museum. Given that legal title was in question, however, the family continued to discuss the property. In the meantime, Revolutionary Guards took possession of it.

easily relinquish major leadership roles to the youngsters. Among the latter, those who most successfully performed in leadership capacities served in deputy-like fashion to the khans; Houman, son of Mohammad Hosain Khan, is the best example.

Men and women of the younger generation, and to some extent of the older, competed for leadership. Some men explicitly denied, on the basis of gender, formal leadership status to women. A published genealogy of "the Qashqa'i ruling family," which included only men, was offered as proof that no women had ever been tribal leaders (Oberling 1974:237–40). All were aware of historical precedents for female leadership in this family, however, and its most recent expression in Khadijeh Khanom (widow of Isma'il Khan and mother of the four khans), two of her daughters, and two granddaughters. The ninety-three-year-old Khadijeh Khanom (Bibi Khanom) was still a functioning leader. Her daughters Farrokh Bibi and Molki Bibi tended to exert power through men of the family, while her granddaughters, particularly Homa and Golnar, were more overt in their politics. Farrokh Bibi, still bitter about the lack of family support for her son Bahman's rebellion against the government in the early 1960s and about the lack of organized protest when he was executed in 1966, remained somewhat distant from her brothers but did support the political efforts of two of her surviving sons. Molki Bibi was closely allied with Khosrow Khan, and it was with her that he stayed when he was in Tehran.

Khans of the component Qashqa'i tribes, who had assumed greater political importance when the paramount khans were exiled and who were then stripped of many leadership functions by the state in the 1960s, were now caught in a structural dilemma. On the one hand, they could emerge again as major political figures in south Iran; on the other, they were, and felt they ought to be, politically subordinate to the paramount khans. Some demonstrated no interest in playing active political roles. The paramount khans and many tribespeople regarded the khans at the secondary level as collaborators in the shah's political and economic programs of the 1960s and 1970s. The fact that tribespeople lost pastures and became impoverished while khans gained agricultural land and became wealthy were directly connected in many people's minds. Most khans had provided little concrete assistance to members of their tribes during this period, and some had formed close ties with government officials, including SAVAK agents. The paramount khans, tainted by none of this, could have driven a further wedge between the secondary khans and the tribespeople for their own purposes, but did not. They seemed to be more concerned with re-establishing ties with these khans than with the tribespeople.

The key role in the relationship between the ilkhani and the khans had been played by the kalantar, the most prominent khan of a khan family. Before 1954, he had emerged through a combined process of internal selection and external appointment by the ilkhani. A twenty-five-year hiatus in this process had occurred, and khans now of age to serve as kalantar competed with those who had served in years past. Neither Naser Khan nor Khosrow Khan appointed kalantars from the tribes; they said they wanted them to emerge through internal processes. In reality, they did not always agree on the best candidates, they each wanted to avoid being identified with possibly unpopular ones, and they needed to prevent further conflict within the family and among their supporters.

The main competitors for Qashqa'i leadership between 1954 and 1979 were the Darrehshuri khans, who had become wealthy and connected with the government after the exile of the paramount khans and who had appropriated many of their vast summer pastures. One of Naser Khan's few concrete decisions that affected the Qashqa'i people was to prohibit Darrehshuri pastoralists from migrating into these pastures; this ban served to punish them for the acts of their khans and disrupted the renewal of ties between the Darrehshuri khans and the Shahilu family. In symbolic protest, the Darrehshuri khans, who in the 1970s had established the most elaborate tent encampments of any of the khan families, refused to erect tents and instead set up residence in nearby villages. Many Qashqa'i felt that the Darrehshuri khans had offered less assistance to their tribal sections during the past few decades than any other khan family. Khosrow Khan urged Darrehshuri tribespeople to seize property now owned by the Darrehshuri khans, and, whether or not his urgings were responsible, some Darrehshuri herders did camp on the khans' land. Darrehshuri khans were in conflict on several issues and sought the mediation of the paramount khans. Partly as a result, several councils were formed among the Darrehshuri to handle land disputes between khans and nonelite Qashqa'i, as well as to solve other problems.[19]

19. Councils (sing. *shura*) were simultaneously being organized throughout Iran and were supported ideologically by the new regime.

An unexpected event in December 1979 united both levels of khans. Two Darrehshuri subtribes fought over pastures near the Qashqa'i-Mamassani border north of Shiraz. Local gendarmes, unable to settle the dispute, sought assistance from Ayaz Khan Darrehshuri, who happened to be driving to Mamassani territory on other business. Ayaz Khan agreed to negotiate and entered the area under dispute. As he approached the warring sections unarmed, he was shot and killed without warning, along with another member of his party. The prime assailant was Allahqoli, a young nonelite Darrehshuri who had held grudges against Darrehshuri khans for years, who had been imprisoned under the shah on charges including the theft of a gun from Ayaz Khan's brother, and who had recently attempted to organize leftist activities in Darrehshuri summer pastures. Allahqoli fled to resist capture. Upon hearing the news of Ayaz Khan's death, the paramount khans and other khans descended upon the area to mourn him and to seek revenge against the culprits. Of the Darrehshuri khans, Ayaz Khan had been the closest to the paramount khans and an effective mediator in the rapidly changing political scene. He was the only Qashqa'i known to be a member of a sufi order, and he had independently developed good ties with some nationally prominent clergy. Naser Khan, who had just returned to Iran after a two-month visit to the United States, issued an ultimatum to government authorities that they must arrest Allahqoli and others responsible for the crime or Qashqa'i forces would assume responsibility. Revolutionary Guards entered the area to separate the two groups warring over pastures and prevent a possible fight over Allahqoli. Khomeini appointed a member of the clergy to negotiate. A close Persian friend of the paramount khans, employed as a correspondent for *Time* magazine in Tehran, released news of the confrontation to international wire services in hope of preventing escalating hostilities. No further major confrontation occurred, and the various parties dispersed. Darrehshuri khans, who had earlier found no common ground upon which to agree, spent the winter in Ayaz Khan's winter pastures on the edge of Mamassani and Boir Ahmad pastures in order to prevent others from exploiting his death by seizing his land. Ayaz Khan's death also made the paramount khans realize that their internal disputes were preventing them from attending to wider political issues.

Leftist sentiments had been present among the Qashqa'i for some decades, but Iran's revolutionary process, which enabled a partial resumption of khan rule, brought forth incipient leftist movements calling for its eradication. Leftists in Iran, Qashqa'i and others, declared that the khans supported the old bourgeois landowning and religious classes. They offered as evidence the khans' (initial) support of Khomeini, the new government's frequent use of them as surrogate state officials, and the fact that the Ayatollah Mahallati, one of Shiraz's two major leaders, had mediated in favor of some secondary khans in a land dispute with non-Qashqa'i agriculturalists. Qashqa'i leftists were affiliated primarily with the Revolutionary Organization of Iranian Communists (Sazman-e Engelab-e Komunistha-ye Iran, a faction of the Tudeh or communist party) and with two of the three major parties of the left—the Tudeh (orthodox, pro-Soviet communist party of Iran) and the Fedayi Khalq (var. Feda'iyan-e Khalq; People's Fighters, another offshoot of the Tudeh party and a secular Marxist group that had connections with the Palestine Liberation Organization and Libya). (The third major party of the left—the Mojahedin-e Khalq, Islamic Freedom Fighters—had no representatives among the Qashqa'i.) Qashqa'i leftists were primarily young men and women of both elite and nonelite background. As was also the case among other Iranian leftists, Qashqa'i leftists stemmed primarily from the ranks of the young intelligentsia; many were professionals, including teachers and supervisors in the tribal education program. Nearly all were educated at least through high school, many had urban jobs, and some had army training. A few were army officers who were radicalized during service under the shah in Dhofar (in Oman) and Kurdistan, and several others had been fugitives during the Pahlavi regime. Several of these, along with a few others, were trained in Lebanon by a pro-Syrian faction of the PLO, several fought with Mostoufa Barzani in Kurdistan, and at least one reportedly fought with Dhofar insurgents. None were nomadic pastoralists or agriculturalists.

Although Qashqa'i leftists maintained affiliations and contacts with Iranian and international leftist movements, no non-Qashqa'i leftists—Iranian or foreign—operated in Qashqa'i territory in 1979. By contrast, nonindigenous leftists attempted to recruit members and organize activities among Iran's other major tribal national minorities (Abrahamian 1980:14; Chubin 1980:8, 13, 19). Some Qashqa'i leftists were organized in small, well-armed groups. They spoke in general terms about class struggle, about ridding the area of "khans and feudal lords," and about allowing "the people" to rule the tribe, and they attempted to gather support from the tribal masses. Inspired by leftist rhetoric, some retainers of the Darrehshuri khans fled from their jobs and sought salaried employment from the leftists present in their area. Unsuccessful, they returned shortly thereafter to the khans' service. One leftist group identifying itself as Mount Dina Union circulated xeroxed anti-khan statements.[20] Another group seized several villages and divided the property among the locale's landless. The groups were not unified, and their members were extremely cautious about discussing their affiliations; most Qashqa'i seemed uninformed about them and lumped them together under the label *communist,* a blanket term also used elsewhere in Iran for leftists and even secular non-Marxist parties (Hooglund 1982b:33). Coming as they did from the ranks of the more privileged Qashqa'i, the leftists' attempted identification with "the working class" did not impress many nonelite Qashqa'i, and the suspicion that international powers were at work among the leftists contributed to the Qashqa'i people's lack of support. In addition, these leftists, who utilized the framework of a united Iran, were not overtly supportive of minority rights, despite their groups' doctrinal commitments to such rights.

Some Qashqa'i khans stated that leftists were a greater danger to the Qashqa'i people than the increasingly theocratic state and urged action against them before support for them grew. They feared the leftist presence would provoke a government attack as it had in other minority areas, and they perceived it as a challenge to traditional leadership and to the class interests of khans and other wealthy Qashqa'i. Because the paramount khans owned no land in Fars—it having been totally confiscated by the state in the 1950s and 1960s—leftists presented no immediate economic threat, but these khans hoped to regain some of their lost land and expected to continue as leaders with rights to allocate resources. For other wealthy Qashqa'i, including khans of the Qashqa'i tribes, leftists were immediately threatening.

Within six months of Khomeini's arrival in Iran, government officials produced and distributed wall posters depicting him as the benevolent patriarch of the nation's tribes, represented by men and women in a diversity of tribal dress (including the Qashqa'i). And two of the first postage stamps issued by the Islamic Republic pictured men and women in Kurdish national dress. Other attempts to gain or restore loyalty were also evident. Khomeini offered support for tribal groups,

20. Ettehadiyeh-ye Dina. Mount Dina is the highest mountain in Qashqa'i territory and dominates many summer pastures.

along with condemnation of Kurdish dissidents, in his speeches. But on 5 September 1979, in a televised speech in which he welcomed a delegation of Turkmen tribesmen who had walked from northeast Iran to Qom to present demands, he stated that all groups in Iran—and he named specific tribes, including the Qashqa'i—had suffered under the shah and that none could expect immediate solutions to problems. About this same time, a large delegation of Shahsevan tribesmen, after paying their respects to Khomeini and the Ayatollah Shari'atmadari, demanded dissolution of the forest ranger force, a purging of the gendarmerie of corrupt officials, rights to cultivate and otherwise exploit their lands, development of water resources, nonexploitative loans and credit, veterinary care, establishment of dairy and livestock industries, educational opportunities, health care, and better roads (Taimaz 1979:27–39). Except for some Kurds who were allocated money for public works, these and other tribal groups formally requesting state assistance in such matters as land reclamation, roads, wells, schools, clinics, and cooperatives received no response, and their resentment deepened.

Representatives of some tribal, ethnic, and opposition groups proposed for Iran a federal political system with autonomous ethnic and provincial regions. The Khomeini regime strongly rejected this notion, and the newly adopted constitution made no provision for regional autonomy. No ethnic groups demanded total independence or secession from the Iranian state; most wished to contribute to and benefit from Iranian citizenship, including expected access to oil income. The Kurds, who were the most organized in this regard, formulated the slogan "the self-determination of Kurdistan and democracy for Iran" at a conference in Sanandaj in the summer of 1979. Demands they wanted legislated in the constitution included Kurdish officials for the autonomous region, local police forces under local control, restrictions on the placement and activity of state army forces, constitutional safeguards for the customs and traditions of all national minorities, recognition of Kurdish as an official language on a par with Persian, teaching in the Kurdish language at all levels, a Kurdish university, economic development, improved facilities such as medical services, and freedom of the press.[21] Demands issued by some Baluch in the new Islamic Unity party included regional autonomy, appointment of Baluch to positions in the provincial administration, teaching in Baluchi, and the

21. *Ayandegan*, 20 June 1979; *Kayhan*, 7 July 1979 and 18 April 1980.

right of free contact with Pakistani Baluchistan (Woollacott 1979:8). Linkages among Iran's national minorities, which could have facilitated common efforts, were weak, and the Kurds and Baluch were the only tribal people to possess formal political parties. Khomeini outlawed the Kurdish Democratic party in the summer of 1979; the Marxist-Leninist Komala and Fedayi Khalq continued to function in Kurdistan.

As long as the shah was in power, the paramount Qashqa'i khans were willing to offer verbal support to Khomeini, but the new government's military attacks on the Kurds in the summer of 1979, combined with Khomeini's call for holy war (jihad) against them, abruptly altered their stance. Although these khans had earlier demonstrated little interest in speaking with visiting Kurdish leaders, they were now outraged by the government's military aggression and recognized that it could be directed toward them as well. They were distressed that the Islamic Republic was perpetuating the Persian chauvinism of the Pahlavi era, so destructive to them in the past, and expressed concern that Khomeini demonstrated no interest in Iran's diverse minorities. Noting that he usually spoke of Muslims rather than Iranians, they remarked that it was ironic that the Qashqa'i—a minority that had been accused in the past of lacking patriotism—were stronger Iranian nationalists than was Khomeini. In fact, the turn to Islam in Iran can be viewed as a rejection of nationalism in the historical sense (Tabari 1982:113). Some Qashqa'i, noting the non-Iranian nature of the Islamic Republic, spoke jokingly of the new regime as the "second Arab invasion" (the first Arab invasion being the initial sweep of Islam into Iran many centuries ago).

The paramount khans astutely articulated their feelings about the relationship with Khomeini. The problem, as they saw it, was one of the degree of support to be offered and the extent of identification with Khomeini, the Islamic Republic, and even Islam. While these khans were not devoutly religious and did not use religious functionaries in their leadership, they had found occasion in the past to ally with Muslim clergy. By mid-1979 they saw that support for the increasingly repressive theocratic state was rapidly eroding in some segments of Iranian society, including those with which they shared some interests, such as other non-Persians, the secular elite, and Western-oriented and formally educated professionals. Those who had thought that diverse forms of political activity could survive in the provinces, now that the heavy-handed rule of the shah was gone, viewed with dismay the trends toward recentralization of government in Tehran and Qom on increasingly narrow ideological lines. Fars was becoming increasingly peripheral to the center of revolutionary activity and to the consolidation of state power and authority. The paramount khans noted that, in Qashqa'i history, whenever state authority had been threatened, their ancestors had always backed what eventually turned out to be the side that lost and were punished for years later as a result (a generalization not always true, as previous chapters demonstrate). They planned not to make this mistake again. In the case of Khomeini, however, they could not estimate how long he would remain in power, and therefore did not know how much they should be identified as his supporter. Khomeini's military attacks on Kurdistan seemed to indicate his true colors, and they withdrew from direct expressions of support. Malek Mansur Khan pessimistically remarked, "the Qashqa'i don't take sides; sides take the Qashqa'i." In the past, he noted, the Qashqa'i had been swept up in national events and manipulated into positions they had not specifically sought. He believed it was happening again.[22]

The establishment of the Islamic Republic of Iran in 1979 introduced new dimensions to historical patterns of relationships between tribes and the state in Iran. The emerging threat was theocracy and the forced imposition of Shi'i Islamic politics and world view on primarily rural, agricultural and pastoral, non-Persian, and only nominally religious people who doubted that they would receive benefits from being absorbed into the state commensurate with the price extracted from them. Where Sunni Muslims were involved, the state military undertook to suppress incipient protests. For the Shi'i Qashqa'i, the renewal of historical links with the Shi'i clergy had sheltered and temporarily set them apart from the Sunni minorities, but as fundamentalist conservative clergy increased their power in Iran and were able to suppress alternate forms of power, even the Shi'i Qashqa'i were soon to draw their fire.

The lack of organized, coordinated Qashqa'i leadership and the ambiguous political response of the paramount khans during the first year of the Islamic Republic can be explained by a combination of factors. First, unstable national politics, competing parallel governments, and disunified national leadership had prevented Qashqa'i leaders from establishing effective, predictable ties with the center. The processes of state centralization and decentralization in the previous twenty-six

22. Malek Mansur Khan, personal communication, 28 August 1979, Tehran.

years had meant discontinuous relationships among tribal leaders, tribal members, and old and new state authorities. By their own reckoning, the paramount Qashqa'i khans had played limited roles in leadership during this year, and one remarked that "the only thing we have done is that we have not moved against this government."[23] They expressed reluctance about taking any political stance, given their thoughts that the Islamic Republic might be short-lived. Naser Khan stressed his obligation to stand by his words of support to Khomeini, even though he no longer intended to provide such support, and other khans felt that actions on behalf of the Qashqa'i, whatever their intentions, could easily be interpreted by central authorities as threats to the state. The khans seemed not to want to jeopardize even an ambiguous position, which did, after all, give them time to work out their interrelationships and assess contemporary conditions.

Second, Naser Khan and Khosrow Khan had been absent from tribal and national affairs for twenty-five years, during which time Iran had been economically and politically transformed. They no longer allocated land rights or had economic ties with supporters and clients, and the Qashqa'i people had developed various strategies to cope with pacification, state encapsulation, and capitalist expansion. The Qashqa'i had become more diverse economically, and many had become wage laborers and had adapted to urban and village residence. A sizable portion of the young generation was formally educated and some had entered new jobs and professions. New classes that undercut former political interests and allegiances had emerged. One non-Qashqa'i observer of Naser Khan and Khosrow Khan in 1979 noted that "khans as viable figureheads and leaders were somewhat irrelevant" under these new conditions.[24] While many Qashqa'i were eager to make a political, even a military, statement about fifty-five years of repressive Pahlavi rule, not all were eager to return to the political and economic conditions of the past, and those in the higher socioeconomic levels did not want to risk their interests in a confrontation with the state. Those who desired to achieve local self-rule before central authority became reestablished were frustrated by the khans' lack of leadership. The paramount khans were caught between a center that could not be located and a people whom they had not directly led for many years. They complicated the process for themselves and for the people by not defin-

23. Malek Mansur Khan, personal communication, 5 September 1979, Tehran.
24. This person chose to remain anonymous.

ing what, if any, their new leadership functions were to be. Their triumphant return to Qashqa'i territory held an explicit promise of leadership; it created expectations that went unmet.

Third, the circumstances under which the paramount khans had last been effective, powerful leaders (1941–54) included a set of factors no longer present: people dependent on allocated pastures and comprehensive mediatory leadership, a weak and inexperienced shah, a prime minister (Mosaddeq) who supported them, and interfering foreign powers. But it could also be said that the Islamic Republic in its first year presented an equally fruitful set of circumstances for an assertion of leadership.

THE IMPACT OF A CONSOLIDATING ISLAMIC REPUBLIC IN 1980–1982

The uncertainty with which the paramount Qashqa'i khans dealt with the potential of resumed tribal and national leadership in 1979 had some chance of partial resolution in the 1980 national parliamentary elections. The outcome of these elections, however, was to alter irreparably the position of the Qashqa'i khans in Iran.

Members of the Shahilu family believed that parliamentary elections, for which they would prepare a slate of Qashqa'i candidates, would lead to the establishment of formal, effective ties with the new state, ties that had up to this point been lacking. Their ambiguous relationship with the state was a factor behind the dissension among them and their lack of political aggression. Early in 1980 the family gathered to choose candidates and discuss possible districts from which to run. Naser Khan declined to run, and others agreed that his age of seventy-eight was a restricting factor; service in what was expected to be a clergy-controlled parliament would require energy and stamina. Abdollah, another likely candidate, was temporarily out of the country, to the chagrin of family members who supported him. Houman also chose not to run. They considered that running in the district of Firuzabad would guarantee a Qashqa'i victory. Because Khosrow Khan was the best known Qashqa'i likely to win, they selected another district, Eqlid (west of the Shiraz-Isfahan road), for him. Shapur and Manuchehr, sons of Farrokh Bibi, agreed to run in Firuzabad and Lar (southeast of Firuzabad), respectively. All expected Khosrow Khan and Shapur to win, and possibly Manuchehr also. Members of the family had represented these or neighboring districts in parliament in the past and had owned land in these areas. In the nineteenth century their ancestors governed these districts.

In the first round of elections in March, in which ninety-seven candidates received the necessary 50 percent or more of the votes in their districts out of the hundreds who ran nationally, Khosrow Khan won 70 percent of the vote in his district and a seat in the new parliament. He attained a new source of legitimacy in national politics and stated publicly his opposition to the continuing American hostage crisis.[25] Shapur and Manuchehr, neither of whom campaigned much or were well known, gained only 20 to 30 percent of the votes in their districts and lost the chance to run again. In the case of Shapur, who ran against a member of the clergy, voting irregularities occurred and further elections were suspended. (A year later a member of the clergy who was a candidate of the Islamic Republican party was elected as representative of Firuzabad; Shapur chose not to run again.)

Parliament held the right to accept or reject the credentials of candidates before formally allowing them to assume their seats. In May 1980 some members of parliament accused Khosrow Khan of having associated with SAVAK and the shah's minister of court and of having recently cooperated with the United States Embassy and the CIA. In the case built against him, they accepted as testimony statements from the interrogation of Thomas Ahern, an American hostage then being held at the United States Embassy and identified by his captors as a CIA agent. Ahern was said to have named his high-level Iranian contacts as Khosrow Qashqa'i and Abbas Amir Entezam.[26] Copies of documents, including some seized from the embassy, were circulated as evidence. Embassy employees had hastily shredded some documents, but the hostage takers later reconstructed them and, with the help of Ahern, were able to decipher many of those written in code. None of these documents was particularly incriminating for Khosrow Khan; most simply contained his name. Pro-Soviet leftist groups, who accused Khosrow Khan of being a feudal landlord, actively joined the

25. International wire services carried Khosrow Khan's comments: "the hostage issue has become a tool for 'usurping power and power plays' in Iranian politics" (*Salt Lake Tribune*, 16 May 1980).

26. *The New York Times*, 15 July 1980; *Time*, 28 July 1980, p. 43. Entezam was summoned from his post as ambassador to Sweden, arrested on arrival in Iran, and imprisoned.

hostage takers in supporting the campaign to discredit him (Zabih 1982:67).[27]

On 5 June 1980, Revolutionary Guards went to the house in Tehran where Khosrow Khan stayed to report that his presence was requested at a meeting of parliament. He was suspicious; it was Thursday, a day of few official functions, and he knew of no meeting. Having only two bodyguards with him at the time, he felt obliged to accompany the Revolutionary Guards as requested; he took his bodyguards with him and hid a handgun in his jacket as they left. He was also suspicious about the route taken and the speed of driving; when they met another vehicle containing additional Revolutionary Guards he knew he was being kidnapped. He drew his gun and grabbed the driver. Revolutionary Guards seized him, shooting broke out, and they overpowered him and took him off to guard headquarters, where they beat and imprisoned him.

One of Khosrow Khan's bodyguards who escaped during the shooting rushed to inform Molki Bibi and Homa of the capture. Homa telephoned President Bani Sadr to report the news and urge assistance; when Bani Sadr seemed unable to effect the release, she telephoned Khomeini. (Homa had Khomeini's private telephone number from the time her brother, Abdollah, was Khomeini's escort for the Sandinistan.) News of the arrest spread rapidly to other family members, who took evasive action on the assumption they too could be arrested. Recent allegations against Khosrow Khan as a CIA contact had created a negative political climate for the whole family. Houman collected a reluctant Naser Khan, who had long-standing plans to fly to the United States the following day, and drove him to safety in the Semirom area of summer pastures. News of Khosrow Khan's arrest preceded them, and Naser Khan and Houman were quickly able to assemble armed Qashqa'i to block all roads leading to Semirom and summer pastures in order to prevent government forces from entering. Revolutionary Guards attacked Abdollah, who had taken the same action in and around Firuzabad and Shiraz. Government sources angrily proclaimed Abdollah personally responsible for the guards who were killed. Guard commanders and other officials were apparently surprised

27. Dr. Habibollah Peiman, a dentist who had written an account of the Qashqa'i people (1968) at a time when he was highly politicized in his opposition to the shah, was apparently the mastermind of the successful attack on the United States Embassy (Zabih 1982:42–61).

by these military moves; they perceived them as a "tribal uprising" in support of Khosrow Khan. Under pressure from Khomeini and Bani Sadr and possibly for other reasons, they released Khosrow Khan after only twenty-four hours. Guards drove him to the Tehran airport for a flight to Shiraz but changed their minds and returned him to prison in Tehran, at which point he bribed a prison guard and escaped. In the meantime, armed Qashqa'i had protected the road leading into Shiraz from Isfahan and had surrounded the Shiraz airport to prevent Khosrow Khan from being seized on his arrival in Fars, but he had traveled south through the mountains on secondary roads. Armed Qashqa'i from all parts of the territory descended on Firuzabad. Simultaneously, guards sought and arrested those Qashqa'i who they suspected would pose military threats, and they rushed to Mehr-e gerd, the Darrehshuri khans' summer settlement, to confiscate all vehicles.

Khosrow Khan's arrest was described in Iran and abroad as a gun battle in the streets of Tehran between Revolutionary Guards and Qashqa'i forces in which many were killed and wounded. Government officials and the government-controlled press denigrated Khosrow Khan and the Qashqa'i people and labeled them as counterrevolutionaries. Foreign news services picked up parts of the story from government sources and media reports, and in typical fashion contributed their own dramatic highlights.[28] Many assumed that if the Qashqa'i tribe "rose," other tribes would follow. In this political climate, many Qashqa'i, especially family members of both levels of khans, were harassed. Revolutionary Guards sought khans of the component tribes, action inspiring some of those who had not already gone to Firuzabad to go. Some khans were arrested while others turned themselves in to authorities to avoid arrest.

Qashqa'i forces—including all paramount khans, some of their family members (including some women), many other khans, and many other Qashqa'i—and some Boir Ahmad and Basseri khans and tribespeople convened in a defensible area near Firuzabad and established an armed camp. This gathering repeated the one commemorating Naser Khan's return to Iran in January 1979; the earlier camp could be considered a dress rehearsal. Some Qashqa'i who had remained uncommitted when the paramount khans returned from exile now offered their

28. The *London Observer* (20 July 1980) reported: "When the tribal leader Khosrow Qashquaie was arrested, Bani-Sadr leapt in to get him released. If the Qashquaie tribe rose, others might follow. That would spell disaster."

support. Differences among the Shahilu were for the moment suspended, as were differences among others in the camp. For two years the group successfully held off attacks by Revolutionary Guards.

The establishment of the insurgency marked changes both in the relationship between the paramount khans and the state and in the image of these khans. The government viewed the group as an insurgent force threatening the revolution and the Islamic Republic and urged its defeat and elimination and the arrest of its members. Since the revolution, the paramount khans had been viewed by some Qashqa'i, and many non-Qashqa'i, as individuals pursuing local and private interests; many now saw them as men committed to opposing and defeating the Khomeini regime. As on some previous historical occasions, their identity as leaders operating on a national level superseded their identity as specifically tribal leaders.

On 13 July 1980, parliament met to consider the assembled case against Khosrow Khan. Deputies had earlier summoned him to testify at a hearing that he had been a SAVAK agent; he had refused to attend. By a vote of 189 to three, parliament members rejected his credentials and officially expelled him.[29] Admiral Ahmad Madani, elected representative from Kerman, who was also accused of having had SAVAK connections and who refused to testify, defended Khosrow Khan against the charges made by stating that Qashqa'i leaders and tribespeople had fought the Pahlavi regimes for fifty-seven years and that men who had served their country all their lives should not be mistreated.[30]

The same month, shortly after the establishment of the insurgent camp in the south, forces in opposition to the Khomeini regime were accused of planning a military coup. Bakhtiyari khans living in Tehran were among those suspected; the government executed several, and Revolutionary Guards and other mobs ransacked their homes. *The Times* of London reported (incorrectly on many counts), "a dozen homes in Tehran belonging to prominent Qashqai families have been ransacked despite the danger of a full rebellion by 10,000 Qashqai tribesmen in central Iran."[31]

Also in July, Rudabeh Khanom, wife of Naser Khan, fell victim to diphtheria and died. Government authorities in Firuzabad, where she

29. *Iran Times*, 25 July 1980.
30. Ibid.
31. *The Times* (London), 25 July 1980.

resided, had not permitted her to be hospitalized or seen by a doctor. Her son, Abdollah, trapped in the insurgent camp, was unable to provide medical assistance.

The insurgents maintained a camp for two years, from June 1980 to July 1982. They remained in Hengam (south of Firuzabad) and Farrashband for more than a year and then moved to the Sorkhi-Kuhmarreh region to the southwest of Shiraz (between the Shiraz-Kazerun and Shiraz-Firuzabad roads), which offered better protection from attacks.[32] Winter pastures, covering an area twice as large as summer pastures, are better protected, have few major roads, and offer unimpeded access to the gulf and its arms traffic, while summer pastures are surrounded by Persian settlements, major roads, and state military facilities. Winter pastures also offer better ground cover than summer pastures, which are located in wide open valleys. The insurgents gradually moved to higher altitudes and denser ground cover during these two years. As government attacks increased in the spring of 1982, the Sorkhi camp proved to be too vulnerable, and the insurgents dispersed in small groups in the mountains. They were no longer able to use tents or large vehicles, which are easily spotted. In the early summer of 1982 the insurgents were high in the hills and sought protection in caves.

Core members of the insurgent force included Khosrow Khan, Naser Khan, and Abdollah, all of whom were restricted in their movements because of government warrants for their arrest. Other core members were more mobile and could travel, albeit with care and in secrecy, to Shiraz and Tehran. These included Malek Mansur Khan, Houman, Homa, Shapur, Manuchehr, and Kaveh. Other family members visited periodically. The number of insurgents, ranging from two to six hundred, varied according to wider political circumstances. Beyond members of the Shahilu family, they included members of the khan families of the component Qashqa'i tribes (particularly Kashkuli Bozorg, Darrehshuri, Kashkuli Kuchek, and Farsi Madan), some headmen, members of Qashqa'i subtribes, and some Boir Ahmad and Basseri. Included also were a few Qashqa'i who had been part of leftist groups (now disintegrated) in Qashqa'i territory in 1979. Many other Qashqa'i and others visited the camp for short periods but did not offer longterm or reliable support. In the summer of 1981 many new supporters joined the insurgents, an influx connected with the success of Moja-

32. Isma'il Khan's brother, Ali Khan, had taken refuge for twenty years in this same location.

hedin forces in challenging the regime by killing and attacking prominent clergy. Some who thought the regime was weakening took this occasion to ally with the Qashqa'i insurgents, but several months later most had left, and by the summer of 1982 the insurgent group was small.

Those who joined the khans in their insurgency were variously motivated. As were many Iranians, they were inspired by the recent revolution and the potential for action and change inherent in it. For many who had expected to join the paramount khans in resurgent Qashqa'i politics in 1979, the resistance belatedly offered them the opportunity. The insurgency began at a point when many other Iranians had already been forced out of revolutionary activity. By now the repressive nature of the new Islamic regime was apparent, and many joined the Qashqa'i group out of opposition to rule by clergy. Given the past military successes of the Qashqa'i and their military prowess, they expected that they could defeat Khomeini's forces; they entered the fight expecting to win. The insurgents were also motivated by historical events and by memories of the oppressions of the Pahlavi shahs. The insurgency offered them a chance to avenge family members who had died or suffered under the shahs, to restore what they perceived were the ideal conditions of the past, and to regain power in Fars. Many thought that by supporting the khans in their resistance they could reestablish the political and economic conditions of earlier periods; they nostalgically evoked the 1940s as a model of the conditions they sought to achieve. During the past decades, pressures to assimilate into a modernizing Persian society had been intense, and many Qashqa'i had been regarded with prejudice because of their Turkic, tribal, nomadic heritage. The insurgency offered them an opportunity to restore their self-esteem and their place in society. Finally, the insurgents held great respect for and were inspired by the paramount khans and their families who abandoned comfortable lives in the West and Tehran for an uncertain future among fellow Qashqa'i in Fars.

Revolutionary Guards periodically attacked the insurgent camp during these two years and attempted to police roads in the vicinity to prevent reinforcements from reaching it. Their commander, a Bolvardi Qashqa'i, sought leadership of the Qashqa'i for himself through the defeat of the insurgents.[33] Although the government assigned gen-

---

33. His father was a Qashqa'i nomadic pastoralist and his mother a Shiraz-based Bolvardi Qashqa'i.

darme and army forces to the vicinity, they did not play a direct role in these attacks and suffered only one casualty in the two years of fighting; a gendarme officer accidentally ran into the line of fire, was shot (by which side is unknown), and died before he could be given medical attention. In a major attack on the camp in 1980, the Qashqa'i force took seventy Revolutionary Guards as hostages and then used gendarmes as mediators to negotiate their release. Since their origin in 1979, Revolutionary Guards had differed in aim and motivation from gendarmes and army forces, and the tension inherent between the new overzealous force and the established but demoralized ones was also apparent in Fars during the Qashqa'i struggle. Some army officers even suggested to Khosrow Khan that Qashqa'i forces take over army posts in the region in order to compete more effectively against the guards.

The major battles between Revolutionary Guards and the Qashqa'i force occurred in the summer and fall of 1980, the spring of 1981 (at Farrashband), and the spring (at Jahrom) and summer of 1982, with up to six hundred guards participating in the largest ones. In the most recent of these battles, guards used helicopters to carry forces into the mountains where Qashqa'i fighters had taken cover. When guards attacked the Qashqa'i group, other Qashqa'i in the wider area, unconnected with the camp, joined in the defense by coming from behind, threatening the guards with entrapment and forcing their retreat. Guards also attacked Qashqa'i groups elsewhere. In 1981 they seized the settlement of the Kashkuli Bozorg khans in summer pastures and prevented them from entering the area, and they attacked a Farsi Madan force at Padena in the center of summer pastures.

Iraq's invasion of Iran in September 1980 temporarily deflected the attention of Revolutionary Guards and other government forces away from the Qashqa'i. The attacks resuming again in the spring and early summer of 1982 coincided with renewed efforts to repel and defeat Iraq. The increasing strength of the guards also corresponded with the political consolidation of fundamentalist clerical rule in Iran, the increased pressure on the opposition, and the elimination of moderates (such as Bani Sadr, friend of the paramount khans) from government. By early 1982 the government had formed a special staff to plan operations against the Qashqa'i insurgency, including an attempted economic embargo on the region, and increased efforts to gather intelligence data.

By 1982 the Qashqa'i insurgents were the only localized, armed opposition to the regime left in Iran outside of Kurdistan, which partly explains the state's intense efforts to capture the force. Certainly the threat this group posed was unequal to the military might brought against it. From the time of the group's formation, government officials saw it as a plot against the regime and the revolution still underway; they considered the insurgents counterrevolutionaries. In September 1980 a news account entitled, "Smell of Tribal Revolt Fills Air in Fars," typified official sentiment in Iran by noting that "the government was anticipating a movement by the tribesmen to take control of something more than the few hilltops they occupy now."[34] The Governor of Fars worried about a "second front" among tribesmen in Fars while simultaneously noting the "great contribution of the tribesmen to the revolution."[35] Opposition forces in exile, in Europe and elsewhere, as well as foreign nations hoping to weaken the Khomeini regime, also saw the Qashqa'i force in an exaggerated light and sought to enlist its support in their own struggles, without any apparent success. For the insurgents, however, the attention they drew from government military forces, opposition groups in exile, and foreign states indicated their importance and provided some incentive to continue the resistance.

Total Revolutionary Guard casualties approximated two hundred killed and over two hundred wounded in this two-year period. Khomeini and other clergy incited others to avenge them and to sustain the hostilities, a strategy also utilized in the Iraq-Iran hostilities. In both cases a vicious cycle of attacks and killings resulted. Qashqa'i casualties, numbering approximately fourteen, included Gholam Hosain (Amaleh), Shapur Khan Kashkuli, Shapur's son Mehrdad, and Ibrahim Khan Namadi's son. The fervor with which guards entered battle astonished the Qashqa'i. In one early battle, when Qashqa'i fighters heard the guards shout, "Allahu akbar" (God is great), they assumed they had recognized defeat; however, the guards attacked even more vigorously and took risks, which partly explains the number of fatalities. At no previous time in history have Qashqa'i forces met such an inspired, motivated opposition force. In previous battles, they had always fought against relatively uninspired troops who were forced or hired to fight the battles of other powers. Guards, however, identified closely with the cause for which they were fighting, sought to avenge their comrades' deaths, and expected to enter heaven immediately if they died as battleground martyrs. In their eyes, these Qashqa'i were enemies of God, Islam, Khomeini, and the Islamic Republic. Also,

34. *Iran Times,* 5 September 1980.
35. Ibid.

never before in history had Qashqa'i forces been in a similarly long-
term defensive position. They found themselves trapped by a force they
could not defeat.

Members of the insurgency were responsible for their own military
provisions and secured weapons and ammunition privately. All kinds
of weapons were available on the regional market, supplied primarily
by smugglers from the gulf. Prices, already steep, steadily increased
during these two years. The insurgents had little opportunity to capture weapons; the promise of such bounty had been a major goal of
Qashqa'i fighters in past history. In the fall of 1980 rumors circulated
in Washington and London that Israel was supplying the Qashqa'i directly with arms, including anti-helicopter weapons, by agreement
with the CIA, which sought to avoid direct involvement. Shipments
were said to have lasted a month, when Iraq's invasion overtook events
in the area. Members of the insurgency say they received no such arms
and deny that they secured arms or money from any outside power.
They, too, had heard these rumors and suggested that the CIA had
planted them intentionally, along with other rumors unconnected with
the Qashqa'i, in order to increase hostilities in Iran, weaken the Khomeini regime, and eventually bring about the release of the American
hostages.

Each camp was located near Qashqa'i who offered some support. The
Hengam camp was near the Kashkuli Kuchek, the Sorkhi camp near
Farsi Madan khans and Sorkhi headmen. Each camp was, however, an
isolated, independent body, which contrasted markedly with earlier ilkhani camps. Camp members were responsible for their own tents,
bedding, food, and water. Procurement of supplies was difficult, given
travel restrictions on some members, constant danger of ambush and
attack, and the camp's physical isolation. Those who regularly visited
the camp brought supplies, and occasional visitors brought food. But
the frequency with which people had given gifts to the ilkhani in the
past did not recur. Camp members purchased sheep (for meat) and pastoral products from nearby Qashqa'i pastoralists. The circumstances in
which the paramount khans found themselves, in financial difficulty
and sometimes without adequate food, were in marked contrast with
all earlier periods of Qashqa'i history. That fellow Qashqa'i did not
supply them with necessities was a major disappointment and indicated to them how small and isolated their resistance movement was.

Camp members slept in canvas tents and erected kitchen, bath, and
latrine tents. No goat-hair tents were used. A man who had previously
served Khosrow Khan as a cook left his family and work to join the

insurgents. He cooked communal noon meals consisting of rice and stew, and others assisted. Other meals were arranged privately. No retainers or workers were present, another sharp difference from earlier ilkhani camps, and individuals tended to their own personal needs. Khosrow Khan bought several Mercedes-Benz trucks to move the camp and carry supplies. Groups of supporters took turns guarding the camp and nearby roads, including night watch, and used motorcycles to report quickly on approaching forces; a Darrehshuri group took night watch one night, the Boir Ahmadis the next, and so forth.

Several incidents in the camp demonstrate the group's hostility toward the attackers and their supporting regime. After the battle in which the insurgents took seventy Revolutionary Guards hostage, several in the camp wanted to kill them, but Khosrow Khan suggested instead that they simply shave off half the beards of each and send them away. Beards identified guards and other devout supporters of the Islamic Republic, and this act was meant to humiliate them. And one day when a camp member, cousin of Naser Khan and someone who had made the pilgrimage to Mecca years before, began to say his prayers, Naser Khan snapped at him, "We don't do prayers here."

Prior problems within the Shahilu family were subordinated to the issue of survival and the need for sustained, careful action. Changed circumstances helped to restructure power relationships, yet different groups within the family continued to compete—although at a less sustained level due to the precarious situation—for recognition as the major wielder of power and authority and representation of the Qashqa'i vis-à-vis external powers. Naser Khan continued as figurehead of the family and the Qashqa'i as a whole but did not play an active political or military role, primarily because of his age and health. Khosrow Khan, although having an excellent reputation as a leader and military commander from the struggle against the shah in 1953, had not cooperated well with most other family members upon his return to Iran in 1979. Under the trying conditions of his arrest and expulsion from parliament and in the organized resistance thereafter, however, he performed admirably. The tension between Naser Khan and Khosrow Khan and their respective supporters in 1979 had been partly resolved. From May 1980 most members of the family, the Qashqa'i in general, and outsiders considered Khosrow Khan the major Qashqa'i leader. Some family members who had strongly criticized his behavior in 1979 became part of his staunchest supporters in 1980 and thereafter. Malek Mansur Khan joined the insurgent group some forty days after its formation and remained with it throughout the two years. He played a low-key political role, as had been the case in 1979, and took military action only when the camp was attacked directly. Mohammad Hosain Khan, in London during this period, was involved, as before, in issues connected with general Iranian politics and various opposition forces in exile. He was the European connection, which became increasingly important when Bani Sadr and Massoud Rajavi, leader of the Mojahedin, went into exile.

Members of the younger generation played similarly diverse roles and competed for power and authority. Abdollah, as Naser Khan's son, was in a structural position to succeed him but did not easily gain support from others. He had lived outside Iran longer than other family members who had returned, and some were unfamiliar with him. As a physician, he was indispensable; he treated the wounded and sick and saved many lives. As the government's prime fugitive because of his role in the deaths of Revolutionary Guards at the time of Khosrow Khan's seizure, he was greatly restricted in movement. Houman, Mohammad Hosain Khan's son, was active in political and military affairs in the camp and outside. Being mobile, he was able to disseminate information among the camp, Shiraz, and Tehran. In December 1981 he escaped from Iran on horseback, via Kurdistan, in order to seek political and possible military assistance from opposition groups in exile. He established contacts throughout Europe with a wide range of groups and political figures. Homa, daughter of Naser Khan, served in many ways on his behalf and on behalf of her cousins Manuchehr and Shapur but was also politically active in her own right. She divided her time between Shiraz and the camp and was present when fighting occurred. Guards kidnapped her at one point but she escaped. She was medically trained and assisted her brother Abdollah in his work. She performed in a way expected of a child of the ilkhani; her problem was largely one of being the wrong sex. Some objected to her as one whose political activities competed with theirs, but they often phrased their sentiments in terms relating to gender.

A turning point in the Qashqa'i insurgency was a major battle near Firuzabad in April 1982. In the dead of the night hundreds of Revolutionary Guards who had been transported by helicopters and tanks surrounded the sleeping insurgent camp. An ayatollah accompanying them shouted to Abdollah to disarm and surrender; in response Abdollah shot him dead. Shooting broke out on all sides and possibly hundreds of guards were killed (government sources claim thirty). The guards could no longer fight due to these heavy losses, and the Qashqa'i force, including Gholam Hosain who had been badly wounded, took cover at higher altitudes. All equipment, including medical supplies, had been abandoned at the camp, and Abdollah was distressed about his inability to render proper medical assistance. When Gholam Hosain died, Abdollah pledged to fight to the "last drop of blood." Some Qashqa'i in the vicinity brought food to the exhausted fighters. Abdollah, who was the first to eat (an orange), complained of internal pains and died. Some suspected that the food had been poisoned (the orange by a lethal injection), while others speculated that he had suffered a heart attack. Naser Khan appointed two people to bury his son secretly so that guards and government authorities would not discover his death. They left the grave unmarked and kept its location secret even from other members of the camp. (When rumors spread during the next few weeks about Abdollah's death, family members in Europe hoped that these were diversionary tactics to allow Abdollah to escape from Iran and expected to see him appear in Paris or London. Hearing of his death, Iranian authorities, especially at borders, would not be looking for him. The death was finally confirmed in May.) The loss of Abdollah was devastating to Naser Khan. Family members convinced him to attempt an escape from Iran; he successfully exited through Kurdistan, assisted by leaders of the Kurdish Jaf tribe. Others in the camp, although despairing at the loss and viewing the severity of the guard attack as boding ill for the future, still held on in their mountain stronghold.

In July, Khosrow Khan decided to negotiate a settlement with the government and sought the assistance of a Bolvardi Qashqa'i who was a bank vice-president based in Shiraz and a nephew of Isma'il Khan's chief secretary. The mediator went on Khosrow Khan's behalf to the Governor of Fars and to Shiraz's leading ayatollah to talk terms. The government agreed to offer a general amnesty if the Qashqa'i force disarmed and surrendered. Neither Khosrow Khan nor the mediator trusted the government but suggested that the plan be tested. Malek Mansur Khan volunteered to turn himself in to authorities; the government accepted his surrender and granted amnesty. Khosrow Khan then negotiated pardons for all camp members; he stayed behind in the camp with ten others so the rest could be processed. The next day, after he sought refuge in a supposedly "safe" house in Shiraz, government forces who had been tipped off about his location seized and arrested him, along with five others. He had been betrayed by an acquaintance and former member of the insurgency who was said to have been paid well by the authorities for his information.[36] Khosrow Khan was jailed and then secretly moved to Tehran. In mid-September an Islamic Revolutionary Court in Shiraz condemned him to death on charges that he fomented trouble in Fars province, was responsible for the death of a high-ranking clergyman and many guards, and was a CIA agent. Others from the camp, by now in Shiraz and other towns, went underground, were arrested, or were kept under surveillance and ordered to report to the police daily. Authorities especially sought those who still influenced tribal politics. The major figure evading arrest and the government's prime fugitive was Homa, who hid in the mountains. Authorities attempted to bribe those close to her into divulging her whereabouts. She eventually escaped from Iran through Baluchistan. Khosrow Khan's sister, Molki Bibi, and the Bolvardi mediator flew to Mashhad in northeast Iran to seek assistance from the Ayatollah Shirazi (Mashhad's leading ayatollah) in securing Khosrow Khan's release. He agreed to help and wrote to Khomeini asking him to free the Qashqa'i on the grounds that he had been in exile for twenty-five years and had never opposed Khomeini directly. Guards arrested the mediator in Tehran and kept Molki Bibi under surveillance.

The Islamic Revolutionary Court that condemned Khosrow Khan to death wanted to execute him by firing squad in a public demonstration in Firuzabad, but apparently decided that the risk of revolt in this predominantly Qashqa'i area was too high. On 8 October 1982, they hung him publicly in a major square in Shiraz. No Qashqa'i attended the hanging. Religious leaders in Shiraz arranged for (some say paid) Persian men to wear Qashqa'i hats and peasant clothes at the hanging in order to prove to the nation that the Qashqa'i people had opposed the khans and their insurgency. Malek Mansur Khan went afterward to claim the body for burial. Revolutionary Guards refused him access and arrested him instead. They held him in prison for many months despite the amnesty he had been granted, and threatened to and eventually did exile him to Qom, where he was subjected to a rigorous religious indoctrination. Authorities also arrested and imprisoned other members of the family, including Malek Mansur Khan's daughter Nazli, Molki Bibi, her son Kaveh, Naser Bayat (husband of Molki Bibi and son of

---

36. This person, of a Boir Ahmad father and a Kashkuli mother, had been a SAVAK agent under the shah. Claiming to be pro-Qashqa'i, he had joined Khosrow Khan in the insurgency.

Mosaddeq's sister), and Manuchehr. Others were subjected to internal exile, usually to religious towns. Five other members of the insurgency who had been captured along with Khosrow Khan were also executed; they included Jehanpulod Kashkuli (a cousin of Khosrow Khan's mother), Jafar Kashkuli, and a Persian army officer who had joined the insurgency.[37]

The government, concerned about the incidents of "unrest" in Qashqa'i territory and the Kuhgiluyeh-Boir Ahmad region in the month following Khosrow Khan's execution, attempted to prove its charges against him and justify the execution. Officials aired on television Khosrow's "confession" taped a month before his death. In the forced statement extracted after he had been tortured, Khosrow "admitted" that he had received money from the United States to collect information against the Khomeini regime, had plotted with Bani Sadr and Madani against Khomeini, and had received money from SAVAK under the shah.[38]

Family members and friends held a memorial service for Khosrow Khan in New York City at the residence of his niece. They intentionally avoided any religious elements in the service. Members and supporters of the National Front, with which Khosrow Khan and his brothers had been affiliated in the 1950s, suggested simultaneous memorials elsewhere in the United States and in Europe, but Naser Khan stated that this would jeopardize National Front members still in Iran.

The degree of support for the insurgents from the Qashqa'i people is difficult to assess. Qashqa'i came from all parts of tribal territory and the region as a whole, every major sociopolitical group, and every level of the sociopolitical hierarchy. But the Qashqa'i people did not rise in support or defense of the insurgents, and the actual number of supporters, compared with the total population size, was very small. Many specific individuals expected as supporters did not appear, while many who joined them had not been expected, and their presence is still somewhat of a puzzle to the core members. The general lack of support can be explained in four ways.

---

37. As of October 1985, one member of the Shahilu family was still imprisoned. Murad, son of Farrokh Bibi's eldest son, Amirbahador, had been arrested in 1980 at the time of Khosrow Khan's arrest and subsequent escape from Tehran, when Revolutionary Guards searched the houses of members of the Shahilu family. Guards claim to have discovered in Murad's house literature published by the Mojahedin.

38. *Frontier* 1 (34–35), 10 November 1982, p.7.

First, no activity—including military—of the paramount khans in history has ever attracted more than a small percentage of the total Qashqa'i population. Second, the paramount khans returned to Iran and potential leadership roles without a specific plan, on their own admission, and they never proceeded to develop one. "We came back empty-handed," said one. They also lacked a sustaining, articulated ideology beyond the time-worn, nonspecific one associated with the besieged, virtually nonfunctioning National Front, and many Qashqa'i and others were puzzled about what they stood for. The Qashqa'i people, diverse in occupation and socioeconomic status, had lived without paramount leadership for twenty-five years and had developed strategies independent of this overarching institution. In order for them to have accommodated their lives to some form of paramount leadership, they needed to be offered something concrete in material and/or ideological terms. Therefore, with regard to both points, to ask why the Qashqa'i people did not support the khans in their resistance is partly a misguided question, for it assumes that they would or should have. It is probably more essential to ask why certain people did join the resistance, especially given the risks involved.

A third explanation concerns the explicit policy of various branches of state government to alienate the Qashqa'i people from the paramount khans. From June 1980, when it became clear that the resistance was only a small group and not a general response, the government carefully distinguished between "feudal lords and chiefs" and "impoverished Qashqa'i brothers and sisters" in its official pronouncements, including speeches by Khomeini and media reports.[39] The government labeled the paramount khans as exploiters of the Qashqa'i masses and claimed they were agents of the shah and the CIA. Officials implemented this policy by threatening the khans with physical annihilation while ignoring the rest of the Qashqa'i people. They made no effort to prevent or obstruct seasonal migrations, interfere with or change land-use patterns, allocate pastures, prevent travel to cities and towns, or forbid gatherings, to the surprise of many Qashqa'i and non-Qashqa'i. Most crucially, they made no attempt to disarm the Qashqa'i. To counter frequently circulating rumors that the government planned to confiscate Qashqa'i weapons, the state radio periodi-

39. The "impoverished ones" (*musta'zafin*), with whom the clergy and their supporters claimed to be deeply sympathetic, was a category used widely by the Khomeini regime.

cally broadcast reassurances that no action would be taken against the Qashqa'i masses for the crimes of the khans. One khan remarked that the government must have been getting "good" advice on these matters and suggested that Bahmanbegi was possibly involved. Taking action against the Qashqa'i people, especially attempting to remove their weapons, would probably have driven many to support the opposition. By leaving them to pursue their livelihoods without either state or khan interference, under conditions of an expanding market for pastoral products, the government assured that almost all Qashqa'i would keep their distance from the insurgents. It could also be argued, with sufficient evidence, that state forces were incapable of controlling the activities of the Qashqa'i people during this period.

The Qashqa'i people, having rapidly rearmed in late 1978 and 1979, were probably the best armed population in southwest Iran. Armed might, combined with their ongoing organization in sociopolitical groups (subtribes and their sections), enabled many Qashqa'i to reclaim or seize pastoral and agricultural land. As a result, they once again exercised supremacy in land use and military strength in strategic parts of the region over other pastoralists and some other agriculturalists, especially those at some distance from Persian-controlled towns. Both levels of khans had functioned most actively in the past when they had negotiated relationships between the Qashqa'i people and the state and other powers. Between 1980 and 1982 these khans lacked productive ties with the Iranian state and hence could offer no viable strategies in alternative to the ones the Qashqa'i people were currently developing independently. Rural-based Qashqa'i did not support the Islamic Republic or its policies, but neither did they have any immediate reason to organize activities against it. Offering support to the insurgents would have jeopardized the freedom of migration, land use, and arms holding they already enjoyed. Khans had not helped them in these matters and were in no position to improve conditions. Therefore, many Qashqa'i, especially nomadic pastoralists and small-holding agriculturalists, were better off without khans than if they came under their authority. The government intentionally ignored these people in order to reach the paramount khans directly.

And fourth, the lack of Qashqa'i support for the insurgents can also be explained by the high risks and low rewards involved. Many Qashqa'i feared to support those who were already in deep political trouble with the existing regime. By the summer of 1980 the regime no longer appeared to be short-lived; the rapid consolidation of power in the hands of fundamentalist clergy and their supporters boded ill for any local insurgency. Although the means by which the regime maintained power at this point were uncentralized, multifactional, and vulnerable to manipulation by those interested in personal power, its combined might and resolve more than equaled the Qashqa'i force. Potential Qashqa'i supporters, lacking the protection provided by state borders that some other minorities enjoyed, would risk their lives and livelihoods by joining the resistance. Also, war at the side of the ilkhani in the past had meant captured arms and other wealth; current conditions offered no promise of material reward. In addition, while some Qashqa'i were already negatively inclined toward the paramount khans, many others were influenced by attitudes found in the region. Loeffler notes that "quite generally in Boir Ahmad [territory] and in Shiraz, the medley group gathered around Khosrow Khan was considered an agglomeration of outcasts and misfits supporting themselves by opium growing and opium peddling. They were not . . . identified with revolutionary ideals of any sort."[40]

The Amaleh, largest of the Qashqa'i tribes and the body affiliated to the ilkhani in the past, was notably absent from the resistance movement. Few Amaleh tribespeople, including headmen, offered physical or material support to the insurgents. Assistants and retainers, historically supporting the ilkhani's leadership, did not reappear in 1980. Some had offered services to Naser Khan and other khans in early 1979 in the enthusiasm of the return from exile and the shah's ouster, but except for bodyguards these offers had been rebuffed, lessening the likelihood that they would be offered again. Naser Khan and others found it difficult to comprehend their absence. One reason the paramount khans so readily entered into a state of war with the most dedicated military arm of the government in 1980 was their assumption that adequate numbers of armed Qashqa'i, especially from the Amaleh, and other regional forces would join in this encounter and ensure their success. The Amaleh had, however, suffered economically and politically during the previous twenty-five years. Other Qashqa'i sections well organized by tribal khans had taken over much of their land, and they had lacked high-level leaders who could prevent these confiscations and assist them with state services. Although the shah's government had apparently given the Amaleh top-priority consideration in certain kinds of development projects (Kortum 1979b:74), the policies

40. Reinhold Loeffler, personal communication, 8 March 1985.

behind these projects aimed to encourage settlement, lessen tribal attachments, and assimilate its members into Persian/Iranian society. By 1979 many Amaleh had found new livelihoods and affiliations and were more settled and assimilated into the wider society than most other Qashqa'i, which militated against their appearance at the side of the paramount khans in 1980.

Many Qashqa'i khans who had in the past joined the paramount khans to fight government and foreign troops were also notably absent from the resistance. Although some did join, others, equally expected, did not. Khans who had offered the ilkhani military support in the past did so through their own supporters, primarily members of their Amaleh sections. These Amaleh, however, were as reluctant as members of the Amaleh tribe to enter the fight. Khans no longer had many supporters, and it was said that many did not even visit the insurgent camp because they were ashamed to go unaccompanied.

One person who was anxious to join the insurgents was Mohammad Zarghami, leader of the Basseri tribe and a man repeatedly imprisoned under Mohammad Reza Shah. Anxious to be politically active in 1979, he sought to ally himself with Naser Khan, but because he was regarded as militarily reckless, Naser Khan and others tried to avoid much contact with him. Mohammad Zarghami had figured in the outbreak of fighting between Basseri and Shish Boluki over pastures in 1979 at a time when the paramount Qashqa'i khans were playing peace-keeping roles in Fars and avoiding armed conflict. In 1980 or 1981, he was killed in his own battle with Revolutionary Guards.

A number of Boir Ahmad had joined the insurgents, including the son of the late Abdollah Zarghampur, who had allied with Naser Khan in the 1940s. Serafras Nikeqbal, son of Ali Aqa Nikeqbal, the dominant landlord/khan of the Boir Ahmad village of Sisakht, and groomed as his heir, fled from the village and joined the Qashqa'i insurgents when the regime arrested his father for participating in or sympathizing with the aborted coup of the summer of 1980. Serafras was later captured and executed by the regime. According to the government, and apparently the majority of Sisakhtis, the landlord/khans of Boir Ahmad expected that the revolution would restore their power and possessions and were motivated by personal gain, not communal goals. When news of the execution of Serafras reached Sisakht, the people there were unmoved and even expressed satisfaction that he was not allowed to be buried in the village cemetary. In contrast, "when the bodies of executed Mojahedin youths were returned to the village it was a major tragedy. While people in general did not sympathize with Mojahedin ideals, it was nevertheless recognized that the youths had died for ideals rather than for private gains."[41]

Qashqa'i headmen, who had gained and then lost power and authority in the 1960s and 1970s due to rapidly changing government policy, emerged again after the revolution as essential political figures. Government officials regarded them as representatives of the Qashqa'i people and used their office as their point of access. As before, most affairs internal to Qashqa'i society were handled without government knowledge or involvement, while land disputes and other matters between Qashqa'i and non-Qashqa'i were settled by Qashqa'i headmen and sometimes by local officials. Some headmen provided liaison for the insurgents, but they visited the camp informally and offered little more than information. Other headmen, including some who had been closely affiliated with khans and the ilkhani in the past, never went to the camp. With neither khan nor government control of migrations, headmen were the highest authority available to handle these movements, and they acted on behalf of their own groups. Untimely spring migrations meant that some herds grazed new growth, which jeopardized herds that depended on mature growth later in the year. Khans, hearing these reports, felt they could have prevented this problem had they been able to exercise their leadership.

Leftist groups emerging within Qashqa'i society in early 1979 began to disintegrate by the end of the year and were gone by the middle of 1980. One reason for their failure to attract supporters was similar to the paramount khans' own failure; leftists offered little, if anything, concrete to potential supporters. After 1980 leftists either resumed urban occupations or went underground. One small leftist group consisting mostly of Darrehshuri people split up in November 1979 because of internal disputes. In December one member assassinated Ayaz Khan Darrehshuri and evaded capture. Later, Revolutionary Guards sought him for this and other deeds, and in the summer of 1982 he was underground somewhere in Qashqa'i territory and said to be politically inactive. Guards arrested and later released another member of this group, the son of one of the wealthiest Qashqa'i khans, on the guarantee that he remain in Tehran and report to the police daily. No leftist activity among the Qashqa'i was reported in 1982. Those with leftist

41. Ibid. Ali Aqa Nikeqbal was imprisoned in Tehran for three months and repeatedly interrogated but was then released.

sentiments, such as many tribal schoolteachers and other professionals, who were not organized in leftist groups or undertaking leftist activities in 1979, continued to be unorganized in 1980–82. They still opposed khan rule and claimed, along with some other Qashqa'i and many non-Qashqa'i, that the khans were fighting the government in order to regain economic supremacy in the region.

Tribal schools in Qashqa'i territory continued to function into 1982 but at a decreased level of activity, as did most other institutions in Iran. The regime forbade coeducational classes in the teacher-training program and Tribal High School in Shiraz and in tent schools in Qashqa'i territory and imposed restrictive dress codes on female students and teachers. Both restrictions served to decrease significantly female participation in the program. The director of the Office of Tribal Education in Shiraz, a Boir Ahmad Lur who had assumed the post in 1979, raised the standards for tribal teachers by requiring an additional two years of regular school and one more year of normal school. Bahmanbegi stayed in semiseclusion in Tehran and did not return to Fars; he was said to hold no hope of resuming his former post.

Qashqa'i pastoralists enjoyed unimpeded access to regional markets during this period, and many prospered. Meat and dairy prices increased from 300 to 800 percent between 1978 and 1981. Grain prices continued to be subsidized heavily by the state, as under the shah, and agriculturalists did poorly (Loeffler 1982). Both these factors, combined with the renewed military power of Qashqa'i individuals and small sociopolitical groups and the absence of state control over land use, led many Qashqa'i who had settled under the previous regime and begun new livelihoods to resume nomadic pastoralism. Many nomadic and settled Qashqa'i continued to cultivate in order to avoid buying grain at any price. The market in woven goods fluctuated, depending on conditions of export and overseas prices, both of which were affected by sanctions brought against Iran because of the hostage taking and later by state restrictions against the exporting of valuable goods, particularly carpets. Demand for woven goods of the kind typically made by Qashqa'i women greatly decreased in Iranian markets, but these weavers continued to produce goods for household use and local exchange. Weapons were expensive, but practically all Qashqa'i men owned at least one, sometimes spending five thousand dollars for a Soviet-made Kalashnikov; in 1979 many pastoralists sold all their flocks in order to buy a gun.

The spread in the land of a new ethos inspired by fundamentalist conservative interpretations of Shi'i Islam led to the banning of Western and celebratory music and dancing, especially on the part of women. Military marches and patriotic music were permitted. The ban extended to the music and dancing traditional to Qashqa'i weddings. The sounds of drums and reed horns, heard for miles and indicating festivity, reached ever vigilant village mullahs and roaming Revolutionary Guards, who demanded their cessation on threat of punishment. Some Qashqa'i were arrested and imprisoned for performing music at weddings. Feats of gunmanship had been part of Qashqa'i weddings until the 1960s when guns were confiscated, and following the revolution they once again became the main entertainment, demonstrating, as before, the military prowess of Qashqa'i men and standing as an explicit challenge to the armed might of the state.

In 1984 the future of Qashqa'i leaders and tribespeople depended on the Iranian state. Qashqa'i leaders above the level of headman were unable to function effectively in any leadership capacity. The paramount leaders had no chance, and khans of the component tribes were under close government surveillance. Nevertheless, some khans were able to serve former supporters in private capacities, as some had done in the 1960s and 1970s, and most continued to frequent tribal territory in order to tend to their land and private economic pursuits. Qashqa'i settled in cities, towns, and predominantly non-Qashqa'i villages continued to assimilate into these settings, and the attempted resumption of paramount Qashqa'i leadership had little impact on them. They fared under an increasingly theocratic and repressive Islamic Republic as their non-Qashqa'i neighbors and coworkers fared. For pastoral nomadic Qashqa'i, their ability to continue to migrate and utilize traditional pastures depended on the course of the state's centralizing process. State officials, having successfully suppressed the insurgency, viewed with distrust the virtually independent, heavily armed nomads.

Land tenure in and near tribal areas in Fars following the revolution was chaotic and suffered from thousands of conflicting claims. In September 1979 the Revolutionary Council approved a moderate land-reform bill and in April 1980 enacted a more radical measure; but in October 1980 Khomeini prohibited the implementation of some articles of the new bill, for unauthorized land confiscations had spread, uncertainty over ownership was detrimentally affecting agricultural production, and, most importantly, some leading clergy had declared land reform to be in violation of Islamic law. Members of the ruling Islamic Republican party were divided over the issue of land reform; some supported further distributions and had long promised an "Islamic" land reform, while others stressed the inviolate nature of private property. Khomeini submitted the issue of land to the parliament, which approved a conservative measure in December 1982. The Council of Guardians, however, vetoed this measure in January 1983, and the issue of land reform remained unresolved. Government policy in the Iranian countryside continued to be inconsistent; in some areas land was distributed to peasants who articulated their demands, while in others, particularly in areas posing security problems for the state (such as Kurdistan and Baluchistan), the government allied with large landowners to reject the requests of peasants demanding land.[42] The most recent land regulations decreed that control over land was to remain "as is" as long as the land was tended by those who currently owned or controlled it, and the government implemented few changes in Fars, including Qashqa'i territory.[43]

The Reconstruction Crusade (Jihad-e Sazandegi), a loosely organized volunteer corps active throughout Iran in small-scale development projects, operating under the auspices of the Islamic Republican party, and often supportive of peasant demands vis-à-vis the government, was not sent to Qashqa'i areas. Many Qashqa'i, well armed and organized in lineages and subtribes, had seized their former lands and retained control of them. Because many non-Qashqa'i who also claimed or sought this land supported key members of the ruling clergy, moves in favor of their interests were anticipated. Attempts of government officials from 1980 to 1982 to ally with "impoverished Qashqa'i brothers and sisters" had been markedly opportunistic and had not represented true sentiments. Those in control of the state were unsympathetic toward non-Persians, and the fact that the Qashqa'i were not religiously devout provided state authorities with a moral justification for moving against them, as they had moved against Kurds, Bahais, and other minorities.

In early 1983, with the insurgency crushed and Khosrow Khan and others executed, imprisoned, or driven into exile, the regime began to implant Revolutionary Guards among the Qashqa'i people, which until this point had not occurred. It recruited young Qashqa'i men of the poorer and impoverished families by offering them a regular salary,

42. See Bakhash (1984:195–216); Ferdows (1983); Loeffler (1982:61); McLachlan (1980); *Hannoverische Allgemeine*, 6 February 1981.

43. In May 1985 parliament approved a bill giving peasants and squatters rights over land they had seized or were allotted after the 1979 revolution. The bill was partly intended to increase security of tenure and decrease migration to urban areas (*The New York Times*, 21 May 1985).

guns, ammunition, uniforms (identical to those worn by Revolutionary Guards elsewhere in Iran), and the power and authority to serve as the government's representatives in Qashqa'i territory. Their function was to conduct surveillance on the Qashqa'i and control any emerging opposition, and they were to report suspected individuals and groups to the guard center in the nearest town, which would relay information to Shiraz and Tehran and invoke wider authorities. The young men continued to live with their families in the customary ways and migrated with their groups to seasonal pastures. Much conflict was reported between these new authorities and the more established headmen, who also continued to serve the government and their groups in some of the same capacities as they had in the past, particularly in land use. By 1985 it was said that each Qashqa'i coresident group of from ten to twenty families was represented by one of these new Revolutionary Guards. And once again, as under real and suspected surveillance by SAVAK under the shah, distrust among the people was prevalent. Qashqa'i youngsters were also recruited into the army and sent to the Iraq-Iran front; some were killed, and hatred for the Islamic Republic among their families and groups was intense.

The paramount Qashqa'i khans had represented unambiguous authority figures for a wide spectrum of the Iranian people upon their return to Iran in 1979. Their antagonism to the despised Pahlavi regimes was unquestioned; their popularity, even charisma, was based on the stand they took against repression and despotism and their identification with Mosaddeq and Khomeini. In 1979 these positive attitudes had also extended to the Qashqa'i people. After 1980 and the establishment of the insurgency, however, government authorities worked diligently to revive the prejudiced beliefs, which had flourished under the Pahlavi shahs, that the Qashqa'i khans were feudal barons and brigand chiefs. Once the insurgency was crushed, these prejudices were again turned against the Qashqa'i people, who were viewed as counterrevolutionaries and again were considered as bandits and highway robbers. Years ago Abdollah noted that the Qashqa'i are "a minority who can easily be painted as deserving the barbaric treatment accorded them" (Gashgai 1954:7). So once again the Qashqa'i people and their leaders have been made to suffer by a state that offers them nothing but repression in exchange for obedience and service to an alien ideology.

Conclusion

$\mathcal{I}$n this study I have analyzed the historical vicissitudes of a regional elite caught up in the shifting waves of national—sometimes international—and revolutionary politics; and I have linked a discussion of long-term transformations in Qashqa'i tribal leadership and the nature of Qashqa'i identity to state and dynastic politics.

Relationships between the Qashqa'i polity and the Iranian state have been characterized by three patterns. In the first, the Qashqa'i polity was one of many locally competitive entities in Iran that fulfilled necessary functions for the state. These entities were, in effect, parts of the state apparatus. The decentralized Iranian state was partly a result of the efforts of the elites connected with such entities to establish control over particular territories, resources, labor forces, and other vested interests. Without these efforts the state could not have maintained its rule. The relative success of the Qashqa'i polity in these matters was largely attributable to the rich environment, the strategic setting, and the ability of the Qashqa'i elite to secure and maintain power and authority on the local level and to create effective ties with state officials and other elites. The Qashqa'i elite was one of many locally and nationally competitive elites through whose activities the state maintained its continued existence. The relevant historical periods discussed here include Zand rule (second half of the eighteenth century), much of Qajar rule (nineteenth century), and the months during which the fall of the

348

last Pahlavi dynasty and the establishment of the Islamic Republic took place.

The second pattern, in which the state and the Qashqa'i polity were opposed, featured efforts by rulers of a centralizing Iranian state to destroy the military capability and local autonomy of the Qashqa'i polity and the power of its elite. State rulers viewed Qashqa'i political institutions and elites, which had emerged as instruments of state administration, as threats and hence attempted to eliminate them. This pattern occurred under Reza Shah Pahlavi (1926 to 1941), under Mohammad Reza Shah Pahlavi (between 1953 and 1978), and during the second phase of the Islamic Republic (1980 through 1985).

The third pattern emerged when the Iranian state was weak, decentralized, and under the occupation or strong influence of foreign powers. During these periods the Qashqa'i polity neither particularly supported nor opposed the Iranian state. Rather, its primary ties were formed with foreign powers, which interacted with the Qashqa'i elite as state rulers had, their relationships being ones of either alliance or opposition. This pattern could be found from the end of the nineteenth century to the rise of Reza Shah (including World War I), during World War II, and briefly in 1953.

The circumstances leading to these three patterns, as they have appeared and reappeared in the last two hundred years, help to explain not only the changing roles of the Qashqa'i elite on the national, regional, and local scene but also the relative importance of the Qashqa'i confederacy for its members and in the region and nation. The Qashqa'i tribal confederacy as it has continually evolved and changed can be best explained by these complex historical, contextual, and sociological factors.

The phenomena that social scientists have usually labeled as "tribes" have been assumed to be self-contained entities created by autochthonous factors and somehow inherently opposed to states and to nontribal society. The information and analysis offered here, however, indicate that the Qashqa'i and similar kinds of polities in Iran and elsewhere were in fact formed and sustained by broad external forces, and that the resulting sociopolitical structures were ultimately ways of integrating the affiliated people into state structures. That such polities were sometimes perceived as threats to the state is a secondary phenomenon. The coresident units and lineages embracing the Qashqa'i people at the local level functioned continuously regardless of the extent of the centralization of the confederacy and the state; yet the ties of kinship,

political alliance, intermarriage, coresidence, cooperation, and contract binding individuals to one another also served varying purposes
depending on wider circumstances.

Members of the Qashqa'i confederacy often had more advantages
than other inhabitants of rural Iran. They enjoyed land security and
protection from incursion. State institutions in Iran did not adequately
protect the rights of those who worked and those who owned or controlled the land, and when local and state regimes changed, individuals
were even more vulnerable. Those in Iran who were part of other polities such as tribes and confederacies, however, often enjoyed security in
land use and were protected from competitors and changes in land tenure brought about by shifting regimes. Thus, tribal affiliations provided a degree of permanence in land use in a context in which the state
was incapable of providing this security. Through these same affiliations, the Qashqa'i escaped many oppressions suffered by other rural
Iranians at the hands of extortive government officials, military officers,
land grantees, and landlords. Landlords typically extracted 20 to 80
percent of their peasants' yearly production; the tax Qashqa'i leaders
levied was much less burdensome. Qashqa'i political institutions provided the people with mechanisms of defense and offense and with institutionalized forms of redress that were lacking for the peasantry.
Qashqa'i who were dissatisfied with tribal leaders could easily "vote
with their feet"; they could sever political ties and form new ones, a
possibility that kept leaders' actions in check. Iranian peasants tended
to lack such options (Kazemi and Abrahamian 1978).

The Qashqa'i elite were also often advantaged compared with the
nontribal elite of Iran. They based their power more on tribal numbers
and strength than they did on land, which usually saved them from the
fate suffered by landed nontribal elite when changes in land tenure were
effected by new regimes. Because of consistent policies of indirect rule
over tribal people from one regime to the next, tribal elite with enduring local ties had a greater chance of long-term political and economic
fortune than nontribal elite, who were more apt to lose economic and
political standing when the regimes they formed or supported fell.

Conflicting tendencies are found in the state's and the khans' rule of
tribal people. The state was a mechanism for extorting wealth from
people; but it was also a mechanism for protecting people from extortion. Strong state institutions could in fact do both. Khans were also
vehicles for extorting wealth from people; they owed their positions,
in part, to the state's bequeathing this privilege to them. But they also

limited, at times prevented, the state's extortions. Strong tribal leadership could in fact do both. Khans sought to achieve a balance between viable contacts with the state, as this was a basis for their power and wealth, and viable contacts with the affiliated people, another basis of power and wealth. Amiable ties with both were to the advantage of all three parties. Most Qashqa'i khans were able to maintain this balance; those who did not were usually mired in international politics, over which they exercised little or no control. The strength of this tribal elite was based on convincing the national elite and interested foreign parties, themselves possessing rapidly changing abilities to manage political events, of its control over the Qashqa'i constituency while at the same time convincing this constituency of the soundness of its decisions. Tribal leaders were more secure in their ties with the Qashqa'i people, with whom they enjoyed a permanent base, than with the state.

These conflicting tendencies also demonstrate the ambiguities and dilemmas involved in state rule and tribal rule. For much of the historical period under discussion, the incorporation of tribal leaders into state structures blurred the distinction between tribal and national political systems. A state might have been unable to rule, to perform its defined functions, while a non-state polity such as a tribal confederacy might have performed many state functions. A state, in order to administer a people, was forced to rely on tribal leaders because it lacked other means of administration; but in doing so it created powerful competitive forces that might eventually contribute to its own collapse. The state, having delegated authority to tribal leaders in the past, created residual effects in periods when the state chose *not* to rely on tribal leaders, and it, too, was threatened by their potential power. Tribal leaders, by assisting the state in its rule, were able to control the state's access to the tribe and hence helped to defend the tribe against the state. Simultaneously, however, they helped the state to impose centralized order on the tribe and to increase its own power (Gellner 1983:439) and thus facilitated the state's efforts to control or eliminate the tribe as well as the tribal leaders. Also, tribal leaders, as agents of the state, were forced or enticed into practices that could undermine the indigenous bases of their rule. The most effective leaders were those who understood these ambiguities and dilemmas and were skilled enough to balance their conflicting aspects.

These issues help to explain the consequences of the return of the paramount leaders to the Qashqa'i people in 1979. In the past they and their ruling ancestors had enjoyed a triple base of support: a powerful and independent tribal base, a political center to which to relate, and an economic base somewhat independent of either the tribe or the state. In 1979 the paramount leaders lacked all three of these advantages. Had they possessed one, they could have possibly gained a second and even a third, but they were not so fortunate. In the end they fought— some to the death and all to a political death—against a hostile state, without a supporting tribal body or means of financial support. They had retained their reputations, and even their charisma, but these proved to be inadequate in the face of the self-proclaimed moral authority and coercive power of the Islamic Republic of Iran.

Bibliography

Abbott, Keith Edward
    1857   Notes Taken on a Journey Eastwards from Shiraz to Fessa and Darab, Thence Westwards by Jehrum to Kazerun, in 1850. *Journal of the Royal Geographical Society of London* 27:149–84.

Abrahamian, Ervand
    1975   European Feudalism and Middle Eastern Despotisms. *Science and Society* 39(2):129–56.
    1979   The Causes of the Constitutional Revolution in Iran. *International Journal of Middle East Studies* 10(3):381–414.
    1980   The Guerrilla Movement in Iran, 1963–1977. *MERIP Reports* 10(3):3–15.
    1982   *Iran between Two Revolutions.* Princeton, N.J.: Princeton University Press.

Additions and Corrections to Who's Who in Persia. Vol. 4, *Persian Baluchistan, Kerman, stan, Kerman, Bandar Abbas, Fars, Yezd, and Laristan.*
    1924   Delhi: Government Central Press.

Ahmed, Akbar S.
    1980a   Afghanistan and Pakistan: The Great Game of the Tribes. *Journal of South Asian and Middle Eastern Studies* 3(4):23–41.
    1980b   *Pukhtun Economy and Society: Traditional Structure and Economic Development in a Tribal Society.* London: Routledge & Kegan Paul.

Amanolahi, Sekandar
    1985   The Lurs of Iran. *Cultural Survival Quarterly* 9(1):65–69.

Arfa, General Hassan
    1965   *Under Five Shahs.* New York: William Morrow.

353

Asad, Talal

1972   Political Inequality in the Kababish Tribe. In *Studies in Sudan Ethnography,* edited by Ian Cunnison and Wendy James. New York: Humanities Press.

1979   Equality in Nomadic Social Systems? Notes toward the Dissolution of an Anthropological Category. In *Pastoral Production and Society,* edited by L'Equipe ecologie et anthropologie des sociétés pastorales. Cambridge: Cambridge University Press.

Asaf, Mohammad Hashem Rostam ol-Hokama

1969   *Rostam et-tavarikh.* Edited by Mohammad Moshiri. Tehran.

Aubin, Jean

1955   References pour Lar medievale. *Journal Asiatique* 243:491–505.

Avery, Peter

1965   *Modern Iran.* New York: Praeger.

Bahmanbegi, Mohammad

1945–46 *Orf va adat dar ashayer-e Fars* (The customs of the nomads of Fars). Tehran: Azar Publishing Company.

1971   Qashqa'i: Hardy Shepherds of Iran's Zagros Mountains Build a Future Through Tent-School Education. In *Nomads of the World,* edited by Melville Grosvenor. Washington, D.C.: National Geographic Society.

Bakhash, Shaul

1984   *The Reign of the Ayatollahs: Iran and the Islamic Revolution.* New York: Basic Books.

Balayan, B. P.

1960   K Voprosu ob obshchnosti etnogeneza Shakhseven i Kashkaytsev (To the question about the common origins of the Shahsevan and Qashqa'i). *Vostokovedcheskiy Sbornik* (Yerevan) 1:331–77.

Bani Hashimi, Abdolreza; Alireza Ayatollahi; et al.

1977   *Ilat-e ashayer-e Fars* (The migratory tribes of Fars). Shiraz: Pahlavi University, Department of Sociology.

Barker, Paul

1981   Tent Schools of the Qashqa'i: A Paradox of Local Initiative and State Control. In *Modern Iran: The Dialectics of Continuity and Change,* edited by Michael Bonine and Nikki Keddie. Albany: State University of New York Press.

Barth, Fredrik

1959   The Land Use Pattern of Migratory Tribes of South Persia. *Norsk Geografisk Tidsskrift* 17:1–11.

1961   *Nomads of South Persia: The Basseri Tribe of the Khamseh Confederacy.* London: Allen and Unwin.

Barthold, Wilhelm

1984   *An Historical Geography of Iran.* Princeton, N.J.: Princeton University Press.

Bates, Daniel

1974   Normative and Alternative Systems of Marriage among the Yoruk of Southeastern Turkey. *Anthropological Quarterly* 47(3):270–87.

Baver, Mahmud
  1945   *Kuhgiluyeh va ilat-e an* (Kuhgiluyeh and the tribes there). Gachsaran,
            Iran.
Beck, Lois
  1978   Women among Qashqa'i Nomadic Pastoralists in Iran. In *Women in the
            Muslim World*, edited by Lois Beck and Nikki Keddie. Cambridge and
            London: Harvard University Press.
  1980a   Herd Owners and Hired Shepherds: The Qashqa'i of Iran. *Ethnology*
            19(3):327–51.
  1980b   Revolutionary Iran and Its Tribal Peoples. *MERIP Reports* 10(4):14–20.
  1980c   Tribe and State in Revolutionary Iran: The Return of the Qashqa'i
            Khans. *Iranian Studies* 13(1–4):215–55.
  1981a   Economic Transformations among Qashqa'i Nomads, 1962–1978. In
            Modern Iran: The Dialectics of Continuity and Change, edited by Michael
            Bonine and Nikki Keddie. Albany: State University of New York Press.
  1981b   Government Policy and Pastoral Land Use in Southwest Iran. *Journal of
            Arid Environments* 4(3):253–67.
  1981c   The Qashqa'i People of Southern Iran. UCLA Museum of Cultural His-
            tory Pamphlet Series, no. 14. Los Angeles: UCLA Museum of Cultural
            History. Photographs by Nikki Keddie.
  1982   Nomads and Urbanites, Involuntary Hosts and Uninvited Guests. *Jour-
            nal of Middle Eastern Studies* 18(4):426–44.
Bell, Mark S.
  1885   *Military Report on South-West Persia, Including the Provinces of Khuzistan
            (Arabistan), Luristan, and Part of Fars.* Simla: Government Central
            Branch Press.
Bestor, Jane
  1979   The Kurds of Iranian Baluchistan: A Regional Elite. M.A. thesis, De-
            partment of Anthropology, McGill University.
Bill, James
  1975   The Patterns of Elite Politics in Iran. In *Political Elites in the Middle East,*
            edited by George Lenczowski. Washington, D.C.: American Enterprise
            Institute.
Blok, Anton
  1974   *The Mafia of a Sicilian Village, 1860–1960: A Study of Violent Peasant
            Entrepreneurs.* New York: Harper & Row.
Bode, Baron Clement Augustus de
  1845   *Travels in Luristan and Arabistan.* Vol. 1. London: J. Madden and Com-
            pany.
Bosworth, C. E.
  1968   The Political and Dynastic History of the Iranian World (A.D. 1000–
            1217). In *The Cambridge History of Iran.* Vol. 5, *The Saljuq and Mongol
            Periods.* Edited by J. A. Boyle. Cambridge: Cambridge University Press.
Bosworth, C. E., and G. Doerfer
  1978   Khaladj. *Encyclopedia of Islam.* New edition. Vol. 4. Leiden: E. J. Brill.
            Pp. 917–18.

Bourdieu, Pierre
1977   *Outline of a Theory of Practice.* Cambridge: Cambridge University Press.
Boyle, John Andrew
1976   Introduction. In *The Qashqa'i of Iran.* Manchester: University of Manchester, Whitworth Art Gallery.
Bradburd, Daniel
1980   Never Give a Shepherd an Even Break: Class and Labor among the Komachi. *American Ethnologist* 7(4):603–20.
1981   Size and Success: Komachi Adaptation to a Changing Iran. In *Modern Iran: The Dialectics of Continuity and Change,* edited by Michael Bonine and Nikki Keddie. Albany: State University of New York Press.
Brooks, David
1983   The Enemy Within: Limitations on Leadership in the Bakhtiari. In *The Conflict of Tribe and State in Iran and Afghanistan,* edited by Richard Tapper. London: Croom Helm.
Burnham, Philip
1979   Spatial Mobility and Political Centralization in Pastoral Societies. In *Pastoral Production and Society,* edited by L'Equipe ecologie et anthropologie des sociétés pastorales. Cambridge: Cambridge University Press.
Busse, Heribert, trans.
1972   *History of Persia under Qajar Rule* (translation of Hasan-e Fasa'i's *Farsnama-ye Naseri*). New York: Columbia University Press.
Cahen, Claude
1965   Ghuzz. *Encyclopedia of Islam.* New edition. Vol. 2. Leiden: E. J. Brill. Pp. 1106–11.
Chick, Herbert George
1916   Past History of the Qashqais and Their Khans. In Arnold Talbot Wilson, *Report on Fars.* Simla: The Government Monotype Press.
Christian, Captain A. J.
1919   *A Report on the Tribes of Fars.* Simla: The Government Monotype Press.
Chubin, Shahram
1980   Leftist Forces in Iran. *Problems of Communism* 29(4):1–25.
Cohen, Abner
1969   *Custom and Politics in Urban Africa: A Study of Hausa Migrants in Yoruba Towns.* Berkeley: University of California Press.
1974   *Two-Dimensional Man: An Essay on the Anthropology of Power and Symbolism in Complex Society.* Berkeley: University of California Press.
Cohn, Bernard
1980   History and Anthropology: The State of Play. *Comparative Studies in Society and History* 22(2):198–221.
1981   Anthropology and History in the 1980s. *Journal of Interdisciplinary History* 12(2):227–52.
Coon, Carleton S.
1955   The Nomads. In *Social Forces in the Middle East,* edited by Sydney Fisher. Ithaca, N.Y.: Cornell University Press.

Cronin, Vincent
   1957   *The Last Migration*. London: Rupert Hart-Davis.
Cunnison, Ian
   1966   *Baggara Arabs: Power and the Lineage in a Sudanese Nomad Tribe*. Oxford:
           Clarendon.
Curzon, Lord George Nathaniel
   1892   *Persia and the Persian Question*. Vol. 2. New York: Barnes and Noble
           [1966].
Demorgny, Gustave
   1913a   Les Reformes administratives en Perse: Les tribus du Fars. *Revue du Monde
           Musulman* 22:85–150.
   1913b   Les Reformes administratives en Perse: Les tribus du Fars. *Revue du Monde
           Musulman* 23:3–108.
   1914   *Les Institutions de la police in Perse*. Paris: E. Leroux.
Department of the Environment, Tehran, Iran
   1977   Case Study on Desertification, Iran: Turan.
Diamond, Stanley
   1970   Reflections on the African Revolution: The Point of the Biafran Case.
           Journal of Asian and African Studies 5:16–27.
Dillon, Robert
   1976   Carpet Capitalism and Craft Involution in Kirman, Iran: A Study in
           Economic Anthropology. Ph.D. dissertation, Department of Anthropol-
           ogy, Columbia University.
Douglas, William O.
   1951   *Strange Lands and Friendly People*. New York: Harper.
Duncan, David Douglas
   1946   Life Goes on a Migration with Persian Tribesmen. *Life* (July 29): 99–
           105.
   1982   *The World of Allah*. Boston: Houghton Mifflin Company.
Dupré, Adrien
   1819   *Voyage en Perse, fait dans les années 1807, 1808 et 1809*. Vol. 2. Paris:
           J. G. Dentu.
Eickelman, Dale F.
   1981   *The Middle East: An Anthropological Approach*. Englewood Cliffs, N.J.:
           Prentice-Hall.
Enloe, Cynthia
   1980   *Ethnic Soldiers: State Security in Divided Societies*. Athens: The University
           of Georgia Press.
Evans-Pritchard, E. E.
   1949   *The Sanusi of Cyrenaica*. Oxford: Clarendon Press.
Fasa'i, Hasan-e
   1895–96a *Farsnama-ye Naseri*. Vol. 1. Reprint, Tehran, ca. 1965.
   1895–96b *Farsnama-ye Naseri*. Vol. 2. Reprint, Tehran, ca. 1965.
Fatemi, Faramarz
   1980   *The U.S.S.R. in Iran*. South Brunswick and New York: A. S. Barnes and
           Company.

Fazel, Golamreza
    1971   Economic Organization and Change among the Boir Ahmad: A No-
              madic Pastoral Tribe of Southwest Iran. Ph.D. dissertation, Anthropol-
              ogy Department, University of California, Berkeley.
    1979   Economic Bases of Political Leadership among Pastoral Nomads: The
              Boyr Ahmad Tribe of Southwest Iran. In *New Directions in Political Econ-
              omy: An Approach from Anthropology,* edited by Madeline Barbara Leons
              and Frances Rothstein. Westport, Conn.: Greenwood Press.
Fazel, Golamreza, and Nader Afshar Naderi
    1976   Rich Nomad, Poor Nomad, Settled Nomad: A Critique of Barth's Sed-
              entarization Model. Unpublished paper.
Ferdows, Emad
    1983   The Reconstruction Crusade and Class Conflict in Iran. *MERIP Reports*
              13(3):11–15.
Ferrier, Ronald
    1977   The Development of the Iranian Oil Industry. In *Twentieth-Century Iran,*
              edited by Hossein Amirsadeghi. New York: Holmes and Meier Publish-
              ers.
Field, Henry
    1939   *Contributions to the Anthropology of Iran.* Chicago: Field Museum of Nat-
              ural History.
    1954   Tribal Maps of Iran. Mimeographed.
Fraser, David
    1910   *Persia and Turkey in Revolt.* Edinburgh and London: William Blackwood
              and Sons.
Fraser, James B.
    1825   *Narrative of a Journey into Khorasan in the Years 1821 and 1822.* London:
              Longman, Hurst, Rees, Orme, Brown, and Green.
Fried, Morton
    1967   *The Evolution of Political Society: An Essay in Political Anthropology.* New
              York: Random House.
    1975   *The Notion of Tribe.* Menlo Park, Calif.: Cummings.
Frye, Richard
    1963   *The Heritage of Persia.* Cleveland and New York: The World Publishing
              Company.
Gagon, Glen S.
    1956   A Study of the Development and Implementation of a System of Ele-
              mentary Education for the Ghasghi [*sic*] and Basseri Nomadic Tribes of
              Fars Ostan, Iran. Master's thesis, Brigham Young University.
Garrod, Oliver
    1946a   The Nomadic Tribes of Persia Today. *Journal of the Royal Central Asian
              Society* 33(1):32–46.
    1946b   The Qashqai Tribe of Fars. *Journal of the Royal Central Asian Society*
              33(2):293–306.
Garthwaite, Gene
    1975   Two Persian Wills of Hajj 'Ali Quli Khan Sardar As'ad. *Journal of the
              American Oriental Society* 95(4):645–50.

1981   Khans and Kings: The Dialectics of Power in Bakhtiyari History. In *Modern Iran: The Dialectics of Continuity and Change,* edited by Michael Bonine and Nikki Keddie. Albany: State University of New York Press.

1983   *Khans and Shahs: A Documentary Analysis of the Bakhtiyari in Iran.* Cambridge: Cambridge University Press.

Gashgai, Abdollah

1954   The Gashgais in Iran. *Land Reborn* 5(5):6–7.

Gazetteer of Persia, Part 3, *Including Fars, Luristan, Arabistan, Khuzistan, and Yazd.*

1918   Simla: General Staff of India.

Gellner, Ernest

1969   *Saints of the Atlas.* Chicago: The University of Chicago Press.

1981   *Muslim Society.* Cambridge: Cambridge University Press.

1983   The Tribal Society and Its Enemies. In *The Conflict of Tribe and State in Iran and Afghanistan,* edited by Richard Tapper. London: Croom Helm.

Ghashghai, Houshang Bahadori

1981   The Question of Settlement of Nomads of Iran. Ph.D. dissertation, School of Human Behavior, United States International University.

Godelier, Maurice

1977   The Concept of the 'Tribe': A Crisis Involving Merely a Concept or the Empirical Foundations of Anthropology Itself? In *Perspectives in Marxist Anthropology.* New York: Cambridge University Press.

Goldsmid, Maj. Gen. Sir Frederic John

1874a   Notes on Recent Persian Travel. *Journal of the Royal Geographic Society of London* 94:183–203.

1874b   *Telegraph and Travel.* London: Macmillan and Company.

Good, Mary-Jo DelVecchio

1981   The Changing Status and Composition of an Iranian Provincial Elite. In *Modern Iran: The Dialectics of Continuity and Change,* edited by Michael Bonine and Nikki Keddie. Albany: State University of New York Press.

Haig, T. W.

1934   Salghurids. *Encyclopedia of Islam.* Vol. 4. Pp. 105–06.

Hand, Captain Robert P.

1963   A Survey of the Tribes of Iran. Counterinsurgency Department, United States Army Special Warfare School. Mimeographed.

Harrison, Selig S.

1981   *In Afghanistan's Shadow: Baluch Nationalism and Soviet Temptations.* New York: Carnegie Endowment for International Peace.

Helfgott, Leonard M.

1977   Tribalism as a Socioeconomic Formation in Iranian History. *Iranian Studies* 10(1–2):36–61.

1980   The Structural Foundations of the National Minority Problem in Revolutionary Iran. *Iranian Studies* 13(1–4):195–214.

Helm, June, ed.

1968   *Essays on the Problem of Tribe.* Proceedings of the 1967 Annual Meeting of the American Ethnological Society. Seattle: University of Washington Press.

Hendershot, Clarence
1964   *White Tents in the Mountains: A Report on the Tribal Schools of Fars Province.* Tehran: Communications Resource Branch.
Hooglund, Eric
1982a   *Land and Revolution in Iran, 1960–1980.* Austin: University of Texas Press.
1982b   Social Origins of the Revolutionary Clergy. In *The Iranian Revolution and the Islamic Republic,* edited by Nikki Keddie and Eric Hooglund. Washington, D.C.: Middle East Institute.
Hooglund (Hegland), Mary
1980   One Village in the Revolution. *MERIP Reports* 10(4):7–12.
Iran Almanac and Book of Facts, 1963
1964   3d ed., edited by J. Behrouz. Tehran: The Echo of Iran.
Iranfar, Javad
1970   Management and Improvement of Rangelands in Iran. In *Proceedings of the CENTO Conference on National and Regional Livestock Development Policy, Islamabad, 1969.*
Irons, William
1974   Nomadism as a Political Adaptation. *American Ethnologist* 1:635–58.
1975   *The Yomut Turkmen: A Study of Social Organization among a Central Asian Turkic-Speaking Population.* Anthropological Paper no. 58. University of Michigan Museum of Anthropology. Ann Arbor: Univeristy of Michigan.
1979   Political Stratification among Pastoral Nomads. In *Pastoral Production and Society,* edited by L'Equipe ecologie et anthropologie des sociétés pastorales. Cambridge: Cambridge University Press.
Katouzian, Homayoun A.
1978   Oil versus Agriculture: A Case of Dual Resource Depletion in Iran. *Journal of Peasant Studies* 5(3):347–69.
1981   The Political Economy of Modern Iran: Despotism and Pseudo-Modernism, 1926–1979. New York: New York University Press.
Kayhan, Mas'ud
1932–33 *Joghrafiya-ye mofassal-e Iran.* Vol. 2. Tehran: Matba'e-ye Majlis.
Kazemi, Farhad, and Ervand Abrahamian
1978   The Nonrevolutionary Peasantry of Modern Iran. *Iranian Studies* 11(1–4):259–304.
Keddie, Nikki
1972   Stratification, Social Control, and Capitalism in Iranian Villages: Before and After Land Reform. In *Rural Politics and Social Change in the Middle East,* edited by Richard Antoun and Iliya Harik. Bloomington: Indiana University Press.
Keyes, Charles F., ed.
1981   *Ethnic Change.* Seattle: University of Washington Press.
Khazanov, A. M.
1984   *Nomads and the Outside World.* Cambridge: Cambridge University Press.
Khurmuji, Hajji Mohammad Ja'far Khan
1859   *Fars Nameh.* Tehran. Lithograph.

Kinneir, John Macdonald
1813   *A Geographical Memoir of the Persian Empire.* London: John Murray.
Kortum, Gerhard
1975   Siedlungsgenetische Untersuchungen in Fars. *Erdkunde: Archiv für wissenschaftliche Geographie* 29(1):10–20.
1979a   *Entwicklungsprobleme und -projekte im bäuerlich-nomadischen Lebensraum Südpersiens. Fragenkreise 23523.* Paderborn: Ferdinand Schöningh.
1979b   Zur Bildung und Entwicklung des Qašqai-Stammes 'Amale im 20. Jahrhundert. In *Interdisziplinäre Iran-Forschung: Beiträge aus Kulturgeographie, Ethnologie, Soziologie und Neuerer Geschichte,* edited by Günther Schweizer. Beihefte zum Tübinger Atlas des Vorderen Orients, series B, no. 40. Wiesbaden. Pp. 71–100.
1980   Bergnomadismus und Ansiedlung der Qašqai (Zagros/Iran). Tübinger Atlas des Vorderen Orients Map A, 12.2. Wiesbaden: Tübinger Atlas des Vorderen Orients, Universität Tübingen.
1982   Entwicklungskonzepte für den nomadischen Lebensraum der Qashqai in Fars/Iran: Ein perspektivischer Rückblick. *Nomadismus: Ein Entwicklungsproblem?* Edited by Janzen Scholz. Abhandlungen des Geographischen Instituts, Anthropogeographie, vol. 33. Berlin.
Krader, Lawrence
1968   *Formation of the State.* Englewood Cliffs, N.J.: Prentice-Hall.
Lambton, Ann K. S.
1953   *Landlord and Peasant in Persia: A Study of Land Tenure and Land Revenue Administration.* London: Oxford University Press.
1960   Ilat. *The Encyclopedia of Islam.* 2d ed. Vol. 3. Leiden: E. J. Brill. Pp. 1095–1110.
1967   The Evolution of the Iqta' in Medieval Iran. *Iran* 5:41–50.
1969   *The Persian Land Reform 1962–1966.* Oxford: Clarendon.
1977   The Tribal Resurgence and the Decline of the Bureaucracy in the Eighteenth Century. In *Studies in Eighteenth-Century Islamic History,* edited by Thomas Naff and Roger Owen. Carbondale: Southern Illinois University Press.
Lancaster, William
1981   *The Rwala Bedouin Today.* Cambridge: Cambridge University Press.
Lane, D. Austin
1923   Hajji Mirza Hasan-i-Shirazi on the Nomad Tribes of Fars in the Fars-Nameh-i-Nasiri. *Journal of the Royal Asiatic Society of Great Britain* (April): 209–31.
Layard, Sir Henry
1846   A Description of the Province of Khuzistan. *Journal of the Royal Geographical Society* 16:1–105.
Leacock, Eleanor
1972   Glossary. In F. Engels, *The Origin of the Family, Private Property and the State.* New York: International.
Lenczowski, George
1949   *Russia and the West in Iran, 1918–1948.* Ithaca, N.Y.: Cornell University Press.

Le Strange, Guy

1905   *The Lands of the Eastern Caliphate: Mesopotamia, Persia, and Central Asia from the Moslem Conquest to the Time of Timur.* London: Frank Cass & Company.

1912   *Description of the Province of Fars in Persia at the Beginning of the Fourteenth Century A.D.* (From the *Fars Nameh* of Ibn al-Balkhi). London: The Royal Asiatic Society.

Le Strange, Guy, trans. and ed.

1926   *Don Juan of Persia: A Shi'ah Catholic, 1560–1604.* New York: Harper and Brothers.

Lindberg, K.

1955   *Voyage dans le sud de l'Iran.* Lund: C. W. K. Gleerup.

Lindner, Rudi Paul

1982   What Was a Nomadic Tribe? *Comparative Studies in Society and History* 24(4):689–711.

Loeb, Laurence

1977   *Outcaste: Jewish Life in Southern Iran.* New York: Gordon and Breach.

Loeffler, Reinhold

1973   The National Integration of Boir Ahmad. *Iranian Studies* 6(2–3):127–35.

1978   Tribal Order and the State: The Political Organization of Boir Ahmad. *Iranian Studies* 11(1–4):145–71.

1982   Economic Changes in a Rural Area since 1979, Supplementary Remarks, and Discussion. In *The Iranian Revolution and the Islamic Republic,* edited by Nikki Keddie and Eric Hooglund. Washington, D.C.: Middle East Institute.

McCagg, William O., and Brian D. Silver

1979a   Introduction. In *Soviet Asian Ethnic Frontiers,* edited by William O. McCagg and Brian Silver. New York: Pergamon Press.

McCagg, William O., and Brian Silver, eds.

1979b   *Soviet Asian Ethnic Frontiers.* New York: Pergamon Press.

McLachlan, Keith

1980   Postscript. In Cyrus Salmanzadeh, *Agricultural Change and Rural Society in Southern Iran.* Cambridge, Eng.: Middle East and North African Studies Press.

Magee, Lieutenant G. F.

1948   *The Tribes of Fars.* Simla: Government of India Press.

Mahamedi, Hamid

1979   On the Verbal System in Three Iranian Dialects of Fars. *Studia Iranica* 8:277–97.

Mahdi, Muhsin

1957   *Ibn Khaldun's Philosophy of History.* Chicago: The University of Chicago Press.

Malcolm, Sir John

1829   *The History of Persia.* Vol. 2. London: J. Murray.

Marlowe, John

1962   *The Persian Gulf in the Twentieth Century.* New York: Praeger.

Marsden, David
1978   The Social Structure of the Amaleh Tireh. Unpublished manuscript.
Meeker, Michael
1980   The Twilight of a South Asian Heroic Age: A Rereading of Barth's Study
         of Swat. *Man,* n.s. 15(4):682–701.
Military Report on Persia. Part 2, *Fars, the Gulf Ports.*
1922   Simla: General Staff.
Ministry of Education, Department of Tribal Education
1972   Statistics on the Qashqa'i. Tehran. Mimeographed.
Minorsky, Vladimir
1934a   Lur. *Encyclopedia of Islam.* Vol. 3. Pp. 41–46.
1934b   Shulistan. *Encyclopedia of Islam.* Vol. 4. Pp. 391–92.
1939–42 The Turkish Dialect of the Khalaj. *Bulletin of the School of Oriental and
         African Studies* 10:417–36.
Minorsky, Vladimir, ed. and trans.
1943   *Tadhkirat al-Muluk: A Manual of Safavid Administration.* Cambridge,
         Eng.: E. J. W. Gibb Memorial Trust.
Monteil, Vincent
1966   *Les Tribus du Fars et la sedentarisation des nomades.* Paris: Mouton & Com-
         pany.
Moore, Arthur
1914   *The Orient Express.* London: Constable and Company.
Morier, James
1816   *A Journey through Persia, Armenia, and Asia Minor.* Philadelphia: M.
         Carey.
1818   *A Second Journey through Persia, Armenia, and Asia Minor.* London: Long-
         man, Hurst, Rees, Orme, and Brown.
1837   Some Account of the I'liyats, or Wandering Tribes of Persia. *Journal of
         the Royal Geographic Society* 7:230–42.
Mounsey, Augustus Henry
1872   *A Journey through the Caucasus and the Interior of Persia.* London: Smith,
         Elder and Company.
Napier, Captain G. S. F.
1900   *Military Report on Southern Persia.* Simla: Government Central Printing
         Office.
Oberling, Pierre
1960   The Turkic Peoples of Southern Iran. Ph.D. dissertation, History De-
         partment, Columbia University. Ann Arbor: University Microfilms.
1964   The Turkic Tribes of Southwestern Persia. *Ural-Altaische Jahrbucher*
         35:164–80.
1974   *The Qashqa'i Nomads of Fars.* The Hague: Mouton.
O'Connor, Sir Frederick
1931   *On the Frontier and Beyond.* London: John Murray.
Paynter, Robert, and John W. Cole
1980   Ethnographic Overproduction, Tribal Political Economy, and the Ka-
         pauku of Irian Jaya. In *Beyond the Myths of Culture: Essays in Cultural
         Materialism,* edited by Eric Ross. New York: Academic Press.

Peiman, Habibollah
  1968   Tousif va tahlili az sakhteman eqtesadi ejtema'i va farhangi il-e Qashqa'i
          (A description and analysis of the economic, social, and cultural aspects
          of the Qashqa'i confederacy). Publication no. 34. Tehran: University of
          Tehran, Institute of Health.
Pelly, Sir Lewis
  1865a   A Brief Account of the Province of Fars. *Transactions of the Bombay Geo-
          graphical Society* 17:175–85.
  1865b   Remarks on a Recent Journey from Bushire to Shirauz. *Transactions of the
          Bombay Geographical Society* 17:141–74.
Perry, John R.
  1975   Forced Migration in Iran during the Seventeenth and Eighteenth Cen-
          turies. *Iranian Studies* 8(4):199–215.
  1979   *Karim Khan Zand: A History of Iran, 1747–1779.* Chicago: The Univer-
          sity of Chicago Press.
Petrosian, Angela, et al.
  1964   *The Health and Related Characteristics of Four Selected Village and Tribal
          Communities in Fars Ostan, Iran.* Shiraz, Iran: Pahlavi University.
Picot, Lieutenant Colonel H.
  1897   *Persia: Biographical Notices of Members of the Royal Family, Notables, Mer-
          chants, and Clergy.* Tehran.
Planhol, Xavier de
  1968   Geography of Settlement. In *The Cambridge History of Iran.* Vol. 1, *Land
          of Iran,* edited by W. B. Fisher. Cambridge: Cambridge University
          Press.
  1972   Regional Diversification and Social Structure in North Africa and the
          Islamic Middle East: A Geographic Approach. In *Rural Politics and Social
          Change in the Middle East,* edited by Richard Antoun and Iliya Harik.
          Bloomington: Indiana University Press.
Price, Barbara
  1978   Secondary State Formation: An Explanatory Model. In *Origins of the State:
          The Anthropology of Political Evolution,* edited by Ronald Cohen and Elman
          Service. Philadelphia: Institute for the Study of Human Issues.
Ramage, Darlene
  n.d.   The Quashqkai [*sic*]. Unpublished manuscript.
Roosevelt, Kermit
  1979   *Countercoup: The Struggle for the Control of Iran.* New York: McGraw-Hill
          Book Company.
Rosenthal, Franz, trans.
  1967   *Ibn Khaldun's The Muqaddimah.* 2d ed. Bollingen Series, 43. Princeton,
          N.J.: Princeton University Press.
Royce, William
  1981   The Shirazi Provincial Elite: Status Maintenance and Change. In *Modern
          Iran: The Dialectics of Continuity and Change,* edited by Michael Bonine
          and Nikki Keddie. Albany: State University of New York Press.
Safiri, Floreeda
  1976   The South Persian Rifles. Ph.D. dissertation, University of Edinburgh.

Sahlins, Marshall
   1963   Poor Man, Rich Man, Big-Man, Chief: Political Types in Melanesia and Polynesia. *Comparative Studies in Society and History* 5:285–303.
   1968   *Tribesmen.* Englewood Cliffs, N.J.: Prentice-Hall.
   1972   *Stone Age Economics.* Chicago: Aldine.

Salzer, Richard
   1974   Social Organization of a Nomadic Pastoral Nobility in Southern Iran: The Kashkuli Kuchek Tribe of the Qashqa'i. Ph.D. dissertation, Anthropology Department, University of California, Berkeley.

Sandford, Stephen
   1977   *Pastoralism and Development in Iran.* Pastoral Network Paper 3c. London: Overseas Development Institute.

Schulze-Holthus, Berthold
   1954   *Daybreak in Iran, A Story of the German Intelligence Service.* Translated by Mervyn Savill. London: Staples Press.

Service, Elman
   1975   *Origins of the State and Civilization: The Process of Cultural Evolution.* New York: W. W. Norton.

Shafii, Forough; Manouchehr Mohseni; and Mansour Motabar
   1977   Formal Education in a Tribal Society, Iran. *Sociologia Ruralis* 17(1–2):151–57.

Shahshahani, Soheila
   1986   History of Anthropology in Iran. *Iranian Studies* 19 (1) (in press).

Sheil, Justin
   1856   Notes on Russia, Koords, Toorkomans, Nestorians, Khiva, and Persia. In Lady Mary Leonora Sheil, *Glimpses of Life and Manners in Persia.* London: J. Murray.

Shor, Jean, and Frank Shor
   1952   We Dwelt in Kashgai Tents. *National Geographic Magazine* 101(6):805–32.

Southall, Aidan
   1970   The Illusion of Tribe. *Journal of Asian and African Studies* 5:28–50.

Spooner, Brian
   1976   Flexibility and Interdependence in Traditional Pastoral Land Use Systems: A Case for the Human Component in Ecological Studies for Development (Tauran). *Proceedings of an International Meeting on Ecological Guidelines for the Use of Natural Resources in the Middle East and South West Asia.* International Union for the Conservation of Nature and Natural Resources Publication, n.s., no. 34. Morges, Switzerland.

Stack, Edward
   1882a   *Six Months in Persia.* Vol. 1. New York: G. P. Putnam's Sons.
   1882b   *Six Months in Persia.* Vol. 2. New York: G. P. Putnam's Sons.

Sümer, F.
   1978   Kashkay. *The Encyclopedia of Islam.* New edition. Vol. 4. Leiden: E. J. Brill. Pp. 705–06.

Swee, Gary Michael
1981   Sedentarization: Change and Adaptation among the Kordshuli Pastoral
        Nomads of Southwestern Iran. Ph.D. dissertation, Anthropology De-
        partment, Michigan State University.
Swidler, Nina Bailey
1969   The Political Structure of a Tribal Federation: The Brahui of Baluchistan.
        Ph.D. dissertation, Department of Political Science, Columbia Univer-
        sity.
Sykes, Christopher
1936   *Wassmuss "The German Lawrence."* London: Longmans, Green and Co.
Sykes, Sir Percy Molesworth
1930   *A History of Persia.* 3d ed. Vol. 2. London: MacMillan and Co.
Tabari, Azar
1982   Mystifications of the Past and Illusions of the Future. In *The Iranian
        Revolution and the Islamic Republic,* edited by Nikki Keddie and Eric
        Hooglund. Washington, D.C.: Middle East Institute.
Taheri, Atta
1976   *Ashayer-e Kuh-e Giluyeh va Boir Ahmadi* (The nomads of Kuhgiluyeh and
        Boir Ahmad). Kermanshah, Iran: The Office of Research, Planning, and
        Budget of Kermanshah.
Taimaz, S.
1979   *Seh maqaleh dar bareh-ye Turkman-sahra, Dasht-e Moghan, va rustaha-ye
        digar* (Three essays on Turkman-sahra, Dasht-e Moghan, and other vil-
        lages). Tehran: Ilm Publications.
Tapper, Richard
1971   The Shahsavan of Azarbaijan: A Study of Political and Economic Change
        in a Middle Eastern Tribal Society. Ph.D. dissertation, University of
        London.
1979   *Pasture and Politics: Economics, Conflict and Ritual among Shahsevan Nomads
        of Northwestern Iran.* London: Academic Press.
1983   Introduction. In *The Conflict of Tribe and State in Iran and Afghanistan,*
        edited by Richard Tapper. London: Croom Helm.
Tribal Development Office, Office of the Governor of Fars
1967   Map of the Migratory Routes of the Tribes of Fars. Shiraz.
Ullens de Schooten, Marie Therese
1954   Among the Kashkai: A Tribal Migration in Persia. *Geographical Magazine*
        27(2):68–78.
1956   *Lords of the Mountains: Southern Persia and the Kashkai Tribe.* London:
        Chatto and Windus.
van Bruinessen, Martin M.
1978   Agha, Shaikh and State: On the Social and Political Organization of
        Kurdistan. Ph.D. dissertation, Utrecht University, Netherlands.
1983   Kurdish Tribes and the State of Iran: The Case of Simko's Revolt. In *The
        Conflict of Tribe and State in Iran and Afghanistan,* edited by Richard Tap-
        per. London: Croom Helm.

Waring, Edward Scott
    1807   *A Tour to Sheeraz by the Route of Kazroon and Feerozabad.* London: T. Cadell and W. Davies. Reprint 1973, New York: Arno Press.

Whitworth Art Gallery, University of Machester
    1976   *The Qashqa'i of Iran.*

Who's Who in Persia. Vol. 4, *Persian Baluchistan, Kerman, Bandar Abbas, Fars, Yezd, and Laristan.*
    1923   Simla: General Staff.

Wills, Charles James
    1883   *In the Land of the Lion and Sun.* London: Macmillan and Company.

Wilson, Sir Arnold Talbot
    1916   *Report on Fars.* Simla: The Government Monotype Press.
    1932   *Persia.* London: Ernest Benn Limited.
    1942   *SW Persia: Letters and Diary of a Young Political Officer 1907–1914.* London: Readers Union.

Wirsing, Robert G., ed.
    1981   *Protection of Ethnic Minorities: Comparative Perspectives.* New York: Pergamon Press.

Wolf, Eric
    1982   *Europe and the People without History.* Berkeley: University of California Press.

Woods, John
    1976   *The Aqquyunlu: Clan, Confederation, Empire.* Minneapolis and Chicago: Bibliotheca Islamica.

Woollacott, Martin
    1979   Baluchistan's Chance to Assert Its Identity. *Manchester Guardian* 120:8.

Yapp, Malcolm E.
    1983   Tribes and States in the Khyber, 1838–1842. In *The Conflict of Tribe and State in Iran and Afghanistan,* edited by Richard Tapper. London: Croom Helm.

Zabih, Sepehr
    1982   *Iran since the Revolution.* Baltimore: The Johns Hopkins University Press.

Index

369